☆ ☆ ☆

THE

AMERICAN

MOVIE

INDUSTRY

The Business of Motion Pictures

Edited by Gorham Kindem
The University of North Carolina at Chapel Hill

Southern Illinois University Press
Carbondale and Edwardsville

Copyright © 1982 by The Board of Trustees,
Southern Illinois University

All rights reserved

Printed in the United States of America

Edited by Joyce Atwood

Production supervised by John DeBacher

Library of Congress Cataloging in Publication Data
Main entry under title:

The American movie industry.

Bibliography: p.
Includes index.
1. Moving-picture industry—United States—Case
studies.   I. Kindem, Gorham Anders.
PN1993.5.U6A872   384'.8'0973   81-23317
ISBN 0-8093-1036-8   AACR2

85 84 83 82   5 4 3 2 1

Contents

Illustrations

Tables

Preface

This collection of case studies surveys the history of the American movie industry. Each chapter has been thoroughly researched by a recognized business, law, mass communications, or film scholar. The authors have carefully examined relevant business records, legal proceedings, government and industry statistics, and trade papers in an attempt to evidence their theses about important historical developments with primary as well as secondary source materials. Several studies explicitly cite relevant models and theories, which help to order and explain the causes and effects of important economic, legal, and social developments in American film industry history. In short, many of these case studies are seminal works in the field.

The anthology is organized both chronologically and topically. Parts One, Two, and Three basically follow the history of the film industry's marketing strategies, structural changes, and product innovations: from exhibition in Kinetoscope arcades to film "acts" in vaudeville, nickelodeons, small-time vaudeville, and movie palaces; from states' rights marketing schemes to block-booking and chain-store exhibition strategies; from a production and distribution monopoly based upon the pooling of major patents to an oligopoly among vertically integrated (production, distribution, and exhibition) firms; and from the rise of feature films, the star system, and the studio system to Hollywood's conversions to sound and color.

Parts IV through VI examine major topics, such as regulation and censorship, interaction with television, and America's role in the international film industry. These topics include several major historical developments: NRA policies which endorsed monopolization of the industry by major studios in the 1930s, the divorcement of production and distribution from exhibition and the rise of television in the late 1940s and early 1950s, and Hollywood's involvement with television and foreign film industries (Canada and the Common Market in particular) in the 1960s and 1970s.

While most of the case studies in this volume focus upon developments and events of relatively short duration, a few trace several decades
of historical change in one specific area, such as antitrust, self-censorship,
the star system, or color. Taken together these long and short views suggest that restricting the scope of study to specific areas (the case study
approach) dramatically improves the depth of our understanding about
problems in film industry history. The diversity of methods and perspectives in this anthology are intended to be representative of the field and
suggest that American film industry history is really a collection of histories, rather than a monolithic, single-strand chronology of events.

One of the pitfalls of taking a narrow view, however, is that individual
scholars may fail to consider all of the relevant factors involved in major
historical change. The reader can sometimes overcome this limitation by
examining several chapters which deal with different aspects of and approaches to the same topic or period in American film industry history.
The overlap between studies often reveals the true complexity of historical events, when viewed from several different perspectives simultaneously. If the reader learns nothing more from this collection of case
studies than the fact that film industry history is complex and myths per-
petrated by earlier historians should be questioned, the editor and the
other contributors will know that their efforts have not been in vain.

I want to thank the contributors to this anthology and the previous
publishers of their works; Joyce Atwood for her meticulous editing of the
manuscript; and Kenney Withers, James Simmons, and Southern Illinois
University Press for their firm commitment to film scholarship.

Chapel Hill, North Carolina   Gorham Kindem

Acknowledgments

Reprinted by Permission:

Allen, Robert C. "Vitascope/Cinematographe: Initial Patterns of American Film Industrial Practice," *Journal of the University Film Association* 31, no. 2 (Spring 1979):13–18.

————. "Motion Picture Exhibition in Manhattan: 1906–1912: Beyond the Nickelodeon," *Cinema Journal* 18, no. 2 (Spring 1979):2–15.

Ayer, Douglas; Roy E. Bates; and Peter J. Herman. "Self-Censorship in the Movie Industry: An Historical Perspective on Law and Social Change," *Wisconsin Law Review*, 3 (1970):791–838.

Cassady, Ralph, Jr. "Monopoly in Motion Picture Production and Distribution: 1908–1915," *Southern California Law Review*, 32 (1959): 325–90.

Gomery, Douglas. "The Movies Become Big Business: Publix Theatres and the Chain Store Strategy," *Cinema Journal* 18, no. 2 (Spring 1979): 26–40.

————. "The Warner-Vitaphone Peril: The American Film Industry Reacts to the Innovation of Sound," *Journal of the University Film Association* 28, no. 1 (Winter 1976):11–19.

————. "Hollywood, the National Recovery Administration, and the Question of Monopoly Power," *Journal of the University Film Association* 31, no. 2 (Spring 1979): 47–52.

Guback, Thomas H. "Film as International Business," in *Communication and Class Struggle; Volume 1, Capitalism, Imperialism*, edited by Armand Mattelart and Seth Siegelaub, (New York and Paris: International General, 1979):359–67.

Kindem, Gorham. "The Demise of Kinemacolor: Technological, Legal, Economic, and Aesthetic Problems in Early Color Cinema History," *Cinema Journal* 20, no. 2 (Spring 1981): 3–14.

————. "Hollywood's Conversion to Color: The Technological, Economic, and Aesthetic Factors," *Journal of the University Film Association* 31, no. 2 (Spring 1979): 29–36.

Le Duc, Don R. "The Common Market Film Industry: Beyond Law and Economics," *Journal of Communication* 29, no. 1 (Winter 1979): 44–55.

Litman, Barry R. "The Economics of the Television Market for Theatrical Movies," *Journal of Communication* 29, no. 4 (Autumn 1979): 20–33.

Pendakur, Manjunath. "Cultural Dependency in Canada's Feature Film Industry," *Journal of Communication* 31, no. 1 (Winter 1981): 48–57.

Phillips, Joseph D. "Film Conglomerate 'Blockbusters,'" *Journal of Communication* 25, no. 2 (Spring 1975): 171–82.

Staiger, Janet. "Dividing Labor for Production Control: Thomas Ince and the Rise of the Studio System," *Cinema Journal* 18, no. 2 (Spring 1979): 16–25.

Stuart, Fredric. *The Effects of Television on the Motion Picture and Radio Industries* (Arno Pr., Inc., 1975).

Whitney, Simon N. "Motion Pictures," in *Antitrust Policies: American Experience in Twenty Industries*, (Twentieth Century Fund, Inc., 1958), 2: 145–95.

Introduction

Why study American film industry history? The study of cinema history can provide an insight into current film problems. Film is an important contemporary art form and communications medium, with a rich aesthetic tradition; but it is also a major entertainment business and industry. Feature films are both cultural *and* commercial products; and owing to this duality economic considerations are inextricably interwoven with political, social, and aesthetic aspects of film history. Study of the American feature-film industry, which has played a significant role in cinema history, provides a unique opportunity for both students and scholars to examine the complex interaction of these factors from an industrial perspective.

The American film industry has traditionally dominated world feature-film markets, but its economic success has also been the object of scorn and concern both at home and abroad. While some of these objections to American film-industry practice are simply expressions of envy on the part of less successful competitors, others are legitimate concerns about industry priorities, such as the pursuit of profits at the expense of art, culture, or social well being. Certain public interest groups, independent domestic and foreign film businesses, and government agencies have been genuinely concerned about the structure of the American feature-film industry, the concentration of power in the hands of a few, and the content of American films. Films, they argue, are cultural and aesthetic artifacts that have social and political effects. They are not commercial products pure and simple, although the American courts defined films in this way until 1952, prohibiting them from participating in First Amendment protections against censorship. This tension between film culture and film commerce lies at the heart of American film-industry history and makes the study of this subject of particular interest to students and scholars of arts' management and business in general.

While the feature-film industry has experienced much economic success during the past century, it is important to keep its financial status and growth in perspective. The American feature-film industry reached the apex of its growth in domestic markets during the mid-1940s. Today its gross sales are less than half those of the television industry and less than one third of video games' sales. Compared to the sales and assets of major American industries, such as steel and automobiles, the feature film industry is quite small, but financial comparisons provide a poor index of its overall significance. An evaluation of the importance of this industry must also consider the fact that films, unlike many other manufactured products, have significant social, political, and aesthetic value. The images projected by Hollywood have had a profound impact on the entire world, and American films have been an amazingly resilient form of popular entertainment throughout the twentieth century.

The relatively recent case studies presented in this book offer at least two general insights into American film-industry history. First, although the feature film industry has grown and changed rather dramatically during the past century, its basic motivation to maximize profits through specific policies and strategies—such as technological innovation, cooperation and competition with related entertainment industries, self-censorship, and the concentration of power in a few companies that dominate both foreign and domestic markets—have remained remarkably unchanged. Second, film industry history is complex; it can be productively approached from many different perspectives. Alternative, sometimes contradictory, explanatory models that emphasize different sets of economic, social, political, legal, and aesthetic factors, which can effect industry change, offer slightly different but often equally valid perceptions into major historical problems. While few problems in film industry history have been definitively answered, recent scholarship, such as that presented here, greatly improves upon prior knowledge by looking at many causative factors from various points of view and by applying relevant models and research methods to newly discovered information and documentation.

A persistent effort to maximize profits along with other entrepreneurial motivations helps to explain film industry policies and tendencies favoring a concentration of power, self-censorship, technological innovation, interaction with related entertainment industries, and America's dominant position in world feature-film markets. A tendency toward monopoly or oligopoly market structure has obtained throughout the history of the American feature-film industry. Ralph Cassady has carefully documented the formation and dissolution of an early film trust, known as the Motion Picture Patents Company (MPPC), in which major film-equipment manufacturers in 1908 pooled their patents to control both film equipment and film production by licensing film distributors (exchanges), and exhibitors (theater owners) so long as they handled only MPPC authorized films. Jeanne Thomas Allen suggests several alternative explanations of MPPC policies and points out some important research gaps and omissions in her thorough critique of Cassady's study. Independent film businesses appear to have bitterly fought the MPPC's monopolistic trust, stimulating a government antitrust suit that was not concluded until 1916. By the time this early trust was dissolved, an oligopoly among major "independent" concerns based on film-studio acquisitions of exhibition outlets or theaters, major movie stars, feature films, and the vertical integration of production, distribution, and exhibition was being formed.

By the 1930s the movie industry was largely controlled by five major companies (Loew's [or Metro-Goldwyn-Mayer], Warner, Paramount, Twentieth Century–Fox, and RKO) that were linked symbiotically with three smaller companies (Columbia, United Artists, and Universal). As Douglas Gomery's study of the effects of Roosevelt's National Recovery Act (NRA) policies on Hollywood indicates, this noncompetitive market structure was in effect reinforced and encouraged, although it was not openly sanctioned, by the federal government in an attempt to stimulate certain industries specifically and the economy in general. But by the late 1930s disgruntled independents encouraged the Department of Justice to initiate an antitrust suit against Paramount Pictures and the other major studios, who were accused of collusion and unfair practices in restraint of trade.

Simon Whitney's examination of antitrust litigation in the motion picture industry concentrates upon the *Paramount* case and documents the adversary relationship that existed between government and industry at the time. Analyzing the effects of the decrees against Paramount and the other studios, Whitney, like Cassady, questions the ability of government legal action to ensure free competition. Joseph Phillips argues that when the decrees forced the studios to divorce their exhibition holdings from production and distribution the locus of power in the film industry simply shifted to distribution. Today the major distributors are responsible for the vast majority of film receipts in both foreign and domestic markets. While power in the film industry shifted from MPPC control of equipment and production to control of exhibition outlets and vertical integration among the major studios in the 1930s and 1940s, and finally to major film distributors linked symbiotically with about ten leading theater chains, the general tendency toward a concentration of power among a few persisted throughout the industry's history. This fact raises several important questions which are examined closely in this book. Is government the film industry's advocate or adversary? Is government antitrust action an effective means of ensuring free competition? What are the effects of the concentration of power in the hands of a few as opposed to free competition?

Efforts of the film industry to censor itself are also largely explained by the desire to maximize profits. Faced with the threat of film boycotts by the Catholic Legion of Decency in the 1930s, the film industry established its own production code, which prohibited certain types of film content. The dissolution of the studio system and the resulting ineffectiveness of its code stimulated a proliferation of local and regional legal suits, which attempted to ban specific films in specific parts of the country. The film industry responded by establishing its own rating system in the 1960s. In both the 1930s and the 1960s the industry sought to avoid short-term and long-term financial losses by policing itself. In responding to social pressures and social change, as Douglas Ayer et al. point out in their insightful study of industry self-censorship, the film industry tried to maximize its profits and prevent outside control.

In their respective studies Douglas Gomery and Gorham Kindem discuss the film industry's adoption of sound and color and show that technological conversion has been a rational response of profit-maximizing oligopolists to technological, economic, and social change. The simple fact that a new piece of film technology is perfected and readily available does not explain innovation and conversion. Innovation occurs when a company has little to lose and much to gain by undertaking the profound risks of initiating technological change. Industry conversion to this new technology only occurs when the major, usually somewhat more conservative, companies determine that previous innovation has justified the added cost of new technology by establishing new markets and demand. In the case of sound, demand increased at the box office, while in the case of color a new demand and market were created by the conversion of the television industry to color. In both cases, profit-maximizing oligopolists reacted deliberately and wisely.

Technological change and media interaction have been closely related phenomena throughout film industry history. As Robert Allen points out in his thorough study of early film exhibition, with the advent of film projectors the film industry initially depended quite heavily on vaudeville for exhibition outlets. The development of film exchanges and storefront theaters or nickelodeons devoted exclusively to presentation of motion pictures, as Allen points out, brought increased specialization to the production, distribution, and exhibition aspects of the industry. This exclusivity also brought greater product differentiation, as films became longer and longer in duration. While the film industry still worked cooperatively with vaudeville and the theater industry throughout the 1920s in terms of exhibition and performers, as Douglas Gomery notes, in about 1910 it began to develop its own star system, examined by Gorham Kindem, which helped films attract larger and larger audiences. The growth of film audiences, particularly middle class audiences, as Ralph Cassady points out, coincides with the rise of other marketing strategies, such as feature films and picture palaces, as competition intensified between theater and film.

The tremendous growth of the film industry and its cooperation and competition with other media were facilitated by the adoption of specific production and marketing strategies. Borrowing concepts from other industries, the film industry's adoption of the studio system in the teens, as examined by Janet Staiger, increased labor specialization and production control, while the adoption of a chain-store, "big business" strategy in exhibition during the 1920s, as Douglas Gomery suggests, effected economies of scale through the exercise of monopsony (single-buyer) power. The coming of sound initially encouraged cooperation and dependence on Broadway and radio for story material and talent, but declining audiences, perhaps resulting from competition with radio as well as the Depression in the early 1930s, stimulated new marketing strategies, such as double features and giveaways. Competition with television and Hollywood's increasing exploitation of and dependence upon foreign markets since the 1950s encouraged major distributors and film conglomerates to adopt the "blockbuster" movie as a marketing strategy, as Joseph Phillips points out.

Between the 1950s and 1970s technological innovations, such as widescreen, 3-D, and color processes, and the production of fewer movies but more blockbusters in the 1950s reflected an initially competitive policy toward television, which is carefully documented by Fredric Stuart. These marketing strategies were designed to increase product differentiation. But during the late 1950s and 1960s Hollywood began to cooperate with television by leasing older films and becoming involved in the production of television programming. As Barry Litman indicates, increased cooperation with the television industry and policies of early sales of television rights have also increased the film industry's dependence on television and the likelihood of its capitulation to the demands of the television industry.

Today cable television, video tapes, and video discs offer both new markets and new competition. Film producers, distributors, and performers recognize them as new sources of revenue, while film theater owners are fearful of the threat they pose to theatrical exhibition. The history of media interaction suggests that technological change is directly related to media interaction. The film industry will continue to interact with new

technology industries both competitively and cooperatively as each segment of the film industry tries to maximize its profits.

Stimulated by the desire to maximize profits through international distribution, America's position in world film markets was also aided and
abetted by two world wars and various types of government support and
cooperation. As Thomas Guback explains, shortly after World War I
the American film industry's penetration of foreign markets was helped
by the disruption of foreign industries and the passage of the Webb-
Pomerene Export Trade Act, which allowed American companies engaged in world markets to form cartels, which were prohibited in domestic markets. By the 1920s American film companies dominated the
international film industry and began to entice away the best foreign talent. Capitalizing on the disruption caused by World War II and further
stimulated by the decline in domestic film attendance after 1946, the
American film industry expanded its penetration of foreign markets until
by 1950 over 50 percent of its total distribution receipts came from foreign distribution. Foreign subsidies stimulated American involvement in
production overseas and also ensured foreign distribution of cooperatively financed products. But America's dominance in world feature-film
markets was also the result of the "universality" (other scholars, such as
Joseph Phillips, might call this "homogeneity" or "inoffensive neutrality")
of its product and its possession of the largest domestic market, where it
could amortize massive production costs. Foreign film industries, even
within the European Economic Community (EEC), or Common Market,
which has for the most part encouraged collective cooperation in major
industries, have remained largely autonomous, maintaining their unique
cultural identities. As Don Le Duc points out, European feature films have
possessed unique cultural values that sometimes limit their international
economic value. European film industries seem to have consciously refused to cooperate with each other in order to compete with the major
American film companies. But it can also be argued, as it is by Thomas
Guback and Manjunath Pendakur, that American advertising and America's control of international distribution outlets have crippled foreign
film industries and made them dependent on the American film industry.
U.S. government foreign policy and aid may also have helped the film industry in its efforts to maximize profits and dominate world markets. In
return American films have sometimes performed political propaganda
functions throughout the free world.

The history of the American film industry is one fraught with contro-
versy in which few questions have been definitively answered. No theoretical approach has attained the status of a scientific paradigm, which
fully and comprehensively explains every problem. The authors repre-

sented in this book have explicitly or implicitly adopted a particular theoretical stance, with their interests, concerns, and general "world view" in large part determining their approach or model. Applying a more general theory to a specific area or problem, each researcher selected a pertinent set of "facts" or explanatory (social, political, economic, legal, or aesthetic) factors, thus allowing each study to be partially judged and evaluated on the basis of the logical consistency of its implied or explicit theory and the ability of that theoretical approach to explain the specific historical problem under consideration.

Case study authors Whitney, Cassady, Litman, Kindem, Gomery, and Le Duc express a basically neoclassical economic approach in their studies of antitrust procedures, television strategies, technological innovation, and the international business of film. J. Allen, Guback, Pendakur, Gomery, and Staiger, on the other hand, present a basically Marxist approach in their studies of antitrust procedures, the international film industry, NRA policies, and the rise of the studio system. In some studies, such as those by Gomery, Litman, and Staiger, a specific theoretical model is cited, while other authors use either a general neoclassical or general Marxist approach. Differences inherent in these alternative approaches to the study of film industry history are apparent in the contrast between Gomery's approach to government regulation (NRA policies) and Whitney's approach to this same general problem. A similar contrast exists between Le Duc's approach to America's role in the international business of film (the EEC, specifically) and those of Guback and Pendakur.

Douglas Gomery's study of the effect of NRA policies on the film industry in the 1930s deals with the problem of government regulation from a perspective that obviously contrasts with Simon Whitney's approach to this same general problem. Gomery applies a specific Marxist economic model which suggests that capitalist governments and monopolists are mutually supportive. Whitney's study of antitrust action in the motion picture industry, like Cassady's study of the MPPC, applies an implicitly neoclassical economic model which suggests that government and monopolists are generally adversaries in terms of regulation. Government agencies attempt to preserve free competition and stimulate a "healthy economy" through legal antitrust actions involving the Sherman and Clayton antitrust acts. Gomery's Marxist model helps explain the effects of NRA policies, while Whitney's neoclassical approach helps explain the effects of the *Paramount* case. The contradiction between Gomery's and Whitney's models and explanations of film industry history reveals a duplicity inherent in government interaction with American industry. The U.S. government has been both an advocate and an adversary of major companies and monopolies. NRA policies implicitly advocated and supported a noncompetitive market structure as a means of stimulating economic recovery, while the 1948 *United States* v. *Paramount et al.* antitrust decrees attempted to stimulate the economy through renewed competition. Neither government policy appears to have been very effective in accomplishing its ostensible goals—to reinvigorate the economy in general or to bring renewed competition to a specific industry, however. Taken together these events seem to indicate that it is difficult to regulate the feature film industry—to curb its tendencies toward oligopoly or to stimulate healthy economic growth. It is quite likely that taking a Marxist approach to the *Paramount* case and antitrust action in general or a neoclassical approach to NRA policies would provide us with additional insights into these problems. Gomery's own application of an explicit neoclassical economic theory of technological innovation to help explain the coming of sound illustrates the fact that a scholar can apply different, even contradictory theoretical models to different problems (sometimes the same problem) and obtain satisfying results. In some instances, one specific explanatory model may provide the best possible means of organizing and explaining a problem, while in another case two or more explanatory models may be equally illuminating.

Valuable insights obtained from alternative approaches characterize studies in other areas of film industry history. Thomas Guback, Manjunath Pendakur, and Don Le Duc approach the problem of America's role in the international film industry from different perspectives. Le Duc's study of the European Economic Community adopts an implicitly neoclassical approach while Guback and Pendakur adopt generalized Marxist approaches in their studies of the international film business and Canada's cultural dependency upon the U.S. film industry, respectively. The approach of Douglas Ayer et al. to movie censorship emphasizes social changes rather than legal precedents and offers a sharp contrast to the majority of legal research in this area. Fredric Stuart's study of television's effect on the film industry uses empirical, quantitative analyses of industry statistics to isolate television's economic impact on the film industry. It fails to explore fully factors related to general social change, however, and the reader would do well to examine the study by Ayer, et al. of censorship and social change, as well as Whitney's study of antitrust action to broaden the overall perspective to include many other causes of significant economic change in the film industry during this period.

The complexities of the American film industry are revealed by viewing its history from several different perspectives. The overlap among the case studies in this book is expansive rather than redundant. Different approaches highlight various economic, social, political, legal, and aesthetic forces. The portrait of film history that emerges is similar to a cubist painting. Many different perspectives on American film industry history are projected simultaneously, revealing the richness and complexity of the subject. Film scholarship and research is an ongoing, collective process. These case studies establish a context for further historical research that will add significantly to current film scholarship. A thorough familiarity with the collective histories presented in this anthology also sets a context for the study of contemporary film developments and problems.

PART ONE

Initial Patterns of Production,
Distribution, and Exhibition

Vitascope/Cinématographe:
Initial Patterns of American Film
Industrial Practice

Robert C. Allen

The earliest patterns of American film distribution and exhibition have remained obscured by historical inattention. Gordon Hendricks' detailed studies of the invention of the Kinetograph, Kinetoscope, and Biograph leave relatively unexamined the contexts in which these initial cinematic devices were commercially exploited. In most survey histories of American cinema, discussion of this period focuses on the Koster and Bial exhibition of the Vitascope on 23 April 1896. This event is included in most chronicles of early film history because it demonstrates the popularity of film as a vaudeville attraction. Yet missing from these histories is the integration of this single event into a systematic analysis of the early history of the film industry. What factors led up to the Koster and Bial exhibition, and what was its full significance as a precedent for the marketing of motion picture technology?

By using data collected from the contemporaneous trade press and business records of the Vitascope Company and the Edison Manufacturing Company, I shall consider the first year (1896–97) of large-scale commercial exploitation of cinema as a projected medium. The two principal companies involved, the Vitascope Company (licensees of Edison) and the Lumière Company, represent divergent marketing strategies for the American cinema. The success of the Lumières and the concomitant lack of it by the Vitascope Company attest to the determining influence vaudeville exerted on early practices of the motion picture industry.

The history of American commercial screen exhibition begins with the invention of the Kinetograph camera in the laboratories of Thomas Edison. Developed between 1887 and 1891, the Kinetograph was the camera with which, as Gordon Hendricks has noted, "every subject known to us up to May 1896" in the United States was shot. The Kinetograph films were not projected, however, but viewed by means of a peep-show device, the Kinetoscope, which was first marketed in April 1894. During the spring and summer of that year, Kinetoscopes were installed in penny arcades, hotel lobbies, summer amusement resorts, and phonograph parlors.[1] By 1895 the Edison Company had demonstrated the practicability of motion photography, begun regular production of films for use in the Kinetoscope, and established the commercial usefulness of the motion picture as a popular entertainment novelty.

It was not until five years after Edison had patented the Kinetograph in 1891 that his laboratory produced its own movie projector. Journalist Terry Ramsaye's widely quoted explanation for Edison's delay was that the Wizard reasoned, "If we put out a screen machine, there will be use for maybe about ten of them in the whole United States. . . . Let's not kill the goose that lays the golden egg."[2] There is reason to doubt that Edison thought in terms of the Kinetoscope as his magic goose and thus discounted the profitability of opening up motion picture exhibition to group audiences. It is much more likely that the Kinetoscope scheme was perceived as a *turkey* rather than a magic goose; records of the Edison Manufacturing Company show that its supply of golden eggs lasted but a few months. Edison probably doubted the commercial value of the Kinetoscope from the beginning, and when returns from the device began to dwindle after a brief success, he turned his attention to the myriad other projects he was working on. Even before the first Kinetoscope had been placed into commercial service, Edison wrote Eadweard Muybridge, "I have constructed a little instrument which I call a kinetograph with a nickel slot attachment and some twenty-five have been made out. I am very doubtful if there is any commercial feature in it and fear that they will not earn their cost."[3]

Ohio businessmen Norman Raff and Frank C. Gammon became exclusive American marketing agents for the Kinetoscope on 1 September 1894.[4] The following May Raff wrote, "The demand for Kinetoscopes (during 1895) has not been enough to even pay expenses of our company. . . . In fact our candid opinion is that the Kinetoscope business—at least as far as the regular company is concerned—will be a 'dead duck' after this season."[5] Public interest in the peep show was waning, and the owners were selling their machines, further depressing the market for new Kinetoscopes.[6] To make matters worse, by May 1895 news had reached Raff and Gammon that Frenchmen Louis and Auguste Lumière had patented and publicly exhibited a camera/projector, the Cinématographe.[7]

With their Kinetoscope business a failure and the prospects of a successful commercial projector imminent, during the summer and fall of 1895 Raff and Gammon pleaded with the Edison Company to develop its own projector, but to no avail. Just when the partners were trying to sell their business and cut their losses, they learned of a projector, the Vitascope, invented by two men from Washington, D.C., Thomas Armat and Francis Jenkins. In January 1896 Raff and Gammon concluded negotiations by which they received the license to market the device on a territorial-rights basis. To avoid potential patent litigation and to assure a supply of films, they also contracted for the Edison Company to manufacture the projector and provide films.[8]

The marketing plan devised by Raff and Gammon for the Vitascope was based upon that initially used for the Edison phonograph. In June 1888 the North American Phonograph Company was formed for the purpose of exploiting the Edison phonograph and a competing machine, the graphophone. This company was authorized by Edison to grant exclusive territorial licenses for the lease of the phonograph and the purchase of recording cylinders. Within two years, North American had issued franchises to thirty-three state or regional companies. This territorial-rights marketing scheme was based on the assumption that the phonograph would be used primarily as a piece of office machinery: a stenographic aid. Within a short time, however, it was discovered that the phonograph, as then designed, was not particularly useful as a dictating machine. Rights holders resorted to attaching coin-in-the-slot devices to their phonographs in an effort to recoup their investment. By 1892 most phonographs were being used, not in offices, but in saloons and penny arcades, a development which made the territorial-rights plan outmoded.[9] Rights holders discovered that as the demand for phonographs increased with their popularity as entertainment devices, their clients began purchasing cheap copies of the Edison machine rather than leasing the original from them.

There is no discussion of the merits of the territorial-rights marketing scheme among the Raff and Gammon correspondence; its dubious usefulness in marketing entertainment devices did not deter them from resorting to it. The scheme devised for marketing the Vitascope called for the selling of franchises in the United States and Canada. For an initial advance payment, an agent could purchase exclusive rights to the Vitascope for a state or group of states, including the right to lease projectors (for from $25 to $50 monthly, per machine) and buy Edison films. The manner and location of the exhibitions were left entirely to the franchise holder. The agents could exploit the Vitascope themselves, or as Raff and Gammon repeatedly pointed out in their correspondence, the territories could be further divided and subfranchised.[10]

The exhibition context Raff and Gammon had in mind for the Vitascope is unclear from their correspondence with prospective rights purchasers. In their initial catalogue, they suggest that a twenty-five or fifty-cent admission charge could be made for a brief program of Vitascope subjects.[11] What they do not seem to have had in mind was the use of films in vaudeville theaters on a regular basis. The films were to be sold, not rented. Raff and Gammon told prospective customers that the films could be used "for a long time." With a stock of only fifteen to twenty films at the beginning of their marketing campaign, Raff and Gammon were not in a position to supply vaudeville managers with the regular change of program their audiences had come to expect. The two types of exhibition outlets Raff and Gammon envisioned for the motion picture seem to have been the penny arcade, or phonograph parlor, and presentations by itinerant showmen. Several people who bought territorial rights were operators of phonograph parlors. A. F. Reiser, the Vitascope agent for Pennsylvania (exclusive of Philadelphia and Pittsburgh), operated a publishing company that specialized in providing books for public libraries. If the community did not have the funds, Reiser would help them raise the money by sponsoring musical concerts. He wanted to use the Vitascope in rural Pennsylvania to assist him in these fund-raising efforts.[12]

Raff and Gammon did not aspire to a relationship with vaudeville; it was thrust upon them. The public and commercial debut of the Vitascope at Koster and Bial's Music Hall in New York on 23 April 1896 was a result of a hurriedly made decision, arrived at in the face of news that several vaudeville managers were attempting to secure the Lumière Cinématographe for their theaters.[13] Realizing the adverse publicity value of having another machine open in New York ahead of the Vitascope, and, no doubt, the potential economic advantages of a combination between vaudeville and foreign motion picture interests, Raff wrote to Abraham Bial on 7 April offering him the use of the Vitascope "at a largely reduced compensation," out of consideration for "a certain benefit to us from your advertising, etc."[14]

The interest of vaudeville managers in the movies was by no means coincidental. For decades vaudeville, with its modular program of brief, self-contained acts, had featured visual novelties of all sorts: pantomime, shadowgraphy, puppetry, *tableaux vivants*, and lanternry, among others. By 1896 vaudeville was rapidly becoming the preeminent American popular entertainment form, with competition among theaters growing intense, especially in New York. Two seasons before (1894/95), New York vaudeville managers had begun an all-out battle for patronage. F. F. Proctor presented opera stars at his Twenty-Third Street Theatre. B. F. Keith countered by securing the state luminaries to appear in condensed dramatic vehicles at his Union Square Theatre. The warfare intensified when Oscar Hammerstein opened his Olympia Theater in the fall of 1895, importing French chanteuse Yvette Guilbert at a cost of $3,000 per week.[15] By April 1896 the five major New York vaudeville entrepreneurs were frantically trying to surpass each other with more lavish theater environments, more acts on the bills, and especially, novel attractions. It was perhaps the most auspicious moment in the history of vaudeville for the introduction of a new visual curiosity.

Raff and Gammon, however, were much less interested in providing vaudeville with its latest sensation than in generating publicity on the eve of distributing the first Vitascopes to the state-rights holders. The Koster and Bial exhibition was preceded by three weeks of press coverage, beginning with a press screening at the West Orange Laboratory of Thomas Edison on 3 April.[16]

The only thing Edison had contributed to the development of the Vitascope was the imprimatur of his name, yet Raff and Gammon promoted the projector as the latest marvel from the Wizard's workshop—a ruse which, no doubt, was largely responsible for the generous publicity given the Vitascope.

The second purpose of the Koster and Bial exhibition was to attempt to preempt foreign competition. In this, Raff and Gammon failed for several reasons: it was already too late; by demonstrating that the motion picture could be adapted successfully to form a vaudeville act, they helped to spawn a demand from vaudeville managers that benefited not only them but also advocates of other machines; and the tremendous demand for motion picture demonstrations that arose after the Koster and Bial exhibition was premature for Raff and Gammon; they were unable to satisfy it and left a growing market ripe for competition.

Despite Raff and Gammon's assurances to actual and prospective franchise holders that they would be protected from competing projectors entering the market, competition with the Vitascope developed almost immediately. In May the Lumière Cinématographe opened at Keith's Union Square Theatre, where for several weeks each performance was "wildly applauded."[17] Even with New York sweltering in a June heat wave, the Cinématographe enabled the Union Square to double its weekly box office receipts.[18]

During the summer and fall of 1896 Raff and Gammon's Vitascope

Company fared badly. Their first problem was that their marketing strategy militated against a strong connection between vaudeville and the Vitascope in that their state-based franchise plan conflicted with the institutional structure of vaudeville. By 1896 vaudeville was in a period of interstate circuit building—growth which ignored the political boundaries at the very basis of the Raff and Gammon scheme. Unlike other vaudeville acts the Vitascope could be booked into a circuit of theaters only with great difficulty. Separate deals had to be negotiated with rights holders in each state. The states-rights arrangements explains why no franchises were sold to vaudeville circuits. The Lumières, on the other hand, used no such territorial plan. All engagements in the United States for the Cinématographe were booked through a single New York office.

Secondly, even before the Koster and Bial exhibition, Raff and Gammon had begun making commitments to their agents on delivery of Vitascopes. Unfortunately, Raff and Gammon could not control the manufacture of the machines at the Edison factory, and late deliveries were a problem almost from the start.[19]

Even prompt delivery of the projector did not assure the debut of the Vitascope as advertised. The Vitascope arrived at Ford's Theatre in Baltimore the day of its scheduled opening. The manager had sold out his house long in advance. But when the electrician sent along to set up the Vitascope saw that the house electricity operated on alternating current and the projector on direct, he refused to install the machine. The franchise holder, who had arranged the exhibition with the theater manager, blamed the problem on the ineptitude of the electrician, but the problem was in the design of the Vitascope:[20] all the early Vitascopes were made to work only on direct current, and in 1896 municipal lighting systems were a hodge-podge of incompatible currents and voltages. Throughout the summer and fall exasperated Vitascope agents complained to Raff and Gammon about the situation, the agent for the Maritime Provinces writing, "If the small towns of the continent are to be worked, a radical change will have to be made in the construction of the machines so that exhibitions can be utterly independent of electric power companies." Otherwise, he said, "it is simply working for nothing."[21] On the other hand the Cinématographe needed no electrical current, being hand-cranked and illuminated by limelight or another nonelectrical source.[22]

While Raff and Gammon provided a trained projectionist to set up and operate the Vitascope for early exhibitions at Koster and Bial's, they offered no such assistance to their agents, only "detailed instructions" on the operation of the machine. In many instances, the success of a Vitascope exhibition depended far less on the projector itself than on the skill of its operator.[23]

The most serious obstacle facing the Vitascope agents, and, in turn, Raff and Gammon, was obtaining a regular supply of new films. The franchise holders needed to be able to count on regular shipments of new films whose contents were as appealing as those of the Lumière films. Raff and Gammon's inability to meet this demand resulted in a rising chorus of frustration and anger from their agents. The Pennsylvania franchise holder chided them, "the museum people were so much disappointed that they stopped the Vitascope. They expected eight new subjects and I only had three and they were poor." [24] The Wisconsin agents wrote in August, "It seems singular to us that our orders are so long about being filled. We are not safe in promising anything. . . . With . . . the cinématographe and others menacing us, we ought to be accomodated [*sic*] promptly." [25]

The design of the Cinématographe gave it a considerably wider range of subject matter than the Edison camera. The latter, still called the Kinetograph, was a bulky, electrically driven apparatus weighing several hundred pounds. [26] The production situation devised for its operation was the famous Black Maria open-air studio behind the Edison works in West Orange. The principal components of the Edison repertoire were condensations of vaudeville turns, circus acts, and minute extracts from popular plays. These reenactments had limited popular appeal, however, and there is evidence that their popularity as Kinetoscope peep-show subjects had begun to decline even before the Vitascope appeared. [27]

The hand-cranked Lumière Cinématographe was both camera and projector, and weighed slightly over sixteen pounds. The Lumières sent cameramen all over the world and could offer their patrons scenes of the Czar's coronation, Venice as seen from a moving gondola, and Trafalgar Square. These travel films were so popular that in August 1896 Raff and Gammon resorted to having the English agents for the Vitascope surreptitiously purchase Lumière films shot in Russia, Italy, and France for use with the Vitascope in the United States. [28] Also with camera/projector/printer in one, the Lumière operator could take, develop, and show films while on tour. The ability to take these "local actualities," as they were called, was of no small benefit to the Lumières. It also speaks to fundamental differences in business organization between the Lumières and the Vitascope Company—differences that gave the Lumières significant advantage in the vaudeville market.

Raff and Gammon had control over only one part of the Vitascope operation. The Edison factory manufactured the machines and films; these were distributed by Raff and Gammon, who did not engage themselves in exhibition, but often sold off parts of their territory to others. As the Raff and Gammon correspondence shows, the route from source of supply to its final destination could be, and too often was, a long and uncertain one.

Exhibition was separated from production by distance, business and legal arrangements, and technology—the Vitascope was not able (without substantial and illegal modifications) to serve as a camera.

With the Cinématographe, although the distance from the Lyons factory to the exhibition site in the United States was certainly greater, this problem was alleviated to a large extent by the collapsing of some of the functions of filmmaker, distributor, exhibitor, and projectionist into a single individual: the "operator" sent out from Lyons to tour in the United States. Felix Mesguisch, the first Lumière operator to arrive in the United States, stated that in the first six months of exploitation there were some twenty-one projectionists/cameramen/developers on tour with the Cinématographe.[29] The Lumière representative in New York was an employee of the Lumière Company, not a rights speculator. He arranged for exhibitions, scheduled tours, and distributed films to the operators, acting very much like the booking agent for a vaudeville act. The operator with his Cinématographe and films was not *like* a vaudeville act, he *was* one—a self-contained unit which could travel an interstate circuit as easily as an acrobat or a trained-dog act.

The marketing scheme for the Vitascope failed because it did not anticipate the use of the motion picture as a popular entertainment device exhibited in a theatrical setting. Moreover, the territorial-rights plan could not be easily adapted to the institutional structure of vaudeville. All the blame for the demise of the Vitascope Company cannot be attributed to the unsuitability of its marketing plan, however. Certainly design limitations of the Vitascope itself contributed to Raff and Gammon's troubles. Another part of the problem was Raff and Gammon's desire to reap short-term profits through rights' speculation rather than engaging in exhibition themselves. Edison's lack of foresight regarding the motion picture is well known, and the Edison Manufacturing Company did its share toward placing the Vitascope in an impossible position within the vaudeville exhibition market. Films were slow in being delivered, and the subjects prepared at West Orange were unsuitable for urban vaudeville performances. Clearly Edison did not anticipate the relationship between vaudeville and film.

He did see, however, that Raff and Gammon's attempt to market the Vitascope was a failure. Thus when the Edison laboratory developed its own projector, the Projecting Kinetoscope, Edison sold the machine outright with no territorial restrictions. He further undercut Raff and Gammon by selling films for the Projecting Kinetoscope at a lower price than Raff and Gammon were offering to their Vitascope customers.[30] Raff and Gammon's agreement with Edison and Armat prohibited their selling the

Vitascope, and they had sold the rights to it for most of the United States for five years. By the end of 1896, the Vitascope enterprise was no more.

Clearly, the Lumière operation was better adapted to servicing the American vaudeville market, but their victory was short-lived. In the spring of 1897 the Lumières left the American market, presumably under the threat of patent litigation from Edison.[31] But they left behind them a pattern of industrial practice that survived through the next decade: the providing of vaudeville theaters with a complete "act," consisting of projector, films, and operator. This marketing plan formed the basis for much of the success by the Edison and Vitagraph Company of America film companies before 1905.

The Lumière approach to marketing we might call preindustrial. The Lumières, Biograph, and Vitagraph were providing a service to vaudeville. This dependency upon vaudeville temporarily obviated the need for the American cinema to develop its own exhibition outlets, but it also prevented film from achieving industrial autonomy. The industrial structure of vaudeville did not call for a division of labor in the usual sense. Rather, the division came within the vaudeville presentation itself: each act was merely one of eight or more functional units—one cog in the vaudeville machine. Hence it is not surprising that a machine would quite literally replace the acrobat, animal act, or magician on vaudeville bills. Neither did the use of films in vaudeville require a division of the industry into distinct production, distribution, and exhibition units. In fact, it favored the collapsing of these functions into the "operator," who, with his projector, became the self-contained vaudeville act. It was not until American cinema achieved industrial autonomy with the advent of store-front movie theaters that a clear separation of functions became the dominant mode of industrial organization, and film entered its early industrial phase.

Motion Picture Exhibition in Manhattan, 1906–1912: Beyond the Nickelodeon

Robert C. Allen

On 19 June 1905 on Smithfield Street in Pittsburgh a vaudeville entrepreneur, Harry Davis, and his partner, John P. Harris, opened a theater devoted to the showing of motion pictures. Audiences on that opening night sat in seats salvaged from a defunct opera house and, for their five-cent admission charge, watched *The Great Train Robbery* unroll on the screen to piano accompaniment.[1] There was little more to the performance. The Nickelodeon, as the theater was called, could boast only ninety-six chairs, a piano, projector, and screen. Yet, with the possible exception of Koster and Bial's Music Hall, the Nickelodeon Theatre is the most famous theater in which motion pictures were shown before 1914. It was here, according to most film historians, that movies in America entered a new era. Inside this dingy little storefront and the thousands like it that, we are told, sprang up in the wake of its success, the motion picture found its own exclusive exhibition outlet and a new audience of working-class Americans. The movies had outgrown their role as minor adjuncts to vaudeville performances, and while the middle-class patrons of variety thumbed their noses at this upstart amusement, the nickelodeon proceeded to revolutionize American mass entertainment in only a few years' time.[2]

Most students of American film history are familiar with the descriptions of nickelodeons in secondary sources. "Concentrated largely in poorer shopping districts and slum neighborhoods," writes Jacobs, "nickelodeons were disdained by the well-to-do. But the workmen and their families who patronized the movies did not mind the crowded, unsanitary, and hazardous accommodations most of the nickelodeons offered."[3] Sklar locates the nickelodeons ("crowded, dark, and smelly rooms") in working-class neighborhoods and says their programs of films and illustrated songs "lasted no more than fifteen or twenty minutes."[4] Hampton also describes nickelodeons as "crowded, poorly ventilated" places in which film programs lasting approximately twenty minutes were given.[5] North places the nickelodeons mostly "in big industrial cities with large foreign populations of poorly paid laborers."[6] Sklar and other film historians maintain that a large portion of the nickelodeon audience was made up of newly arrived immigrants. He notes, "what was distinctive about the movies as they entered their second decade, . . . was their success in providing entertainment and information to an audience that did not need English or even literacy to gain access to urban popular culture for the first time."[7]

While both Sklar and Jowett go into more detail on the nature of early film exhibition than previous historians, we still know relatively little about this crucial stage in the development of the American film industry. As Russell Merritt has put it, "The nickelodeon era, for the most part, has been ignored in the current literature of film history."[8] We have yet to answer the following questions. Were nickelodeons located exclusively in working-class neighborhoods? Did immigrants form a large portion of the nickelodeons' audience? How long was the nickelodeon the primary form of motion picture exhibition? Did exhibition patterns vary from city to city and between urban and rural areas or both? How do we explain the alleged nickelodeon "explosion": the establishment of as many as 7,000–10,000 nickelodeons in a two- or three-year period?

Studies by Merritt and Gomery cast doubt upon the characterization of early motion picture exhibitions as taking place in "crowded, dark, and smelly rooms." Merritt found that in Boston nickelodeons were located along busy commercial thoroughfares, rather than in working-class residential areas. He also found that Boston exhibitors were much more interested in attracting middle-class patrons than in serving working-class moviegoers.[9] Gomery discovered the location of Milwaukee nickelodeons to be determined not so much by the socioeconomic status of particular neighborhoods as by proximity to mass-transit lines and previously established shopping areas.[10]

Remarkably, there has been no study of early motion picture exhibition in New York City, the popular entertainment capital of America during the early years of this century. In dealing with conditions of exhibition in Manhattan between 1906 and 1912, two matters are of particular concern here: whether the usual characterization of nickelodeons offered in secondary sources apply to those in New York City, and what elements determined the locations of nickelodeons in the city. And as the hub of the nascent motion picture industry and the largest urban center in the country, with considerable demographic and other data available, New York seemed the logical choice for this study. In the words of urban historian Thomas Kessner, "New York represented the Immigrant City *sui generis*," so that it is here of all cities that the relationship between immigrant neighborhoods and motion picture exhibition should be revealed most clearly.[11] Also, much of our mythology of early American exhibition originates in New York because theater magnates William Fox and Adolph Zukor were products of the city's Lower East Side Jewish ghetto, although the "great man" emphasis in early exhibition history hardly presents an accurate indication of the economic, social, and demographic forces that shaped their first business ventures and those of the myriad other New York exhibitors as well.[12]

As I shall discuss in the remaining pages of this chapter, our picture of the nickelodeon is at best sketchy, at worst misrepresentative; no single factor accounts for the location of nickelodeons; and the "nickelodeon era," as usually conceived, was much briefer than generally believed—in that important changes in the exhibition format after 1908 radically altered the nature of moviegoing in New York City, if not in the entire country.

☆
The Lower East Side

While storefront motion picture theaters date back to 1896, it does not appear that they were established in any numbers until around 1906. The first trade press notice of the nickelodeon phenomenon comes in the 17 March 1906 issue of *Variety*, to effect that several storefront theaters giving fifteen-minute shows had recently opened "along the main thoroughfares" in New York City. Early in 1907 a "conservative estimate" of the number of nickelodeons in the United States was 2,500, but as *Variety* pointed out, "they are increasing so rapidly that positive figures are unobtainable."[13]

The 1908 *Trow's Business Directory* lists 123 motion picture exhibitions in Manhattan, exclusive of vaudeville theaters. Of this number, 42 were located in the Lower East Side, an area bounded roughly by the East River, Catherine Street on the south, the Bowery on the west, and Fourteenth Street on the north. It is here that we find the nickelodeons so beloved of film historians: they were almost certainly proletarian and immigrant oriented.

In 1908 the Lower East Side was heavily populated by recent Jewish immigrants. (By 1900 there were already 654 persons per acre, the highest population density in the city, and crowding did not peak until 1910.) Living conditions ranged from bad to intolerable; 95 percent of the families lived three or more to a room.[14] But as Thomas Kessner has pointed out, "congestion also produced economic dividends" for peddlers and small shopkeepers, whose potential market numbered in the hundreds of thousands.[15] It is difficult to prove whether the nickelodeons located along Delancy or Rivington streets were dingy or crowded, but it is fairly certain they were small. Detailed fire insurance maps from the period reveal that the size of most nickelodeons on the Lower East Side did not exceed 25 by 100 feet.[16]

Of the Lower East Side nickelodeons, nearly one-third (thirteen of forty-two) were not located in the residential blocks per se, but were strung along the Bowery. For decades the Bowery had been a center of popular entertainment. Before 1875 it was the locus of New York's legitimate theaters; thereafter it became a prime location for cheaper amusements: vaudeville, burlesque, dime museums, shooting galleries, and approximately six saloons per block.[17] A civic reformer wrote of the street a few years before the nickelodeon boom, "The Bowery is the main artery of night life on the East Side. At night it is a blaze of light from one end to the other. It is a center for saloons of every order, from gin-palaces to bucket-shops; theatres, concert-halls, 'free-and-easys,' and dime museums abound, all of them profusely ornamented with every device of colored light. . . . In and out of these resorts pours a constant crowd."[18]

Although not a part of the Lower East Side proper, the Union Square area at Fourteenth Street and Broadway was nearly adjacent to it. Like the Bowery, Union Square had been a major New York entertainment center for years. Seven movie theaters were crowded around the square, cheek-by-jowl with two important vaudeville theaters (Tony Pastor's and Keith's), several legitimate and burlesque theaters, and a number of penny arcades. Union Square was but a short walk from the tenements of the Lower East Side, but several of the movie theaters there bore little resemblance to those in the heart of the Jewish ghetto. William Fox's Dewey Theatre, a former legitimate house acquired by him in 1908, seated nearly one thousand persons. Fox gave a show lasting almost two hours, including five reels of film and five vaudeville acts. Twelve uniformed ushers were among the fifty employees at the Dewey.[19]

To repeat, of 123 New York movie theaters in 1908, only 42 were located in the heavily immigrant-populated Lower East Side. The sites of the 13 theaters along the Bowery were probably owing as much to the traditional entertainment orientation of the boulevard as to its proximity to the nearby tenements. The same might be said of the 7 other theaters clustered around Union Square.

☆
Other Neighborhoods

Proximity to public transportation lines helps to explain the location of some movie theaters, especially along the east side of the island. Some nineteen theaters were scattered along Second and Third avenues between 23d Street and their termination at 129th and 130th streets. It was along Second and Third avenues that major East Side streetcar lines ran. Interestingly, however, we do not find a high correlation between subway or streetcar lines and movie theaters elsewhere on the island, leading to the speculation that most New York theaters were probably patronized by those who lived or worked in the immediate area. This neighborhood orientation is supported by the fact that large numbers of movie theaters were centered around four easily identifiable ethnic or socioeconomic (or both) areas of the city: Yorkville, 125th Street, Jewish Harlem, and Little Italy.

Nine theaters were located in the Yorkville section of the East Side. This neighborhood, bounded by Seventh-Fourth and Eighty-Ninth streets, Third Avenue and the East River, was in 1909 a German and Irish enclave where "many of the residents were small merchants or tradesmen." [20]

There were also concentrations of nickelodeons in two other clearly defined ethnic communities on the Upper East Side: Jewish Harlem and Little Italy. The first of the so-called New Immigrants groups (non-Northern European) to move into Harlem was the Italians. During the 1890s Italians began congregating in an area bordered by 99th and 119th streets, Third Avenue, and the East River. In this area in 1910 there were 60,897 Italians out of a total population of 113,920. The heart of Little Italy was between 114th and 119th Streets, and First and Third avenues, where Italians constituted 72 percent of the population.[21] E. Idell Ziesloft, writing in *The New Metropolis* in 1899, described this neighborhood as "one of the most flourishing and picturesque Italian colonies in New York. . . . The tenements that line these streets are not much to look at in themselves, but the quaintly furnished rooms in them, . . . the gay lines of wash, the small shops and street scenes make up a picture that never loses interest. . . . These are the peaceful Italians from the north of Italy, and the stiletto is rarely brought into play here."[22] Although clearly an ethnic community, Little Italy seems to have been much more affluent than the immigrant ghettos of Lower Manhattan. There were thirteen movie theaters here in 1908.

Ten more nickelodeons were located in nearby Jewish Harlem. This neighborhood of first- and second-generation Jews was bounded by 98th and 118th streets, Park Avenue, the northeast shoulder of Central Park, and Lenox Avenue. Its residents were the more prosperous and Americanized Jews who had been able to escape from the Lower East Side. The illiteracy rate among males in Jewish Harlem was less than one quarter of that on the Lower East Side.[23]

North of these two areas was Harlem proper, in 1908 still a middle and lower-middle class neighborhood, although the transformation of the area into a black community had just begun.[24] As late as 1902 in the East Harlem Twelfth Ward, only 10,786 families out of 103,570 were New Immigrants.[25] For over a decade the principal crosstown street of Harlem had been 125th Street—a street which also formed the community's primary entertainment district.[26] By 1908 twelve movie theaters had pushed in among the Harlem Opera House, the Gotham Theatre, Hurtig and Seamon's Music Hall, and Keith and Proctor's 125th Street Theatre.

In all, some forty-four movie theaters were located in Yorkville, Little Italy, Jewish Harlem, and on 125th—two more than were located on the Lower East Side in 1908.

Smaller Concentrations of Theaters

The major groupings of movie theaters discussed above (lower East Side, Union Square, Second and Third Avenues, Yorkville, Little Italy, Jewish Harlem, 125th Street) account for 102, or 83 percent, of the 123 movie theaters listed in the 1908 *Trow's Business Directory*. The remaining theaters were scattered around the island in smaller clusters. There were a few along 23d Street between the subway stops at Seventh Avenue and Broadway. Three were established a few blocks northwest, in the area of Miner's Eighth Avenue (vaudeville) Theatre. Four more theaters were further up Eighth Avenue, between 38th and 49th streets. All of these movie theaters were located in or adjacent to traditional entertainment districts.

But in addition to accounting for the location of nickelodeon concentrations, we must also account for areas where nickelodeons were not to be found. We do not, for example, find a single movie theater along Fifth or Madison avenues, from Union Square to 100th Street, a fact not difficult to explain given the character of these two streets. French novelist Paul Bourget wrote of Manhattan in 1894, "It is but too evident that money cannot have much value here. There is too much of it. The interminable succession of luxurious mansions which line Fifth Avenue proclaim its mad abundance. No shops—unless of articles of luxury . . . only independent dwellings, each of which including the ground on which it stands, implies a value which one dares not calculate. . . . This avenue has visibly been willed and created by sheer force of millions."[27] Madison Avenue was "second only to Fifth as a residential thoroughfare," and was also termed "the Avenue to the Gods."[28]

The absence of movie theaters on the Upper West Side might be owing to two factors. First, this area was much slower to develop than the Upper East Side. It was not until the completion of the Ninth Avenue "El" in the 1880s that large-scale residential building began. Second, by 1900 the social character of the Upper West Side was set: mansions along Riverside Drive, handsome houses along West End Avenue, and fashionable apartment buildings spreading westward from Central Park; in other words, the area was solidly middle and upper class.[29]

The large concentration of movie theaters in the Lower East Side is not surprising; however, it is somewhat puzzling not to find significant numbers of nickelodeons in the equally dense and immigrant-dominated Middle West Side (roughly marked by Thirty-Fourth and Fifty-Eighth streets, Eighth Avenue and the Hudson River) and the neighborhood immediately west of the Lower East Side (bounded by Canal and Houston, the Bowery and Sullivan). Both areas housed newly arrived immigrants— mostly Italians—of the poorest means. In the former we find but one movie theater; in the latter, only three. The combined area of these two neighborhoods makes them nearly equal in size to the Lower East Side, but, omitting those theaters located along the Bowery, there were seven times more movie theaters in the Jewish area than in the Italian. Yet, the more affluent Italian and Jewish neighborhoods on the Upper East Side are roughly equal in the number of movie theaters in each. This seeming paradox might be explained by differences in immigration patterns between the two ethnic groups during this period.

Many Italians who came to the United States around the turn of the century did not come to stay; they earned what money they could and returned to Italy. Between 1907 and 1911, seventy-three out of every one hundred Italians landing at Ellis Island repatriated. That most Italian immigrants in New York City were either working toward building a personal nest egg or supporting families in the old country is indicated by the fact that between 1880 and 1910 80 percent of Italian immigrants to the city were male, most between the ages of fourteen and forty-four. Children made up an insignificant portion of the immigrant population.[30] It is plausible, therefore, that many of the Italians who lived in the Middle West Side or Lower Manhattan were unlikely to spend part of their paltry earnings on something so frivolous as the movies.

On the other hand, as Thomas Kessner has pointed out, "statistics on the Eastern European Jewish immigrants show no comparable repatriation." The average repatriation for all New Immigrants was 42 percent, but among Jews only 7 percent. Among 295,000 Russian Jews who entered the United States between 1908 and 1912, only 21,000 re-emigrated to another country. Further, Jewish immigration was a movement of families. Between 1899 and 1910, 43 percent of arriving Jewish immigrants were female and nearly one-third were under the age of sixteen.[31] Other factors need to be investigated—child-rearing practices, possible religious sanctions against certain forms of entertainment—but it does appear that the family-oriented, American-minded Jewish community was a more lucrative location for a nickelodeon than the transient, predominately male Italian neighborhoods. We do not find this to be the case in Little Italy, probably because it was the most prosperous and hence most stable Italian enclave in the city.

Small-Time Vaudeville

Comparing the listings under "moving picture exhibitions" in the extant *Trow's Business Directories* between 1906 and 1912 reveals that the patterns established by 1908 do not substantially change. The total number of movie theaters increased only slightly (to 138), and the proportional distribution among geographical areas generally remained stable. The increase in the total number of theaters was largely owing to their establishment in the upper reaches of Harlem. In 1908 only 6 theaters were located north of 125th Street; in 1912 there were 19.

What these data do not show, however, is an important qualitative change in motion picture exhibition between 1908 and 1912—a change wrought by the growth of what came to be called small-time vaudeville. As we have seen, just as all movie theaters were not located in immigrant ghettos, not all of them were the small, sawdust-floored dives of historical legend. As early as 1907 enterprising entrepreneurs saw that huge profits could be made by converting large-capacity theaters into movie houses, where audiences enjoyed not only movies but the trappings of theatrical entertainment. Moreover, as Russell Merritt found in Boston, improvements in theater decor and comfort led to increased patronage by middle-class citizens.

By early 1908 several New York theaters had been converted into movie houses. In November 1907, William A. Brady took over the 1,200-seat Alhambra Theatre on Union Square and renamed it the Unique, making it, according to *Variety*, "the newest and easily the handsomest popular priced vaudeville theatre in the city." The Unique offered movies and vaudeville acts for from ten to twenty-five cents.[32] A few weeks later, a group of investors, led by Philadelphia theater entrepreneur Felix Isman, rented the Manhattan Theatre for $25,000 annually. Its transformation into a movie theater was an immediate success; on opening night "a capacity attendance took up all the available space." Almost simultaneous with the above, the New York entertainment industry was shocked to learn that Keith's Union Square Theatre and Proctor's Twenty-Third Street Theatre, two of the premier vaudeville houses in the city, were to be made into movie theaters. By February 1908, the Twenty-Third Street Theatre, renamed the Bijou Dream, was attracting 2,000 people daily. Of motion picture exhibition in New York *Variety* commented, "the tendency is clearly toward fewer, bigger, cleaner five-cent theatres and more expensive shows."[33]

What evolved from this movement toward spacious, middle-class oriented theaters and away from the converted storefront was small-time vaudeville: the showing of a mixed program of film and vaudeville acts in large-capacity theaters for between ten and thirty-five cents. Several film historians have mentioned attempts by some exhibitors to upgrade the quality of nickelodeon presentations and surroundings between 1906 and 1912.[34] Almost no attention, however, has been given to the growth of small-time vaudeville as an autonomous entertainment form, despite the fact that by 1910 it was a major factor in motion picture exhibition in New York and in the country as a whole. As early as August 1909, *Moving Picture World* predicted that the "storeroom" shows would shortly disappear, their place being taken "by especially built theatres, seating five hundred to a thousand, most of them giving a mixed bill of vaudeville and motion pictures."[35]

The mixing of vaudeville and film in large, often ornate theaters was a result of three factors: the saturation of large cities (including New York) with nickelodeons, leading to a highly competitive exhibition market; a scarcity of new films; and a desire on the part of some exhibitors to attract more middle-class customers.

The clustering of movie theaters in residential neighborhoods, along commercial thoroughfares, and in traditional entertainment districts led to fierce competition among them. Early in 1907 *Variety* correspondents from around the country began commenting on the battles for movie patronage raging in large cities. Managers employed many gimmicks to differentiate their house from the one across the street. Some gave longer bills or promised daily changes of movies; some even tried lowering admission to three cents. One of the most popular ploys was the addition of a few vaudeville acts to the nickelodeon program. In November 1907, *Moving Picture World* acknowledged that "a vaudeville act or two interspersed between the changes of reels has been a means of doubling the receipts of many moving picture theatres." [36]

The use of vaudeville on movie theater programs was also spurred by a shortage of new films, resulting from the tremendously increased demand for them by the thousands of nickelodeons established between 1906 and 1908. Since 1896 motion picture producers had been supplying each of several hundred vaudeville theaters with approximately 1,800 feet of film each week. By 1908 the number of exhibition outlets had increased to several thousand, each using two or three reels and changing programs three or more times each week. Although the amount of new film placed on the American market weekly increased from 10,000 feet in November 1907 to 28,000 feet in March 1908, there was still not enough product to satisfy exhibitor demand at the established price level. [37]

The addition of vaudeville acts to the nickelodeon program meant that exhibitors could expand the length of their shows without increasing the number of reels of film required. The acts could also be used to bolster a weak film program: if, for some reason, the exhibitors' films were not particularly attractive one week, they could attempt to attract patronage on the basis of the variety portion of the bill.

Vaudeville acts also made movie theaters more palatable to middle-class audiences, offering them a version of what they went to Keith's, Proctor's, and other vaudeville theaters to see. In August 1908, *Moving Picture World* noted that theaters presenting more than "the average nickelodeon" were able to raise their prices to ten cents, and were "in addition blessed with a better and cleaner patronage." [38]

Presenting vaudeville acts in movie theaters did present some problems for exhibitors, however. Additional salaries had to be paid. In some cases ticket sales per day declined as the vaudeville acts lengthened each show presented. Because of municipal theater licensing laws, nickelodeons in New York and other cities were limited in seating capacity (in New York to 199 seats). With costs up and performances per day down, nickelodeon managers who could not expand their seating capacity were hardpressed to keep their houses profitable. In the face of stiff competition, they were reluctant to increase ticket prices. Some managers found that by moving into larger buildings or leasing former vaudeville or legitimate theaters, they could cover increased costs with larger capacity, and even raise the price of admission to ten cents or more.

New York quickly became a major center of small-time vaudeville activity, largely owing to the growth of two theater circuits: those belonging to William Fox and to Marcus Loew. Fox became an exhibitor in 1906, when he purchased a failing nickelodeon in Brooklyn. By 1908 he had joined the trend toward the use of vaudeville and film in large-capacity theaters. As noted previously, he leased the Dewey Theatre on Union Square and turned it into "the best run and most profitable" movie theater in New York. On Thanksgiving Day 1908 the Dewey sold 12,000 tickets, a feat believed by *Variety* to be the largest business ever done by a movie theater. By the end of 1910 Fox owned a circuit of fourteen theaters in the New York area. The Fox theaters offered long programs (often including as many as seven or eight vaudeville acts), comfort, and low prices (ten and twenty-five cents). The Fox audiences included many middle-class patrons. When Fox's Nemo Theatre opened in October 1910, *Variety* remarked, "The audience was one of real 'class,' . . . dinner coats were in evidence in the auditorium."[39]

In 1903 Marcus Loew, a New York furrier, was persuaded by fellow businessmen Adolph Zukor and Morris Kohn to invest in their penny arcade business. In 1904, Loew opened arcades in New York and Cincinnati and later operated several nickelodeons. As Bosley Crowther tells the story in *The Lion's Share*, Loew made the discovery of many nickelodeon managers, that theaters offering vaudeville acts as well as pictures had a competitive edge. "Loew went along with this fashion, but he soon saw that the small size of the 'stores' limited the attraction and the variety of such tabloid vaudeville. He sensed that he might get a jump on his competitors if he could do it on a somewhat larger scale."[40] In the summer of 1907 Loew saw an opportunity to move his style of entertainment into more pretentious quarters. He leased Watson's Cozy Corner burlesque theater in Brooklyn, and after redecorating it, opened it in January 1908 as the Royal Theater, a small-time vaudeville theater. By the summer of 1909, Loew's People's Vaudeville Company operated "one of the largest of the big small-time circuits," with twelve houses in New York City alone.[41]

The locations of small-time vaudeville theaters in Manhattan are significant in that they demonstrate an increasing movement toward a middle-class audience. Small-time theaters were located where earlier movie theaters had been (Union Square, 125th Street, Yorkville), but also at Columbus Circle, Riverside and 96th Street, 145th Street and Amsterdam Avenue, 110th Street and Broadway, and 165th Street and Broadway—previously unbreached middle-class bastions. The extent to which small-time vaudeville attracted middle-class patronage is indicated by the fact that as early as 1910, New York theaters on the Loew circuit were actively competing with those belonging to members of the United Booking Office, the "high-class" vaudeville syndicate.[42]

Small-time vaudeville theaters also attracted patronage away from smaller movie theaters. The old nickelodeons, restricted to a few hundred seats by the size of the building or municipal fire regulations, simply could not compete in many cases with the huge, luxurious small-time vaudeville theaters. *Variety* noted in December 1909, "anyone who overlooks this 'small time' is falling into a great error. . . . It has driven out the 'picture place' and how."[43]

☆

Conclusion

In light of the findings of this study, as well as those of Gomery and Merritt, it is obvious that accounts of early motion picture exhibition contained in secondary sources are grossly inadequate. As is too often the case in motion picture history, easy generalizations serve to hide complex historical issues. In Manhattan moviegoing between 1906 and 1912 was by no means an exclusive activity of the poor or the immigrant. Our one-dimensional image of early exhibition taking place in the dingy, converted cigar store does not hold in Manhattan. Some patterns do, however, emerge. Most movie theaters were located near large working-class and middle-class populations. Few theaters were found in exclusively middle- and upper-class neighborhoods. Like vaudeville theaters, burlesque houses, and dime museums before them, many movie theaters were located in traditional entertainment districts. It is difficult to generalize about the relationship between movie theaters and public transportation. Major shopping areas, such as Union Square and 125th Street, were of course serviced by transit lines. The low correlation between transit lines and nickelodeons outside of established retail and entertainment districts seems to indicate that these movie houses drew their patronage from the immediate area. Small-time vaudeville theaters show a higher correlation with subway and streetcar lines, indicating, perhaps, that these larger theaters drew from a wider area than the nickelodeons. While the heavy concentration of nickelodeons on the Lower East Side indicates that moviegoing was popular among the immigrant population there, the sparsity of theaters in other immigrant neighborhoods suggests differences among ethnic groups in their moviegoing behavior.

The growth of small-time vaudeville indicates that the middle-class embraced the movies much earlier than is generally believed—several years before the advent of the feature film. The nature of small-time vaudeville, with its large, often ornate theaters, uniformed attendants, and long programs, makes it an important link between the storefront shows of 1906 and the picture palaces of the late teens.

The extent to which the findings of this study can be generalized beyond Manhattan is a moot question. New York might well turn out to be typical only of New York; factors quite alien to the situation there might prove to be decisive elsewhere. What is needed are studies of exhibition in other cities—large and small, polyglot and homogeneous, in all parts of the country. Only when this task has been accomplished can we safely make generalizations about the nickelodeon era.

Monopoly in Motion Picture
Production and Distribution:
1908–1915

Ralph Cassady, Jr.

I. Introduction

By the end of 1907 motion pictures were being presented in thousands of storefront shows (nickelodeons) throughout the country and it appears that the industry was extremely profitable. In view of the high commercial value of motion pictures, it is not surprising that many patent battles were fought in the courts during the next few years to establish prior rights to the various inventions. At first, it was Edison against the field. The Edison Manufacturing Company was involved in numerous suits between 1897 and 1907 in an attempt to protect its position.[1] While the decisions were far from clear-cut evaluations of the strength of Edison's patent rights, the early decisions were favorable enough to attract most of the manufacturers, distributors, and exhibitors into the Edison camp.

But by 1908 the industry was divided mainly into two hostile camps. On the one side were Edison and its licensees, Essanay, Kalem, Lubin, Méliès, Pathé Frères, Selig, and Vitagraph; on the other were Biograph and its licensees, Williams, Brown and Earle, Kleine Optical Company, Charles E. Dressler, and through a contractual licensing arrangement, Armat Moving Picture Company. The Biograph licensees, unlike the Edison licensees, were importers, rather than domestic producers. It appears from the Record[2] that the Biograph Company was offered a license by Edison in early 1908 at the same time the other principal manufacturers were licensed, but refused to accept. It is clear from the evidence that the deterrent to an agreement between Edison and Biograph was that Biograph demanded half of the royalties, and Edison would not agree to such a division. The battle continued between Edison and Biograph until late 1908, when the two factions joined forces through the organization of the Motion Picture Patents Company. According to Terry Ramsaye,[3] the Biograph Company was almost at the end of its rope when the armistice was finally signed, but despite this near failure it bluffed its way through and secured terms almost, if not actually, equal to Edison's. Thus began a move toward monopolization of the motion picture industry in America.

II. The Motion Picture Patents Company

The Motion Picture Patents Company was incorporated on 9 September 1908 under the laws of the State of Maine, to effectuate the coalition between the Edison and Biograph forces. Stock in the company was to be wholly owned by Edison and Biograph, except for four shares qualifying the directors.[4] Authorization was given under terms of the company's charter to acquire motion picture patents and inventions and to license others to use the devices so acquired.[5] Thus, in effect, the Patents Company was a patent-pooling and licensing organization.

After numerous preliminary discussions with patent holders and industry members concerning proposed arrangements with the various functionaries, the company was activated on 18 December 1908 by the assignment by their owners of the various patents to the Patents Company and the issuance by the Patents Company of certain licenses under these patents.[6] The stage was set for Patents Company domination of the industry.

A. Agreements for Assignment of Patents

In late 1908 the ownership of the various motion picture patents was in the hands of four companies. Since these patents were the *sine qua non* of the Motion Picture Patents Company, the first order of business of the Patents Company at its initial meeting was the acceptance of the assignment of a total of sixteen patents from the four manufacturers— Armat, Biograph, Edison, and Vitagraph.[7] The patents assigned, which represented fundamental discoveries as well as relatively minor improvements in the art of manufacturing and projecting motion pictures, were as follows:

(1) Film patent-reissue No. 12192 (from Edison);

(2) Camera patents-reissue No. 12037 (from Edison) and No. 629,063 (from Biograph); and

(3) Projecting machine patents—Nos. 578,185; 580,749; 586,953; 588,916; and 673,992 (from Armat); Nos. 707,934 and 722,382 (from Biograph); and Nos. 673,329; 744,251; 770,937; 771,280; 785,205; and 785,237 (from Vitagraph).[8]

The assignment agreements between the Motion Picture Patents Company and the several assignors covered all of the patents of any importance in the early-day motion picture industry. These agreements, while necessarily different from one another in certain particulars, were generally similar. In each such agreement, the assignor related that it owned the rights and titles to specifically mentioned patents and indicated that it was willing to and did, in fact, assign these to the Motion Picture Patents Company for a consideration, typically of one dollar and other material benefits. In assigning the patents to the Patents Company, the assignor agreed to cancel all other licenses if any, but reserved the right to use its own patents without royalty payments.

One important aspect of the assignment agreements, it appears, was the specific reference in each document to the other patents which the Patents Company agreed to acquire in order to complete its holdings of motion picture patents. Thus in the Edison agreement reference is made of the intended acquisition of patents held by Armat, Biograph, and Vitagraph. It is clear from this statement that the assignee and each of the assignors recognized the importance of acquiring all patents if control of the industry was to be effective.

Each assignment agreement reported that the Motion Picture Patents Company contemplated establishing the following royalty scheme:

1. Royalties to be collected on a per-machine basis from manufacturers of projecting machines under patents covering such machines, i.e., "machine royalties";

2. Royalties to be collected on a per-theater basis from exhibitors under patents covering projecting machines, i.e., "exhibitor royalties"; and

3. Royalties to be collected on a per-foot basis from manufacturers and importers of motion pictures under patents covering cameras and films, i.e., "film royalties."

By terms of the assignment agreements the Motion Picture Patents Company contracted to keep account of and distribute royalties at the end of each year to the various recipients, as follows:

1. Net royalty figures were to be derived by (a) subtracting Vitagraph royalties, one dollar per projecting machine manufactured, from total machine royalties, (b) deducting 24 percent from gross exhibitor royalties for distribution to motion picture manufacturers and importers other than Biograph and Edison, and (c) deducting general litigation expenses from film and other royalties;

2. Net royalties were to be paid to a trustee for distribution (a) to Edison in an amount equal to "net film royalties," (b) to Biograph two-thirds and to Armat one-third of the remainder up to an amount equal to "net film royalties," and

3. Any balance after the division indicated above was to be paid to Edison, Biograph, and Armat on a basis of one-half, one-third, and one-sixth, respectively.

The assignment agreements provided that the contract between assignor and assignee should normally continue until the expiration of all the patents. However, the continuation of the agreements was conditional upon satisfactory performance and provided, "that if during the life of this agreement either party should knowingly or through gross neglect or carelessness be guilty of a breach, violation, or nonperformance of its covenants, conditions, and stipulations resulting in substantial injury to the other party, and should for the period of thirty days after notice thereof from the other party, persist therein or fail to correct, repair, or remedy the same, then and in such case the party aggrieved may terminate this agreement by giving thirty days' notice in writing to the guilty party of its intention so to do."[9] The agreement also provided that upon the termination of the agreement "all of the right, title, and interest in and to the said . . . [patents] shall be reassigned by the . . . [assignor] Company."[10]

B. Agreements with Licensees

In late 1908 or early 1909, the Motion Picture Patents Company entered into agreements with most of the key factors in the early-day motion picture industry.[11] Thus contractual arrangements were made with (a) the supplier of raw film, (b) the most important producers of motion pictures, (c) the several manufacturers of projecting machines, (d) the great bulk of rental exchanges, and (e) the leading exhibitors. These agreements provided a basis for the control of the motion picture industry by the Patents Company.

1. Agreement with Raw Film Manufacturer. Raw film was, as it is today, the *sine qua non* of motion picture production. At the time of the organization of the Motion Picture Patents Company, the Eastman Kodak Company was the principal, if not the only, domestic manufacturer of this commodity. It was, therefore, a simple matter to control the supply of raw film and hence motion picture production by entering into an exclusive licensing arrangement with Eastman.

The Patents Company agreement with the Eastman Kodak Company was entered into 1 January 1909. On the basis of the sixteen patents it controlled, the Patents Company extended to Eastman "the sole and exclusive authority . . . to manufacture the 'Licensed Film' . . . and sell such 'Licensed Film' to the 'Patents Company [manufacturer] licensees' . . ." under specific conditions laid down in the agreement.[12] This seeming deference of Eastman to the Patents Company in permitting the Patents Company to give it the right to produce its own film may have been owing to the fact that Edison appears to have collaborated closely with Eastman in the development of motion picture film and indeed may well have been mainly responsible for the joint product.[13]

The Eastman Company, by terms of this agreement, was authorized to charge producers a maximum price of three cents net per running foot for licensed nonperforated nitrocellulose film, one and three-eighths inches (i.e., 35 mm) wide, and three and one-quarter cents net per running foot for perforated film of the same width. While Eastman paid no royalty to the Patents Company under this agreement, the contractual arrangement required that Eastman should collect a royalty for the account of the Patents Company of one-half cent per running foot, subject to certain quantity discounts, from each of the licensed motion picture manufacturers, except Edison. The absence of a provision in the Eastman–Patents Company agreement calling for royalties to be paid the latter by the former may have simply been owing to the fact that Eastman was considered an important collaborator in the development of motion picture film, or possibly to the fact that the collecting of royalties from motion picture manufacturers by Eastman was a valuable service and constituted a *quid pro quo*.

While the Eastman Company was given the sole right to sell licensed film to Patents Company licensees, it reserved the right to sell its product to certain other customers not engaged in the business of distributing or dealing in motion pictures. It appears to have been the intention of the agreement, however, to confine sales of licensed motion picture film mainly to Patents Company licensees and to exclude nonlicensed manufacturers. There is evidence, too, that suggests the existence of contracts between Eastman and the individual licensed manufacturers that, in general, conformed to the Eastman–Patents Company agreement.

This licensing agreement was to continue until 31 August 1914, the date of expiration of reissued Letters Patent Nos. 12027 and 12192; however, either party was free to terminate the agreement upon sixty days' written notice. Bankruptcy or dissolution of the Patents Company was also to be a ground for termination of the agreement. There is, interestingly enough, no mention of involuntary termination of the Eastman–Patents Company pact for violation of the terms of the agreement as in the case of licensing compacts with other types of functionaries.

 2. *Agreements with Motion Picture Manufacturers and Importers.* As has been mentioned earlier, motion picture films have always been an indispensable element of motion picture distribution and exhibition. The Motion Picture Patents Company, immediately after its organization, licensed all important motion picture manufacturers, as producers were then called. These manufacturers, of course, included both the former Edison licensees and the former Biograph licensees (e.g., Kleine Optical Company, an importer of the foreign films of Gaumont and Urban Eclipse).

 As of 18 December 1908 the Patents Company granted licenses to nine manufacturers and importers of motion pictures: American Mutoscope and Biograph Company, Edison Manufacturing Company, Essanay Film Manufacturing Company, Kalem Company, Inc., Kleine Optical Company, Lubin Manufacturing Company, Pathé Frères, Selig Polyscope Company, and Vitagraph Company of America. A tenth manufacturer, Gaston Méliès, was licensed a few months later, on 20 July 1909. The agreement provided that the Motion Picture Patents Company grant licenses to manufacture motion picture cameras and to manufacture and lease motion pictures. The licensees were required to mark cameras manufactured as "patented," to give the patent dates, to print the licensee's trademark in at least one scene of each motion picture, and to mark the film container "licensed motion picture," including appropriate dates on which the basic letters patent were issued.[14]

 The manufacturer licensees also contracted to use only "licensed film" in manufacturing motion pictures and to lease, not sell, motion pictures to their customers, the rental exchanges. They were not to deal with distributors who handled unlicensed films or to make "dupes" of existing motion pictures. The last stipulation was undoubtedly included to thwart the efforts of nonlicensed producers. In leasing films to exchanges, the manufacturers (lessors) were further required to stipulate that the rental exchanges (lessees) rent the motion pictures only to those exhibitors using projecting machines licensed by the Patents Company.

 Although importer licensees were limited in the footage that they were permitted to release, manufacturer licensees were not restricted in the amount of motion picture film they were permitted to produce and sell. (For minimum prices of films leased to rental exchanges by licensee manufacturers and importers for ordinary releases see table 3.1.) The prices to be charged by the exchanges for motion picture service to exhibitors were not specified, and thus were based on what the traffic would bear.

By terms of the licensing agreement, as was mentioned, royalties were to be paid to the licensor, the Motion Picture Patents Company, on one-and-three-eighths-inch (35 mm) film by each of the licensees, except Edison, in accordance with a scale of charges that declined as the film footage increased. More specifically, the licensees paid a royalty charge, through Eastman as agent for the Patents Company,[15] of one-half cent on all footage up to 4 million running feet, four and one-half mills on all footage from 4 to 6 million running feet, four mills on all footage from 6 to 8 million running feet, three and three-quarters mills on all footage from 8 to 10 million running feet, with a minimum charge of three

Table 3.1 *Minimum Prices of Films Leased to Rental Exchanges**

Category	Ordinary Film	Nonflammable Film
	(*in cents per running foot*)	
List[†]	13	14
Standing order[‡]	11	12
Topical	9	
Films leased between 2 and 4 mos. after release date	9	
Films leased between 4 and 6 mos. after release date	7	
Films leased after 6 mos. following release date	any price net	

* See also the modification in the agreement and schedule of prices of 6 June 1912. Record, 7:3729–30.
† A 10 percent rebate allowed except on topical pictures and those selling at a price of 7 cents or lower.
‡ A standing order is an order for one or more prints of a motion picture subject that remains in force at least 21 days. Section 5 of the exchange agreement defined a standing order as "one or more prints of each and every subject regularly produced, and offered for lease by such manufacturer or importer as a standing order subject and not advertised as (a) special." Record, 7:3517–18.

and one-quarter mills on all footage of over 10 million running feet. Royalties on "licensed film" which was wider or narrower than the standard 35 mm were greater or less in proportion to the variations in width.

On its part the licensor, Motion Picture Patents Company, agreed to institute suits against infringers of patents at the request of a majority of the licensees. The licensor also agreed to institute suits against any and all licensees who breached or violated any terms or conditions or covenants of the license agreement. All legal expense incurred by the licensor up to $20,000 was to be borne by the manufacturer-licensees on a pro rata basis.

The licensor Patents Company by terms of the agreement was permitted to grant not more than nine manufacturer-licenses except by a majority vote of the licensees.[16] Any additional licenses were to be granted on terms and conditions no more favorable than those extended to any other manufacturer; i.e., each was accorded "most-favored-nation" treatment. In case of a breach or violation of any of the terms or conditions of the agreement by either party resulting in substantial injury to the other that continued for a period of forty days after written notice, the aggrieved party was permitted to terminate the agreement. In case of a second breach, an aggrieved party might terminate after giving thirty days' notice. In any case, termination was to occur on 20 June 1910, with the provision for yearly renewal by the licensee giving notice to the licensor on or before 20 April of each year, except that the right of renewal was not to extend beyond 26 August 1919, the date of expiration of Letters Patent No. 707,934.[17]

3. Agreements with Projecting Machine Manufacturers. Motion picture projecting machines were, and still are, key elements in the conversion of motion picture films into motion picture entertainment. The patents on projecting machines held by the Motion Picture Patents Company allowed it to control the manufacture and sale of such equipment; and through control of the thirteen projecting machine patents mentioned earlier, the Patents entered into licensing agreements with ten manufacturers of such machines. Some of these, Edison Manufacturing Company, Lubin Manufacturing Company, Selig Polyscope Company, Spoor and Company (George Spoor was the "Ess" in Essanay), and Vitagraph Company of America manufactured motion picture films. The others, Armat Moving Picture Company, Edengraph Manufacturing Company, Enterprise Optical Manufacturing Company, Nicolas Power Company, and Eberhard Schneider, did not. Four other companies became licensees later on: American Moving Picture Machine Company (in February 1909), Gaumont Company (in March 1909), Biograph Company (in April 1909), and Precision Machine Company (in June 1912). By terms of these agreements, the licensor, Motion Picture Patents Company, granted the licensees the right to manufacture and sell motion picture projecting machines under certain conditions specified in the agreements.

The agreements provided that the licensees would sell projecting machines under the restriction and condition that the machines were to be used solely for exhibiting or projecting motion pictures containing the invention of reissued Letters Patent No. 12192, i.e., the film patent. It was further agreed that the licensees would attach to each machine a plate containing the patent number and date and the conditions of use under which the equipment was sold. It is interesting to note that the licensor placed no further restrictions, such as requiring that they be sold only to licensed exhibitors, on the sale of the machines.

The licensee agreed to charge a fixed price for each projecting machine it sold— $150 list, after 1 May 1909, for machines using transmitted light and film of a width greater than one inch. It agreed further to pay royalties of $5 per machine which included $1 per machine to be paid directly to Vitagraph for the use of the projecting machine patents, with certain exceptions specifically noted, and to submit a statement of units sold at specified intervals, when Patents Company royalties would be due.

Under terms of the projecting machine manufacturer agreement, the licensee was not to make or sell repair parts for motion picture exhibiting machines that had been manufactured or imported by any person or firm other than that which was licensed to manufacture and sell such equipment. However, the agreement permitted the licensor to grant further licenses to manufacture and sell projecting machines under the patents, but provided that such licenses should not be issued under any more favorable terms than those given others; i.e., again the "most-favored-nation" provision was to apply.

Breach, or violation, of any covenant or condition of the licensing agreement or nonperformance thereof was a ground for termination if there were no correction of the breach after notice was given by the licensor. Moreover, bankruptcy or dissolution of the licensor company would result in termination of the agreement. The agreement was to continue until 20 June 1910, unless termination occurred sooner, but was renewable during the life of the patents.

4. Agreements with Rental Exchanges.[18] The rental exchanges, as now, provided the channel through which motion picture films passed in the movement from manufacturer to exhibitor. It was important, therefore, if control of the industry was to be effected, to regulate distribution activities. This control was first accomplished by the licensing of exchanges by the Patents Company on a basis of the Edison film patent, reissue No. 12192.

In the weeks following its organization on 18 December 1908, the Motion Picture Patents Company granted licenses to over one hundred film exchanges.[19] The terms of the agreements permitted the exchanges to lease, but not purchase, licensed motion pictures from licensed manufacturers and to sublease such films to licensed exhibitors. The agreements also provided that after 1 February 1909 the exchanges should sublease their films only to exhibitors using projecting machines "regularly" licensed and on which license fees had been paid. However, there was nothing in the license agreement that restricted the exchange in regard to the geographical area it was to serve; i.e., the distributors were not given franchises which circumscribed the market areas within which licensees were permitted to do business. However section 15 of the agreement read as follows: "This agreement shall extend only to the place of business for the subleasing of motion pictures maintained by the licensee in the city for which this agreement is signed, and the licensee agrees not to establish or maintain a place of business for the subleasing of motion pictures . . . in any other city, unless an agreement for such other city, similar to the present agreement, is first entered into by and between the Licensee and the Licensor."[20]

It should be noted that the exchange licenses provided that the motion pictures only be leased, not purchased, from suppliers and, in fact, required the eventual return of the films to the manufacturer. By terms of the agreements, the exchanges were not permitted to sell or otherwise to dispose of the films to anyone who was engaged in selling or renting motion pictures, but were permitted only to sublease to exhibitors. This, of course, was an attempt to prevent bootlegging of licensed films.

Under the terms of the agreement, the licensee was not only restricted in subleasing the films in his possession but he was also prohibited from dealing in unlicensed film. Moreover, he was required to "purchase" a minimum of $2,500 worth of licensed films per month, and he was prohibited from becoming involved in the making of additional film copies, commonly known as [unlicensed] "dupes."

The licensed distributor under this agreement was not to deal with any individuals or companies that had violated any terms or conditions of the licensor's agreements. Upon notice of any nonpayment of royalties by exhibitors for use of projecting machines, the distributor licensee was required to cease supplying such exhibitor with film service. The licensee moreover should not "deliberately remove the trade-mark or trade name or title from any licensed motion picture, nor permit others to do so."[21]

As was mentioned earlier, the exchange licensing agreements called for a schedule of prices to be charged by the manufacturers. According to this schedule, the price to be paid by the exchanges for regular releases purchased on release date, printed on ordinary stock, was to be thirteen cents per running foot.

The licensee was required by terms of the agreement to exact a contract from each exhibitor before dealing with him, which was to "conform to all the conditions and stipulations of the present agreement applicable to the exhibitor." [22] The licensee agreed, if called upon to do so, to mail to the licensor company the names of exhibitors, the names and locations of exhibiting places, the dates of commencement of service and any other information which might be requested by the Patents Company. While the first exchange agreements did not require it, by terms of a Patents Company directive dated 7 April 1909 the rental exchanges were appointed "agents" of the Motion Picture Patents Company in collecting "exhibitor royalties." [23]

It is significant to note that, unlike the licensing agreements with most other types of functionaries, there was no provision for royalties to be paid by exchange licensees. It may be that the cooperation of the exchanges in adhering to Patents Company regulations was so important in exacting market control that this release served as a *quid pro quo* for granting of the license. It must be remembered, also, that beginning in May 1909 the exchanges assumed the task of collecting royalties from the motion picture exhibitors, and it may have been that the Patents Company, anticipating this event, felt that the collecting service was a sort of royalty paid "in kind."

All licenses to rental exchanges were to be similar in terms but might be altered at the option of the licensor Patents Company upon fourteen days' written notice to the licensee. Under terms of the agreement, an exchange license might be terminated upon fourteen days' written notice also, and the name of the exchange might be placed on a "suspended list." If the agreement were terminated for any breach of any condition contained in the agreement, e.g., selling film to infringers or leasing to nonlicensed exhibitors, "the right to possession of all licensed motion pictures . . . [reverted] . . . to the respective Licensed Manufacturers and Importers from whom they were obtained." [24]

5. Agreements with Motion Picture Exhibitors. Because the theaters were the primary source of revenue in the early days of the motion picture industry, exhibitors were, as today, the key functionaries. It is not surprising, therefore, that the Motion Picture Patents Company decided to license the exhibitors and exact a royalty as a *quid pro quo* on the basis of the patented projecting machines used by the theaters so licensed.

Licenses were required of all exhibitors wishing to use licensed film, and in the weeks following the organization of the Motion Picture Patents Company in December 1908 licenses were granted to thousands of motion picture theaters.[25] The licensing agreements between the Patents Company and the exhibitors were very informal and the terms simple. The principal elements in these agreements were as follows:

a) The licensee was licensed to operate "one or more motion picture projecting machines" under certain of the projecting machine patents controlled by the Patents Company;

b) Only motion pictures manufactured or imported by licensees of the Motion Picture Patents Company and rented from a licensed exchange could be exhibited in theaters licensed by the Patents Company;

c) Licenses were at all times to be prominently displayed in the place of exhibition and together with the projecting machines used were subject to inspection by the Motion Picture Patents Company;

d) Licensed exhibitors were required to pay a royalty which at first was supposed to be "graded according to the relative business of each of the licensed theatres," but was later standardized at two dollars per week; and

e) The exhibitor "in no case . . . [was] permitted to sell or sublet or otherwise dispose of said licensed motion pictures."

The Patents Company regulations were to some extent *ex post facto* in nature because they purportedly applied to exhibitors who had previously acquired projecting equipment as well as those purchasing machines after the Patents Company was organized. To the extent that this was true, the regulations were of questionable legal validity. Licensed distributors of film were required by terms of the exchange agreement to exact a contract from each exhibitor in connection with each theater operated and supplied "satisfactory in form to the Licensor [Patents Company]."[26]

Not only were licensed theaters not permitted to show unlicensed film, but the film licensed by the Motion Picture Patents Company was restricted to use in licensed theaters only. Showings of licensed film in unlicensed theaters purportedly constituted a breach of the license agreement under which the manufacturer leased the film and gave the licensed manufacturer the right to immediate possession of the film through replevin suits.[27] Licensed theaters were encouraged to report such showings to the Patents Company so that remedial action could be taken to the advantage of both the Patents Company and the exhibitor.[28]

Since exhibitors were required to lease films from licensed exchanges exclusively, they had to be continually supplied with information concerning the issuance and cancellation of exchange licenses in order to permit adherence to Patents Company regulations re dealing with licensed exchanges only. Conversely, any violations by licensed exhibitors in the form of failure to pay royalties, the showing of unlicensed films, or the subrenting or subleasing of films, were cause for exhibitor-license cancellation, and licensed exchanges were then ordered to cease serving exhibitors whose licenses were canceled.[29] There was no mention made in the Patents Company—exhibitor license agreement of "bicycling," but this practice must have been at least frowned on by the Motion Picture Patents Company and may actually have been proscribed in the agreements between the exchanges and the exhibitors. "Bicycling" (the means by which films were transported from one theater to another, thus the term) consisted of the use by exhibitors of a film program ostensibly purchased for one theater in several houses controlled by a multitheater operator, without additional payment to the distributor. Although exhibitors had no voice in determining whether additional licenses should be granted in their areas, as was true in the case of some other types of licensees, i.e., the motion picture manufacturers, the Motion Picture Patents Company had a sort of "public convenience and necessity" policy of protecting established theaters "as far as possible," and of seeking the advice of rental exchanges before granting new licenses.[30]

It may be inferred from the record that exhibitors would continue as Patents Company licensees just as long as they adhered to the conditions of the licensing agreement. For a breach of any of the conditions, however, the licensee was subject to fines and indeed to cancellation, and purportedly at least, the Patents Company had "the right to proceed against said [licensed] machines for infringement of said patents."[31]

C. The Patents Company in Operation

It should be evident from the foregoing that the Patents Company was not a manufacturing concern, a mercantile firm, or even a service-performing organization in the usual sense. Nor did the Patents Company control any such operations through the ownership of licensee—company stock or assets. The company was, rather, simply an agency organized for the purpose of (*a*) holding title to patents governing motion picture film, cameras, and projectors; (*b*) licensing individuals and companies to conduct motion picture operations under its jurisdiction; (*c*) regulating the conduct of business of those licensed;[32] (*d*) preventing infringement by those not licensed by the Patents Company; and (e) collecting royalties from various functionaries in exchange for the privilege of operating as licensed companies in this field.

The Patents Company did not, therefore, have exclusive possession of any product or service, except for the patents it held in trust, but was an instrument through which industry control was effected through the "interlocking" agreements of the Patents Company and its licensees. The company, whose stock was wholly owned by Edison and Biograph, had four officers—a president and a secretary, representing the Edison interests, and a vice-president and a treasurer, representing the Biograph interests. These four men also served as the board of directors. These officers, who appear not to have received any salary from the Patents Company,[33] made the major decisions in connection with Patents Company operations and employed a staff to assist them in the performance of the firm's functions.

After the assignment of the patents and the licensing of the various participating functionaries, the business of the Patents Company, directly or through counsel, consisted mainly of repelling the efforts of infringers, requiring adherence to operating standards applicable to the various licensees, and collecting royalties from those obligated to pay them. It appears from the record that the most important Patents Company activities in terms of expenditure of time and energy were those that were regulatory in nature, including those that were exclusionary in purpose as well as those that were designed to raise industry standards.

Patents Company licensees were free to operate as they pleased in many respects. Thus licensed manufacturers made their own decisions regarding the number and length of pictures to be produced and sold.[34] Distributors were free to operate in any market area they pleased and to charge the exhibitor any price they thought they could get for the film service offered. Exhibitors were free to purchase any class of service they desired from licensed distributors and to use their own discretion regarding admission charges to their theaters. It may have been, however, that the class of film service available to an exhibitor was influenced by the admission price charged by the theater. According to a statement by W. W. Hodkinson, an early-day licensed distributor and later organizer of Paramount, he attempted with considerable success, it would seem, initially to raise the level of admission prices, from five cents to ten cents.

While licensees were not completely regimented, they were required to function within a framework of regulations prescribed by the Patents Company that included a listing of those with whom certain of the licensees were permitted to deal. Regulations governing the activities of the licensees stemmed largely, though not entirely, from the provisions of the licensing agreements. While such regulations were based on provisions of the licensing agreements, the penalties for violations were devised and administered by Patents Company officers. Some of the Patents Company regulations governing competitive practices transcended the provisions of the license compacts but, in the main, these usually were quite reasonable in terms of efficient operation and possibly even public policy. These included not shipping films before specific release dates, and not using advertising materials that were unapproved by the manufacturer.[35]

An integral part of the regulatory function of the Motion Picture Patents Company was enforcement of Patents Company operating rules. Enforcement involved obtaining information concerning the activities of those under regulation, and taking remedial or punitive action designed to correct abuses and to promote adherence to regulations. The Patents Company reportedly did not have an espionage division for the purpose of detecting violations, but rather relied largely on reports from the various licensees for such information. However, mention has been made in certain historical accounts about the activities of Patents Company "spies," and it may be that some undercover work was carried on, especially in conjunction with infringement suits.[36]

Written communications were used to remind licensees of existing Patents Company rules, to inform licensees of new regulations, and to notify licensees of violations and of the punitive or remedial action (fines or cancellations of licenses), if any, taken by the Patents Company. Thus the gathering and dissemination of information was an important Patents Company activity, perhaps the most important single activity of the company.[47]

Communication between the Patents Company and its licensees was a particularly important function in connection with the cancellation of licenses. In such instances, not only the licensees but usually their suppliers and customers, had to be notified. In the case of the cancellation of an exchange license, indeed, communiques might be sent to (a) the exchange whose license was canceled, (b) the licensee-manufacturer or licensee-importer who supplied the exchange with film, (c) the licensed exhibitor-customers of the disfranchised exchange who had to find new suppliers, (d) the erstwhile competitors of the disfavored exchange which could be expected to supplant that company as suppliers of film service, and (e) rental exchanges generally, presumably as a deterrent to violations of Patents Company regulations in the future. In addition to this system of communications, the erstwhile suppliers of film, manufacturers and importers, often notified their customers of discontinuance of supplier relations as a result of Patents Company action.

One of the most important functions of the Motion Picture Patents

Company—perhaps the most important from the standpoint of those participating in the receipts—was the collection of royalties from the various licensees obligated to pay them: projecting machine manufacturers, motion picture producers, and motion picture exhibitors. The film royalties were, of course, collected by Eastman at the time the raw film was produced and hence should have presented few difficulties. This procedure applied to the manufacturers, not the importers. The record is not at all clear in regard to the method used to collect royalties on imported films, if indeed there was one, but the collection of the machine royalties should have been simple enough if only because of the fewness of the licensees.

The most difficult task in connection with this program undoubtedly was collecting the two-dollar-per-week fee from the thousands of widely-scattered and reluctant exhibitors. The difficulties in this connection were by no means lessened by the absence of enthusiasm on the part of the rental exchanges in acting as Patents Company agents for the collection of these payments. One reason for their reluctance was undoubtedly because it was an unpleasant task for which there was no compensation; but in addition some exchanges may have felt that competition would in time force them to absorb the two-dollar fee[38] and in some instances their judgment was unquestionably sound.

The penalty for nonpayment of royalties was, of course, cancellation of exhibitor licenses. It might well have been to the exchanges' advantage in some instances to assume the burden of absorbing exhibitor royalties in order to retain the patronage of an exhibitor customer and thus continue to receive the rental revenue even at a slight discount represented by the two-dollar-per-week fee.

Despite collection difficulties, the royalty program was not without some degree of success. Total royalties from manufacturers and exhibitors amounted to approximately $800,000 in each of the years 1910 and 1911, and they were close to $1 million in each of the years 1912 and 1913.[39] While no figures exist for machine royalties, i.e., from projecting machine manufacturers, the amount involved must have been very small. In the years for which figures exist, exhibitor royalties were much greater than film royalties; in fact, typically, exhibitor royalties exceeded film royalties by a ratio of two to one.[40]

As has been mentioned, Biograph and Edison were the sole stockholders of the Patents Company, except for the qualifying shares held by the directors, and they were the main recipients of royalty payments by the Patents Company licensees. Thus royalty revenue was equally divided between these two companies after payment of Patents Company expenses and the allocation of 24 percent of exhibitor royalties to the manufacturers and importers other than Biograph and Edison. It may be concluded that all licensed manufacturers benefited from the exclusionary nature of the licensing arrangement and each participated, to a limited degree at least, in the royalty program created by the Patents Company.

☆

III. The General Film Company

The license agreements discussed in the previous section were the sole basis of control of the industry until 18 April 1910. At that time, the first step was taken toward outright ownership of the rental exchanges by the Patents Company manufacturer licensees, through the formation of the General Film Company, which was incorporated under the laws of the State of Maine. The charter provided for ten directors—one for each of the licensee manufacturers controlling the voting shares of the firm: Frank I. Dyer (Edison), J. A. Berst (Pathe), Gaston Méliès (Méliès), Colonel William N. Selig (Selig), George K. Spoor (Essanay), Siegmund Lubin (Lubin), Jeremiah J. Kennedy (Biograph), William T. Rock (Vitagraph), George Kleine (Kleine) and Samuel Long (Kalem).[41]

The purpose of this company in general was to engage in the distribution of licensed motion picture films in competition with other licensed rental exchanges. What the precise motivation of the industry leaders was in organizing this company is unknown. The government claimed that it was a move toward more complete monopolistic control of the industry. Industry members, on the other hand, contended that it was merely an attempt to provide more satisfactory film service to exhibitors and to the public.[42] Undoubtedly, both points of view were represented among those promoting the scheme. In fact, some individuals may have been motivated by a genuine desire to improve the industry as well as to monopolize one segment of it.

A. License Agreement Between Patents Company and General Film Company

During the period of Patents Company control, any individual or firm wishing to distribute licensed motion pictures had, of course, to be licensed by that company. Accordingly, on 21 April 1910 an exchange agreement was entered into between the Motion Picture Patents Company and the General Film Company that was basically the same as the other agreements between the Patents Company and the licensed exchanges although somewhat broader in scope.[43]

By terms of this agreement, the Patents Company, through its control of basic patents, granted the General Film Company a license to acquire positive motion pictures from ten specifically mentioned licensed manufacturers,[44] under the aforementioned letters patent, and the right to import some motion pictures from abroad. By terms of the license, General Film Company was also permitted to lease such motion pictures to exhibitors in the lease territory, on condition that they would be used solely on machines containing Patents Company inventions, and to sell such motion pictures for export.

Under terms of its licensing agreement with the Patents Company, the General Film Company also agreed not to make motion pictures available to anyone dealing in unlicensed films or to dispose in any way of whatever unexposed positive or negative motion picture film the company happened to have in its possession. Moreover, General Film Company agreed not to use the films for the purpose of giving exhibitions for profit, "directly or indirectly," except, of course, to prospective lessees or purchasers. This proscription, note, was undoubtedly designed to preclude the "evil" of providing favored film service to affiliated theaters so prevalent in the industry at that time.[45] It, of course, prevented distributor-exhibitor integrated operations by the General Film Company.

As in the case of other exchange licensees, the General Film Company was required to return all films to manufacturer-suppliers at stated intervals, thus indicating that technically the company was not actually a purchaser of motion picture films from, but rather a lessee of, the suppliers. The terms of the agreement also provided that the General Film Company was to lease, or perhaps better, sublease, motion pictures to exhibitors only on the condition that such films would not be disposed of or subleased; no reproductions, or "dupes," would be permitted to be made; and no trademarks, trade names, or titles would be removed from the films so leased. Any violation of such provisions entitled the sublessor, General Film Company, to immediate repossession of the films without liability.

Unlike the arrangements with independent distributors, the General Film Company was required under terms of its agreement to pay royalties on a footage basis to the Patents Company for the right to operate as a distributor of licensed motion pictures. This stipulation would seem to suggest that film royalties were to be exacted twice by the Patents Company—once from the manufacturer (through Eastman) and once from the distributor, General Film Company. This provision is particularly difficult to understand because no royalties were charged the other licensed exchanges, and because such a requirement would have placed the General Film Company at a competitive disadvantage with other licensed exchanges. The licensee, Patents Company, and the licensor, General Film Company, agreed that the contract should continue for one year, until 20 June 1911, but that the licensee might renew the agreement "thereafter from year to year upon the same terms, conditions, and stipulations . . . by giving notice to the Licensor on or before April 20, of each year . . . of the Licensee's election to so renew" until expiration of Letters Patent No. 707,934 covering the Latham slace-forming rollers, popularly known as the Latham loop. The agreement provided, however, that the contract might be terminated, upon due notice, if reissued Letters Patent No. 12192 were held invalid, or if either party should be guilty of a breach of its covenants.

B. Agreements Between General Film Company and Licensed Manufacturers

The licensing agreement between Motion Picture Patents Company and General Film Company, just discussed, merely permitted the General Film Company to conduct an exchange business if and when it could make the proper arrangements with licensed manufacturers. It appears that such arrangements had been made in advance of the granting of the license, for on 21 April 1910—three days after the license was granted—manufacturer-distributor agreements were executed between the General Film Company and each of the ten manufacturers and importers of licensed motion picture films.[46]

Under terms of these agreements each manufacturer agreed to supply as many copies of each film released by it as the General Film Company required in its distribution business. The General Film Company requirements were to be determined by the number of exhibitor customers that it served; e.g., the Edison contract specified that General Film would lease one reel of approximately one thousand feet of film for each sixty-two customers served in any two consecutive weeks from any place of business operated by it. The minimum quantity of film to be leased by the General Film Company varied with the number of releases of film of each of the several manufacturers.

By terms of its contracts with manufacturers, the General Film Company agreed to use its best efforts to extend the use of licensed motion pictures in general. However, in signing with any one licensee-manufacturer, the company of course reserved the right to lease such licensed motion pictures from Patents Company manufacturer-licensees. No mention was made in the manufacturer-distributor contract of specific prices and terms that were to apply to films leased by distributors from manufacturers, except that they were to be the same as those charged "other person, firms, or corporations," i.e., other licensed exchanges, that were supplied by the manufacturer. This price schedule, incidentally, did not include special releases (such as the Teddy Roosevelt African pictures), which were not issued as regular releases and which commanded much higher rates.[47] By the same token, distributors were able to exact substantial supplementary charges from exhibitor-customers for specials, so-called. For example, the famous serials *Perils of Pauline* and *Exploits of Elaine*, made by Pathé in and around 1914, brought very high rentals. More specifically, the Chaplin comedies made by Essanay in early 1915 and issued as "specials" often commanded a rental fee of $500 from exhibitors in addition to the regular weekly payment charged for regular programs supplied by the distributors. It might be added that the exhibitors in their turn were often able to increase box office prices for the showings of special releases and thus recoup the extra investment in such pictures.

The General Film Company by terms of the contracts with manufacturers, agreed to make payment each Monday for such licensed motion pictures shipped the previous week, upon receipt of invoice. The General Film Company agreed also to pay the suppliers at the end of each year any net profit earned from leasing and subleasing motion pictures in excess of the amount required for payment of dividends, if any, on the 7 percent preferred and the 12 percent common stock. The proportion of such residual profit was to be determined by the percentage of licensed motion pictures leased from each supplier to the total leased from all companies.

The agreement between the General Film Company and the manufacturers and importers of motion picture films was to continue until 26 August 1919, the expiration date of Patent No. 707,934 covering the Latham loop, except in case of termination of the license granted the General Film Company by the Motion Picture Patents Company, or a breach or violation of conditions or covenants by either party after due notice, or bankruptcy of the Patents Company. In case of termination before the expiration date, the suppliers (manufacturers or importers) were entitled to their share of the net profit for the year in which expiration took place.

C. General Film Company in Operation

As was mentioned earlier, rental exchanges have always been key factors in the industry for the successful distribution of motion picture subjects.

Unfortunately, during the early years some distributors did not discharge their responsibilities properly, with the result that the entire industry, as well as the general public, was adversely affected.

In early 1909 shortly after the start of Motion Picture Patents Company operations, there were 116 licensed exchanges in the United States. During the period January 1909 and June 1910, many exchanges had their licenses canceled[48] for violations of Patents Company regulations, and some voluntarily withdrew from the Patents Company organization.[49] At the time of the organization of the General Film Company, after allowing for withdrawals and correcting for new licensees, there were 69 licensed rental exchanges in the United States.[50] These exchanges, as we know, were independent of "Trust" ownership, although their activities were, of course, circumscribed by licensor-licensee contractual arrangements.

The General Film Company, which was controlled by the Patents Company licensees and not by the Patents Company per se, began operations on 6 June 1910. Since the basic purpose of the company was to improve the generally deficient motion picture rental service then in existence, it follows that the concern had two main functions at the outset—establishing of and acquiring exchanges and running them on a basis of sound operating principles. There is no question that the rental service of independent exchanges was deficient in many respects previous to the establishment of the General Film Company. For example, many exchanges sent out worn prints, were undependable in the matter of getting films to the exhibitor on time, were careless about giving competitive houses conflicting service, and in some instances gave preferential treatment to affiliated theaters. It is reasonable to assume that the establishment of a model exchange might well have resulted in improved conditions. According to Jeremiah J. Kennedy, onetime president of General Film Company: "[T]he object [of the General Film Company] was . . . to provide a means whereby the exhibitor could obtain a reliable and impartial supply of motion pictures. The intention was to try this experiment in localities where these abuses were greatest in an effort to help the exhibitor protect himself.[51]

The administration of the company's affairs was in the hands of five officers: a president, vice-president, treasurer, clerk, and secretary, selected from and responsible to the board of directors. An executive committee, consisting of the president and two members of the board of directors, was created to carry on the company's business between meetings. A general manager, assistant treasurer, assistant secretary, and auditor were appointed by the board to aid in the management of the company.[52] Other staff members included the managers of the various distribution units as branch exchanges were established.

1. Acquisition of Exchanges. Since the General Film Company was organized for the purpose of conducting motion picture exchange operations, the establishing or acquiring of exchange facilities was a necessary first step in its operating program. Consequently, the company lost no time in acquiring exchange facilities. It was the policy of the General Film Company to acquire exchanges by purchase rather than by the establishment of new units and to make payment in cash and in preferred stock of the company.

The General Film Company began its distribution operations in early June with the purchase of two exchanges from George Kleine, one located in Chicago and the other in New York,[53] and one from Siegmund Lubin, located in Philadelphia. Further acquisitions were made in rapid succession. The Transcript of Record in the Motion Picture Patents Company case shows that within one month the company had purchased eleven additional exchanges and within three months had bought twenty-three distributive units out of a total of sixty-nine.

Eighteen months after beginning operations, the General Film Company had purchased fifty-eight American exchanges, and during the same period the Motion Picture Patents Company canceled the licenses of ten rental exchanges,[54] leaving only William Fox's Greater New York Film Rental Company outside of the General Film Company organization. Efforts were made by the General Film Company to purchase the Greater New York Film Rental Company from Fox beginning in September 1911, but the parties were unable to agree on a price. On 14 November of that year the Motion Picture Patents Company served Fox with a notice of cancellation of the Greater New York Film Rental Company's exchange license. The cancellation notice contained no mention of the cause for the action, but Albert E. Smith's testimony indicates that at a meeting of the licensees of the Patents Company, held on 13 November, the discussion of cancellation of Fox's license brought out several violations.[55] Subsequently, on 1 December 1911 the termination notice was rescinded after, so Fox claimed, he agreed to accept the previously offered purchase price of General Film Company. However, after conferring with his attorneys, Fox says he sent word to the General Film Company that he could not sell on the terms specified and, as a consequence, reportedly, on 7 December, he received a second notice of cancellation, effective 25 December.[56] When Fox failed to receive a shipment of film from Biograph, he applied for an injunction and thus initiated a lengthy period of litigation during which he continued to operate as a Patents Company licensee. Action was finally taken to terminate relations between Fox and the Patent Company in 1913, but the evidence is not clear whether the General Film Company ever acquired the Greater New York Film Rental

Company by purchase. By 12 January 1912, after consolidation of operations in cases of duplication of facilities, the General Film Company operated forty-two exchanges in thirty-two cities.[57] Thus, except for the New York market, there was a single source of supply of licensed film available to exhibitors in the United States which, of course, meant that the General Film Company enjoyed a near-monopoly of licensed film distribution.

It has been contended that the relationship between the Motion Picture Patents Company and the General Film Company was solely that of a licensor and a licensee. While this may understate the closeness of the relationship to some extent,[58] there is no substantial evidence of any collusion between the two companies in the matter of Patents Company cancellation of exchange licenses in order to pave the way for General Film Company operations. One fact that tends to contradict the collusion theory is that the great bulk of cancellations, thirty of forty-two, occurred before the organization of the General Film Company.[59] Moreover, if collusion between the Patents Company and General Film Company had been practiced, one would think that the pattern of General Film growth would have been to arrange the cancellation and then either to establish new branches or to purchase disfranchised firms at bargain prices. Actually, the pattern was to acquire going concerns from willing vendors at what appear to have been fair prices, although there is no way of telling to what extent those offering to sell to General Film Company were motivated by fear, even if groundless, that their licenses would be canceled if they did not sell.

2. Operating Practices. The General Film Company was a motion picture distributing concern whose main operating function was to acquire films by lease from licensed producing companies, or manufacturers, as they were called in the early days, and sublease them to licensed exhibitors. The latter activity included, of course, selling, pricing, physical distribution, and collection of accounts. Regardless of any other motive, there is no doubt that one aim of the company was to improve the quality of motion picture service to exhibitors with a resulting salutary effect on the industry generally and also on the theater-going public.

While certain activities had to be centralized, i.e., acquisition of exchanges and the formulation of major operating policies, the administration of most of the General Film Company's affairs was highly decentralized, and the company gave its exchange managers a great deal of discretion in handling its distributing business. Thus, an individual exchange manager had complete autonomy in the selection of films to be distributed by his branch.[60] The exchange manager, or his booker, had the sole authority in making up film programs for theater customers. Finally, managers of exchanges had full say about the prices charged exhibitors for film service and, presumably, were fully responsible for collection of accounts. Rates charged exhibitors for film service were based on the number of program changes; the newness of the films contracted for; and, undoubtedly, the number of showings per week, the size of the theater, the box-office price charged by the exhibitor, and the relative bargaining ability of the trader.

In order to serve its customers effectively it was necessary for General Film Company to: (1) have an adequate supply of popular subjects and makes of films available to exhibitor customers, (2) keep its motion picture films in good repair so as to ensure a good showing, (3) provide exhibitors with fair and impartial service, (4) give exhibitors advance knowledge of scheduled programs in order to provide a basis for consumer advertising, (5) furnish nonconflicting programs to neighboring exhibitors,[61] (6) get films into the hands of exhibitor customers in time for scheduled showings, and, in some instances at least, (7) educate exhibitors in the advantages of extending runs in order to derive full benefit from word-of-mouth advertising.[62]

There is little question that General Film Company provided improved rental service to licensed exhibitors as compared to that supplied by predecessor companies. The evidence is conflicting, however, about whether prices charged for service by the General Film Company were higher than those charged by predecessor exchanges. Undoubtedly, opportunities for increasing prices of motion picture service tended to become greater with the disappearance of the independent licensed exchanges. Actually, however, there is no evidence that exhibitor customers were charged inordinately high prices, probably owing to the existence of alternative sources of supply represented by increasing numbers of unlicensed exchanges as time went on.

The General Film Company was evidently efficiently organized and, in short-run terms, appears to have been a profitable venture. Total undivided net profits for General Film Company after payment of dividends on preferred and common stock, for 1911, for example, were $1,055,579.98.[63] By terms of the company's agreements with the manufacturing concerns, the motion picture producers participated in the profits after payment of the common and preferred dividends to stockholders.[64] Although the amounts received by the several manufacturers from the General Film Company were substantial, these may have been offset by a reduction in producing-company profits resulting from a decrease in the number of prints required by the more efficient distributing organization as compared with the previous independently operated exchanges.[65] There is no question that the General Film Company monopolized one segment of the motion picture industry. There is no doubt, however, that the improved marketing conditions made for a healthier industry in certain respects at least. It is interesting that the licensed manufacturers were quick to detect and correct the deficiencies of their distribution system in 1910 but a few years later were not sufficiently alert to adjust their policies to the basic changes that were taking place in the industry, and thus suffered competitive losses to independent distributors and, indeed, finally "went to the wall."

IV. Rise of the Independents

Thus far we have discussed the "trust" operations without consideration of the activities of nonlicensed competitors. We now turn to an analysis of the activities of those operating independently of the Patents Company organization.

A. The Early Independents

One may easily obtain the mistaken impression from a superficial study of the Patents Company case that there were no independent operators left after organization of the Motion Picture Patents Company in mid-December of 1908. However, an intensive examination of the trade papers for the first half of 1909 throws a somewhat different light on this matter.

1. Competitive Position of Early Independents. The independent segment of the industry in early 1909 was composed of perhaps four or five domestic manufacturers of motion picture films, an equal number of importers of European films, 10 or more rental exchanges, and an estimated 2,000 to 2,500 motion picture exhibitors. Although there was a nucleus of independent producers and importers at this early date, there was very little product available from these sources, possibly owing to a shortage of raw stock; a lack of know-how on the part of independent producers; and the restrictive effect of Patents Company legal action against infringers. The domestic companies produced only an occasional film, and the importing companies had not as yet secured sufficient numbers of European films to supply the independent market.[66]

Within six weeks after the Patents Company commenced business, a super importing concern, the International Projecting and Producing Company, was established for the purpose of supplying the film requirements of the independents.[67] The plan was to import films from manufacturers located in various European countries and sell them outright to independent exchanges. The first advertisement of International listed the names of eighteen foreign manufacturers for which it claimed to be the exclusive distributor in this country.[68] The evidence suggests, however, that for some unexplained reason the supply of films available from this company was considerably smaller than promised. While the International Projecting and Producing Company possessed limitations as a direct supply factor, the company, which was only in existence for about a year, did perform a valuable incidental service in behalf of the independent cause by preventing the imposition of heavy import restrictions on motion picture films from abroad.[69]

Despite quality limitations of the independent offering[70] and the efforts of the Patents Company to prevent nonlicensed companies from gaining a foothold in the market,[71] the independent segment of the industry gradually gained strength. The evidence seems to indicate that the independent movement at the exhibitor level was stronger in some parts of the country than others. One of the trade papers reported in May of 1909 that nearly 75 percent of the exhibitors in the country were licensees of the Patents Company and that the percentage was as high as 90 percent in many parts of the East; in the Chicago area only about 50 percent of the houses were licensed, while on the West Coast, licensees were again in the majority. The trade papers mention new entrants at the manufacturing level from time to time throughout 1909, so that by the end of the year there were a dozen or so unlicensed manufacturing companies scattered throughout the United States, although admittedly none was very productive. This inactivity may have been, in part at least, owing to the difficulty of obtaining supplies of raw film stock. However, the foreign film supply increased substantially during the year. The record shows that additional rental exchanges joined the independent ranks from time to time as a result either of Patents Company license cancellations[72] or of voluntary withdrawal from the "trust" organization.[73] The evidence suggests, finally, that the ranks of independent exhibitors expanded along with the growth of supplier companies.

2. Competitive Problems and Methods of Early Independents. During 1909, and even later, the supply of films was the basic problem of the independents. American-made independent films were particularly limited. In these early days most exhibitors demanded twenty-one reels per week, i.e., seven changes of three reels each per week. As late as October 1909 the record indicates that only about seven reels per week were available from domestic firms,[74] although of course these were supplemented by films from foreign sources. In addition, it appears that the independent foreign and domestic product was augmented by stocks of "Trust" film remaining in the possession of renters whose licenses were canceled, even though the Patents Company made every effort to prevent subsequent film use.[75] It appears also that individual licensed films found their way into the independent segment of the industry through the connivance of sympathetic licensees who were not averse to augmenting their income by bootlegging licensed films.[76] In addition, undoubtedly some licensed films were "duped" and circulated among independents in that form, although this procedure was not as simple as it sounds because of the shortage of raw stock as well as the practice of "Trust" manufacturers of photographing their trademarks into every scene of each picture produced, thus readily identifying them as licensed films.

The type of competitive activity engaged in by independent vendors was determined to a considerable extent by their competitive position in the industry. The market for independent company films was limited largely, if not entirely, to functionaries who were not licensed by the Patents Company. One might expect, therefore, that independent suppliers concentrated their efforts to entice licensed exhibitors into the independent ranks in order to broaden the market and also to emphasize any differential advantages these vendors might possess.

The evidence suggests that the independent competitive pattern took several forms:

a) While independent exchanges of necessity competed against one another, individual sellers placed more emphasis on seeking custom from licensed rather than unlicensed exhibitors. Thus typically independent exchanges admonished licensed exhibitors in their advertising to assert their independence and free themselves from "trust" control.[77]

b) Typically, the independent exchanges offered exclusive service, thus taking advantage of the weakness of the "trust" exchanges, which before the organization of the General Film Company, at least, often provided conflicting service. Moreover, most, if not all, of the independent exchanges emphasized that the pictures offered by independents were "different" from those offered by their competitors.[78]

c) Independent exchanges, conscious of the importance of a sound product to the success of the independent operation, soon inaugurated production programs. In doing so they raided the "Trust" plants for technical know-how.[79] At least one independent, Carl Laemmle of the Independent Motion Picture Company (IMP) successfully wooed licensed companies' featured players, thus strengthening his own offerings as well as those of independents generally. Although the star system was not as yet in effect in the motion picture industry in 1909, some players were known to the public by a general designation rather than by a specific name. For example, the very popular Florence Lawrence was known as the "Biograph Girl" by the public even though she remained anonymous. Laemmle appears to have been astutely aware of the value of well-known players in attracting patronage for his distributing and producing companies in particular, and for the independent cause in general. He therefore acquired the services of Miss Lawrence, advertised the coup in the trade papers,[80] and subsequently planted a sensational news story (actually a hoax) designed to publicize the imminent appearance of this "star" in IMP pictures.

Later on (in mid 1910) Mary Pickford, known as "Little Mary" to the general public, was enticed from the Biograph Company at a salary of $175 per week. "Laemmle further undertook to let the public know . . . that 'Little Mary' had a second name. . . . [Moreover] thenceforth Miss Mary Pickford began to appear in 'copy' sanctioned by the IMP publicity bureau." It may be added that Miss Pickford's first appearance for IMP was publicized in an advertisement.[81]

At least one of the reasons for the slowness in the development of the star system in the early motion picture industry was the reluctance of "Trust" companies to feature players and thus be faced with an inevitable demand for higher salaries. It is an interesting fact that in England distributors of American films supplied fictitious names for the featured players in response to a public demand for their identity. It is interesting, too, that in America before the manufacturers gave way to demands of their patrons, the fan magazines had departments devoted to answering the questions of motion picture devotees and at least some of these questions concerned the identity of the movie "stars."

d) Price evidently was not typically employed by independents as an aggressive competitive weapon; however, considering the quality of their offering and the position of the independent buyers, it might be expected that independent prices would be somewhat lower than those of the licensed manufacturers and importers. Generally speaking, the evidence does suggest that the independent prices were lower than those of the "trust,"[82] at least at the exchange level, if only because the independent exhibitors generally were smaller and thus were not able to pay so much. In addition, in their sales promotional efforts independent sellers stressed certain semiprice advantages, such as not having to pay a license fee and allowing renters to sublease independent films.[83]

3. Consolidation of Early Independent Sales Effort. During the first few months of Patents Company activity, the various nonlicensed suppliers operated independently of one another in getting their product into the distribution channels. In the fall of 1909—less than a year after the Patents Company commenced operations—the nonlicensed operators organized the National Independent Moving Picture Alliance to foster cooperative sales activity. The alliance was a loose-knit organization that, nevertheless, laid down certain rules of competitive behavior, including, reportedly, adherence to a schedule of minimum prices at the manufacturer level.[84] This association, which was in existence only a few months, was replaced by a much more formal organization that acted as a centralized sales agency for independently produced motion picture film at the pre-exchange level. Superficially, the organization was similar to that of the General Film Company; but fundamentally it was quite different because the latter was an exchange-operating company, and the former was merely an agent of the manufacturers that distributed goods to independent exchanges.

This concern, the Motion Picture Distributing and Sales Company, was organized in the spring of 1910 by the top officials of two leading unlicensed manufacturers, the Independent Motion Picture Company and the New York Motion Picture Company. There were undoubtedly various reasons for the formation of this company; one unquestionably was to provide a solid front of independent competitive activity. But the most important reason, one would surmise, was the recognition by the company's organizers that successful independent effort necessitated a dependable film supply source,[85] which, in turn, at this stage at least, necessitated a centralized competitive activity.

The Sales Company, as it was commonly called, would act as a super-distributing agency and assume most, but not all, of the sales activities of the producers. The physical distribution of the motion picture film to the exchanges was handled by the Sales Company, and it also engaged in sales promotional activity in behalf of the independent offering in general. Each manufacturer, however, had the responsibility of promoting his own brand of films either by direct contact with distributors or by advertising or both.

Thus a new level was added to the independent motion picture distribution structure with the result that the manufacturers would be able to concentrate on producing pictures while the exchanges, relieved of supply problems, would be free to expand the market for independent films. This policy, note, was not true with respect to the General Film Company, which was simply a superexchange concern that competed with and even replaced existing exchanges.

Several independent manufacturers joined the Sales Company almost at once, but the scheme was openly derided by others. Some of the independents announced that they would distribute their films individually.

Indeed, an organization called the Associated Independent Film Manufacturers was formed to lend support to this policy.[86]

After some months, a compromise was reached between the Sales Company and the dissident faction, with the result that the Motion Picture Distributing and Sales Company was reincorporated under a new charter that gave equal representation to Sales Company and Associated Independent interests. Under the terms of the agreement between the company and its members, each manufacturer was required to be sold in accordance with a uniform schedule of prices,[87] and a fee was to be levied on each release as a distribution charge to the manufacturers. Thus by concerted activity reminiscent of "trust" behavior, the independents consolidated their sales effort and by so doing enhanced their chances of succeeding against "trust" opposition.

The Motion Picture Distributing and Sales Company program consisted of twenty-seven reels per week from twenty or more domestic and foreign manufacturers. By mid-July of 1910 the Sales Company had entered into distribution arrangements with forty-seven nonlicensed rental exchanges located in twenty-seven cities in the United States and Canada. These rental exchanges, in turn, served approximately 4,000 theaters, which by that time were operating without benefit of Patents Company licenses.[88] Thus eighteen months after the formation of the Patents Company, there was a substantial and well-organized segment of the industry operating independently of "trust" control.

The independent motion picture concerns presented a solid front through the agency of the Sales Company for almost two years. The first sign of a schism in the independent ranks was the announcement in early April 1912 that certain manufacturing interests had organized a company, Mutual Film Corporation, for the purpose of acquiring rental exchanges. This notice was followed shortly by an announcement of the organization of the Film Supply Company of America and the securing by that company of the exclusive rights to the product of some of the more important Sales Company manufacturers.[89]

Some of the manufacturers were opposed to the exchange-acquisition program as well as to other policies of the new regime, and remained in the Sales Company temporarily. Shortly, however, this faction organized the Universal Film Manufacturing Company, with a policy of releasing motion picture films direct to independent exchanges rather than through the Sales Company. Thus "Half of the members of the Sales Company organized a new program, while the other half organized another program and, withdrawing simultaneously, left the Sales Company [merely] a shell."[90]

The independents were mainly now in two groups. Thanhouser, Gaumont, American Film Manufacturing Company, Great Northern, Reliance, Eclair, Solax, Majestic, Lux, and Comet, releasing a total of twenty reels per week, were allied with the Film Supply Company; while New York Motion Picture Company, IMP, Powers, Rex, Champion, Republic, and Nestor became part of the Universal organization. Thus there were in mid-1912 about the time the petition was filed in the government's case against the Motion Picture Patents Company, two strong[91] independent groups dealing in the same type of product-service as the "trust" organization, i.e., programs made up of a variety of short films.

Generally speaking, therefore, despite "trust" effort to the contrary, the early independents were able to compete sufficiently effectively in the marketplace to survive and to protect their position against legal interferences. However, by this time a new development was already taking place in the form of multiple-reel offerings, which would eventually relegate all the producers of short films to secondary positions in the industry.

B. The Later Independents

In the year 1911 the motion picture market consisted of millions of customers, known as movie fans, who were accustomed to pay five cents, or at the most ten cents, for motion picture entertainment composed of a variety of inexpensively produced short films. To serve this market were some 11,500 theaters[92] whose owners contracted with one or more of the 150 or so rental exchanges to supply them with a specified number of program changes per week. Each program consisted of a number of reels of film of a specified age. While there was some preference for certain programs over others, owing in part at least to consumer familiarity with certain companies' players, there was relatively little preselection of subjects by exhibitors.

The early independent effort was really a simulation of "Trust" company activities with minor variations owing to differences in competitive positions of the traders. Later independent effort was quite different; in fact, it was revolutionary in nature and began a new era in motion picture production and distribution.

1. The Feature-Length Film. It should be clear from the foregoing that the first wave of independent competitors of the Patents Company manufacturer-licensees was composed of firms that produced the same type of product as they, i.e., short films. The feature-length picture involved an innovative concept of motion picture entertainment; namely, that consumer interest in a motion picture subject could be sustained for a considerable period of time. Thus instead of attending performances consisting of a ten-minute comedy, a fifteen-minute society drama, a five-minute scenic film and a twenty-minute western, the public might be induced to patronize theaters which featured hour-long dramatic offerings. Indeed, the theory was that if the picture were well made, "movie" patrons would pay a premium price for such entertainment. For one thing, some imaginative individuals must have realized that the feature-length picture would provide an ideal medium for the development of the star system with its opportunities for exploiting popular players. If the theory of feature-length pictures was sound, of course, the producers of such films possessed a product that might in time replace the programs of short subjects in motion picture theaters.

While general acceptance of the feature film did not come until considerably later, the first appearance in America of this type of production occurred in 1907 with Adolph Zukor's distribution of Pathé's three-reel *Passion Play*. Then in 1909 Vitagraph produced a five-reel version of *The Life of Moses*, which the company was forced to issue as a five-part serial.[93] This latter experience may have conditioned the behavior of the licensed producers generally because, with few exceptions, these gentry took very little interest in the promotion of the feature film, preferring to concentrate their efforts on the well-established short film.

Movement toward the acceptance of the feature film began in 1911 when two European feature films were imported into the United States: *Crusaders* in four reels, and *Dante's Inferno* in five reels. These feature-length motion pictures were followed in 1912 and early 1913 by other imports, including the four-reel *Queen Elizabeth*, starring Sarah Bernhardt, and by a considerable number of American made feature pictures. It was in early 1913 that the famous Italian eight-reel film *Quo Vadis* was successfully presented in this country. This picture, interestingly enough, was imported by George Kleine, one of the Patents Company licensees; but the venture appears to have been quite apart from his short-film operations. According to Ramsaye, the film ran for twenty-two weeks in New York City's Astor Theater, to mention only one booking, at a top admission price of one dollar.[94]

Most of these multireel pictures were the products of companies that were operating independently of "Trust" affiliation, indicating perhaps that Patents Company restrictions tended to stultify innovations. However, the independents who were promoting feature productions and those who were producing or importing short films were usually entirely different individuals.

2. Initial Methods of Feature Distribution. The problems of marketing feature-length pictures in the early days must have been very difficult, for most of the theaters, or "shows" as they were sometimes called, were small and provided little profit potential for the feature film. In addition, the owners of such theaters tended to be satisfied with the status quo, i.e., programs composed of short subjects, for the reason, perhaps, that nickelodeons were money-makers. But some theaters, usually Motion Picture Patents Company licensees, were large and well appointed and thus provided a potential market for the features; consequently, the impact of the feature film was greater on the licensed segment of the industry than on the unlicensed. Their size and attractiveness also indicated that their owners were progressive and therefore receptive to innovation. And although at first there was little chance of completely replacing the short-film programs with features, it became a common practice to book a feature in a theater for a one- to three-day run without disturbing the contractual relations between the theater owner and his regular exchange.[95] Occasionally, of course, a theater manager would show a feature-length film by drawing on the supply of the various feature distributors and by shelving the regular program, for which he had already paid. Managers of licensed theaters frequently followed this practice because Patents Company regulations forbade the showing of unlicensed films, and the theater owners were not ready to "burn their bridges" behind them. Because feature films required individual promotion efforts instead of the complete-program promotion used by orthodox exchanges for short films, new methods of distribution were introduced and producers of such films sought distributors to represent their product in each market area.

The earliest arrangements between feature producers and distributors were made on what was, and still is, known as a states-rights, or territorial-rights, selling basis. The term *states rights* is a more common name, but when greater accuracy is required the term *territorial rights* is employed. Territorial rights might extend over an area of more than one state, e.g., the entire Pacific Coast, or they might be sold for only one part of a state, e.g., southern California. The origin of states-rights selling is discussed in a story appearing in one of the trade papers in mid-1914.[96] According to this account, a multireel picture was first offered to exchanges sometime in 1910 or 1911 at the rate of so much per foot but the exchanges were reluctant to handle it because they thought it was too long to be much in demand. However, this disadvantage could be partially offset by the sale of exclusive rights to one distributor in each area, thus making worthwhile any intensive sales effort the distributor might wish to exert on the film. There were two steps in this process: sale by a vendor to a theater or exchange operator of the exclusive right to distribute the picture in a particular territory, usually on a fixed-fee basis[97] and leasing the film by a states-rights buyer to individual theaters in his territory for exhibition purposes on a flat-rental or percentage basis. Some of the feature-length films were rented to these theaters on an exclusive basis, at least for a limited time. In the early days of feature distribution, vendors were not much concerned with box-office prices. As time went on, however, the distributors became increasingly aware of the relationship between prices charged by exhibitors and potential rental payments, and in many instances specified the minimum admission prices to be charged. The earliest example of this practice that I have found is the restriction in 1912 by the distributors of Max Reinhardt's *The Miracle* that the picture be shown only in houses charging twenty-five cents or more admission.[98] Eventually, the standard contracts of motion picture distributors contained a price-maintenance clause, which became one of the grounds for the government charge of trade-restraining activities on the part of producer-distributors in a case against Paramount and other producer-distributors many years later—*United States* v. *Paramount Pictures, Inc.* (S.D. N.Y. 1946).[99]

It may be inferred from the foregoing that states-rights selling provided quick revenue with little sales effort; but at least in its original form, it presented little opportunity for the original seller to share in any unusual profits that might develop at the distribution level. Rights sold on a percentage basis or for a limited period rather than in perpetuity helped to offset the disadvantage when the buyer could be persuaded to accept such terms.

Another distributive scheme used almost from the outset, and which even persists today, was the road-showing technique, in which the producer or distributor assumed the responsibility for the exhibition of the film at the consumer level, unlike the states-rights system in which the producer or importer took responsibility of distributing the films to theaters.

Road-showing could be successfully used only for outstanding productions on a percentage-of-gross basis, which was undoubtedly a continuation of the traditional arrangements between theatrical impresarios and theater owners in the production of stage plays. It also involved taking over the actual operation of the theater, which included furnishing projecting apparatus and assuming the publicity function. Such showings were often conducted on a hard-ticket (reserve seat) basis, and made possible the utilization of the relatively large and well-appointed legitimate theaters for the showing of motion pictures.

While the road-show and states-rights selling methods of distribution were basically different, they were not necessarily mutually exclusive.

For one thing, a vendor might first road-show a strong picture and later sell states rights to it, as was done with the twelve-reel *Birth of a Nation*. For another, a distributor might buy the territorial rights for such a picture and then road-show it himself before renting it to other exhibitors. It should be emphasized that both of these methods developed out of the inability of short-film distributors to market feature-length pictures effectively. When Vitagraph, a Patents Company licensee, started producing films and had no way to distribute them, it arranged for General Film Company to handle them. According to Albert E. Smith, president of Vitagraph: "We released eight feature pictures through General Film. Some were very good, but none made any money. General Film's method of handling was the reason for the loss in almost every instance."[100]

   3. Improved Methods of Distribution. It was in 1912 that Adoph Zukor, an erstwhile exhibitor, organized the Famous Players Film Company to implement his idea of making motion pictures featuring "Famous Players in Famous Plays." Zukor's first move was to purchase the rights of the four-reel *Queen Elizabeth*, starring the immortal Sarah Bernhardt. According to Zukor, he even underwrote the production costs of this film, or at least part of them, in exchange for the North American rights. In his book he said: "Louis Mercanton, a French producer, wanted to make a four-reel picture with the world-famous Sarah Bernhardt in her successful play *Queen Elizabeth* . . . [but he] was being delayed for lack of money. . . . I got in touch with Mercanton's American agent. We discussed the possibility of securing the North American rights. In the end I agreed to pay forty thousand dollars for them, advancing the money to enable Mercanton to go ahead."[101] Later in the same year, Famous Players produced its first feature picture, the five-reel *Count of Monte Cristo*. According to Alexander Lichtman, in a recorded interview, *Count of Monte Cristo* was the first film produced by Famous Players, but because of some litigation over the story rights to this picture, the second company film, *The Prisoner of Zenda*, was evidently released ahead of it. This was not Zukor's first experience with feature films because, as was mentioned above, sometime earlier he acquired the rights to a three-reel version of the European-made film *Passion Play*, and presented it (on what might be termed a "road show" basis) in Newark. As he later remarked, "The *Passion Play* had a good run in Newark and afterwards at our other theaters. It satisfied me that feature pictures would be successful even though my colleagues were as skeptical as ever."
   It is an interesting fact that Adolph Zukor, who was a sort of "outlaw" in the eyes of the Patents Company in connection with his *Queen Elizabeth* venture, attempted, at first unsuccessfully, to get a license for his

domestically-produced feature films, but following a successful trade showing of *The Prisoner of Zenda* received word from the Patents Company that it would license this production at least.[102] The following year, in 1913, Bosworth, Inc., made the first feature-length version of Jack London's *Sea Wolf*. Shortly thereafter, the Jesse L. Lasky Feature Play Company, which was controlled by Jesse L. Lasky and Samuel Goldfish, now Goldwyn, produced that company's first picture, a multireel version of the famous stage play, *The Squaw Man*. The Jesse L. Lasky Feature Play Company ran the first advertisement for *The Squaw Man* offering it to distributors on a states-rights basis in January 1914. Practically all the rights were disposed of before the film was exhibited which indicates, perhaps, that there was an active demand for feature-length motion pictures at that time or, possibly, that Sam Goldfish was a super salesman (as he undoubtedly was).

Independent feature-producing companies were not entirely free from Patents Company interference, despite the action taken in August 1912 against its monopolistic activities. For example, in August 1914 the Patents Company reportedly sued Lasky, but the suit was settled out of court and Lasky was permitted to continue operations.[103] Similarly, the Patents Company took action against Famous Players in a suit that was also settled out of court with the payment of "damages."

Several other companies entered the feature-film field in 1913. Some of these ventures appear to have been predicated on the principle of offering exhibitors programs of features at regular intervals rather than single features from time to time. Thus, Warner's Features, Inc., predecessor of present-day Warner Bros., and Box Office Attractions Company, predecessor of Fox Film Corporation, later Twentieth Century–Fox, were organized to acquire films from various independent producers and to distribute them through their own or franchised exchanges.

The inefficiency of the states-rights selling system manifested itself particularly at the exchange level. There were two reasons: the rental price of a single feature was often not sufficient to carry the selling and distribution costs incurred, and the total number of rentals that might be expected was very small since most of the theaters were nickelodeons having little interest in showing feature-length pictures. Although the states-rights system continued to be used by companies producing only an occasional film, a more efficient method of distribution was required by more stable concerns. The first method used by Famous Players Film Company to overcome the weakness of the single-picture states-rights deals was to adopt a policy of releasing a program of thirty pictures and selling the distribution rights for the season's output to various exchanges throughout the national market. Under this scheme, which was in effect during the 1913/14 season, supplies were assured buyers and per-unit selling costs were reduced. Exchange men acquiring rights under such a program were thus able to sell a season's output to exhibitor customers at a greatly reduced cost per picture, providing, of course, that the buyer took the entire offering. A few months later, Adolph Zukor reflected on this move. "[After experimenting with states-rights distribution] we devised the plan of selling a year's output to an exchange for a certain territory at a fixed price, per annum, instead of obtaining a varying scale for each picture." [104] This early version of block-booking developed out of the distributors' need for a more efficient method of selling film. Block booking, now largely proscribed by law, *United States* v. *Paramount Pictures, Inc.* (1948),[105] was the sale of films in a block rather than as individual pictures, often before the pictures were produced. The main difference between block booking of features and program booking of short films was that the former usually related to specifically mentioned titles and the contractual relationship between distributor and exhibitor was for a whole season's product, while the latter had to do with a weekly supply of usually unspecified films for an indefinite period of time.

In May of 1914 the trade papers announced the formation of Paramount Pictures Corporation to handle the distribution of films for Famous Players Film Company, Jesse L. Lasky Feature Play Company, and Bosworth Inc.[106] This company, which was controlled by a group of feature distributors operating in various parts of the United States, was granted exclusive distribution rights by the producing companies, which agreed to provide a certain number of pictures per season for the distributor to market, and the producers and the distributors were to share on a 35-percent-to-distributor—65-percent-to-producer basis in the gross revenue derived from rentals and receipts, if any, from "subfranchise" distributors.

Although feature films were leased to theaters almost exclusively on a flat-rental basis before 1914, in that year Paramount announced in the trade press that the corporation was working on a percentage plan similar to that existing between legitimate theaters and theatrical companies that would provide for the exacting of a certain percentage of the gross receipts as rental for feature films.[107] Paramount was owned by five exchangemen whose operations covered approximately 80 percent of the domestic market. The remaining territories were covered by subfranchise holders, who shared the gross rentals with the franchise holders on a 25-percent—75-percent basis, respectively. In addition, the franchise agreements between Paramount and the producing concerns provided for a cash advance by the distributor to the producer on the release date of each picture, to be liquidated by the producer's share of the receipts.

The agreements also guaranteed a minimum return to the producer. The franchise arrangement, incidentally, paved the way for the later acquisition of distribution facilities by producing companies, and hence, for the integration of motion picture production and distribution.

Other companies roughly similar to Paramount entered the feature-film field in 1914. One of these was the Alco Film Corporation, predecessor to Metro Pictures Corporation, which subsequently became part of Metro-Goldwyn-Mayer. Alco was a sales company that did not produce films but acquired them from various producers and distributed them through franchise arrangements with exchanges in various markets. Another was the World Film Corporation, an important competitive factor in the early days of feature-length films. This company, which was aggressively managed by Louis J. Selznick, the father of present-day producer David O. Selznick, had contractual arrangements with producing companies (probably on some percentage basis) and distributed the films directly to exhibitors through the firm's own branch offices. In 1915 the famous but short-lived Triangle Film Corporation was organized by Harry S. Aitken, with Thomas H. Ince, D. W. Griffith, and Mack Sennett as the vertexes of the triangle. Also in 1915 four of the Patents Company licensees organized a distributing company for feature-length films called V.L.S.E. (Vitagraph, Lubin, Selig, and Essanay), but this company was subsequently taken over by Vitagraph.[108] While improved methods of distribution had been developed as early as 1914, there was still some states-rights selling, particularly by companies having only an occasional picture to release.

It is clear from the record that the public acceptance of feature-length pictures in America was a gradual process. Even as late as mid-1914, some prominent picture makers were not convinced that the feature-length picture would prevail. For example, in July 1914, Colonel William N. Selig, whose blockbuster *The Spoilers* had only recently had its premiere at New York's Strand Theatre, complained of "padded" features and revealed an affinity toward the short film productions when he said, "Personally, I believe that long features are doomed. . . . I predict that the general clamor for a diversified program (which has been experienced in Europe) will soon sweep this country."[109] It is equally clear that by the end of 1913 the competition of feature companies was beginning to affect Patents Company licensees and unlicensed short-picture companies as well.[110] Patents Company licensees should have realized that the feature picture would in time pose a serious threat to the short-film programs, and that they would have to adjust themselves to the trend if they were to maintain their position in the industry. It may well be that the insidious pattern of the acceptance of feature-length pictures worked to the disadvantage of the short-film producers because they were not forced to alter their production programs as they would have been if the change in consumer response had been abrupt.

While the short films were still predominant in small theaters throughout the country in 1914, "movie palaces" were beginning to replace store shows in large cities, two of the earliest of which were the Strand and the Vitagraph theaters in New York City.[111] The efficient operation of the large houses required the showing of feature films that would attract large audiences at prices considerably higher than those usually charged for motion-picture entertainment. The prices at the Vitagraph Theater in 1914 ranged from twenty-five cents to one dollar. The prices at the Strand ranged from ten to fifty cents.[112] It should be obvious that once they were opened, such theaters automatically provided a market for feature-length pictures and by the same token contracted the market for short films. By 1915, the year that the lower court decision was handed down in the government's case against the Motion Picture Patents Company, feature producers were well entrenched in the motion picture industry; and by December 1916 feature-length pictures were predominant.[113] New feature companies listed in mid-1916 included Metro Pictures Corporation, Selznick Pictures Corporation, and K.E.S.E. (Kleine, Edison, Selig, and Essanay). Within a few years all but three of the erstwhile short-film manufacturers had disappeared from the scene, and these three, Pathé, Vitagraph, and Universal, had shifted to the production of feature films. At this writing, only Universal, now known as Universal International, is extant.

Famous Players—Lasky Corporation was incorporated in 1916 about the same time that Artcraft Pictures Corporation was organized to market the producing company's better pictures. As a result of a merger between Artcraft and Paramount Pictures Corporation in 1917, production and distribution became fully integrated, although there were still a considerable number of states' rights companies operating.[114] It was about this same time that Samuel Goldfish (not yet Goldwyn) withdrew from Famous Players—Lasky and established his own company. Goldwyn Pictures Corporation subsequently became part of Metro-Goldwyn-Mayer, but without the services of Mr. Goldfish, who had been deposed some time previously.[115]

It is very difficult to obtain a clear-cut view of the beginning years of the integration of production, distribution, and exhibition in the film industry. A former official of First National in an interview with one of the author's research assistants suggested that in an effort to block the competition that arose after Famous Players—Lasky acquired some theaters in several key cities, leading theater owners throughout the country organized in 1917 the First National Exhibitors' Circuit at first to contract for the production of motion pictures and later to produce them. There is evidence, on the other hand, that these same exhibitors made the move to resist Famous Players–Lasky's block-booking policy, as revealed in Famous Players–Lasky Corp., F.T.C. (1927).[116] Zukor, however, states that "exhibitors [entered production because they] argued that the rental costs of big-star films was too high." Regardless of the precise reasons for the First National organization, the record indicates that in 1919 Famous Players–Lasky adopted a policy of theater acquisition in retaliation to the First National move.[117] It should be noted that the integration of First National was the backward type (from exhibitor to distributor to producer) while the Famous Players–Lasky integration was of the forward type (from producer to distributor to exhibitor). Within a very few years another "monopolistic" combination would be giving the government antitrust agencies cause for further worry.[118] Thus one monopolistic combination would soon be replaced by another consisting of erstwhile independents.

☆

V. Conclusion

The original petition in the government's case against Motion Picture Patents Company was filed on 15 August 1912,[119] under the enactment of 2 July 1890, commonly known as the Sherman Act—i.e., "SEC. 1. Every contract, combination in the form of a trust or otherwise, or conspiracy, in restraint of trade or commerce among the several States, or with foreign nations, is hereby declared to be illegal. . . . SEC. 2. Every person who shall monopolize, or attempt to monopolize, or combine or conspire with any other person or persons, to monopolize any part of the trade or commerce among the several States, or with foreign nations, shall be deemed guilty of [violation of this section]."[120] In its complaint, the government charged the existence of a combination in unlawful restraint of trade and prayed for remedial action by power of the law in the form of cessation of the unlawful activities of which the combination was accused. Various documents in the case were filed by the defendant in late 1912,[121] and the case went to trial in the District Court of the United States for the Eastern District of Pennsylvania 15 January 1913, when testimony was given by the first witness subpoenaed by the petitioner.[122] The decision in this case was handed down by the lower court on 1 October 1915.[123]

In its decision, the court first described the rights of patent holders exclusively to use, make, or vend the patented article for a limited time, and to withhold the article from sale or even part with its possession without parting with its ownership. The court then went on to state that a patent holder may protect itself by reasonable means against infringement and even to seek the aid of the law to enforce the exclusion of others. However, the court stated that patent holders may not with impunity impose unreasonable restraints on commerce and through such restraints monopolize an industry under the guise of defending themselves against encroachment.

The court decided that "the agreements and acts of the defendants in the present case went far beyond what was necessary to protect the use of the patents or the [government-granted] monopoly which went with them, and that the end and result . . . was the restraint of trade condemned by the law." The court did not spell out the specific actions which were in violation of the Sherman law but it must have had in mind, among other things:

1. The attempted control of all industry activities through the use of interlocking agreements;

2. The attempted exclusion of new competitors (in certain phases of the industry at least) by vesting the power of granting entrance to those already in the industry;

3. The attempted elimination of independent distributors and their replacement with the "Trust" affiliated General Film Company exchanges;

4. The fixing of prices for raw film (sold to manufacturers) and for motion pictures (leased to exchanges); and

5. The employment of various types of harassing tactics designed to impede the activities of would-be independents in all branches of the industry.[124]

While granting that the motives of the defendants were in certain respects meritorious,[125] the court found that the primary motivation of the combination was "domination of the motion picture business itself" and indeed "to reap the commercial advantages" of monopoly for themselves while ostensibly protecting their patent rights. The court further decided "that the contracts enumerated in the petition, and the combination there described, were a conspiracy in restraint of trade . . . among the several states . . . and were and are illegal, and that the defendants . . . [with the exception next noted][126] have attempted to monopolize, and have monopolized, and have combined and conspired, among themselves and with each other, to monopolize, a part of the trade or commerce among the several states and with foreign nations, consisting of the trade in films, cameras, projecting machines, and other accessories of the motion picture business, as charged in the petition of complaint filed."[127]

It appears from the foregoing decision that the court was stressing the conspiracy and the attempted monopolization of the motion picture business rather than the market results which actually obtained at the time the decision was handed down. It will be recalled that by the time the petition was filed in August 1912, the independents had established themselves firmly in the market despite exclusionary tactics by the "Trust," and that by the time the decision was handed down in October 1915, little monopolistic control remained in the industry. It is true, however, that the Patents Company had practiced various trade-restraining activities, in violation of SECTION 1 of the Sherman Antitrust Act, and attempted to monopolize and did in fact succeed in monopolizing one segment of the industry (the trade in licensed film), in violation of SEC. 2 of the Sherman Act.

The court therefore concluded that the petitioner was entitled to relief and stated that it would entertain a decree in keeping with this finding. This decree, which was filed 24 January 1916, enjoined the defendants and their officers from continuing the unlawful combination. An appeal from the district court's decision by the Patents Company was subsequently dismissed on stipulation of the parties in 1918.[128]

The legal record in this case would not be complete without reference to another decision in a case involving the Motion Picture Patents Company that was handed down a few months after the government's case was decided in the lower court. This decision revolved around the Patents Company requirement of the use of licensed film in licensed projecting equipment. The court in this case decided against the Patents Company's purported restriction of the use of unlicensed film in projecting machines whose patents were held by the company,[129] on the basis of SEC. 3 of the Clayton Act, rather than on any provision of the Sherman Act. SEC. 3 of the Clayton Act reads as follows: "That it shall be unlawful for any person engaged in commerce, in the course of such commerce, to lease or make a sale or contract for (the) sale of goods, wares . . . or other commodities, whether patented or unpatented, for use, consumption or resale within the United States or any . . . on the condition, agreement or understanding that the lessee or purchaser thereof shall not use or deal in the goods . . . or . . . commodities of a competitor or competitors of the lessor or seller, where the effect of such . . . sale . . . agreement or understanding may be to substantially lessen competition or tend to create a monopoly in any line of commerce."[130]

In affirming the lower court decision, in effect that the Patents Company requirement constituted a tying agreement in violation of Sec. 3 of the Clayton Act, the United States Supreme Court stated that the Patents Company restriction of the type of film used on licensed machines was invalid because "such a film is obviously not any part of the invention of the patent in suit; because it is an attempt, without statutory warrant, to continue the patent monopoly . . . of film after it has expired, and because to enforce it would . . . create a monopoly in the manufacture and use of moving picture films, wholly outside of the patent in suit and of the patent law." [131]

It is an interesting fact that the decision in the government's case against the Motion Picture Patents Company was handed down long after the domination complained of by the government was dissipated by the entrance of unlicensed competitors into the motion picture industry. Indeed, by the fall of 1915 when the government's case was decided, many of the independent companies that had more or less successfully competed with the Patents Company licensees in the early years of "Trust" control, were already giving way to a new type of independent rival—producers of feature films. In fact, within a few months after the decision was rendered, and well before the appeal was dismissed, consolidation of certain feature company interests had taken place, and soon thereafter integration of feature producing and distributing activities was effected followed by producer-distributor acquisition and control of theaters. Thus in July 1916 the Famous Players Film Company (organized in June 1912 by Adolph Zukor) and the Jesse L. Lasky Feature Play Company (organized in November 1913 by Jesse L. Lasky) were merged into what for many years was known as the Famous Players–Lasky Corporation. This company, shortly thereafter, acquired the stock of two other producing companies and thus effected vertical integration of production and distribution. This activity, interestingly enough, led within a few years to antitrust action in the form of a complaint by the Federal Trade Commission on 30 August 1921, against grounds that it now was dominating the industry. Famous Players–Lasky Corporation and a dozen or more related concerns on the grounds that they were dominating the industry through such things as block-booking contracts and theater control, actual or threatened. [132] This antitrust action was the first of many taken by the government to stop monopolistic practices by feature companies in the years following the demise of the Patents Company monopoly.

It might well be argued, then, that the long-run problem of monopoly control as in the case of the Motion Picture Patents Company is self-correcting; that, given time, new competitors and, indeed, new methods result in a dissipation of monopolistic control. But while this hypothesis may be valid generally, the case discussed here is no proof of its soundness. In fact, the antitrust action taken by the government against the Patents Company occurred early enough both to thwart the company's own accomplishments and to stimulate the activities of independent competitors. One cannot know the results had there been no antitrust action.

But even if it could be established that in the long run monopolistic combinations are eventually dissipated by inexorable pressure of would-be entrants, government interference might still be warranted because of short-run social benefits to be derived from such action. That is, the long-run theory dismisses the short-term monopoly problem as insignificant, when actually trade-restrictive activities on the part of a temporarily dominant firm might result in the elimination of competent but vulnerable competitors before they have a chance to exert their beneficial influence on the industry. One may conclude, then, that the invocation of the antitrust laws in the Motion Picture Patents Company case, though apparently redundant, may well have had some remedial effect on the monopolistic activities of others in the field, and that our antitrust laws with all their limitations may play an important role in the promotion of vigorous competition in American industry.

Afterword
Jeanne Thomas Allen

Scholars frequently describe their research as an ongoing process of dialogue or debate with other scholars. This description makes the important point that scholarship is a collective activity. It seeks to expand, challenge, and refine current knowledge through close scrutiny and questioning. An important aspect of this approach to scholarship is the belief that published research is not finished or complete in any absolute sense no matter how "permanent" the printed word arranged in paragraphs with titles and headings appears to be. The readers' task is to open a dialogue with a published work that continues the research process. The purpose of this afterword is to begin such a dialogue. It will not present a completed argument or position to compare with another. Instead, it will examine a previously published piece of research by asking four questions: what is the scholar's model of explanation and its limitations?; is the evidence presented consistent with the researcher's conclusions?;

what questions remain unanswered?; and what model of explanation might better address them?

Ralph Cassady, Jr.'s, "Monopoly in Motion Picture Production and Distribution: 1908–1915" represents an important contribution to film scholarship and was initially published in the *Southern California Law Review* in the Summer of 1959. It was not the first piece of extensive research on the Motion Picture Patents Company. William I. Greenwald's dissertation ("The Motion Picture Industry: An Economic Study of the History and Practices of a Business," New York University, 1950) provides an economic history of the motion picture industry and devotes a chapter to the MPPC. Floyd Vaughn's study of the economics of the U.S. patent system (*Economics of Our Patent System* [New York: Macmillan, 1925]: 52–58, 107–25) examines this first trust in the motion picture industry. Cassady's own dissertation ("The Motion Picture Patents Company and Anti-Trust Law in the United States," UCLA, 1930) is devoted to this same subject. What stands out about Cassady's 1959 article is its thorough reference to the voluminous court record which led to the legal dissolution of the MPPC: 3 Transcript of Record 1700–1, United States v. Motion Picture Patents Co., in the District Court of the United States for the Eastern District of Pennsylvania (transcript is available at the Law Library, UCLA, and Princeton University Library).

The significance of this use of legal records lies in the fact that Cassady was working with documents which would not provide a unified perspective on the MPPC but rather conflicting interests and reports which he would have to weigh and synthesize. MPPC lawyers were interested in showing the beneficial effects of the patents trust on the industry as a means of bringing order to competitive chaos and improving service with greater efficiency. The prosecution representing the government sought to demonstrate that the MPPC conspired to restrain trade, and indeed the court found the business arrangements and practices of the MPPC to be in violation of the Sherman Act. Like the court, Cassady as historian seeks to reach conclusions by interpreting conflicting testimony. Because his evidence, which is mentioned in the text as well as in the notes, is extensive, the reader can measure the validity of Cassady's conclusions against the evidence he provides.

Cassady's article does not present an initial argument which is then supported by his evidence and reasoning. It appears, rather, to be purely descriptive, winnowing evidence from secondary sources, trade journals, and court records to *portray* the business practices of the industry. Only at the end of the article does he acknowledge agreement with the court's finding against the MPPC and suggest that despite self-correcting tendencies in "free market" capitalism, antitrust laws help promote vigorous competition. This final statement makes explicit, however, a position which has guided Cassady throughout his "purely descriptive" study and which accounts for much of his selection of pertinent evidence from the record of the court case. Cassady's neoclassical economic philosophy encourages him to view government as largely absent from the operations of a market economy rather than as a positive force encouraging and directing economic development. (See various state laws encouraging corporate concentration in the early twentieth century, particularly Maine and New Jersey for examples of the latter positions.) According to neoclassical theorists, the role of government or the state is to step in only when an imbalance or aberration has occurred, tuning the economy slightly and once again removing itself from market operations. By presenting his narrative history as description and presenting conclusions as though he only then had reached them, it is not readily apparent to the reader that his economic philosophy informs his selection of pertinent details. One must read both the text and notes closely, questioning the conclusions reached and noting the inconsistencies between the data cited and the generalizations drawn from them, to uncover his implicit theoretical approach.

For example, Cassady concludes that antitrust law enhances competition in the market. Although independents were flourishing before the case was decided, knowledge of the suit may have strengthened the independents' position in some incalculable but significant way. This conclusion would be almost impossible to prove in light of two cases in the teens involving independents as infringers, which, Cassady tells us, were settled out of court *in favor* of the MPPC. These cases suggest that knowledge of the 1912 suit did not strengthen the independents' bargaining position. Cassady mentions that the court stressed conspiracy rather than market results (p. 66), which may very well imply that market results were not as effective in this vein as the structure of MPPC agreements seems to suggest. In fact, there is little evidence which supports Cassady's conclusion and considerable evidence against him, both within his text and elsewhere. The inconsistency here makes clear that a theoretical position or economic philosophy has been used as a screen or guiding force for his selection of data.

The availability of film stock from Eastman as early as 1911 may have been more significant in encouraging the independents' resistance to the MPPC and operation outside it than the suit initiated in 1912. Reese Jenkins in his study of the American photographic industry and Eastman Kodak in particular (*Images and Enterprise: Technology and the American Photographic Industry 1839–1925* [Baltimore: Johns Hopkins Univ.

Pr., 1975]:52–58, 107–25) has researched the role of Jules E. Brulatour, who represented the interests of film industry independents. Although he was unsuccessful in 1909 and 1910 in securing a supply of Eastman film, Brulatour managed to produce contracts with the independents for substantial quantities of cine film. These contracts convinced Eastman early in 1911 to make a *modification in the contract* with the MPPC that allowed Eastman Kodak to sell to the independents. This modification can be interpreted as an admission that the original strategy of the MPPC had failed. Jenkins writes: "The flow of Eastman film to the independents spelled the first of a series of defeats for Motion Picture Patents and signalled the ultimate failure of the first attempt at the rationalization of the cinematographic industry" (p. 291).

Relying so heavily on the court record not only commits Cassady to weighing conflicting perspectives and evidence but it also sets up the terms of the discussion of the MPPC as a question concerning the intentions of the business executives involved in the 1908 formation: were they conspiring to restrain trade by crushing the nonlicensed industry or were they committed to improving the quality of service with a resulting salutary effect on the industry? At various points in his discussion Cassady acknowledges that both statements are true, but he does not seek to recast the terms of the debate from those set by the antitrust suit. These statements of intent—the one a description of predatory aggressive business practices and the other a claim to humanitarian service—indicate the problems of taking the divergent statements of prosecution and plaintiff at face value and treating the legal record as a unified document. Given the charged atmosphere of a court case that is attempting to ascertain legal liability, it would seem to make more sense to ask what the *structure* of the MPPC arrangements suggests, rather than what the stated intentions of the opposing sides in a courtroom are.

One could argue that the MPPC's structural design, as outlined by Cassady, points to the predictable goal of securing continued profitability for Edison and Biograph interests in a manner conventional to large businesses of this period: first, license or lease equipment, rather than sell it outright, to ensure continued income rather than short-term profit; second, diffuse the means of production to expand the market while retaining legal machinery to profit by that expansion; and third, ensure a continued flow of income in royalties and licensing fees in order to expand productivity through predictable long-term planning and investment. In other words, the MPPC may have been less interested in eliminating independents than guaranteeing that it be "cut in" on any and all operations. The latter approach would allow the MPPC to proceed with those techniques of standardization, cost accounting, and scientific management that enhanced efficiency and profit for businesses throughout the economy, a condition that a Price, Waterhouse report on the industry at the time substantiates (Price, Waterhouse and Company, *The Motion Picture Industry* [New York: Price, Waterhouse, 1917]). A public image of competition between trusts and independents was popularly celebrated during this period. "Big business" and its power was the major domestic issue. But documented financial arrangements (such as silent-partner investments) seem to indicate that trusts were less interested in stamping out competitors than in containing their operations and sharing their profits in order to direct or dominate the market.

One might argue, then, that the structure of the MPPC agreements with its various branches suggests less a quest for total control than a desire to regularize and standardize income, demand, and profits in order to ensure the possibility of long-term planning for rationalized production. For example, the MPPC was apparently not interested in policing exhibitors. The exchanges had the job of regulating the exhibitors, and since they were simultaneously dependent on exhibitors as clients, one wonders what incentive exchanges had to be concerned that exhibitors be licensed. The exchanges had the opportunity of dealing with a single client, the MPPC, and in return had to buy $2,500 worth of film per month which allowed the manufacturer-producers to standardize the cost of production. Licensed exchange standardized the demand for the product by setting a minimum purchase regardless of seasonal flux or other factors of public demand. Cassady suspects that exchanges may have paid the $2 per week licensing fee themselves or passed it on in costs for service in an attempt to woo exhibitors for whose business they competed in certain areas. The issue clearly was not disciplining the exhibitors so much as it was guaranteeing a steady income.

This situation would help to explain the apparent glaring inconsistency of the MPPC not requiring licensed manufacturers to sell projecting equipment exclusively to licensed exhibitors, a surprising omission considering how it would have simplified the regulatory work of the exchanges. One can hardly imagine that an entrepreneur as legally knowledgeable and tenacious as Edison would have allowed such an arrangement, unless it was not absolute control but rather expanded, stabilized market demand that interested him. Exhibitors were disciplined by the riskiness of depending upon independents. Independents' productivity was threatened until 1911 by the difficulty of obtaining raw film stock and by the possibility of patent suits for infringement. Other loopholes in arrangements with exhibitors support the same conclusion: exchanges and manufacturers both kept the books on sales, not the MPPC; controls on bootlegging, duping, and bicycling appear to be very weak particularly if the exchanges stood to gain from illegal copies; and royalty payments by exhibitors who bought projectors before 1908 were illegal, and exhibitors seem to have been aware of this. The view that the MPPC was designed to ensure a standardized cash flow seems to be supported by Cassady's own figures about the revenues that the MPPC gained. Cassady does not compare these figures with any figures for potential income.

This brings up a closely related issue concerning the limited degree to which Cassady examines the MPPC in actual operation as opposed to its financial and legal arrangements. Legal historian James Willard Hurst, among others, points out that law as written represents a description of relations in the ideal or abstract. Such a statement provides us with information about the image of power relations, its ideology, but not necessarily about its practice. One of the areas that Cassady does not present in significant detail is the degree to which the MPPC actually backed up its threats to sue and remove licenses; nor does he examine the resulting economic effects. Removing licenses, we know, provided a stimulus to independent operations despite the fact that this action actually may have been designed to inhibit independents. How frequent were suits against infringers and what were their results? In addition, we probably cannot ascertain the seriousness of being "unlicensed" without a more detailed history of how many unlicensed manufacturers there were, and how much finished film they supplied at what times. Why could William Fox operate successfully without a license from the MPPC when the other ten unlicensed exchanges could not do so, for example?

The influence of a neoclassical position is apparent when Cassady argues that there was "no question" that the MPPC did improve service to exhibitors and offered a generally salutary effect on the industry as a whole. Nevertheless, when he reaches the discussion of feature films he cites evidence that contradicts this conclusion: "According to Albert E. Smith, president of Vitagraph: 'We released eight feature pictures through General Film. Some were very good, but none made any money. General Film's method of handling was the reason for the loss in almost every instance'" (p. 159). Again, if there is conflicting evidence of beneficial effect of MPPC policy, how does Cassady conclude the overall effect was salutary? He does not seem to be sufficiently conscious of these discrepancies in his own text to explain his judgment. He merely asserts the necessary existence of a salutary effect as though there is no conflicting evidence.

This problem of both a denial of conflicting evidence and the failure to explain how conclusions are reached in the face of conflicting evidence points to a rhetorical pattern in Cassady's article, which can serve as a "red flag" to other scholars. He repeats phrases that deny the need for evidence or that inhibit the perception of conflict within the evidence he supplies. Sometimes, Cassady suggests, the probability of accuracy is so great that no evidence is needed. For example, he suggests that competing exchanges paid exhibitors' license fees. "This latter contingency unquestionably materialized in some instances." Cassady could make a case for high probability given the economic goals and interests of those involved. But if it did happen, he probably could have cited evidence from the legal record—the testimony of exchange personnel—if not, then it is not "unquestionable." A legal historian cannot substitute rhetoric for argument or evidence. Again, Cassady states that there is no doubt that the MPPC improved quality of service generally (p. 481) but "no doubt" substitutes for testimony and evidence. Readers then must ask, why is there no doubt? Or again Cassady states, "there is no question that the rental service of independent exchanges was deficient in many respects previous to the establishment of the General Film Company." What is the evidence that General Film improved the quality of service to exhibitors? It might as easily be questioned what incentive a monopoly operation would have to go to any expense to improve service. "There is *no doubt* . . . that improved marketing conditions made for a healthier industry in certain respects at least" (p. 491). (Emphasis mine.)

These denials become red flags attracting the healthy skepticism of historians given that: (a) the record presented conflicting evidence in the context of a legal suit; (b) some of the evidence which Cassady himself presents seems to be at odds with his conclusions; (c) there are serious evidentiary omissions for which Cassady substitutes the force of rhetorical absolutes. Cassady mentions that in 1909 a dozen or so unlicensed manufacturing companies were scattered throughout the United States, although "admittedly none was very productive"; yet once again no evidence for the degree of productivity is offered. Cassady claims there is "no evidence" of collusion with General Film to show that the MPPC used threat of suit to get exchanges to accept the MPPC's offer to buy, although it seems probable that it did so as leverage machinery, and Cassady also gives the example of the MPPC using suits and the threat of losing licensure when negotiating terms of sale.

If it is important to Cassady to assert the beneficial effects of the MPPC on the industry in terms of improved efficiency, it is just as important that we scrutinize the notion of "efficiency" which is so important to the neoclassical economic position. In neoclassical economics, efficiency is frequently mentioned as an abstract principle or value for both business in general and the "public" rather than as a goal for one segment of an industry or society whose interests may not be universal. Since the ostensible goal of business in neoclassical philosophy is making maximum profits through productivity and since profits are not equally shared, efficiency as a means to profits must be seen within the perspective of "efficiency for whom?" Cassady seems to assume that effects of the trust were uniformly beneficial to labor, management, *and* consumers. But a Marxist analysis of the MPPC might very well challenge this notion by questioning whether the "rationalized process of production" was beneficial either in terms of the conditions of work or in terms of the artistic excellence of the product. A criterion of worker control and participation or a philosophy of radical aesthetics that sees art as a process of social relations as well as a fixed entity, might question the simple notion of "efficiency" as an assumed and uniform good.

Finally, it is important to recognize the research areas not investigated in Cassady's article that have been presented here: an examination of how the MPPC arrangements worked out in practice; the history of MPPC's attempts to enforce and discipline sectors of the industry through legal suits, removal of license, and harassment; a statistical survey of the size of independents' operations and the extent of their business at various times; the questions of the degree to which the implementation of a factory production model in the film industry can be attributed to the ability of the MPPC to standardize demand and services; the consequences of this "efficiency" for labor and for the aesthetics of the film product; the degree to which the MPPC's unsuccessful model for vertical integration was later imitated with greater control by a single company; and the "success" of later attempts at "rationalization of the industry" to avoid the problems and loopholes experienced by the MPPC.

I have sought to suggest ways in which scholars enter a dialogue with the work of other researchers. First of all, one needs to identify the position of the research: its argument, theoretical background, and the assumptions from which it is operating. In this case, Cassady presented his argument as conclusions at the end of his study. His theoretical position and its influence on his interpretation and selection of evidence is only apparent implicitly in his choice of words and substitution of conclusions for arguments, in his occasional unresolved discrepancies between evidence and conclusion, and in his selection of terms with which to frame his "description" of the MPPC. We can challenge and yet continue his valuable work by reframing the terms of the description, questioning the relationship of evidence to conclusion, and examining unanswered questions and problems that provide further areas to pursue from alternative positions and approaches. Loopholes in the MPPC's structure and differing interpretations of evidence offer opportunities to continue, refine, and enrich the dialogue.

PART TWO

The Development of
Business Strategies

Hollywood's Movie Star System:
A Historical Overview

Gorham Kindem

In addition to being a social phenomenon, which reflects a particular ideology, the Hollywood star system is a business strategy designed to generate large audiences and differentiate entertainment programs and products, and has been used for over seventy years to provide increasing returns on production investments. As a marketing technique and business strategy, the system was first used in the theater industry. Between 1910 and 1948 Hollywood borrowed and expanded the star system and stock company approaches from the stage;[1] and through the simultaneous exhibition of films throughout the world, the industry eventually established movie studio stables of stars and earned profits well in excess of those of the largest theatrical companies.

Significant historical changes in the status of movie stars have paralleled decisive technological, economic, and social changes that have affected the American film industry as a whole, such as the coming of sound, the Great Depression, and the rise and fall of movie attendance. The contractual terms and salaries for movie stars have also been affected by the same factors.[2] In the highly competitive and expanding market that existed between 1910 and 1920, the most popular silent-movie stars eventually obtained contractual terms that equalled and possibly exceeded their individual contributions to box-office success, and some of them also became involved in film production themselves, although the development of sound and its demand for experienced stage and radio performers ended the careers of many silent film stars. Those working during the early 1930s, when movie attendance declined and industry power was concentrated in the hands of a few studios, were placed in a poor bargaining position, and studios began exercising near autocratic control over the star system.

The Paramount antitrust decrees in the late 1940s resulted in a shift from a mature oligopoly/monopoly, or semicompulsory cartel, involving the Big Five studios (Warner Bros, Loew's/MGM, Paramount, RKO, and Twentieth Century−Fox) and the Little Three (Universal, Columbia, and United Artists), to a bilateral oligopoly with six major distributor/producers and a dozen nationwide theater circuits today. This shift created a slightly more competitive market that benefited the most popular movie stars. Unfortunately, the decline in movie attendance and the rise in production costs, which also occurred during this period, left many less popular contract players unemployed, as stock companies disbanded. In the 1950s and 1960s, although many of the more popular stars remained under studio contract, they also obtained more liberal terms than existed during the studio period, sometimes receiving a percentage of the profits or becoming directly involved financially in film production for both tax advantages and artistic control. During the 1960s and 1970s the absence of studio control forced Hollywood increasingly to rely upon other media, such as television and popular music, to cultivate stars who could then be exploited by the film industry. Eventually some scholars and executives began to question the validity of the star system, embracing instead the "auteur" approach, which suggested that the previous success of a director ensured box-office success better than did the supposed popularity of movie stars.[3]

☆

The Rise of the Movie-Star System

Two factors stimulated the rise of the movie star system: competition between independents and members of a trust that followed the formation of the Motion Picture Patents Company in 1909, and the intense demand of movie audiences for specific performers.[4] Independents like Carl Laemmle began to promote and exploit the public's infatuation with movie personalities about 1910. Patents Company members may have been more reticent to promote their own performers by name because they were fearful of an escalation in star salaries[5] and because they wanted to protect the anonymity of movie performers who themselves worried about overexposure at reduced consumer prices, which might jeopardize their stage careers.[6] The salaries that independents like Laemmle began to offer movie performers to entice them away from the "trust" in fact escalated very quickly and eventually more than compensated for the supposed risks of overexposure.

The specific case of Florence Lawrence, previously known only as the

"Biograph Girl" (Biograph was, of course, a Patents member), who was actively promoted by Carl Laemmle as Florence Lawrence, the "IMP Girl" (Independent Motion Pictures), in February, March, and April of 1910, is probably the first explicit example of the movie-star system as a consciously adopted marketing strategy.[7] Laemmle was an enterprising promoter who engineered a publicity incident in Saint Louis to advertise his recently acquired movie actress and the film in which she was currently starring.

In the 27 February 1910 issue of the *St. Louis Post-Dispatch* an announcement appeared in the same column describing the local performances by stage stars Eva Tanguay and Lillian Russell that "Miss Florence Lawrence, in a new motion picture, will be one of the features of the Gem's new bill this week, THE HARMONIOUS FOUR, in new illustrated songs."[8] Then on 6 March in the Sunday Magazine of the same paper, a feature story on movie actresses appeared which indicated that previous newspaper reports (not explicitly identified) concerning the death of Florence Lawrence in New York had been a ruse.[9] While there is no evidence that these events were ever reported in the press before this time, subsequent trade paper publicity by Laemmle fully exploited this "incident" as an indication of Patents Company interference with independents.[10] Laemmle blamed the ruse upon Miss Lawrence's previous employer, Biograph who was trying to discredit her present employer, IMP. He used this event as an excuse to promote the name of Florence Lawrence and to berate Patents members in trade papers and the popular press and eventually to take Miss Lawrence to Saint Louis in April of 1910 in an attempt to quelch any further belief in her nonexistence.[11]

Perhaps stimulated by Laemmle's new plateau of competition, Vitagraph, another Patents member, revealed the identity of one of its own actresses, the "Vitagraph Girl," Florence Turner, and a full page article, including an interview with Miss Turner, appeared in the Sunday, 15 May 1910, issue of the *North American*.[12] The interview revealed that Miss Turner had received over 3,000 pieces of mail with offers of marriage, and that Vitagraph was besieged with requests for the photos, names, and addresses of its players. By July of 1910 Vitagraph was receiving journalists at its studio, allowing interviews with its stars, and dispensing photos for publication.[13] By September of the same year the Edison Company, another Patents member, was doing the same.[14] Biograph, however, did not fully capitulate to the star system until 1913, relying instead upon strong stories, directors, and an anonymous or feloniously named stock company.[15] In short, some Patents members embraced the star system while others seemed to ignore it.

Perhaps the clearest indication that the rise of the star system was accelerated by competition between Patents Company members and independents was the rapidly escalating salaries that were offered the most popular movie stars by rival companies throughout the period from 1910 to 1920. Laemmle lured Mary Pickford away from Biograph for $175 per week in 1910. After leaving IMP in the same year and Majestic in the next because the quality of the films did not measure up to her production standards, Miss Pickford returned to Biograph for $500 per week in 1912. She then returned to the stage, but was enticed back into films by Adolph Zukor and Famous Players (independent), which paid her $1,000 per week in 1914, $4,000 in 1915, and $10,000 per week by Mutual (independent) in 1916. By 1918 Mary Pickford received over $1 million per year from First National. Charlie Chaplin's rising star was equally meteoric. After working for Keystone (independent) for just $150 per week in 1913, Chaplin was paid $1,250 per week by Essanay (Patents member) in 1914 and $10,000 per week by Mutual in 1916. First National eventually offered Chaplin $1 million for eighteen months work in 1918.[16]

It would be a mistake to attribute the rapid rise of star salaries and the star system in general to a competitive monopoly market structure during the second decade of the twentieth century alone, however. Paralleling the increasing competition between Patents Company members and independents was an increased demand for movies in general and movies featuring the most popular stars in particular. Personal consumption expenditures for motion pictures increased from less than $100 million in 1909 to more than $300 million by 1921.[17] As larger and larger theaters were constructed, exhibitors began to realize that there was a tremendous disparity in drawing power between films featuring different movie players, and exhibitor demand for pictures with the most popular stars continually increased.[18] The rise in star salaries throughout this period was facilitated by both a competitive market structure and an increasing consumer demand.

By 1915 some movie producers, such as Adolph Zukor at Paramount, were attempting to gather together the most popular stars under exclusive contract. Movie stars seemed to represent one of the best means of reducing product uncertainty and effectively differentiating competitive movie products. By this time the practice of block booking several less desirable films along with films featuring the most popular stars was widely practiced.[19] Exhibitors' film choices were significantly limited by producers' package deals. But just as Paramount was in the process of cornering the production market by acquiring the most popular stars, fresh competition arose from the exhibition side of the industry. Zukor's block-booking strategies may have stimulated the formation of the First

National Exhibitors' Circuit. First National soon began acquiring the most popular movie stars, rather than building production facilities, and it controlled an impressive number of first-run and subsequent-run theaters in major metropolitan areas. It financed the production of independent films, which it then exhibited through its franchise theaters. Competition in the film industry spread from the race for control of movie stars and movie products to the race for theater acquisitions and the vertical integration of production, distribution, and exhibition. Movie stars during this intensely competitive and immensely profitable period were offered not only impressive million-dollar yearly contracts but percentages of the net profits as well.

Fears that Paramount and First National might merge to establish a virtual movie monopoly that would jeopardize the strides that movie stars had accomplished in terms of salary, status, and artistic control in the industry stimulated the most popular movie stars to go into business for themselves.[20] In 1919 Mary Pickford, Charlie Chaplin, Douglas Fairbanks, and director D. W. Griffith joined forces and established their own production and distribution company—United Artists. They each financed the production of their own films. At first the popularity of their films virtually guaranteed an exhibition outlet through independent theaters, if Paramount and First National failed to capitulate. United Artists remained committed to independent production and individual artistic control rather than mass production, and even though it acquired theaters in 1926 under a separate company to protect itself from continuing concentration of exhibition power in the hands of a few major companies, it never became a vertically integrated company, as did the major studios that were to dominate the industry in the 1930s and 1940s. Many of the films that United Artists produced during the 1920s, such as Fairbanks' *Robin Hood*, Pickford's *Pollyanna*, Chaplin's *The Gold Rush*, Griffith's *Broken Blossoms*, and Keaton's *The General*, were tremendous commercial and critical successes. The average annual profits after federal taxes of Pickford, Chaplin, and Fairbanks, between 1923 and 1928 were $300,000, $650,000, and $665,000, respectively.[21] The obvious success of United Artists and the apparent vindication of its approach to film production stimulated other major movie stars of the 1920s, like Rudolph Valentino and Gloria Swanson, to try their hand at personal artistic control. In some cases, however, the results fell far short of these stars' commercial expectations. The end of a golden era of movie-star independence and wealth was approaching.

The Star System Under Studio Control

The plight of major movie stars during the 1930s and 1940s changed dramatically from that of the 1920s. As mentioned earlier several factors combined to reduce their independence and incomes severely, including the development of sound in the late 1920s, the Great Depression, income taxes, and the concentration of power in vertically integrated major studios. The coming of sound altered the supply of acting talent, both stimulating the acquisition of experienced stage actors and retarding the careers of silent stars who failed to adapt to the speech requirements of this new medium, and the depression eventually affected movie consumption. By the early 1930s a dramatic decline in admissions and movie attendance occurred. Paralleling this decreasing demand for movies were cutbacks in production expenditures, including the salaries of movie stars. An increasing concentration of oligopoly/monopoly power in the hands of the five major companies, who were linked symbiotically with the three minor companies, was stimulated by several factors, including the tremendous capital investment required for vertical integration the production and exhibition of sound films, and the establishment of the National Industrial Recovery Act and the Code of Fair Competition for the Motion Picture Industry. Although the Supreme Court invalidated the NIRA in 1935,[22] the trade practices which it sanctioned before that time clearly stifled competition between major and independent studios and helped to establish a monopoly structured film industry.

Movie stars in the 1930s and 1940s found themselves at the mercy of studio bosses, who made every attempt to exploit the box-office potential of their movie stars and use monopsony (single buyer) power and the severe economic conditions of the depression as an excuse to discriminate against the stars and to reduce their earnings. While major movie stars in the 1920s had often received a percentage of the net movie profits and substantial artistic control over their films, many movie stars in the 1930s and 1940s were restricted by exclusive, escalating, seven-year contracts, renewable by studios each year, which usually limited maximum salaries to something less than $10,000 per week[23] and with no percentage of the net profits. Movie stars exercised very little artistic control over production decisions other than sometimes rejecting roles. There were basically three kinds of contracts for stars, feature players, and other production personnel: single-picture contracts; multiple-picture contracts for two or more pictures in one year or one or more pictures per year for two or more years, where the time between pictures was not fully

covered; and term contracts for exclusive services for a fixed period, usually seven years, where the studio could renew or not renew each year, and
if it renewed a previously specified increase took effect. Studios disciplined stars who were in disfavor in many ways during this period, including lending them out to appear in inferior pictures for a studio fee well
in excess of their specified salary or not renewing their contracts. Pun-
ished or discarded stars had little hope of being offered better terms by a
competitor than by their current employers. During the 1930s the competition for stars was controlled for the most part by major studios, who
were much more willing to lend them to other major studios, who could
reciprocate in kind or in cash, than to independents, who threatened
their monopoly control. Between 1933 and 1940, for example, Loew's
lent out 610 of its staff and stars to other majors and only 56 to independents, while the figures for Paramount were 439 and 46, respectively.[24]

During the studio era stars became commodities to be shaped, manipu-
lated, exhausted, and discarded, rather than unique personalities to be
catered to as temperamental, talented artists, although, according to Tino
Balio, the studios' mistreatment of stars eventually backfired and turned
Hollywood into a union-minded town.[25] The careers of stars were carefully planned and orchestrated to mesh with popular demand or to promote a new image and create a new demand. A huge publicity apparatus
was developed by the studios to create movie stars and to protect their
investments in performers.

The popularity of stars was continually evaluated. Fan clubs and fan
magazines, which had once been ignored by the studios, were suddenly
given a studio ear.[26] Fan mail was one indication of star popularity. Another indicator was to evaluate response cards filled out by limited audiences after previews of the new films and new stars. Finally, in the late
1930s and throughout the 1940s, the film industry turned to George Gallup, who founded Audience Research, Inc., in 1938 with the ostensible
purpose of conducting research that would reduce some of the risks
incurred in the production, distribution, and exhibition of Hollywood
films. The "Continuing Audit of Marquee Values" was a research program
designed to measure the popularity of movie stars. ARI conducted interviews with a 500- to 1,000-person quota sample that mirrored the demographic characteristics of the movie audience in terms of frequency of
movie attendance. The purpose of this research was not simply to evaluate the potential contribution of movie stars to box-office success as an
aid to casting and other production decisions but also, and perhaps more
importantly, to combine research into movie-star popularity with other
research as an aid in the promotion and marketing of motion pictures.

Data collected on the audience demographics of certain stars might be used in casting a film so as to appeal to the broadest possible audience.

According to Paul K. Perry,[27] former president of the Gallup Organization, Inc., 85 percent of the variation in box-office receipts of Hollywood films during the 1950s was owing to the combined effect of "want to see," 21 percent; penetration (know about), 33 percent; enjoyment, 15 percent; and marquee value, 16 percent; with an unexplained variance of 15 percent. The marquee value of movie stars alone explained about 16 percent of the variance in film revenues, but it also interacted with several other factors, including title and subject matter, in determining the public's "want to see," a composite variable, for a specific motion picture. Perry has suggested that marquee values accounted for 50 percent of the 21-percent variation in film revenue explained by the combined "want-to-see' factor.[28] The purpose of ARI's research was to facilitate marketing decision rather than to predict revenues, but its results also seem to reinforce the validity of the star system in the 1940s by suggesting that marquee values accounted for about 26 to 27 percent of the variation in movie box-office success.

My own research partially substantiates Perry's claims. Using ARI's own value ratings (from Lucille Ball's $13,000 to Clark Gable's $210,000) of over 100 movie stars from the "Continuing Audit of Marquee Values" conducted in January 1942 [29] and *Variety's* list of top-grossing (gross distributor receipts in the United States and Canada) films in 1942,[30] my regression analysis indicates that the combined marquee values explain almost 23 percent of the variation in film revenues, as follows:

N	R^2	Coefficient	df	t	Significance
87	.22739	2.72771	86	25.0	.0001

Perry indicates that the sample size (N) of his multiple regression analysis was N = 73, a relatively small sample drawn exclusively from RKO Radio Pictures, Inc., which inhibits generalizations being drawn from his results, and for which the requisite data were available, but roughly equivalent to the number of top-grossing films released by a variety of studios, which were used in my own regression analysis. The coefficient produced by my analysis indicates that the stars' contribution to gross distributor receipts in the U.S. and Canada alone in 1942 was more than twice the dollar marquee values listed by Gallup for that year. If the Gallup figures were used as a basis for star salaries during this period, they may have grossly underestimated the actual worth of many movie stars.

Thomas Simonet has argued that Gallup's "Continuing Audit of Marquee Values" is a poor predictor of box-office revenues. Simonet examined the relationship between marquee values of representative individual performers and their performance at the box office.[31] He selected a 10 percent sample from the 205 performers' marquee values reported in the "Continuing Audit" of spring 1948 and concluded that the "most dramatic changes in marquee values occurred among performers with top-grossing films in the period. For nine players, marked rises in marquee value occurred after—not before—release of a top-grossing film." [32] Thus marquee value reflected previous hits rather than predicted subsequent success, and it "measured the salience of performers' images more than it indexed future box-office potential." [33]

Simonet's contention that ARI's "Continuing Audit of Marquee Values" may not have been a useful tool for determining the future box-office potential of *specific* movie stars seems valid, but it does not invalidate the strong relationship between movie-star popularity, i.e., the combined effect of several stars on a single film, and box-office revenues. An R^2 of 0.23 is hardly sufficient for accurate prediction of box-office success, but it suggests that during the studio era Hollywood's movie-star system was neither erroneous nor misguided. In fact, given their ability to reduce product uncertainty through both legal and (in retrospect) extra-legal trade practices during this period, the major studios were able to maintain a control over the star system that not only maximized movie-star exploitation but also prevented star salaries from exceeding amounts justified by research analysis of popularity. The industry probably had a more complete and accurate account of the actual contribution of movie stars to box-office success during the 1940s than it had in any previous or subsequent period of film history.

Declining Admissions, Divorcement, and the Star System

The peak year for Hollywood in terms of admissions and movie attendance was 1946, when, it has been estimated, there were over 90 million admissions to movie theaters per week. But between 1947 and 1953 admissions to movie theaters declined dramatically owing to a number of factors, including changing patterns of personal consumption accompanying rising birth rates, the movement of families to the suburbs, purchases of homes and automobiles, and competition with television and radio. The end result was that the film industry found itself holding assets that looked more and more like liabilities. Movie stars and other studio personnel under exclusive, long-term contract and picture palaces in many metropolitan areas suddenly became expendable. Antitrust litigation, such as the Paramount suit begun in 1938 and divorcement decrees in 1948, which divorced production and distribution from exhibition and eventually brought an end to the studio era, aggravated the film industry's economic problems but allowed major studios to rid themselves of costly theater holdings that were becoming financial liabilities in the wake of declining film audiences. More and more movie stars were released from studio contract to reduce overhead and production costs.

For some movie stars the dramatic changes taking place in the film industry were a distinct advantage. Freedom from studio domination and control and renewed market competition gave many stars the flexibility to plan their own careers and once again to become involved in production. Income taxes which had become quite severe since the 1920s, when many movie stars' earnings had been virtually unrestricted, offered an economic incentive for some movie stars to establish independent production companies of their own or to demand a percentage of movie profits that could be paid in smaller amounts over longer periods of time or both. After the breakup of the major studios, the concentration of industry power in distribution, the rise of independent production, and the increasing competition for declining audiences, the film industry found itself confronted by greater product uncertainty. One result was that major studios turned to the production of fewer, but higher budgeted, epics and spectaculars with the most popular movie stars of the time. Greater competition and increased uncertainty also stimulated an escalation of salaries among the most popular stars, as their talent agents bargained for higher and higher salaries and percentages of the profits. This practice culminated in such well publicized examples in the early 1960s as when the producers of *Cleopatra* guaranteed movie star Elizabeth Taylor several million dollars for appearing in the title role. Taylor was to get $125,000 for sixteen weeks' work, plus $50,000 for every week afterwards that *Cleopatra* (which took several years to produce and eventually cost $37 million) ran over schedule. She also got $3,000 per week for expenses and 10 percent of the gross, although the picture, which was given heavy publicity at theaters, barely ran in the black after $5 million in television rentals and high first-run ticket prices.[34]

While the most popular stars were able to turn the changes in the film industry to economic advantage, their success obscures the fact that the demand for and incomes of less popular actors and actresses declined dramatically during this period. The production of fewer pictures and rising costs brought on by labor strikes and concessions and a general inflation in the cost of materials after World War II meant that fewer actors were actively employed in film production. The average percentage of production costs paid to actors dropped from 25 percent to 20 percent in 1948.[35] Many less popular stars moved into television, while the most popular stars, who feared that overexposure might jeopardize their film careers (a parallel to the fears of stage stars between 1910 and 1920) limited themselves to film. In short, the changes that occurred after the war in both consumer demand for movies and the structure of the film industry primarily benefited the most popular movie stars, many of whom obtained greater personal freedom and artistic control over their own productions in the 1950s and 1960s, while others remained under exclusive multiple-year or multiple-picture contracts or both with major studios.[36]

Directors Versus Stars: The Contribution of Production Personnel to Box-Office Success

Beginning in the 1950s and 1960s and coinciding perhaps with the rise of the foreign art film and changes in the demographics of film audiences, personality cults seemed to form around film directors as well as movie stars. In the 1960s American film critics began to talk about directors as *auteurs*,[37] or other analogues to literary authors. It has sometimes been erroneously assumed that young audiences select films on the basis of directors as much as stars, but the evidence that currently exists contradicts this notion.[38] In terms of publicity directors simply cannot compete with movie stars, although their control behind the scenes may be, as the *auteur* theory suggests, a significant determinant of aesthetic quality as well as box-office success.

Hollywood has always been impressed by the prior success of its production personnel, and in the 1970s a new breed of young directors emerged, who seemed to have a tremendous initial rapport with film audiences. Formally trained in film schools or by American International under the tutelage of low-budget, cult filmmakers like Roger Corman, directors Steven Spielberg, Francis Ford Coppola, and George Lukas experienced almost unprecedented box-office success with movies such as *Jaws, The Godfather, Star Wars* and *Raiders of the Lost Ark*.[39] Since many of the "stars" of their films were previously unknown or of questionable popularity (with such exceptions as Marlon Brando) the success of these and many previous films has put both the star system and the contribution of movie stars to box-office success in question. Recently, some executives have turned as much to directors as to stars to reduce product uncertainty, but this approach has also been taken to extremes. The 1960s star system debacle with Elizabeth Taylor in *Cleopatra* has more recently had its 1980s directorial counterpart in Michael Cimino's *Heaven's Gate*."[40] Both incidents reveal the potential hazards of relying too heavily upon any one member of the production team or giving them too much production autonomy or control.

A study of sixty-two Columbia motion pictures released between 1966 and 1968, by Lee Cedric Garrison, Jr.,[41] questions the highly inflated salaries paid for movie stars in these films. His multiple regression analysis of over thirty factors which potentially contribute to box-office success indicates that the box-office ratings given by theater owners to movie stars, which are published in *Motion Picture Herald* each January, are negatively related to box-office success in the case of leading male stars to the same degree that they are positively related in the case of leading female stars. The coefficients of these independent variables (anticipated contribution to box-office success) do not seem to warrant the inflated salaries that some stars receive, although his analysis indicates that experienced and prominent directors significantly contributed to box-office success in comparison to inexperienced directors.

Garrison's study (table 4.1) is partially confirmed by Thomas Simonet's multiple-regression analysis (table 4.2) of the relationship of the previous experience of production staff members (producer, director, original author, screenwriter, and three leading performers) to subsequent box-office success of seventy-three high grossing films made during the

Table 4.1. *Garrison*

Sample Size	R^2 (Full Model)	Independent Variable	Coefficient	df	t	Significance
56	0.727	Leading character, female	2.172	41	4.17	0.01
62	0.727	Leading character, male	−2.321	50	1.78	0.10
56	0.727	Director (exp.)	0.444	41	2.96	0.01
62	0.727	Director (inexp.)	−0.141	50	3.04	0.01

Table 4.2. *Simonet*

Sample Size	R² (Change)	Independent Variable	Coefficient	df	f	Significance
73	0.070	First performer's credits	−0.198	21	8.856	0.004
73	0.010	First performer's box-office results	0.190	21	3.204	0.079
73	0.335	Director's past box-office results	0.478	21	16.457	0.001
73	0.010	Director's credits	−0.057	21	0.280	0.599

last forty years.[42] Experience variables were measures of past box-office results, prior career credits, career Academy Awards and nominations, and a combination factor. Simonet's study reveals a strong positive relation between the prior box-office success of directors and the box-office success of their later films, and a negative relation between the prior credits (prior box-office success is not significant) of movie stars and the box-office success of their later films. As a result, Simonet, like Garrison, questions the validity of the star system, but suggests that the *auteur* theory (the notion that the director is the controlling force, or author, of the film) may have some quantitative, commercial validity in terms of predicting future box-office success.

Garrison's and Simonet's analyses and conclusions regarding the star system can be disputed on a number of grounds, however. First, the index used to measure star popularity and potential contribution to box-office success in Garrison's study is highly subjective. Garrison's star rating is based upon the subjective responses of theater owners. This rating may reflect how well the film in which a movie star appeared happened to fare at box offices around the country. Simonet uses the financial success of stars' previous films (*Variety*'s gross distributor receipts) as an independent variable, rather than theater owners' subjective ratings. If, as the Gallup studies indicate, many other factors contribute to box-office success, using the earnings of a star's previous pictures or some indirect measure of this variable as a predictor of future box-office success is unlikely to be very dependable. Neither Garrison nor Simonet isolates consumer demand for movie stars as an independent variable, and the variables they do select confuse causes with effects.

Gallup's 1940s "Continuing Audit of Marquee Values" may also be an imperfect index of star popularity and box office potential, since as Simonet has pointed out, it is contaminated with the prominence in the popular mind of movie stars who recently had successful films.[43] In short, it is difficult truly to isolate and measure movie-star popularity and potential; it is also difficult to refute the star system with analyses of data that do not properly measure the significant construct of interest, namely consumer demand for movie stars. While Garrison's and Simonet's studies clearly lend support to the *auteur* theory, they do not definitively invalidate the star system. Gallup's analyses and my own, on the other hand, lend some support to the notion that movie stars significantly contributed to box-office success in the 1940s.

The Star System in the 1970s

Lacking the studio apparatus for the development of new movie stars in the 1970s, Hollywood turned more and more to using stars arising in other media, like television and the recording industry.[44] Performers like Sally Field, John Travolta, Goldie Hawn, Olivia Newton-John, Henry Winkler, Barbra Streisand, and Kris Kristofferson became stars on television or in the recording industry before their star status was fully exploited by the film industry. And although film producers lost much of the control over the careers of movie stars obtained in previous eras, they also avoided some of the risks and costs involved in star development and promotion. As the costs and risk of film production dramatically increased in the 1970s, the American feature-film industry was forced to rely upon media where it was less costly to generate bankable performers. This dependence upon other media for stars has also been accompanied by an increasing tendency to capitalize on the simultaneous appearance of stars in different media products. *Saturday Night Fever*, which was produced by recording industry promoter, Robert Stigwood, featured the music of the Bee Gees, and starred John Travolta, is an excellent example of the economic interdependence of these contemporary media with respect to star performers.

Conclusion

Overviewing the history of the star system in Hollywood reveals that changes in three areas—supply, demand, and market structure—accompanied and perhaps precipitated changes in the economic status of movie stars and the nature of the star system. Clearly, the most popular movie stars have benefited from a competitive market. The inception of the star system resulted from competition between independents and Patents Company members and from an intense demand by film audiences for individual performers. The industry's vertical integration and conversion to sound concentrated industry power among the few studios with capital to back these endeavors. The increased power of the studios, declining motion picture attendance, and newly instituted policies of the federal government during and after the depression caused a commensurate loss of power and economic status among even the most popular movie stars, who were sometimes exploited during the studio years. The breakup of the studios following the divorcement proceedings in the late 1940s established a slightly more competitive market once again, but both the star system and the studio system have declined since divorcement, while film directors have acquired increasing importance and popular recognition. The film industry has become increasingly dependent upon other media to develop and promote star performers, and film scholars have questioned the contribution of stars and the star system to box-office success in comparison to that of directors. Although the star system has changed significantly throughout American film-industry history, it still remains a widely practiced strategy for securing and protecting production investments, differentiating movie products, and for ensuring some measure of box-office success.

Dividing Labor for Production Control: Thomas Ince and the Rise of the Studio System[1]

Janet Staiger

Thomas Ince was a classic case of a stage actor who, during a brief period of unemployment in 1910, turned to the fledgling movies as a source of income. Yet his long-term impact on filmmaking would be very great indeed. Working first for IMP and then Biograph, he returned to IMP when promised a chance to direct. He completed his first film in December 1910. Ince soon tired of the one-reel format, however, and accepted a position in the fall of 1911 to direct for Adam Kessel and Charles Bauman's New York Motion Picture Company. He headed for Edendale, California, where a small group of people were already making films. The studio at that time was a converted grocery store: one stage (without even a muslin overhang), a scene dock, a small lab and office, and a bungalow that served as a dressing room. Ince wrote, directed, and cut his first film within one week.[2] From these beginnings, by 1913 he had a fully developed continuity-script procedure; by 1916, a $500,000 studio on 43 acres of land with concrete buildings. There were a 165-foot electrically lit building (which was unique); eight stages measuring 60 by 150 feet; an administration building for the executive and scenario departments; property, carpenter, plumbing, and costume rooms; a restaurant and commissary; 300 dressing rooms; a hothouse; a natatorium; and 1,000 employees and a studio structure essentially like that associated with the big-studio period of later years.[3] Why?

Earlier historians have provided only partial answers. Lewis Jacobs attributes Ince's innovations to the need to standardize large-scale productions through "formula" pictures and publicity: "Essentially a business-man, he [Ince] conducted himself and his film making in businesslike fashion. . . . Planning in advance meant better unity of structure, less chance of uneven quality, and economy of expression." Kalton Lahue, in *Dreams for Sale*, writes, "Ince kept [his studio] functioning at peak effi-ciency by holding a tight rein on everything that was done." Eric Rhode notes that Ince "was among the first film-makers to adapt his craft to the latest ideas in industrial management and to set up the assembly-line type of production."[4]

What historians describe without outlining structure is the division of labor under the control of a corporate manager. Nor do they indicate the steps Ince took in progressing to his final system. Using Paul A. Baran and Paul M. Sweezy's monograph *Monopoly Capital* as a large framework, Harry Braverman, in *Labor and Monopoly Capital*, sets up a model and explanation of how and why labor is divided. As a model it is stochastic rather than deterministic—some amount of variation may occur, but on the whole, the model should account for an individual instance of the historical change and development of a labor structure.

☆

Braverman's Model of Labor in Monopoly Capital

According to Braverman, in the most basic capitalistic situation, humans have a potential labor power that they sell to the capitalist who, in turn, hopes to derive from their labor power the greatest possible surplus. But this potential labor power is affected by "the organization of the process" and "the forms of supervision over it."[5] By selling their labor power, workers no longer control their labor time; that control is ceded to the capitalist, who has purchased the labor time and the potential labor power. Naturally, given the profit-maximization motive, the capitalist will seek to gain as much as possible from that potential in time and power.

Unlike physical capital, however, the results of this purchase are uncer-tain. The original method of the capitalist was to use "labor as it [came] to him from prior forms of production," which usually was the craft or do-mestic system of labor.[6] The capitalist subcontracted for the work he wanted accomplished. But certain problems arose with this system: "ir-regularity of production, loss of materials in transit and through embez-zlement, slowness of manufacture, lack of uniformity and uncertainty of the quality of production."[7]

The first means of controlling of these variables was to centralize em-ployment, which decreased irregularity of production through the threat of loss of employment. This initial step, however, had no effect on the other problems. It is here that the division-of-labor process develops as a second means of solving the other areas of uncertainty.

The division-of-labor process "begins with the *analysis of the labor process* . . . the separation of the work of production into its constituent elements."[8] According to Adam Smith assigning a worker to repeat a single segment of a total task produces three advantages: an increase in dexterity, time saved, and "the invention of a great number of machines which facilitate and abridge labor."[9] A fourth advantage, saving costs, was pointed out by Charles Babbage. Since the task was segmented, only those workers doing the most difficult part of the work had to be paid for their skill rather than paying all the workers for the most difficult part, which was customary under the older craft system. Braverman asserts that these principles have led to separating workers' brains from their hands, and that division of labor promotes an almost systematic elimination of skills required for persons to work.

This division of labor was the second of three steps in monopoly capital's quest for organizing and supervising the potential for labor time and power. The third was "scientific management," which was "the control over work through the control over the *decisions that are made in the course of work*."[10] This advancement in management was initiated, in particular, by Frederick Winslow Taylor, whose work (often called "Taylorism" and typified by the efficiency experts of the first part of the twentieth century) began to be widely disseminated after 1890.

The effects of division of labor and scientific management were multiple—all leading to the separation of the planning phase of work from its execution phase. This separation destroys an ideal of the whole person, both the creator and the producer of one's ideas.[11] Practically, this separation results in certain characteristics that appear consistently in divided labor.

First, there is a physical separation between the conception and production phases. "The concept of control adopted by modern management requires that every activity in production have its several parallel activities in the management center: each must be devised, precalculated, tested, laid out, assigned and ordered, checked and inspected, and recorded throughout its duration and upon completion. The result is that the process of production is replicated in paper form before, as, and after it takes place in physical form."[12] Secondly, not only are conception and execution divided, but specialization results in both planning and producing. Thus there develops the modern corporation which is characterized by: corporate managers, "producing activities which are subdivided among functional departments, each having a specific aspect of the process for its domain,"[13] and extensive development of the marketing process.

Ince had several models of organizing work available to him. He had worked in the theater and might have chosen a labor structure similar to that. Or he might have followed D. W. Griffith's (and most of the rest of the industry's) lead: group units that shot from a brief outline.[14] Instead, he seems to have followed the lead of modern industry. Ince, however, is not unique. He is an innovator, perhaps ahead of others in some respects but not by much. His contributions to the production structure of the film industry need to be placed in perspective by examining the conception/execution process and the labor division in his production unit.

The Separation of Conception and Execution

The first part of this labor structure is Ince's separation of the conception and the production phases of filmmaking. To repeat Braverman's observation: "The concept of control adopted by modern management requires that every activity in production have its several parallel activities in the management center. . . . The result is that the process of production is replicated in paper form before, as, and after it takes place in physical form."[15] For Ince and Hollywood filmmaking, this replication is in the continuity script, a shot-by-shot detailed outline of the film prepared prior to any actual shooting. The framework for the continuity script already existed in the scenarios of the period. In nearly every issue of *Moving Picture World* descriptions of how to write scenarios are given budding screenwriters. Even as Ince was beginning to direct, an article in 1911 advises:

> Follow the cast of characters with the scenario proper. Divide the scenario into scenes, giving each change in the location of the action a separate scene—that is, whenever the plot renders it necessary for the operator to change the position of his camera, as from an interior to an exterior view, begin a new scene. Number the scenes consecutively to the end of the play. At the beginning of each scene, give a brief but clear word picture of the settings of the scene; also the position and action of the characters introduced when the picture first flashes on the screen. . . . Now carefully study out the needed action for each scene; and then describe it briefly, being careful to cut out every act that does not have a direct bearing on the development of the plot.[16]

The article continues to describe many of the characteristics we now associate with classical Hollywood cinema.

Ince had traveled to Edendale in October 1911. According to a trade paper, in June 1912 Ince split his studio into two production units because his staff was increasing in size and becoming unwieldly. At this time Ince was writing scenarios, shooting footage, and editing the films, and the company was averaging one two-reel film per week. Under this new system Ince would direct the two- and three-reel western dramas and Francis Ford, John's older brother, would shoot western comedies and smaller-cast dramas.[17] A later commentator, George Mitchell, attributes the detailed continuity script to Ince's desire for control over what Ford did.[18] This speculation seems plausible: if management desires to control uniformity and quality of product, some means of supervising the individual work tasks must be devised. But there may be more to it than that. The continuity script also provides efficiency and regularity of production. Describing the Ince studio eighteen months later, W. E. Wing writes:

> To the writer the most striking feature of Inceville . . . was its system. Although housing an army of actors, directors and subordinates, there is not a working hour lapse in which all the various companies are not at work producing results. We failed to see actors made up and dressed for their various roles, loafing about the stages or on locations; perturbed directors running here and there attempting to bring order out of chaos, while locations waited and cameramen idly smoked their cigarettes, waiting for the "next scene."
>
> With preparations laid out in detail from finished photoplays to the last prop, superintended by Mr. Ince himself, far in advance of action, each of the numerous directors on the job at Santa Ynez canyon is given his working script three weeks ahead of time.[19]

Ince's scenarios had, by 1913, become continuity scripts. A good number of these scripts, as well as scenarios for Griffith and Mack Sennett films, are available in the Aitken Brothers Papers at Madison, Wisconsin.[20] The earliest Ince script available is for *The Raiders*, which was shot in late 1913, it is as fully developed as later ones, containing the constituent parts of all of his continuities.

Each script has a number assigned to it that provides a method of tracing the film even though its title might have changed. A cover page indicates who wrote the scenario, who directed the shooting, when shooting began and ended, when the film was shipped to the distributors, and when the film was released. This history records the entire production process, allowing for much efficiency and waste control.

Next is a list of all intertitles with an indication of where they are to be inserted in the final print. The location page follows that. It lists all exterior and interior sites, as well as their scene numbers. Pencil lines are drawn through the typed information, which implies that these continuities were used during the filming process.

The cast of characters follows. The typed portions list the roles for the story and penciled in are the names of the people assigned to play each part.

A one-page synopsis follows and then the script itself. Each scene is numbered consecutively and its location is given. Intertitles are typed in, often in red, where they are to be inserted in the final version. The description of *mise-en-scène* and action is detailed. Penciled over each scene is a scribble (presumably marking the completion of shooting), and sometimes on the side is a handwritten number—possibly the footage length of the scene. Production stills for advertising often accompany the script.

Occasionally appearing is the typed injunction: "It is earnestly requested by Mr. Ince that no change of any nature be made in the scenario either by elimination of any scenes or the addition of any scenes or changing any of the action as described, or titles, without first consulting him," although the widely circulated story that once Ince finished a script he had the script stamped "shoot as written" or "produce this exactly as written" is not confirmed by these scripts.[21] Rather, contemporary accounts suggest that Ince, his production manager, the scenarist, and the director discussed and revised the script until it was in final shape for shooting.[22] The continuities include detailed instructions such as special effects and tinting directions for the intertitles. Later, when Ince no longer edited the films himself, the scripts included instructions to the cutters.

Finally, and very significantly, attached to the continuity is the entire cost of the film, which is analyzed in a standard accounting format. First are labor costs, which account for from 80 to 90 percent of the direct costs of production. Second are costs for expendables, such as props, scenery, rentals, and music. Also included is the precise number of feet of negative and positive film, along with a breakdown of cost per reel and per foot.[23]

All of this material demonstrates that Ince's use of the continuity script resulted in a two-stage labor process—the work's preparation on paper by management followed by its execution by the workers. The five problems associated with optional systems—irregularity of production, loss of materials, slowness of manufacture, lack of uniformity, and uncertainty of quality—are controlled by that management. This standardization of the work process was used by Ince's publicity department as a mark of quality and uniformity of the film product: *Ince* became a brand name through the firm's advertising.

The Division of Labor

The second part of this labor structure is the division of labor, which was effected as planning became specialized in the hands of management. When Ince began directing, some division of labor already existed for certain tasks, but the jobs were still flexible. Often the scenario might come from any one of the group.[24] Ince himself performed several of the functions that were to be separated and bracketed as specific tasks: he was the organizer of the work (the producer), the controller of the final script (the scenario editor), the head of shooting (the director), and the film cutter (the editor). As the company expanded operations, he relinquished parts of his work and became a supervisor, using control methods through middle-management personnel to maintain operations as he wanted them.

The first function to be transferred was the basic writing of the script. By spring 1912 Richard Spencer was in charge of writing the scenarios, and *Moving Picture World* called the Edendale scenario department the "most highbrow motion picture institution in town."[25] Ince, of course, still worked on the scripts with Spencer. C. Gardner Sullivan, who was to write many of the scenarios, was hired during this period. By 1915, the writing had been split: Spencer was chief story editor and Sullivan headed the scenario department, which included six writers.[26]

The next of Ince's functions to go was the actual direction of the films. After Francis Ford was placed in charge of a second unit in 1912, the direction staff increased rapidly, and Ince gradually stopped directing. By 1914, Inceville had eight directors, and by 1915, Reginald Barker headed a group of nine, with five or six production units shooting simultaneously. Ince was now titled "Director-General" for the company.[27] By 1915 Ince had relinquished direct control of a third function, that of actually cutting the films,[28] although he still retained final control of a film through continuity script directions and examination of each produced film.

The division of labor did not involve Ince's work alone; the continuing growth in studio facilities and in the scale of production occasioned the segmenting of other work. The management of such a complex organization required more people who were professionally qualified, and in the spring of 1913, George B. Stout became Ince's financial head. After re-organizing the administrative system, Stout turned over the controls to Gene Allen and then transferred to Mack Sennett's studio, which Ince nominally controlled as West Coast head for Kessel and Bauman. There Stout also proceeded to divide Sennett's labor by breaking his studio into ten departments based on work functions.[29] Ince's photography unit expanded rapidly, and set and construction demanded an art supervisor. In 1915 the New York Motion Picture Company aligned with the newly formed Triangle Film Corporation, and Ince, Griffith, and Sennett, became vice-presidents of the corporation. An expansion period followed, and more specialists were hired: a former chief cameraman from Universal was employed "to superintend the development of negative films"; Victor Schertzinger began writing musical scores to accompany the films; and Melville Ellis, described as a "designer and fashion expert of International reputation," was hired for the costume department.[30]

One aspect has been left out of this description of the growth of division of labor and that is the situation of actors and actresses. Stunt people and stock players were replaceable workers. But what about the stars? At an exhibitors' convention both the stars and Ince's control as a mark of quality and uniformity were the central advertising themes. So the stars were not as interchangeable as were the other players.[31] Instead they seemed to serve a function similar in nature to Ince's: product differentiation. For that reason, it would be important that a star be tied to a particular studio so that the star's "unique" qualities would be associated only with that studio's films. At the time of Triangle's formation, Ince disclosed that his idea was "to get stars, teach them the tricks of the camera and then keep them at salaries high enough to restrain them so that they cannot work first for one company and then for another."[32] Even at this time the star as worker was often "bound" to the studio through multiple-year contracts in order to reduce fluctuation in the studio's image. Although a worker in the sense of being an interchangeable part in the script, the star is also a quality or substance in the product itself and fulfills the function of a means to differentiate the pictures of one company from another.

One way to comprehend the growth of the entire studio structure is to recall the initial description of the new studio that Ince built in Culver City in late 1915, at the same time that he was renovating Inceville in Santa Monica: the 165-foot electrically lit building; the eight stages measuring 60 by 150 feet; an administration building for executive and scenario offices; property, carpenter, and costume buildings; 300 dressing rooms; a hothouse; a natatorium; and so forth. But as impressive as this description is, Ince does not seem to have been unique. While he had the best scenario department, others also had them; Keystone, too, was divided into task sections. A special issue of *Moving Picture World* in 1915 describes the growth of the West Coast production companies and lists the New York Motion Picture Company as just one of many whose facilities were expanding.[33] The highly mobile employment patterns in the industry, the widespread publicity, and evidence of the organization of other studios make it clear that Ince was not unusual; that, in fact, most studios were structured somewhat like his.[34]

☆

A Revised Perspective

By 1915 the major divisions of labor had been segmented. A pyramid of labor was the dominant structure with a top manager, middle-management department heads, and workers. This fulfills Braverman's description of a fully organized modern corporation in which "the producing activities are subdivded among functional departments, each having a specific aspect of the process for its domain."[35]

This development was more important to the long-term structure of the film industry and to the development of the form and the style of the films that industry was to produce than was the impact of any individual film or director. Between 1910 and 1920 several models for organizing motion picture labor competed for acceptance, but the model based on a well organized factory, brought to its fruition by Ince, eventually succeeded in dominating the industry. While his system was attacked as potentially producing "mechanical picture[s],"[36] its economical advantages seem to have won over any artistic fears.

Yet we should not create in Ince another great man of history. While he was an innovator of the continuity script, the industry as a whole was departmentalizing its production units. Earlier historians' comments that the continuity script led to economical and efficient production are correct, but the script is only part of the system of the creation of the product. The continuity script works because it is an external manifestation of a more fundamental structure inextricable from modern corporate business—the separation of the conception and production phases of work and the pyramid of divided labor. It is this fundamental structure which explains Ince's production organization, a structure which earlier historians failed to consider.

A question that derives from this analysis is, was there a simultaneous standardization of the product? To answer this question would require an extensive analysis of Ince's films—both the well-known and the lesser works. But it is clear that in the broader model of division of labor and scientific management, the film industry by 1915 had the structure it was to follow for the next fifty years.

The Movies Become
Big Business:
Publix Theatres and
the Chain-Store Strategy

Douglas Gomery

During the 1920s the American film industry developed into a strong oligopoly. Ownership of a large theater circuit provided each vertically integrated Hollywood firm with significant monopoly power. Historian Lewis Jacobs, using a demand-oriented model, argues that since patrons were willing to pay high prices to see first-run films, the large film producer-distributors purchased theater chains to control access to their customers. Such an explanation is one-sided: were theaters acquired regardless of expense? I think not. Motion picture capitalists sought profit and growth, and hence were quite conscious of costs. Second, Jacobs's (implicit) model ignores issues of business organization. How did Hollywood corporations use their new theater holdings to garner higher profits? In this article I argue that during the 1920s the U.S. film industry became a complete "big business" by adopting the strategy of the chain store. Hollywood-owned circuits increasingly presented a more standardized product, on a national level, at decreasing cost—all directed by a central authority in New York. Exhibition was the branch of the industry which could most easily adopt "big business" practices, and thus accumulate the greatest excess profits. Sam Katz, president of the Publix circuit, pushed most strongly for the chain-store system, and by 1929 Publix had become the most powerful theater organization in the United States.

I

Chain stores became a significant force in the U.S. economy during the 1920s. They came first in the form of grocery stores (A&P, Grand Union, Kroger), next variety stores (Woolworth, McCrory, Kresge), and then chains for drugs, auto parts, gas stations, and clothing. (Here I define a retail chain as multiple ownership of four or more outlets with centralized control.) During this period chain units rose from 29,000 to 160,000. Sales skyrocketed: for chain drugstores the increase was 125 percent; for clothing stores growth topped 400 percent. Grocery chains were the largest. By 1925 A&P's red-fronted stores had become one of the dominant icons of American life. In 1912 this chain had only 400 outlets; twenty years later there were 15,700. In 1930 A&P's sales topped $1 billion and accounted for about one-tenth of all food sold in the United States. Business historian Alfred D. Chandler argues that chain store strategy was the major U.S. marketing innovation between 1900 and 1930.[1]

The chief advantage for a chain operation lay in cost reduction through scale economies and monopsony power.[2] Chains could spread fixed costs over more operations and purchase inputs at lower prices. To maximize such savings, chains relied on what was labeled "scientific management." Here large circuits would secure trained managers, experts, and other skilled labor to operate the firm at peak efficiency: no waste, rapid turnover, maximum profits and growth. To assure that a standardized product would be sold in a "clean and dependable atmosphere," the chain's managers, operating from a central office, divided up the firm's activities and had each department perform its specialty at maximum efficiency and minimum cost. Gradually the managers would internalize more and more of the transactions, increase the speed and regularity of operations, and continue to lower costs. Simultaneously, the chain would purchase more outlets, grow more powerful, and garner more monopsony power for necessary inputs. Costs would fall even further. Chains advertised widely and developed trademarks for instant recognition. Large accounting departments provided managers with a continuous flow of information in order to circumvent unneeded expenses. Greater profits facilitated new financing, and chains quickly moved to capture new markets during the 1920s.[3]

The growth of chains of movie theaters, like retail stores, began on the regional level. As late as 1920 there still existed wide differences in movie exhibition. Picture palaces were still the exception, not the rule, and the strategy for live entertainment–movie presentation varied from

106 Development of Business Strategies

city to city. Gradually, during and after World War i, certain regional chains had taken on increasingly more power, and hence a definable set of exhibition strategies arose. The most successful was the Balaban & Katz (hereafter B&K) system. Perfected in Chicago between 1917 and 1923, it enabled B&K to overtake all its larger rivals and thus dominate the Chicago market as well as the rest of Illinois and most of Iowa and Nebraska. In short B&K developed chain store organization for movie exhibition within the city of Chicago.

The B&K system involved the complete operation of exhibition—standardized and controlled from a central office. Like other exhibitors B&K wished to present the most popular films. However, since B&K entered the exhibition market relatively late, other Chicago exhibitors held exclusive contracts with the major Hollywood producers. B&K had to build its chain with states-rights, subsequent-run, and First National films. Consequently, B&K concentrated on the non-filmic factors of exhibition, fashioned a strategy centered on five important inputs and thus developed a large comparative advantage over its competitors.[4]

First B&K recognized the important socioeconomic changes taking place in Chicago (and other American cities). The construction of mass transit in the late nineteenth and early twentieth centuries enabled middle- and upper-middle class (in terms of income) residents of U.S. cities to flee to the new "streetcar suburbs." Consequently, B&K did not build its first large theater, the Central Park, downtown, but on Chicago's far westside in Lawndale. Chicago's elevated system had reached Lawndale in 1902, and what had been a semisuburban area inhabited by a few thousand people, in fifteen years grew to become a crowded urban neighborhood of 100,000 people.[5]

Following the prosperity of the Central Park, B&K sought another outlying location and selected a site at the business center of the far northside neighborhood, Uptown. Here B&K built the Riviera in 1918. Now B&K controlled picture palaces that could draw from Chicago's north and west sides. To reach all areas of the city, B&K needed to build on the southside and in the central business district, the Loop. The southside theater, the Tivoli (ca. 1921), came first. Again B&K located in the largest outlying business center, the southside equivalent to Uptown. With the huge profits from these theaters, B&K built the Chicago Theater in the Loop. Once this matrix of four palaces was in operation, B&K could draw from all parts of the city. No Chicagoan needed more than 30 minutes to reach a B&K theater using the "el" or a streetcar. Thereafter B&K added theaters, reducing the required travel time to 15 minutes. Simultaneously, B&K gained control of all the large theaters in the Loop. Thus by 1925

B&K monopolized movie exhibition in Chicago, not by owning all of the theaters, but by controlling large picture palaces in the major outlying business centers and in the Loop.[6]

The "show" in a B&K theater began before anyone saw a film, or even live entertainment; the building itself served as an important part of the "moviegoing" experience. *Moving Picture World* argued that the Riviera was not so much a theater as a baronial hall, a place to hold teas or benefit balls. Here were buildings in which B&K's upwardly mobile patrons could feel at home in palatial surroundings perhaps unfit for a seventeenth-century monarch but were ideal for a twentieth-century business tycoon. In addition, the exterior of B&K theaters served as a massive advertisement. Huge electric signs identified the theaters. These signs were sometimes three stories high and flashed their message in several colors. Behind the sign an ornate stained glass window and the theater façade reproduced many of the motifs of the interior. In an era when electricity had been common for only twenty years, the exterior sign was quite novel. In contrast, the façades and stained-glass windows of B&K theaters served to remind Chicagoans of conservative institutions like churches or banks.

Inside, the foyers were as spectacular as the exterior and able to accommodate a waiting crowd large enough to fill the theater. Decoration included massive chandeliers, sometimes costing $25,000 each, a painting gallery, elaborate drapery, and space for a pianist to entertain those waiting. No B&K ticket holder needed to stand outside in inclement weather. Numerous ushers serviced the patrons and an intricate network of passageways enabled 8,000 people to enter and exit with relative comfort and speed. In the auditorium B&K prided itself on excellent sight lines, comfortable seats, and good acoustics. The lighting in the auditorium was varied throughout all performances to supplement the mood of the films or live performance. B&K did not ignore a theater's auxiliary services. Rest rooms were spacious, clean, and decorated with paintings and sculpture. In addition B&K provided free baby-sitting. Mothers could leave their children in the care of a trained attendant and a nurse, and enjoy the entertainment. Playrooms were large, well-equipped, indoor playgrounds. B&K advertised this service widely.[7]

The third aspect of the B&K formula was quite special during the 1920s: air-conditioned theaters. Before the Central Park, the nation's first air-cooled movie house, most theaters closed during the summer, or opened to small crowds. Engineers tried to perfect a safe cooling system with adequate power, but available chemical refrigerants proved too dangerous for crowded theaters. Researchers made important progress during the first decade of the twentieth century and by 1911 had developed the technology to cool large buildings safely. Here technological change centered in Chicago because local firms still slaughtered and processed most of America's meat.[8]

B&K placed the newly developed carbon dioxide air-cooling systems in the Central Park and the Riviera. The cool air entered into the auditorium through vents in the floor and rose to the ceiling to be removed by exhaust fans in the roof. In 1921 engineers installed an improved system in the Chicago Theater that included a humidity control using an air washer and cleaner, and a special heater. By 1925, motion picture trade papers constantly noted how air-conditioning seemed to explain the large grosses of B&K theaters. B&K's advertising department continuously reminded Chicagoans of the coolness of its theaters, usually by adding icicles to the names of the theaters in newspaper movie listings. Chicago's health commissioner even argued that the B&K's theaters had better air than Pike's Peak and recommended all Chicagoans to go to a B&K theater several hours each week. Such advertising spurred public acceptance and helped the box office; during the summers B&K frequently experienced larger grosses than during winter months.[9]

Fourth, B&K's system was highly labor intensive, sometimes requiring more than one hundred employees in each house. Most famous were the ushers. B&K recruited corps of male college students, dressed them in red uniforms with white gloves and yellow epaulets, and demanded extreme politeness to all customers (with no tips). B&K regulated and monitored quite closely all actions of its employees. For example, ushers were admonished to refer to a patron as a gentleman, lady, or child, never old man, girl, or boy. Ushers could never shout at customers, and always ended any request with "thank you." Ushers and doormen made up one-third of a theater's staff. Musicians accounted for another third, and projectionists, stage staff, and maintenance the rest.[10]

Rigid control over employees served important functions. First it guaranteed a conservative public image—much like a bank or a fine hotel. Second it kept labor costs low since most employees were either young, black, or female or all three. Labor costs were closely scrutinized and standardized. For example, B&K developed charts specifying precisely the number of janitors it would take to clean any given floor area. Employees provided more than simply service and a good image, however. Ushers maintained "spill cards" to record the number of patrons in all parts of the theater. At any time the chief usher and the manager of the theater knew how many vacancies existed, could instantly move new patrons to those seats, and plan how to avoid empty seats for future shows.

In that way B&K kept its theaters optimally filled, and thus maximized box-office revenue.[11]

Finally B&K presented more than motion pictures. A vast corps of musicians accompanied the films; live stage entertainment filled one-third of the show's two hours. In fact, before B&K had access to popular films it was able to hire important vaudeville entertainers and ensure a constantly attractive entertainment package to its customers. In that way B&K could avoid sustained periods of poor grosses and guarantee a constant flow of revenue. In time B&K became more famous for impressive stage attractions, orchestras, and organists than for any movies it presented.

For musicians and organists B&K developed local stars. B&K stage spectacles offered revues with elaborate settings and intricate, multi-colored lighting effects. The stage show stood by itself as a separate presentation unit of a vaudeville-movie entertainment package. In 1919 B&K tried presentations which interrupted the narrative of the film, but abandoned these experiments after one year. Thereafter B&K tested different combinations of live talent, and in 1923 settled on the pure presentation: a separate, unique musical revue, not tied at all to the film. Such shows were expensive, each costing about $5,000 to set up. To maximize income and to minimize costs, B&K rotated shows. Thus each presentation unit played one week at the Chicago Theatre, then a week at the Riviera, then a week at the Tivoli. Expenses were split on the basis of theater size and run status, so B&K charged off 50 percent of the expenses to the Chicago Theatre, 20 percent to the Riviera, and 30 percent to the Tivoli. Costs fell as B&K took over more theaters. Yet repetition did not hurt business; as many patrons as usual turned out at the Tivoli even though the show had already appeared a week at each of the other two theaters.[12]

II

In November 1925 B&K merged with Famous Players, and Sam Katz took his management team to New York to institute the Balaban & Katz system for the Publix chain.[13] Immediately Katz set in place the five-factored strategy that worked so well in Chicago. Simultaneously, Katz started to run Publix like a "legitimate business." First he took all power from the house managers and centralized it in New York. Wanting to create a logotype as famous as that of A&P or Woolworth, Katz changed the name of many theaters to Paramount. In short, he adapted the principles of chain store operation to the B&K system to create the national Publix chain.[14]

In order to maximize the cost savings which accrue to chain operations, Katz pushed for rapid growth. In five years Publix expanded from approximately 300 to 1,200 theaters.[15] Publix did construct theaters, but most of its growth came from merger or direct takeover. By 1930 Publix dominated film exhibition in the South from North Carolina to Texas, as well as in Michigan, Illinois, Minnesota, Iowa, the Dakotas, Nebraska, and New England. In addition, through Famous-Players Canadian, Publix also controlled Canada. Over 2 million people attended Publix theaters each day. Publix employed more musicians than any other organization in the world—an estimated 12,000. At its peak during the 1930/31 movie season, Publix was the largest motion picture circuit in film history.[16]

Katz supervised all operations. His assistants controlled everything from planning music to advertising, from booking films to acquiring new theaters. (See fig. 6.) The day-to-day activities were handled by four regional managers. Under the regional managers came divisional managers, district managers, and the local house managers. Within this structure, power flowed from the top. Katz, his New York staff, and the four regional managers selected all films for rental, developed and routed all stage shows, picked and trained employees, determined advertising policy, secured supplies, and monitored all expenses.[17]

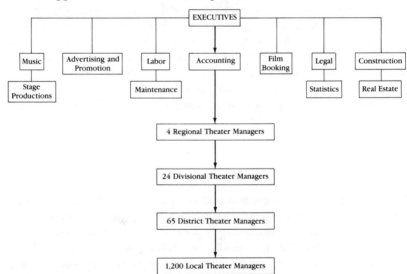

Fig. 6.1. *Organizational chart for Publix Theatres (1926–32)*
Adapted from *Variety*, 7 Aug. 1929, pp. 9–10, and *Film Daily Yearbook, 1927*, p. 665. This is not the official company chart; I created it to simplify the division of labor and management for this period.

All booking was done from New York. Since Paramount did not make enough films to fill Publix screen time, Publix bargained with and obtained favorable terms from the other major producer-distributors. Publix's central buyer relied on data from previous years, which had been compiled in massive detail, and suggestions from managers at all levels. The actual scheduling began six to eight weeks in advance. The regional managers and the booker prepared master booking sheets and then sent them down the line to be commented upon at each level. The divisional, district, and local managers added the "local" touch, eliminated regionally offensive films, and returned the sheets to New York for final approval. Then Katz held numerous meetings to deal with any last minute contingencies. Executive managers at all levels were recruited from the areas they supervised, and visited their territories several times a year. Katz thought experienced local managers made the best executives since they had firsthand knowledge of the "needs" of their communities.[18]

All deluxe first- and second-run Publix houses presented stage shows. Specialists prepared Publix unit shows in New York, selecting all props, costumes, performers, and lighting cues. By 1928 Publix had thirty-three such units on the road. A local manager's only responsibility was to make sure shows began and ended on time. New York executives also hired all organists and pit orchestra members. Although these musicians did not move with the presentation units, Publix could employ the most popular talent, mount expensive shows, and spread the cost over several hundred theaters. Publix effected huge cost savings from economies of scale—as had the Keith-Albee and Orpheum vaudeville circuits in previous years.[19]

Each unit was organized around a central theme or motif. Although none can be judged as typical, the "Say It With Flowers" unit of April 1929 illustrates many of the features of Publix stage shows. The setting was the garden of a summer house, complete with a stage band in brilliant red British military uniforms. Six women in white satin hoopskirts performed an opening dance, after which master of ceremonies Ben Black introduced a female vocalist who sang "All I Want To Know." The stage band followed with a novelty arrangement of "Sweethearts on Parade"; a male comic did a bit with Black; and the six dancers from the opening number encored. All performers appeared in the finale of the thirty-minute show, dancing and singing around a maypole in the garden. The whole stage was covered with multicolored lights, contrasting with the streamers from the maypole. A stage band, several "acts," and a spectacular ending formed the basic structure of all Publix unit shows. Frank Cambria, head of the Publix stage department, and his assistants developed seasonal themes as well as ones tied to current public fads, such as the radio or airplane.[20]

When Sam Katz moved to Publix, he not only instituted the same labor policy that had worked so well for B&K but went several steps farther. He closely supervised the selection and training of all employees and even established a school to train local managers.[21] Publix managers were expected to take an active part in the civic activities of their communities and file regular reports detailing the nature of this participation. All duties performed were recorded; all instructions and emergencies anticipated. Nothing was left to chance. Using such methods Katz guaranteed that the name Publix meant courteous, costless service to all patrons.[22]

In Chicago B&K advertised widely, but with no more frequency than its competitors. Now in a national market Katz determined Publix could not rely on "word of mouth." Advertising and publicity became vital inputs. Katz's experts formulated numerous ambitious advertising programs in order to sell the Publix and Paramount names. The central Publix slogan became: "You don't need to know what's playing at a Publix House. It's bound to be the best show in town."[23] All advertising copy was prepared by Publix specialists at the New York office and sent down the line in the form of a manual, along with the film and stage show. This manual contained model ads, sketches, suggestions on how to place the ads, descriptions of "stunts" to promote the theater's program, and even publicity stories to be planted in the newspaper. The major Hollywood producers supplied a similar press kit, but the New York office required Publix managers to use the Publix manual. Publix local managers simply selected the material appropriate to their market and then executed the advertising campaign within a budget specified from New York. Since local advertising budgets were balanced only once a month, the managers had some flexibility in advertising appropriations. However, in order to conduct any elaborate advertising local managers had to secure permission from the Publix New York office.[24]

Publix buyers in New York purchased all supplies and equipment, and allocated materials from regional warehouses. Of course Publix bought in bulk. In addition, rather than just accepting the going price in any one territory, Publix experts searched the United States for the lowest rate. Supplies were issued against manager's requisitions, but were not allowed to exceed certain budgeted amounts. The New York office reviewed all requests for equipment and repairs, and local managers needed authorization from New York for all major outlays.[25]

By now it is obvious that Publix kept careful control on all expenditures at its theaters. Each theater had a weekly budget detailing all costs. Local managers had to submit weekly reports of actual expenditures, and these figures were carefully scrutinized by accountants in the home office. Any overage had to be explained in a written report. In addition, local managers recorded all nonfinancial aspects of their operations and forwarded such records to the New York office. Here Publix accountants constructed elaborate charts to serve as guides for future decision making. For example, for all deluxe Publix houses, assistant managers recorded the temperature and humidity from the orchestra floor, balcony, lobby, and outside every hour on the hour for the complete operating day. Publix experts then evaluated this data against ideal standards and issued new orders concerning use of the heating and air-conditioning. Local managers also had to hold to strict timing of the theater activities. Publix made heavy use of the "spill cards" perfected by B&K in Chicago. Publix real estate experts planned, built, and acquired all new theaters. Specialists calculated traffic patterns, population densities, income distributions, and recreation habits before a theater site was even considered. When Publix purchased a deluxe theater, air-conditioning was immediately added, and other modifications made so that the house fit the Publix standard.[26]

III

The coming of sound changed the Publix system very little. Filmed "stage shows"—vaudeville shorts—replaced live acts. Orchestras and organists were retained in only the largest theaters. In March 1928 the Publix stage-show circuit reached its acme. Each unit played a guaranteed 33 weeks per year plus 4 weeks vacation. Sam Katz, always quite cost conscious, quickly reasoned that vaudeville acts recorded on sound motion pictures could present the most popular musical entertainment at a huge cost reduction. Thus he lobbied hard for Paramount/Publix to adopt sound.[27] By June 1929 Paramount was producing a continuous supply of sound vaudeville shorts, and Katz began to disband the stage-show units and to lay off musicians, organists, and stagehands. Only the Paramount Theatre in New York and the Chicago Theatre retained live stage shows on a consistent basis. By September 1929 the transformation was complete. Publix's products were all-sound, more standardized, more easily monitored, and more profitable.[28]

With this new profit base Paramount/Publix corporation began to expand toward complete monopoly. Between September 1929 and May 1930 Publix acquired 500 more theaters. In June 1929 Paramount/Publix had purchased 50 percent of the newly formed Columbia Broadcasting System (CBS). Still Zukor and Katz wanted more economic power, and on 1 September 1929 Paramount/Publix agreed to merge with Warner Bros. to form Paramount-Vitaphone. This new combine would control over 1,700 theaters, six motion picture studios, CBS, the Columbia Phonography Company, and Warners' vast holdings in music publishing. Three giants, RCA, the newly merged Fox-Loew's, and Paramount-Vitaphone would then dominate five entertainment industries: motion pictures, vaudeville, music publishing, radio, and phonograph.[29]

The Paramount/Publix–Warner Bros. merger never took place. The new administration of President Herbert Hoover threatened to sue for antitrust violations. This proposed merger signaled the apex of Paramount/Publix power. Business continued to be fine in 1930: Publix grossed $113,000,000; film rental for Paramount reached $69,000,000. However, Paramount/Publix's consolidated balance sheet was heavy with debt. In five short years Publix's expansion had generated $30,000,000 of obligations in the form of bonds and guaranteed repurchase agreements.[30] Late in 1930 box-office revenues began to decline drastically. Zukor and Katz scrambled to meet short-term deficits; still Katz stubbornly clung to the expansionary philosophy which had generated all the debt. However, during the Great Depression chain-store methods could not keep costs low enough to generate sufficient revenue to cover Publix's vast number of mortgages. Sam Katz became Paramount/Publix's scapegoat and was forced to resign in October 1932. Still the Katz system, in a modified form, would be used by Paramount/Publix well into the 1950s.[31]

IV

Before 1920 movie exhibition was primarily a regional, not national, operation. Business practices tended to be those modeled on partnerships or small corporations of the nineteenth century. Following the lead of Publix, movie exhibitors adopted the methods of large modern corporations. Like chains in other industries, Publix operated in a national market using coordinated advertising and an identifiable trademark. Scale economies, and monopsony power enabled it to reduce costs significantly. Publix hired the most popular live entertainment and motion pictures, and sold the package using innovations first developed in Chicago. Expansion proceeded in an orderly fashion: costs fell, profits rose, more theaters were acquired. Other chains copied Publix's methods. The coming of sound altered operations little; the Great Depression would force changes. However, by then vertically integrated movie chains were "big business" in size and operating technique, and thus were able to survive the Depression, dominate U.S. film exhibition for the next twenty years, and serve as the cornerstone of Hollywood's monopoly power.

Afterword

I am quite proud of this essay. Here I think I was able to help integrate the study of the U.S. film industry into the mainstream of business history. Still upon re-reading I gasp at some obvious problems. Time permits me to address several of the more glaring. I must thank the editor for providing me with the space to analyze, evaluate, and correct this re-interpretation of the history of the U.S. film industry.

Two significant drawbacks stand out in 1981. First, I never did spell out in any detail my approach, my theoretical framework. Buried in the third paragraph is one possible economic model for explaining the development of a monopoly in distribution. Theater chains for any retail enterprise could accumulate power and profits based on the twin pillars: economies of scale and monopsony power. Nowhere did I mention that with such a concentration of power "free competition" can break down. Here a failure of the market would call for government intervention, probably in the form of an antitrust suit by the U.S. Department of Justice. Such an action, of course, was instigated in 1938.

I should elaborate on the unfamiliar term, monopsony power. A market for resources in which there exists only a single buyer of a particular product or service from a large number of sellers is defined by neoclassical economists as a monopsony. There seem to be two basic causes. First, monopsonistic purchases of an input may occur when units of the resource are specialized for only one user. Such uniqueness can occur for labor (e.g., performers), and physical capital (e.g., motion picture film stock). A second condition is found because of a lack of mobility on the part of certain resources. For the American motion picture industry, stars offer the most famous examples of monopsony power in that their talents were specialized and were valuable only to movie studios, which to capitalize on their monopsony power in the 1930s signed stars to long-term, exclusive contracts. Theater chains used similar contracts for stage-show performers. Yet little scholarly attention has been given to the effects of monopsony power in the American film industry. The concept of monopolization, represented by eight Hollywood vertically-integrated corporations, dominates the literature. But here, in passing, I do want to argue that concentrated power in resource markets ought to constitute a significant portion of the history of any film industry, especially that in Hollywood between 1925 and 1955. For example, movie industry relations with Eastman Kodak should be studied in detail.

I should like to point out to the contemporary reader of "The Movies Become Big Business" that this article forms a summary of my previous work on movie exhibition. For a more detailed discussion of the important B&K chain, see "The Growth of Movie Monopolies: The Case of Balaban & Katz," *Wide Angle* 3, no. 1, pp. 44–63. I have developed a similar case-study analysis for a dozen other cities. See "The Picture Palace: Economic Sense or Hollywood Nonsense," *The Quarterly Review of Film Studies* 3, no. 1 (Winter, 1978) 23–36; and "Saxe Amusement Enterprises: The Movies Come to Milwaukee," *Milwaukee History* 2, no. 1 (new series) (Spring, 1979):18–28, for more details.

Finally, "The Movies Become Big Business" suggests many avenues for future research. I think film historians have made great strides toward understanding the importance of location and architecture in movie exhibition. But what about the people who worked in these entertainment palaces? We know precious little about labor for such exhibition enterprises. I would suggest one might begin to move in at least two possible directions. First, what were the effects of unionization? In the face of the growing power of the movie chains, would not (at least under John Kenneth Galbraith's theory of countervailing power) there have existed enormous pressure to form unions? And what of IATSE (International Alliance of Theatrical Stage Employees) and its horizontal monopoly on stagehands and projectionists? Moreover, we desperately need a history of stage performers. Who were the stars of the stage presentations? This latter concern directs scholars into uncharted areas of the relationships between film and live performance. Narrative theorists Noel Burch and David Bordwell, for example, have investigated such questions for the Japanese cinema from the same era. The *benshi* "narrated" silent films to audiences in Japan until the mid-1930s. Historians of American cinema, together with those scholars interested in musicals and vaudeville entertainment, should pursue the effects stage shows in the 1920s had on U.S. film exhibition.

PART THREE

Technological Change:
Sound and Color

The "Warner-Vitaphone Peril": The American Film Industry Reacts to the Innovation of Sound

Douglas Gomery

Any revision in film history must begin with the standard account. The most famous description of the reluctant switch to sound by the largest companies in the American film industry, the so-called majors, is in Lewis Jacobs' *Rise of the American Film*. After recounting Warner Bros.' initial activity, Jacobs details the single-minded opposition of Famous Players–Lasky, Loew's, First National, United Artists, and Universal. All resolved to fight the "Warner-Vitaphone peril" on the grounds that:

1. Present equipment would have to be discarded and expensive talking equipment would have to be bought.
2. Such equipment could be obtained only by paying royalties to a competitor.
3. Obeisance to Warner Bros. meant loss of prestige.
4. The technique of production would have to change radically.
5. Long-term contracts with "silent" stars and directors might prove to be frozen liabilities.[1]

Only after the "public's enthusiasm for sound film could no longer be denied" did the majors, on 15 May 1928, sign up. "Now in a panic" they rushed into the production, distribution, and exhibition of talkies, "hoping to make up for lost time." The remainder of 1928 was filled with "chaos, conjecture, and confusion."[2] Benjamin Hampton presents a very similar account, different only in one detail. He dates the panic as the autumn of 1927.[3]

Fitzhugh Green's *Film Finds Its Tongue* is the source of Jacobs' history. Only a minority of film historians have directly cited this source.[4] Yet Green is much more systematic than Jacobs or Hampton. Moreover, he examines the motives of the Big Five—Loew's, Universal, Famous Players—Lasky, First National, and Producer's Distributing Corporation (PDC)—in more detail. Green explains how, once the Big Five decided at a "council of war" in December 1926, to oppose Warner Bros., they hired an engineer at $500,000 and spent a year and a half investigating other devices. All wanted to adopt the same system for "instant" standardization. They also hoped to "squeeze out" Warner Bros. by securing an alternative system.[5] Two later accounts, based on Green, date the "council of war" as 17 February 1927.[6]

Most of the accepted histories originate with Green. Yet there are no notes or bibliographical aids in his basically journalistic narrative. There is no indication of the derivation of his data. N. R. Danielian, an economist writing about the American Telephone and Telegraph Company, has provided a new source in a federal government study. However, Danielian allocates only 20 pages to the transition to sound. Moreover, all of these standard accounts judge, *a posteriori*, that the majors acted as single-minded, irrational monopolists who knew of no strategies other than extermination of the competition.

This article will argue that given their economic station, the majors acted wisely and quite rationally by waiting and signing with Western Electric when they did. Although the switch to sound occurred very rapidly, the majors encountered no substantial problems or loss in profit. Waiting, as others attempt innovation, is often the more rational policy. The more cautious firm can gather valuable data concerning potential revenues and new information concerning costs by observing the actions of the innovator. And although the innovator may initially get an edge on the market over the firm that waits, a powerful firm will suffer little damage by waiting. Thus in 1925 the major studios could afford to wait and gather information, knowing there was no real threat to their oligopolistic position.

☆
Initial Probings

In 1924 when Western Electric was assembling its systems of sound inventions for commercial exploitation, George Cullinan, Western Electric's general sales manager, and Elbert Hawkins, his chief assistant, were convinced that the biggest firms in the motion picture industry would *not* be interested. All were too profitable and had added too much new capital in recent years to attempt such a risky investment. However Edgar S. Bloom, president of Western Electric, overruled Cullinan and Hawkins. The potential profit was far too great. Thus in May 1924 the two Western Electric salesmen approached Sidney Kent, general manager of the film industry's largest firm, Famous Players–Lasky. Cullinan first contacted Kent during Famous Players' annual sales convention in May 1924. Kent's younger brother, employed at Western Electric's Lamp Division, formally introduced the two. Cullinan told Kent of the wonderful promise of talking pictures; Kent was not impressed. Like other leaders of the film industry he knew of the long list of failures of talking-picture experiments compiled during the past twenty years.[7] In a second meeting later in May at Famous Players' New York headquarters, Kent remained opposed. Cullinan and Hawkins did not give up. One by one they approached and tried to interest other leaders of the industry. In each case the reasons for rejection were the same. All reminded Cullinan of past attempts: most recently by DeForest and earlier by Edison and others.[8]

By the autumn of 1924, Cullinan had convinced his superiors that this direct method was not the most fruitful. He suggested Western Electric pursue an alternative strategy by which it would work through an independent promoter from outside the motion picture industry. This type of speculative entrepreneur was common during the boom of the 1920s. The ideal candidate would have a large amount of available private capital and would commit himself to the task for at least three years. In January 1925 Cullinan selected Charles S. Post. During the next few months, Post produced several recordings of vaudeville musical artists. Next he showed these sound shorts to leaders of the industry. He too was rejected out of hand. Discouraged after four months of futile effort and the loss of a large personal investment, Post quit. Cullinan sought a replacement.[9] In May 1925 he reached agreement with Walter J. Rich, then head of a successful corporation producing automobile speedometers. In June 1925 Rich, using Post's shorts as sales tools, duplicated Cullinan and Post's assaults upon the industry's top moguls. He too could not persuade any leader to join with him to form a corporation to create sound films. Only by accident, and with much reluctance on his part, did Rich meet and agree, in June 1925, to link up with Warner Bros. to form the Vitaphone Corporation.[10]

For a year the important film industry moguls continued to concentrate their efforts on immediate and long term problems of growth and generally ignored Vitaphone's efforts. This ambivalence disappeared in August, 1926, with the premiere of the *Don Juan* program. This package of sound shorts, and a feature film with mechanical musical sound accompaniment greatly impressed the leaders of the film industry. Most expected Vitaphone to generate large revenues, especially in conjunction with recordings of vaudeville and presentation acts. In September 1926 Waddill Catchings, Warner Bros.' chief financial officer and investment counselor, with assistance from Harry Warner, easily opened exploratory negotiations toward merger with Adolph Zukor and Sidney Kent. Catchings saw a potential alliance with Famous Players as being consistent with the best interest of Warner Bros. It would give strength and legitimacy to the Vitaphone experiments.[11]

At first Catchings and Warner learned that Zukor and Kent would invest no money in Vitaphone unless Warner Bros. gave up its controlling interest. After long negotiations, Catchings eventually found an opening. He proposed that Vitaphone remain an independent corporation, one-half owned by Warner Bros.; the other half, by Famous Players. The new Vitaphone Corporation would then be at the disposal of both film producers. Silent film production would remain unchanged. Zukor and his associates foresaw that silent features would remain Famous Players' primary product, while sound films would provide only vaudeville presentation material. The new corporation's board would contain three directors from Famous Players, three from Warner Bros., and Catchings would serve as the seventh member. Famous Players would buy out Rich and invest an additional $2 million. In less than one month, at the end of September 1926, all negotiators agreed orally to these propositions and ordered a draft contract printed.[12]

Only one constraint remained. Warner Bros. had to notify Western Electric, as required by the original contract. In the first week of October Catchings notified Western Electric's sales manager, John E. Otterson, of the nature and substance of the agreement between Vitaphone and Famous Players. Otterson became outraged. Many times in the past his company had tried to interest Famous Players in the new inventions and failed. Now this small, unimportant company had succeeded. Otterson went directly to Zukor and offered him a lower royalty rate as a direct licensee. On 24 November 1926 Otterson arranged a meeting between Western Electric president Edgar S. Bloom and Zukor at the University Club in New York City. By then Otterson's persuasive tactics had succeeded. Zukor told Bloom he would not deal directly with Warner Bros. Furthermore, Famous Players would now negotiate in tandem with the other major powers in the industry: Loew's, United Artists, First National, Universal, and Producers Distributing Corporation (then owned by the Keith-Albee vaudeville circuit).[13]

Zukor formed a committee representing these firms in December 1926. He and Sidney Kent represented Famous Players, Nicholas Schenck and David Bernstein represented Loew's, Robert Cochrane represented Universal, John J. Murdock represented Producers Distributing Corporation, and Clifford B. Hawley and Robert Lieber represented First National. United Artists' delegate was Joseph Schenck, brother of Nicholas; however, because he lived in California, he could attend only an occasional meeting. On all matters, Nicholas Schenck looked after his brother's interests. Otterson and Rich represented Vitaphone. Otterson by this time had completely convinced Rich to switch his allegiance from Warner Bros. to Western Electric. Together Rich and Western Electric spoke for Vitaphone, even though they could not effect an agreement without Warner Bros.' approval.[14]

At Otterson's suggestion, this producers' committee began to consider the type of proposal that Zukor had almost adopted when he broke off negotiations with Catchings and Harry Warner. All six producers were reluctant to become direct licensees. Under Otterson's plan the five largest—Loew's, Famous Players, United Artists, Universal, and First National—would share ownership of Vitaphone with Rich and Warner Bros. Rich's share would be 15 percent, one-half his current ownership. Warner Bros.' share would fall from 70 percent to 35 percent. The five new parties would own 10 percent each. For this percentage each would deposit $800,000, to total $4 million in new capital stock. The producers balked at this price, so Otterson reduced their subscription to $600,000. Warner Bros. had already contributed over 90 percent of Vitaphone's $2 million in assets.[15]

Otterson advised Catchings and Harry Warner of the impending agreement. Moreover, he counciled them that Warner Bros. must accept the plan, or Western Electric would announce publicly that Vitaphone had not paid its royalties and thus Western Electric must terminate the original license. Catchings knew such an announcement would severely harm Warner Bros.' credit rating, with the only hope of recovery a prolonged law suit against a very influential and wealthy foe. With some reluctance, Catchings and Harry Warner advised Otterson that Warner Bros. would accept the plan, even though both thought their company was being denied a fair share, given the amount of capital it had invested.[16]

Otterson had waited too long. The producers' committee perceived a deterioration of interest in sound. Long-run profits would not be large enough to support an investment of even $600,000. Moreover, Otterson's proposition seemed too complicated. Several leaders, not wanting to deal with their competitors, demanded direct licenses. They insisted on developing their own individual sound recording operations. None of the producers wanted Warner Bros. to own 35 percent of a corporation in which they would control only 10 percent. All wanted more time to determine the success of Warner Bros.' assault on the marketplace.[17] Only the renegade William Fox—never a party to Zukor's producers' committee—remained speculative enough. Then in the process of developing his own sound-on-film system, Fox signed with Western Electric's newly created subsidiary, Electrical Research Products, Inc. (ERPI), on 31 December 1926. Like Warner Bros. Fox had the necessary banking support to challenge the largest firms in the industry.[18]

Up to this time no manufacturer of sound equipment offered Western Electric any competition in terms of patents owned and controlled, accumulated technical expertise, or significant financial backing. Numerous owners of small firms approached Zukor and the producers' committee in December 1926.

In January, 1927, a major foe entered the arena in the person of RCA's vice-president, David Sarnoff. He not only represented his firm but also the electrical giant, General Electric. The jointly developed Photophone system was well advanced in a technical sense and included rights not only to its own but also to all Western Electric patents, the latter through cross-licensing agreements signed in 1920 and 1926.[19]

Sarnoff reminded the producers that whichever system they chose, it would become the standard for the industry. All equipment at the time was very different: RCA had developed only sound-on-film; Western Electric had not yet demonstrated sound-on-film, using instead sound-on-disc. Moreover, RCA's sound-on-film employed a track significantly wider than Western Electric's still experimental sound-on-film. RCA's reproduction system picked up the sound before the film passed before the lens, while Western Electric's picked it up afterwards. Furthermore, Western Electric's disc required only 33 1/3 rpm; all others ran at the standard 78 rpm. With conversion costs estimated at $30 million Sarnoff easily persuaded the producers' committee to postpone a decision.[20]

On 17 February 1927, Loew's, Famous Players–Lasky, Universal, First National, and PDC signed an agreement to postpone any decision for one year. United Artists tacitly approved since Nicholas Schenck was a signatory. This memorandum was no document of war; it overtly listed none of the reasons Jacobs suggests. Instead it is a rational statement of the issues and the best course of action for six powerful oligopolists. The memorandum opens with a clear statement of the problem. The producers who signed could most profitably present their products in theaters that employed one standardized sound system. They realized it was wasteful for them to let exhibitors install and use more than one system. Simple economies of scale determined it was in the producers' best interest to collude and pressure exhibitors to adopt one system. The producers knew they could do this because of the immense amount of market power they possessed through their distribution networks and ownership of key first-run theaters.

After some self-serving arguments outlining how standardization was also in the public's best interest, the producers agreed to one course of action. First, the signatories would adopt only one system. The producers established a screening committee of five members, one representing each signatory. This subcommittee would accumulate the data needed to determine the best system. The cost of gathering such evidence would be split equally among the five parties. The signatories agreed to consider the subcommittee's recommendation, and given the most reasonable terms, to abide by a majority vote of the full committee. Sidney Kent of Famous Players–Lasky became chairman of the subcommittee, and David Bernstein, vice-president and treasurer of Loew's, became its vice-chairman. The agreement expired on 17 February 1928, but could be continued by majority approval, for up to three years.[21]

☆
The Period of Negotiation

The subcommittee began serious investigations in March 1927. Complete agreement came in May 1928. In this fifteen-month period these large motion-picture firms grew rapidly and further increased their economic power. Loew's, First National, and newly merged Paramount (formerly Famous Players–Lasky) continued a decade-long period of extreme expansion. During the last three years, Paramount had doubled its asset base. By the spring of 1927, all three began to reap the profits from their recent investments. However, that spring the United States' economy experienced a decrease in national income of 2 percent, the first reduction since 1921. During the previous two years America's national income had grown at a rate of 6.4 percent.[22] This small decline had severe repercussions in theatrical box-office demand. Motion picture exhibition receipts fell drastically. The worst decline came for the road-show films, those two-dollar specials like *Ben-Hur* and *The Big Parade*. Revenue from lower priced fare also plunged for the first time since 1919. In areas of the recession's greatest impact, such as New England, receipts fell as much as 45 percent. The leaders of Paramount, Loew's, and First National noticed the change.[23]

The reaction was predictable. Realizing their immense economic power, the majors began to cut expenses wherever possible. The most important component of variable costs, the most easily adjusted in the short run was the wage bill for production, an area where most employees were not unionized.[24] Moreover, alternative employment, especially at high wages, existed only in declining industries—vaudeville and the legitimate theater. Thus Zukor and his cohorts concluded that they could lower wages for these employees and face little effective opposition. All other producers would follow to save money; and many influential bankers who complained of "waste" in the production of films would applaud this move as sensible in these tighter times. Thus on 21 June 1927, Paramount's vice-president for production, Jesse L. Lasky, announced a 10 percent across-the-board salary cut for all of Paramount's production employees earning over $50 a week. The next day every other major producer-distributor, including Fox and Warner Bros., followed Paramount's lead. Zukor estimated this action would save Paramount $1,040,000 per year and would increase profits by 15 per cent.[25]

Unexpectedly, Actors' Equity did not remain passive. On 28 June the executive committee of its Los Angeles branch called the national president, Frank Gilmore, to Hollywood to organize the unhappy film actors. The producers' recently organized company union, the Academy of Motion Picture Arts and Sciences, had already passed a resolution sympathetic to the action of the majors. In the first week of July, Gilmore conducted a series of conferences, climaxed by a mass meeting on 6 July. Equity called for a cessation of all pay cuts, and the adoption of a new basic agreement with minimum guarantees. Groups of writers and technicians held similar protest meetings and demanded similar action. They did not want to negotiate through the Academy, but through established trade unions. The producers feared pressure for a closed shop and reacted quickly. On 29 July Lasky announced that Paramount would rescind all pay cuts if all further labor negotiations would be held *only* through the Academy. The workers agreed. The other major producer-distributors followed; they did not want powerful unions to reduce their monopoly power in crucial labor markets. Expenses would have to be cut in other, less sensitive areas.[26]

However, continued retrenchment proved unnecessary. National income turned up in the fall of 1927 and the "Big Three" experienced a dramatic resurgence in motion picture receipts and profits. Paramount's third-quarter earnings doubled *vis-à-vis* the same quarter of 1926. By the end of 1927 it had accumulated the greatest profits in its history. Loew's, second in the industry, grew less rapidly. It did not acquire a large number of theaters in the mid-1920s. The third giant, First National, also experienced new growth. The firms in the second tier of the industry—Universal, Fox, Warner Bros., PDC, and Film Booking Office—expanded less rapidly. None had major investments in theaters. Fox, with a large commitment in Movietone, had yet to experience any return. Warner Bros.

would secure little profit until 1928. Those small independent producers in the industry's final tier continued to experience extremely poor years, and began to disappear from the industry at an increasingly rapid rate. The strict oligopolistic pattern of the 1930s and 1940s was beginning to crystallize.[27]

☆
The Actual Negotiations

In February 1927, the producers' subcommittee, headed by Sidney Kent, began to investigate available systems. To assist Kent, the producers hired a staff of engineers, lawyers, and technicians. Roy J. Pomeroy of Paramount's special-effects department and Louis Swarts of Paramount's legal staff headed up units concerned with technological and legal questions.[28] Pomeroy was one of the few industry engineers with experience in using sound equipment. In the fall of 1926 he had developed a sound-effects system to be used with the film *Wings*. Pomeroy's method employed six revolving discs, and an automatic mechanism for raising and lowering the tone arm at the beginning and end of each record. However, this system lacked an adequate loud speaker for amplification. While the subcommittee considered different systems in 1927, Pomeroy continued to work on his device. Using RCA loud speakers, *Wings* would play during the fall of 1927 with mixed results. Eventually, the subcommittee would drop Pomeroy's system as being far too cumbersome.[29]

The subcommittee judged all systems by three important standards. First, the equipment had to be technically adequate. It was the Pomeroy unit's job to determine this requirement. Second, Swarts and his assistants had to judge whether the systems' owners controlled the necessary patents to prevent a surge of legal actions against potential users. Both RCA and Western Electric possessed distinct advantages in these areas, controlling hundreds of patents. Moreover under the cross-licensing agreements of 1920 and 1926, each firm had access to the other's patents. Furthermore, both had the vast technological know-how to develop more patents and the legal staff to work out any potential, disruptive technological bottlenecks concerning patents. The final criterion was the most important. The chosen system had to have the financial backing of a large, important firm with substantial manufacturing resources, already existing technical personnel and facilities, and adequate strength in the financial markets. The committee knew the switch to sound would require the output of much technical equipment and the necessary personnel to install and service it. This would be a large undertaking; giants like Paramount did not want to risk their goodwill, capital stock, and strong profit potential by linking to a small, under-financed firm. Sidney Kent put it succinctly: the producer-distributors wanted to buy financial "reputation." [30]

Using these three necessary criteria, the subcommittee easily eliminated all but three firms. It initially considered seriously the Fox-Case system. However, Fox-Case General Manager Courtland Smith had to demand 10 percent of the gross receipts as a royalty; the Fox-Case system depended on a license from Western Electric, and for this Fox-Case paid 8 percent of its gross revenues to Western Electric. Kent soon learned of this rate restriction and dropped the Fox-Case method from consideration, even though Pomeroy had praised its technical performance. After four months of investigation, the only two systems to meet all three criteria were RCA's Photophone and Western Electric's Vitaphone. [31]

In July 1927 Pomeroy and his staff journeyed to Schenectady, New York, to make a complete study of the Photophone system. After about a month of study, Pomeroy returned an exceptionally favorable report. General Electric and its commercial agent, RCA, were strong by all criteria: technical, financial, and patent. Thus Kent sat down with David Sarnoff; Owen D. Young, General Electric's chairman of the board; Paul Cravath, RCA's chief counsel; and their assistants to discuss terms. Chief negotiator David Sarnoff proposed an agreement calling for a holding company, one-half owned by RCA and one-half by the five motion picture producers. This agreement was modeled on the aborted Vitaphone proposal. All of General Electric's sound-film patents would be vested in this one company. Sarnoff and Young sought equality in royalties with Western Electric and demanded 8 percent of the gross revenues. When Kent placed this offer before the full committee, the producers countered with demands for individual licenses and a royalty rate of $500 per reel. For an eight-reel film (90 minutes) with gross revenues of $50,000, the $500 per reel charge equaled 8 percent. As gross revenues rose above $50,000, there would be significant savings. For example, if a film grossed $500,000, then at 8 percent the royalty would be $40,000. The per reel cost remained $4,000. Sarnoff and Young easily accepted the per-reel method of calculation, but not the rate. [32]

For several months the two parties exchanged offers and counter offers concerning the royalty rate. The producers saw as the principle advantage of linking with RCA and General Electric the elimination of legal complications with competitors Warner Bros. and Fox. The six producers would have one system, Fox and Warner Bros. another. As these negotiations wore on, the producers decided not to participate in a joint holding company. They wanted *no* part of the machinery manufacturing.

Each desired only a license to produce and distribute sound films. During September and October 1927 the two parties stalemated over this issue.[33]

In November Kent and Bernstein contacted John Otterson. While the producers' committee was bargaining with RCA, Otterson had worked to strengthen his firm's position. In June 1927 he opened negotiations for a license with the president and general manager of the Music Publishers Protective Association (MPPA), Edwin Mills. On 5 September 1927 ERPI signed a five-year contract with the MPPA giving any ERPI licensee use of MPPA's music. The cost was a function of the number of seats in theaters showing the film. Another provision guaranteed MPPA $100,000 the first year, and $125,000 thereafter. Now Otterson could not only offer prospective licensees his system, he could also tender the rights to a necessary factor of production.[34] Simultaneously, Otterson began conducting talks with the Victor Talking Machine Company to market a nonsynchronous sound system. Later—in January 1928—the two parties would sign an informal agreement granting Victor a nonexclusive license to produce discs for musical accompaniment to films. In turn, Victor would assign ERPI and any potential licensees the right to negotiate with artists under its exclusive contract. With the stress on recording musical artists at the time, Otterson was on the road to acquiring yet another valuable linkage.[35]

Upon opening negotiations with Otterson, the producers' committee requested that Pomeroy inspect and report on the Western Electric system at its present stage of development. In January 1928 Pomeroy spent two weeks in Western Electric's laboratories and rendered a very favorable report regarding both the sound-on-disc and the sound-on-film methods. Pomeroy praised the technical and manufacturing operations already present in Western Electric plants[36] (at this time General Electric possessed no manufacturing facilities); yet the committee desired more data. Thus in February 1928 Otterson shipped two complete recording systems to Pomeroy, then stationed at Paramount's Hollywood studio. In the early part of March, just before their final decision, the committee members journeyed to Hollywood to see a complete demonstration. These two systems would remain at Paramount as part of the deal completed in May.[37] All the relevant technical data for both systems was at hand when the producers' agreement expired on 17 February 1928. The members of the producers' committee anticipated making a favorable decision in some form in the next several months.

The situation had changed little in the early part of January when General Electric purchased part interest in FBO to guarantee studio facilities for its system. Late in February the committee began seriously to bargain with Otterson. Early in the negotiation process, Otterson learned the producers' committee would only consent to one direct license per company. He quickly acceded to this major demand. Although the producers' committee was quite happy with Western Electric's quality and scope of manufacturing operations, many specific contractual arrangements remained to be ironed out. The committee demanded assurance that an adequate amount of Western Electric's manufacturing facilities would be devoted to the production of the needed recording and reproduction equipment. The producers knew they would commit large amounts of capital to this new investment; one estimate reached as high as $100 million. Otterson guaranteed Western Electric would make such a commitment.[38]

The producers were satisfied. They decided in early March 1928 to prepare the final contracts to sign with Western Electric. The two parties, complete with numerous assistants and advisors, began to draw up contractual drafts. The film-industry leaders knew they must make a final decision by May to have any effect on the 1928/29 season. Thus a large group of lawyers, engineers, and executives began holding planning sessions. For four months they drafted long-term schedules and created numerous contingencies for all anticipated mistakes or problems. If and when the producers did sign, the leaders of the Big Five wanted to be assured that their firms would be ready and the transition would be effected smoothly.[39] The major consideration remained price—the royalties the producers would pay.

The producers announced they would not enter agreements in which the basis was a fixed percentage of gross receipts. Under no circumstances would they reveal their revenues to Warner Bros. The current Western Electric–Warner Bros. contract required that Vitaphone receive 37½ percent of the royalties paid to ERPI. Moreover, ERPI's experience with Vitaphone had proven that a percentage method only produced insoluble disputes. If a film was a part-talkie, or only had a synchronized score, what part of the gross receipts would be due to sound? The producers would only accept the reel (of positive film ready for distribution) as the measure. The producers offered $250 per reel; Otterson demanded $1,000. Agreement came at $500.[40]

There remained one final hurdle. Under the current Western Electric agreements with Warner Bros. and Fox, ERPI agreed to charge no new customer a royalty rate lower than 8 percent of gross revenue. The $500 per reel was substantially less. Thus Western Electric would either have to reimburse its old customers and lower current rates or break with the contract. Otterson approached Catchings to see if Warner Bros. would negotiate. Catchings refused. Moreover, Vitaphone and ERPI were locked in a complicated arbitration dispute.[41] William Fox, on the other hand, agreed to a royalty readjustment. By the beginning of April 1928 Otterson was sure he could secure the producers at $500 per reel. This amount would guarantee ERPI millions of dollars in royalties. On 6 April Western Electric terminated its contract with Vitaphone and served its former licensee with a counterclaim in the pending arbitration suit charging that Vitaphone had broken the current agreement.[42]

On 17 March 1928 George Pratt, ERPI's chief counsel; Leopold Friedman, Loew's chief counsel; and Louis Swarts began to meet daily to negotiate the final contracts necessary for licenses for Paramount, Loew's, United Artists, and First National. Robert Cochrane and Carl Laemmle were more conservative; Universal would wait until these four signed to open negotiations. PDC had completely dropped out. John J. Murdock, primarily a vaudeville entrepreneur, alone continued to demand that the producers "freeze-out" Warner Bros. and Fox.[43] The writing of the contract took six weeks. David Bernstein and John Otterson monitored the daily sessions, while other executives from Western Electric, other motion picture moguls, and their lawyers and technical advisors frequently attended. On 19 April First National's president, Clifford B. Hawley, leaked word that his company had secured a license from Western Electric. He revealed that First National had even set up a new subsidiary, the Firnatone Corporation, to handle production of its talkies. The web of secrecy was broken and rumors of an impending, total switch to sound spread to all sections of the industry.[44]

The necessary contracts were not ready until 28 April 1928, however. After two weeks to secure final clearance, the official signings occurred on Friday, 11 May 1928. The public announcement came the following Wednesday morning, 16 May. Quickly other producers signed with Western Electric: Hal Roach on 18 May, Christie Film on 20 June, Universal on 18 July, Columbia on 25 September, and in 1929 several other small independent firms.[45] On 10 May 1928 Western Electric executed an agreement with Fox-Case, retroactive to 2 April 1927, settling all pending royalty questions. Immediately thereafter, Otterson opened negotiations with Fox-Case for a license similar to the four granted on 11 May 1928. Fox-Case delayed its decision, but signed on 14 November 1930, effective 11 May 1928. Their decision finally made, the majors turned to implementing their recently constructed long-range plans.[46]

☆

Conclusion

As profit-maximizing oligopolists, the majors reacted to the innovation of sound wisely and sensibly. There was no "Warner-Vitaphone" peril. There had been no "council of war." There was precious little chaos, panic, or confusion in the fall of 1927 or in the spring and summer of 1928. Instead, after initial albeit quite rational reluctance, Famous Players, reacting to the success of the *Don Juan* show, decided to try the new innovation on a limited, trial basis. Complications arose immediately. Western Electric, represented by John Otterson, presented a better alternative. Two months later, RCA, through David Sarnoff, challenged Western Electric. Standardization, investment, patents and technical expertise arose to become problems that demanded further study. The novelty of sound seemingly had run its course, and the film business began a slight downturn.

Consequently, waiting and gathering information became the most rational strategy. The united majors did not want to "squeeze out" Warner Bros. and Fox. They desired to learn from the innovator's actions. These oligopolists could afford the necessary costs for information, while the possibility of their suffering large loss was slight. The majors had the market power in production, distribution, and exhibition to protect themselves. By the beginning of 1928 conditions in the movie business had substantially recovered, and Warner Bros. and Fox's experience with sound indicated "talkies" indeed had a future.

The Big Five used their fifteen months of waiting wisely. They hired technical and legal consultants, bargained for the best terms, and planned for future contingencies. This careful planning would serve them well in 1928 and 1929. After signing, there was no chaos or panic. Instead, all could make the switch very rapidly and increase their profits and economic power.[47] During this period of waiting, the majors had negotiated very reasonable contracts. Shrewdly, the film industry's negotiators played RCA off against Western Electric and secured much more favorable terms than either Fox or Warner Bros. had. Limited payments for sound licenses and equipment were a small price to pay for the vast profits the majors acquired in 1929 and 1930. Subsequently, much more severe economic problems would threaten the financial well-being of these motion picture giants.

Afterword

Written as the first article from my dissertation, this essay represents a youthful effort. Approaching it for the first time since 1976, I was not surprised to find that my thinking had changed, my writing style improved. Yet the basic argument stood the test of time. Flaws can be found, but nowhere near the number I expected. The writing style, in fact, seemed serviceable and straightforward. I must thank the editor for permitting me the chance to address and comment on a five-year-old monograph.

Two principle limitations of this study are apparent to me in 1981. First I failed to spell out my theoretical framework. Implicit are the assumptions of the neoclassical economic theory of technological innovation. Consequently, since the market "worked," the major Hollywood firms did act "wisely and rationally," given their considerable economic power. Their best interest did dictate waiting, collecting information, colluding, and then innovating sound only when they could expect returns greater than those projected with no change. The neoclassical model did provide the necessary framework to construct a significant reinterpretation of an important question in U.S. film history. But in doing so, I assumed away many other crucial issues. Edward Buscombe agrees. See his piece "Sound and Color," *Jump Cut 17* (April 1978), pp. 23–25.

Second, if I were to rewrite this piece now, I would downplay the "straw-man" technique of organization. My point was not to demonstrate how poorly Lewis Jacobs constructed his book, *The Rise of the American Film*. Indeed not. For more than forty years Jacobs' pioneering tome has defined the contours of what we know and teach about American cinema. The "straw-man" technique simply contrasted my re-interpretations with the dominant position. Implicit within my analysis, then, is a respect for Jacobs' work and its place in the field of film history.

Upon rewriting I would also downplay my use of the narrative elements of structure. I did not intend to author yet another exciting tale of business struggle. The individual corporate chieftains matter-of-factly attempted to maximize their corporation's rate of return. Conflicts were resolved by a process of game theory by which each corporation negotiated the optimal solution. This article should be restructured into a case study of the process of technical change by an oligopoly, and not stand so much as a series of business biographies.

One particular statement violates my current sense of proper industrial analysis. In paragraph two I wrote, "[Walter J. Rich] too could not persuade any leader to join with him to form a corporation to create sound films. Only by accident, and with much reluctance on his part, did Rich meet, and agree, in June 1925, to link up with Warner Bros. to form the Vitaphone Corporation." It is the second sentence which does not sit well in 1981. Aside from a problem of style, I do not believe Rich and Harry Warner met "by accident." Elsewhere I describe and analyze, in some detail, how and why Harry Warner sought out all possible investment alternatives. See "Writing the History of the American Film Industry," *Screen* 17, no. 1 (Spring 1976):40–53. Chance may have had a small role in the exact timing, but should be discounted as a significant variable in the process of technical change.

The reader should be aware that I have written six other articles which clarify questions addressed in the "Warner-Vitaphone" peril. A good overview remains "The Coming of the Talkies: Invention, Innovation, and Diffusion," in *The American Film Industry: An Historical Anthology of Readings*, ed. Tino Balio (Madison: Univ. of Wisconsin Pr., 1976), pp. 193–211. For the activities of Fox Film, see "Problems in Film History: How Fox Innovated Sound," *The Quarterly Review of Film Studies* 1, no. 3 (August 1976):315–30. I have also written about RCA. See "Failure and Success: Vocafilm and RCA Innovate Sound," *Film Reader* 2 (January 1977):213–21. To understand what happened after the 11 May 1928 signing I suggest, "Hollywood Converts to Sound: Chaos or Order," in *Sound and the Cinema*, ed. Evan W. Cameron (Pleasantville, N.Y.: Redgrave, 1980):24–37. Finally, for a view of Hollywood's activities abroad in conjunction with sound see "Economic Struggle and Hollywood Imperialism: Europe Converts to Sound," *Yale French Studies* 60 (Winter 1980): 80–93. (This special issue of *Yale French Studies* is devoted to sound: theory, music, case studies, as well as history. Claudia Gorbman has compiled an impressive bibliography, see pp. 269–86. The coming of sound is treated on pp. 275–78.)

Let me stress that my approach to the coming of sound does not stand alone. Indeed, many scholars have analyzed technical change in the cinema. In *Film Reader* IV, Edward Brannigan has productively compared my methods to the theories and approaches of other historians: Terry Ramsaye, Patrick Ogle, and Jean-Louis Comolli. See "Color and Cinema: Problems in the Writing of History," *Film Reader* IV (1979):16–34, especially the chart on p. 29.

Finally, I think the work in this article ought to be extended in several ways. I'll elaborate on only two in this paragraph. First, we should seek to understand more completely the role of the Academy of Motion Picture Arts and Sciences in the process of this technological change. How did this institution function to mediate disputes and serve as a clearinghouse for information? These questions lead to a puzzle concerning the role of organized labor in the switchover to sound. I describe in the "Warner-Vitaphone Peril" article how the major Hollywood corporations suppressed unionization of actors. But what of other employees? Particularly, I would seek information on the activities of the IATSE. My dissertation ("The Coming of Sound to the American Cinema: A History of the Transformation of an Industry," Univ. of Wisconsin-Madison, 1975) touches on this important organization, but much more research remains to be done.

One cannot expect to resolve all questions of the switchover to sound in one eight-page article. Certainly that is why I continue to research and write about this complex technological transformation in particular and about the process of technological change in the mass media in general. A more extensive study of the innovation of sound would presumably, without sacrificing interest, tell the reader more about the method and theories that can be employed and acknowledge areas for further research.

The Demise of Kinemacolor

Gorham Kindem

Film historians generally agree that Kinemacolor was a significant development in the early history of color motion pictures, but they disagree about why its success was so short-lived. American and British film historians Terry Ramsaye, Rachael Low, Adrian Cornwell-Clyne, and D. B. Thomas each characterize Kinemacolor as the first successful photographic color-motion-picture process. But they offer slightly different explanations for the limited duration of its success. Ramsaye's portrayal of Kinemacolor focuses upon Charles Urban, the American impresario who promoted Kinemacolor throughout the world, and he suggests that the source of Urban's difficulties was the Motion Picture Patents Company, whose disinterest in Kinemacolor prevented him from deeply penetrating American markets.[1] Low examines Kinemacolor's legal problems in Great Britain and argues that the loss of George Albert Smith's original 1906 patent in 1914 forced Urban to voluntarily initiate the liquidation of Kinemacolor's assets.[2] Cornwell-Clyne concentrates upon the technical deficiencies of early additive color processes, including Kinemacolor, and argues that they were all destined to fail, because they were technologically inadequate and perceptually disconcerting.[3] To the technological and legal problems that Kinemacolor encountered about 1915, D. B. Thomas adds economic and aesthetic problems of supply and demand, like the fact that over 70 percent of all British Kinemacolor footage available in 1914 was nonfiction, i.e., newsreel and travel films, and therefore deficient in popular dramatic films and that there were too few Kinemacolor films overall to offer a high-quality, varied, twice-weekly change of program to film exhibitors.[4]

The evidence I have gathered from exhibitor trade papers and other sources indicates that each of these explanations is at least partially valid. Kinemacolor's demise can be attributed to several sets of negative factors: technological, legal, economic, and aesthetic. The deaths of The

136

Natural Color Kinematograph Company, Ltd., in Great Britain and Kinemacolor of America, Inc. (separate but related companies), in 1914 were undoubtedly hastened by the conjunction of technical and economic problems inherent in Kinemacolor production and exhibition, the loss of Smith's British patent, the rising popularity of dramatic feature films (which at Kinemacolor were in short supply), and potential difficulties in international distribution and exhibition accompanying the onset of World War I, although the impact of the war is difficult to assess. Determining the precise contribution of each of these factors to the demise of Kinemacolor is extremely difficult and highly speculative, however, given the paucity of hard evidence that currently exists.

Kinemacolor Technology and Two-Color Theory

Many of the legal and economic difficulties that eventually consumed Kinemacolor have their roots in the specifications for the process G. A. Smith, the Brighton filmmaker/inventor, patented in 1906. British patent No. 26671 was for "improvements in relating to Kinematographic apparatus for the production of coloured pictures."

> An animated picture of a coloured scene is taken with a bioscope camera in the usual way, except that a revolving shutter is used fitted with properly adjusted red and green colour screens. A negative is thus obtained in which the reds and yellows are recorded in one picture, and the greens and yellows (with some blue) in the second, and so on alternately throughout the length of the bioscope film.
>
> A positive picture is made from the above negative and projected by the ordinary projecting machine which, however, is fitted with a revolving shutter furnished with somewhat similar coloured glasses to the above, and so contrived that the red and green pictures are projected alternately through their appropriate colour glasses.
>
> If the speed of projection is approximately 30 pictures per second, the two colour records blend and present to the eye a satisfactory rendering of the subject in colours which appear to be natural.
>
> The novelty of my method lies in the use of two colours only, red and green, combined with the principle of persistence of vision.[5]

In his patent application Smith described the technical and perceptual difficulties inherent in previous attempts to produce natural-color motion pictures with three-color records and argued that two colors, "a certain two, red and green, were sufficient" to have motion pictures exhibited "so as to have the appearance of being in natural colours," that were "apparently" correct. As *The Bioscope*, a major British trade paper, pointed out soon after the first exhibition of Kinemacolor films in 1908, "Messrs. Urban and Smith do not profess to take photographs of subjects in their natural colours, but by the process just described the effects on the eyes of the spectator are as if this had been obtained."[6]

Proponents of classical color theory from Isaac Newton and Thomas Young to many contemporary perceptual psychologists have argued that the reproduction of all natural colors requires *three* different colored lights: red, green, and blue. James Clerk Maxwell put classical color theory into practice when he demonstrated the feasibility of three-color photography in about 1865. Maxwell recorded an original scene through three different color filters attached to three separate cameras on black and white film and then projected the developed positives through their respective color filters onto a single screen. Almost all subsequent experimentation with natural color motion pictures prior to Kinemacolor attempted to apply Maxwell's three-color additive photographic process to motion pictures.

The technical difficulties inherent in three-color additive motion pictures were virtually insurmountable at the turn of the century. In order to produce three-color motion pictures, three separate color records had to be recorded and projected simultaneously in precise registration or consecutively with sufficient speed to fuse the three images into one multiple color scene through persistence of vision. The visual impact of the former could be destroyed by the slightest misalignment, and the rapid film-transport speed required for the latter invariably caused the film to shred. The technological limitations of additive color processes, which are delineated by Cornwell-Clyne in the following quotation, help to explain why this technological innovation was eventually displaced by subtractive processes. "The defects of the additive method were soon obvious to all; the audience suffered from excessive eyestrain, a phenomenon always associated with colour admixture by persistence of vision if the recurrence is only just above the flicker limit of sixteen alternations of the quality of the stimulus per second. The projection speed of 32 pictures per second used for Kinemacolor necessitated a special projector and the life of the film was short."[7] Whether or not additive motion picture color processes caused more eyestrain than conventional black and white films of the period is not clear, although the problem of color fringing (the discrepancy in stopped motion between two adjacent color frames) probably was extremely disconcerting to audiences.[8]

G. A. Smith's solution to some of the technical problems of three-color additive processes presented a direct challenge to classical color theory. His Kinemacolor process attempted to fuse only two color records into one natural color scene through persistence of vision. To accomplish this, panchromatic (red sensitized) black and white film was exposed through alternating red and green filters and then projected at double normal silent speed. During his presentation to the Royal Arts Society on 8 December 1908, Smith argued that two color records seemed to give a range of color equal to three.[9]

The validity of Smith's claim that two color records provide a range of color equal to three is still in doubt today. In the 1950s and 1970s Edwin H. Land experimented with two color photography and attempted to demonstrate that two color records, a long wavelength and a short wavelength, were sufficient to transmit the full range of colors of an original scene.[10] While some contemporary perceptual psychologists agree that there is an "illusion" of multiple color in Land's projected scenes, many argue that the limited saturation of the colors is explained by perceptual processes and optical illusions that do not contradict classical color theory.[11] They argue that even if the eye is fooled into thinking that a wide range of colors is present, the colors only exist in the mind's eye and are much less saturated and more limited in range than three-color projections would be.

Smith's invention and two-color theory were even more controversial in the early 1900s than Land's experiments are today. Many competitors and other inventors doubted that Smith's claims were scientifically valid. By 1911 several competitors began blatantly to infringe upon his patent, and a lack of scientific credibility for his invention did little to discourage them from doing so. Eventually, the disputes over rival claims to two-color motion picture inventions had to be decided in the courts.

Patent Law, Two-Color Technology, and the Dissolution of the Natural Color Kinematograph Company, Ltd.

Rachael Low has demonstrated that by 1911 many of Kinemacolor's competitors had begun to infringe upon Smith's patent with impunity. "Bio-color," a color process invented by William Friese-Green and financially backed by S. F. Edge, published the following challenge in an advertisement in *The Bioscope.* "No attention whatever need be paid to idle threats of legal proceedings. We have been advised by eminent counsel that such threats cannot possibly be enforced."[12] The American Correspondent for *The Bioscope* had publicly declared much earlier that Smith's patent had little or no value. "I do not hesitate to say that the patent as it is published is worthless. In other words, that it would not stand the test of a contest in the courts backed by scientific evidence. That being the case, one of the principle assets of the Kinemacolor Company is of doubtful value."[13] Other competitors found justification for adapting two-color technology to their own purposes in these direct challenges to Kinemacolor. A series of suits and countersuits flooded the courts and bylines of *The Bioscope* until December 1913, when Bioschemes, a competitor owned by S. F. Edge, petitioned for the revocation of Smith's 1906 patent.[14]

This petition was heard before Mr. Justice Warrington on 8, 9, 11, and 12 December before it was dismissed. But Bioschemes persisted in their attack upon Kinemacolor and obtained a hearing with Lord Justice Buckley and the Court of Appeal on 20, 23, 24, and 25 March. Justice Buckley reversed Warrington's decision and revoked Smith's patent on 1 April 1914, staying the order for one month, pending appeal to the House of Lords. Although the matter was eventually brought before the House of Lords, Buckley's decision was upheld.

Justice Buckley argued that Smith's patent failed accurately to specify the color filters that would successfully record and project all natural colors. Smith had indicated that red and green filters were sufficient, and Buckley interpreted the filters Smith intended to be tristimulus red and green, respectively, which were in frequent use in 1906. Between 1906 and 1914, however, Smith and Urban experimented with a variety of different color filters.[15] Projections of objects recorded through tristimulus red and green filters failed to reproduce the color blue. When a "clear red" filter was used, however, the color blue could apparently be reproduced, but Buckley argued that since the filters specified in the patent were tristimulus red and green and these failed to reproduce *all* natural colors, specifically blue, that Smith's patent was inaccurate and hence invalid. He further argued that if Smith intended just any shade of red or green, then his patent was invalid because some red and green filters did not work at all, and that if he intended any two filters that happened to work, his patent was insufficient, and his invention unpatentable.[16] Although the patent suit had been initiated on the grounds of prior use of the two-color process by Friese-Green and others, its resolution was effected by the determination that Smith's two-color process was unpatentable.

The loss of Smith's patent appears to have been catastrophic to Charles

Urban. Within one month he voluntarily initiated the liquidation of The Natural Color Kinematograph Company, Ltd.'s assets to pay off his creditors. Urban then left England for America just before the outbreak of World War I.

The Natural Color Kinematograph Company, Ltd., had begun operations on 16 March 1909 with £30,000 of capital. Between 1911 and 1914 it had profits of £37,000 on receipts of £300,000. Patent rights sold abroad brought in £100,000, and foreign exhibition rights brought in about £21,000 during this period.[17] When Urban initiated his company's liquidation, The Natural Color Kinematograph Company, Ltd., had assets of £150,000 and liabilities of £64,000.[18] The loss of its patent undoubtedly reduced the value of many of its assets, especially the value of color films Kinemacolor maintained for lease and the rights to its color process which it sold throughout the world.

There can be no doubt that Kinemacolor's financial stability and virtual monopoly on photographic color in Great Britain and France depended upon the maintenance of this patent, but it is not at all clear that the demise of Kinemacolor internationally can be entirely attributed to its revocation. For example, one of Kinemacolor's liabilities in April 1914 was £4,000 for half a year's rent at Urban's Paris theater that was past due, and the chairman of the liquidation indicated that this venture had been quite unsuccessful since its opening in December 1913. His Parisian venture cost Urban about £40,000.[19] The Paris theater, which closed in May 1919, was relatively small, charged high admission prices, and was not optimally located.

In short, in 1914 British Kinemacolor encountered financial difficulties with exhibition, attributable, in part, to theater location and exhibition policy, but also undoubtedly caused by its failure to sustain a supply of popular films, like the two-and-one-half hour *Delhi Durbar* newsreel, which grossed more than £150,000 between February 1912 and May 1913.[20] According to D. B. Thomas, Urban was negatively predisposed to the production of "artificial" dramas, and "Kinemacolor was unable to repeat the success of the Delhi Durbar Film with any of its dramatic productions or photoplays."[21]

☆
Kinemacolor's Problems in America

Terry Ramsaye has written at length about Urban's early difficulties with the Motion Picture Patents Company in America and has suggested that Kinemacolor's demise should be attributed in large part to its failure to penetrate American markets. But Ramsaye's account is misleading. Urban in fact sold his U.S. patents outright to Kinemacolor of America for £40,000 in the spring of 1910,[22] and this American company succeeded in forging an agreement with the Patents Co. in 1913.

Kinemacolor of America began a major advertising campaign on 12 October 1912.[23] Over three hundred films had been produced in America in preparation for this event. Kinemacolor enlisted the services of three East Coast production companies, one traveling company, and two dramatic companies in Los Angeles. Many talented performers were brought under contract, including Linda Arvidson Griffith, the former Mrs. D. W. Griffith.[24] In 1912 and 1913 Linda A. Griffith was featured in two major Kinemacolor productions, *The Scarlet Letter* and *The Clansman*, the latter of which was aborted and eventually picked up by D. W. Griffith.[25]

Kinemacolor of America had secured 416 applications for film service only one week after it began offering services in 1912,[26] which attests to its initial popularity, and it eventually signed an agreement with the Motion Picture Patents Company to lease color films and projectors as a licensed supplier on 4 August 1913 (3 Record 1335–51).[27] The Patents Company agreement followed contracts for Kinemacolor films signed by the F. F. Proctor chain of theaters and then by William Fox in April 1913,[28] which suggests that competition with independent exhibitors encouraged the MPPC to sanction the use of Kinemacolor films by its licensees.

Kinemacolor encountered marketing and managerial problems in America despite the fact that it secured access to Patents' licensees. It may have been difficult to persuade exhibitors that there was a sufficient demand for Kinemacolor films to justify the added expense and difficulties involved in removing their conventional projectors each time a Kinemacolor film and projector was leased. In November 1913 Kinemacolor of America, Inc., began selling rather than leasing its projectors.[29] Up until this time its marketing strategy had been to lease Kinemacolor films to one exhibitor in each locale. In England in 1913 a 3,000-foot program, including a projector and operator, which changed twice each week, cost £20 a week in London and £25 outside of London.[30] In America Kinemacolor services cost $20 + a week.[31]

Kinemacolor began selling its projectors in America for $200 to $300 installed, and the same projector could also be used for conventional black-and-white films. But exhibitors may have felt that there was an insufficient demand for Kinemacolor films or an insufficient supply of good dramatic Kinemacolor films to justify the added expense and trouble of acquiring new projectors. In any case, by the end of 1913, Kinemacolor ceased advertising in American exhibition trade papers altogether. In January 1914 Urban made an unscheduled trip to America to sever relations with Kinemacolor of America Vice-President William H. Hickey and publicly announced this action in *Moving Picture World*.[32] In June 1914 an advertisement in *Variety* indicated that the space and production equipment previously used by Kinemacolor in the Mecca Building was available for rent.[33]

Precisely why Kinemacolor of America failed may ultimately remain a mystery, but the scant evidence that currently exists suggests that several factors played important roles in its demise. There was probably a shortage of product—particularly dramatic films for which audience demands were intensifying—like that which existed for British Kinemacolor. The Italian features *Quo Vadis* and *Cabiria* were released in 1913 and 1914, and a strong demand for longer and longer American dramatic films was clearly evident during this period.[34] Dramatic feature-film production magnified the technical deficiencies of Kinemacolor. Twice as much film had to be expended for Kinemacolor as for black-and-white and the film stock had to be chemically treated to be panchromatically sensitive to red light. In common use after 1912, Cooper-Hewitt mercury vapor lighting was very strong on blue light, and this presented difficulties for interior studio production with Kinemacolor.[35] In addition, exhibitors had to be convinced that there was a sufficient supply of[36] and demand for dramatic Kinemacolor films to justify that added expense and technical difficulties of color projection. Managerial conflict between Charles Urban and William H. Hickey severed relations between The Natural Color Kinematograph Company, Ltd., and Kinemacolor of America, Inc., early in 1914, although the two companies had cooperated on film productions like *The Rivals*, in 1913. Finally, it is not at all clear that the dramatic productions offered by Kinemacolor in America and Britain were commercially or critically successful. What evidence does exist suggests that Kinemacolor news documentaries were more successful than the dramatic productions,[37] although the public demand for dramatic feature films generally increased from 1910 to 1915. In short, the failure of Kinemacolor of America was probably caused by the conjunction of negative technological, economic, legal, and aesthetic factors: the technical deficiencies of color recording and projection; the limited supply of and inferior quality of dramatic color films; the loss of Smith's British patent and the dissolution of The Natural Color Kinematograph Company, Ltd.; and Kinemacolor's failure consistently to make color a vital part of commercially and critically successful motion pictures.

In any case, when Urban returned to America just before the outbreak of World War I, he became involved in the production of black-and-white newsreels and scientific documentaries.[38] Kinemacolor of America forfeited its California charter in 1916 for failure to pay back taxes[39] but continued to exist until 1924. Although it was probably commercially defunct in 1914 and never regained its previous stature and commercial success, Kinemacolor of America's primary inventor/researcher William F. Fox, did succeed in improving the process by patenting a new Kinemacolor process in 1918.[40] But these technological improvements were inconsequential in terms of the history of color motion pictures.

Kinemacolor's Contribution to Color-Film History

Kinemacolor played a significant role in film history, not because it made a major contribution to color-motion-picture technology, but because its promoter/owner, Charles Urban, initially demonstrated that a significant market existed for color films, specifically color news and documentary films. Subsequent inventors and entrepreneurs were undoubtedly motivated by the hope that significant profits could be made by offering color services to film producers and color films to audiences throughout the world, especially when a technologically superior process demonstrated the commercial value of color for dramatic as well as documentary films.

Soon after Kinemacolor lost its original patent, color technology began to change and the use of alternating color filters was abandoned entirely. Two-color additive color printing and three-color simultaneous projection methods were the technological heirs apparent to Kinemacolor internationally.[41] But no color process appears to have rivaled the early commercial success of Kinemacolor until Technicolor patented and successfully marketed its subtractive, imbibition dye-transfer process in the mid- to late 1920s. The major technological innovations which succeeded Kinemacolor, i.e., Technicolor and Eastmancolor,[42] obviously benefited from an understanding of Smith and Urban's earlier mistakes. The technological, legal, economic, and aesthetic factors that brought about Kinemacolor's demise were consciously and successfully avoided by Technicolor and Eastman Kodak (Eastmancolor). Technicolor and Eastman Kodak were able to maintain their major color patents for a much longer period of time than Kinemacolor (taken together, for over fifty consecutive years compared to eight years). Unlike Kinemacolor, Technicolor and Eastman Kodak never overextended their financial resources or competed with prospective clients by becoming deeply involved in film production. Instead, they successfully marketed color services to all film producers who wanted and could afford them. In addition, Technicolor films by major producers in the 1930s, like *The Wizard of Oz* and *Gone with the Wind*, clearly demonstrated the commercial value of color for dramatic films. Technologically, Kinemacolor was simply not as significant an innovation as either Technicolor or Eastmancolor. Economically, however, Kinemacolor's successful demonstration of a potential world market for photographic color motion pictures requires that it be allocated more than a footnote in the history of world cinema.

Hollywood's Conversion to Color:
The Technological, Economic, and
Aesthetic Factors

Gorham Kindem

The near total conversion to color in the U.S. film industry between the late 1920s through the 1960s depended on three conditions: technological innovation, economic incentives, and public acceptance. In the early 1930s, unfavorable technological, economic, and aesthetic conditions prevailed, and the use of two-color Technicolor declined almost to nonexistence. Between 1935 and 1955, three-color feature films gradually increased from less than 1 percent to more than 50 percent of the total U.S. output.

Production/distribution costs and potential exhibition markets were economic factors that directly affected the rate of Hollywood's conversion to color film, and it was not until the 1950s that most technological and economic factors favored color over black-and-white films. Between 1955 and 1958 the film industry produced mostly black-and-white films to supply the new television market, which used black-and-white films almost exclusively. Television's conversion to color in the mid- to late 1960s opened up new markets for color feature films (between 1966 and 1970, U.S.-produced color feature films increased from 54 percent to 94 percent); and when network news programs began broadcasting in color in 1965–67, the old associations of color for fantasy and black-and-white for reality no longer obtained.

Color Technology: The Major Inventions

Technicolor and Eastmancolor were major technological inventions for color feature filmmaking. In 1928 Technicolor, Inc., offered a new two-color printing process, and in 1932 it offered a three-color recording and printing process. In 1950, Eastman Kodak marketed its own three-color recording and printing process, Eastmancolor, which greatly simplified color recording and printing. All three of these inventions had a significant impact upon color feature film production.

Technicolor's two-color process solved several technical problems of color films simultaneously. Although 80 percent to 90 percent of all U.S. features in the early 1920s were printed on tinted film,[1] Hollywood's conversion to sound had impeded the proliferation of nonphotographic[2] color processes. Tinting and toning of prints chemically affected the sound track and reduced its overall audio quality. Technicolor's imbibition, dye-transfer process, which basically combined lithography and photography, did not affect the sound track. It also produced prints which were more durable than earlier cemented or double-emulsioned processes, which were alternatives available before the coming of sound (1927), two-color Technicolor (1928), and Kodak Sonochrome, a viable nonphotographic tinted positive film with sound (1929).

In 1932 Technicolor greatly improved the predictability and accuracy of color recording and printing when it offered its three-color process. This three-color process involved a special camera that divided the light coming into the camera so that three separate black-and-white films could record virtually all colors of the spectrum. Each color record would subsequently be transferred to one color print by the same imbibition, dye-transfer process used previously for two-color Technicolor. Technicolor's camera was quite large and required a great deal of light to expose three black-and-white films simultaneously; but the accuracy of Technicolor's process set a rigorous standard for color quality and allowed Technicolor to maintain a virtual monopoly over three-color feature-film services until Eastmancolor appeared in the 1950s.

Eastmancolor greatly simplified color recording and printing, and increased the supply of color available for color feature-film production, since photographic recording on Eastmancolor could be accomplished in conventional black-and-white cameras. This was possible because three-color records were recorded in three different layers of the same film. Like black-and-white, but unlike Technicolor, Eastmancolor was a photochemical printing and processing process. The advantage of Eastmancolor over Technicolor in this respect was that Eastmancolor prints could be made on conventional black-and-white printing machines. Printing and processing facilities proliferated and color supply increased as independent and studio color laboratories adopted Eastmancolor. By the early 1960s, Eastmancolor original film stocks appeared which had a sensitivity to light nearly equivalent to that of black-and-white films and greatly reduced the amount of light necessary for color feature-film production.

Color Economics: Invention, Innovation, and Diffusion

A theory of technological innovation[3] suggests that companies apply new technologies (through invention, innovation, and imitation) to maximize their long-term profits. Invention, by which companies discover and patent new technologies through investment in research; innovation, by which manufacturing and marketing of products resulting from research are accomplished; and imitation, or diffusion, by which competitors manufacture and market similar products—these are the three stages of technological innovation necessary for corporate growth and expansion.

In the specific case of color technologies for feature filmmaking, the companies which invented new color technology were not always directly involved in feature-film production. Color feature-film innovations involved a two-step process from technological innovation among the suppliers of professional film products and services (Eastman Kodak and Technicolor) to technological innovation among feature-film producers.

The Economics of Invention

Investments for research and development of inventions often cause small firms (e.g. Technicolor, Inc.) to take proportionately greater risks than large firms (e.g. Eastman Kodak). Although Technicolor, Inc., accumulated a net loss of $2 million between 1923 and 1935,[4] it continued to invest heavily in research and development, with such investment amounting to $180,000 in 1931.[5] Despite the fact that the firm possessed a virtual monopoly on three-color processes for feature films throughout the 1930s, it did not actually profit after taxes until 1939.[6]

Eastman Kodak, on the other hand, invested over $15 million in color photographic research between 1921 and 1948, but it also had net sales of $435 million in 1948, compared to Technicolor's $20 million. During the same year Eastman Kodak also secured its major patents for colored couplers[7] for Eastmancolor, while it invested $3 million in color research.[8] Obviously, Eastman Kodak never undertook financial risks proportionately equal to Technicolor's in its quest for a virtual monopoly over film color through patent protection of its major inventions.

In the late 1920s and early 1930s Technicolor's inventions and the circumstances surrounding them differed greatly from those of Eastman Kodak in the late 1940s. Technicolor, Inc., was an offshoot of Kalmus, Comstock, and Westcott, a small engineering, research, and consulting firm, and Technicolor's major inventions were superior feats of engineering. Kodak's major inventions resolved longstanding photochemical problems. Simplifying color filmmaking and printing through photochemistry involved chemical-dye research that was well beyond the means of a relatively small firm, like Technicolor. In the late 1940s, Eastman Kodak's major competitors were Du Pont and General Aniline and Film Corporation (Ansco). Eastman Kodak was undertaking color-film research for several potential markets, not the least of which was consumer products. Technicolor, with a market limited to color services for the feature-film industry, did not really diversify as a corporation until the 1960s. Despite its emphasis on engineering, its relatively small size, and its desperate economic straits, Technicolor secured patents for and marketed color services of such quality that it dominated the field of color services for feature film for almost twenty years.

The Economics of Feature-Film Innovation

Since its inception, Technicolor has strived to provide color services of optimal quality for the entire feature-film industry; and although it became involved in feature-film production to a limited degree, it never competed in that area of the business, preferring simply to demonstrate the technological, economic, and aesthetic viability of its color processes. In turn color feature-film producers made few innovations in color-film technology. The split between suppliers of professional products or services and feature-film producers is still widely maintained. For example, film laboratories today do not wish to compete with prospective clients, and film producers are only rarely able to sustain enough volume to justify the maintenance of their own laboratories. Technicolor's ability to sell color services depended on demonstration of the viability of its color process; and when producers did not wish to risk their capital in such investments, Technicolor supported the cost of technological innovation and also enhanced the attractiveness of the agreement by certain incentives, such as the promise of exclusive rights to its process for a given period and occasionally becoming directly involved in feature-film production. Two- and three-color feature-film innovation occurred in three steps: color shorts, color sequences in black-and-white features, and full-color features; and although the firm became financially involved in the production of two-color shorts and a two-color feature, its direct involvement in three-color innovation was limited to the promise of exclusive rights to its three-color process.

Technicolor's early failure to attract a film producer willing to innovate an all two-color feature led to its own involvement in feature-film production. In 1928, Technicolor began producing color shorts, one of which accompanied Chaplin's *Circus* all over the world. By 1929, Warner Bros. and MGM were actively involved in the production of two-color Technicolor shorts.[9] They also began to use two-color Technicolor for color sequences within black-and-white features, like *The Desert Song* and *Broadway Melody*, which encouraged an association between two-color Technicolor and musicals. But before Jack Warner signed a contract to produce twenty features in full two-color Technicolor, Technicolor had begun production on its own all two-color feature, *The Viking*.

Warner Bros.' early success with two-color feature-film innovation stimulated a premature conversion to color. Warner's decision to innovate all two-color features may well have been influenced by Technicolor's *Viking*, which was not actually released until six months after Warner Bros. premiered the first all talking (singing), all two-color feature, *On with the Show*, in May 1929. Warner Bros.' second all-color feature, *Gold Diggers of Broadway*, was released in August of the same year and grossed over $3.5 million, placing it among the top six all-time grossers of its day.[10] By the time *The Viking*, which lacked a synchronous soundtrack, appeared in November, the point that Technicolor had sought to demonstrate by producing *The Viking*, namely that its color process was commercially viable, had already been made. In 1929 and 1930, Technicolor was overwhelmed with new clients. But producers began to have doubts about the value of two-color films in the early 1930s. Audiences were declining, production budgets were being cut, and musicals, the genre with which two-color Technicolor had become so closely associated,[11] were suddenly considered box-office poison.[12] Technicolor also had difficulty expanding rapidly enough to meet both the quantity and the quality of color producers demanded.[13] By 1932 feature-film producers had all but abandoned two-color Technicolor.

In 1932, Technicolor began marketing a new color process, three-color Technicolor. Producers' skepticism about this new process was ag-

Table 9.1. *Technological Economic and Aesthetic Factors That Favored Either Color or Black-and-White*

Decade	Simplicity	Predictability	Availability	Production & Distribution Costs	Theatrical Markets	Television Markets	Fantasy	Reality
1920s	B&W	B&W	B&W	B&W	?		Color	B&W
1930s	B&W	=	B&W	B&W	?		Color	B&W
1940s	B&W	=	B&W	B&W	Color		Color	B&W
1950s	B&W	=	=	B&W	Color	=	Color	B&W
1960s	=	=	=	B&W	Color	Color	Color	Color

Sources: Technological Factors:
    Journal of the Society of Motion Picture and Television Engineers
    American Cinematographer
    Film Daily Yearbook
Economic Factors:
    Film Daily Yearbook
    Variety
    International Motion Picture Almanac
    Television Almanac
    Broadcasting
    JSMPTE
Aesthetic Factors:
    Variety (Gross Distributor Receipts for each year)
    Academy Awards
    American Film Institute *Feature Film Catalogues*

gravated by their previous disenchantment with two-color Technicolor, and Technicolor, Inc., again had difficulty finding a producer willing to innovate a full three-color feature film. Instead of becoming directly involved in film production again, Technicolor offered contractual incentives to two small, independent producers, Walt Disney and Pioneer Films which was owned and operated by Merian C. Cooper and John Whitney.

Technicolor offered Walt Disney the exclusive rights to its three-color process for cartoons from 1932 to 1935. The first three-color Technicolor shorts to be produced and released were Disney's "Silly Symphonies." Disney won Academy Awards for both *Flowers and Trees* and *The Three Little Pigs*, and the latter grossed a quarter of a million dollars and cost only $22,000 to produce.[14] Major studios demanded color for their own cartoons, but they had to wait until 1935 to use three-color Technicolor. By 1934, however, MGM, Twentieth, and Goldwyn were using three-color for sequences in black-and-white films, like *The Cat and the Fiddle*, *The House of Rothschild*, and *Kid Millions*, respectively.[15]

A salient feature of both full two- and three-color feature-film innovations is that the producers who innovated in each case were either previously or subsequently involved in feature-film technological innovations. Innovators of one feature-film technology often innovate another. Warner Bros.' previous feature-film innovation of sound is paralleled by Merian C. Cooper's feature-film innovation of Cinerama subsequent to three-color feature-film innovation. That Warner Bros. did not innovate three-color Technicolor after it had grown to major-studio status, on the other hand, adds support to the contention that large firms often react more conservatively to the risks of feature-film innovation than small firms.

Successful demonstration of three-color's commercial value for features was not immediately obtained. Encouraged by its success with *La Cucaracha*, a three-color short produced in 1934 at a cost of $80,000 which returned a quarter of a million dollars,[16] Pioneer Films completed the first all three-color feature film, *Becky Sharp*, in 1935. Pioneer had signed a contract filled with qualifying clauses with Technicolor in 1933 to produce eight full three-color Technicolor feature films. *Becky Sharp*'s relative lack of commercial success encouraged Cooper and Whitney to join forces with another producer, David O. Selznick, and establish Selznick International, which eventually took over the contract with Technicolor. While other producers adopted three-color Technicolor in feature films with more success than Pioneer Films, it was three extremely successful color features in three successive years by Selznick—*A Star Is*

Born (1937), *The Adventures of Tom Sawyer* (1938), and *Gone with the Wind* (1939)—that clearly established the economic viability of three-color Technicolor.

The Economics of Color Diffusion

Following the commercial success of Selznick's color feature films in the late 1930s, three economic factors continued to limit color feature-film diffusion: Technicolor's virtual monopoly over three-color services for feature films, the high cost of color, and limited markets for color. Technicolor's virtual monopoly over three-color limited the supply of color which was available for feature-film production. Despite the fact that disgruntled producers and others succeeded in initiating an antitrust suit against Technicolor and Eastman Kodak in the mid-1940s, claiming that the two conspired to limit color supplies and specifically delayed the availability of monopack (multilayered color film), it is not at all clear that Technicolor intentionally limited supplies of color to maximize its profits. In fact, evidence suggests that Technicolor's growth was hampered by wartime shortages of materials and supplies and postwar labor strikes.[17] A 1960 study of the effects of the consent decrees in regard to Eastman Kodak in 1948 and Technicolor in 1950[18] suggests that the decrees had little to do with the availability of Eastmancolor monopack film. Post-decree research and patents not covered by the decrees, it was concluded, led to the availability of Eastmancolor and the elimination of Technicolor's virtual monopoly over three-color filmmaking, which was followed by Eastman Kodak's virtual monopoly over color film and chemicals. It seems clear that had Eastmancolor been available in the 1940s or had Technicolor been willing or able to make its color services more generally available, more color feature films would have been made.

The high cost of feature-film production and distribution in Technicolor inhibited three-color diffusion. In 1935 it was estimated that color added 30 percent[19] to the production costs of an average feature (the average negative cost of features in 1935 was less than $300,000).[20] In 1949 it was estimated that using Technicolor added about $100,000 or 10 percent[21] to the production costs of an average feature (which was about $1 million).[22] During the 1940s the distribution cost differential between color and black-and-white feature-film distribution increased. The cost of Technicolor release prints increased from about five cents per foot in 1940 to about seven cents per foot in 1949, while the cost of black-and-white prints remained about the same, almost three cents per foot.[23] In short, in terms of both production and distribution, it was obviously much less expensive to use black-and-white for a feature film than color, and hence, the cost differential between color and black-and-white limited color feature-film diffusion during the 1940s.

The markets for color were not significantly greater for color features than for black-and-white features in the 1940s and 1950s. Of the top-grossing films for each year from 1940 to 1949, five and one-half were in black-and-white and four and one-half were in Technicolor.[24] In 1948 *Variety* estimated that color added about 25 percent to a feature film's earning power.[25] Were this estimate true a film would need distributor rentals of close to $1 million to pay back an estimated $100,000 in additional production costs, plus perhaps almost an equal amount for additional distribution costs, and make $50,000 more than the same feature in black-and-white. According to *Variety*'s gross distributor receipts for 1948,[26] about 50 percent of all features had receipts of $1 million or more, and *Film Daily Yearbook* estimated the average negative cost of feature films at about $1 million in 1948.[27]

While many economic and aesthetic factors complicate this over-simplified picture of color markets, it seems safe to conclude that there was still some uncertainty about the market value of color versus black-and-white as a factor of commercial success. It is doubtful that even a 25 percent increase in revenues would justify the added expense of color in medium- to low-budget feature films. Producer uncertainty about the commercial value of color in the thirties, forties, and fifties[28] undoubtedly placed limits upon color feature-film diffusion.

In the mid-1950s, television began to exert relatively complex market pressure upon the feature-film industry. In the late 1940s and early 1950s producers responded to a decline in audiences by cutting production budgets,[29] but major studios still promoted color as a competitive advantage over television.[30] By 1954 Warner Bros. and other major studios were consciously making fewer but higher-budgeted pictures to attract audiences back into the theaters.[31] In 1956 the feature-film industry began to sell its pre-1948 features to television;[32] and although audiences continued to decline at theaters, to some extent because of competition from television, black-and-white television at the same time began to offer new markets for feature films. Color offered no distinct advantage over black-and-white in an attempt to cut costs without jeopardizing television markets. Despite the fact that Eastmancolor had increased the supply of color and cut some of the production costs, color feature-film production declined in the mid-1950s[33] while black-and-white production increased.

Television's conversion to color had a definite economic impact upon color feature-film production. The major shift to network color began in

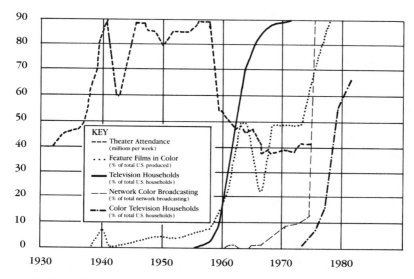

Fig. 9.1. The effects of theater attendance and television on the conversion of feature films to color

Sources:

Theater Attendance:
  Historical Statistics of the United States, 1978 Edition

Feature Films in Color 1938–70:
  Film Daily Yearbooks, 1938–1955
  Screen World, 1950–1970

Technicolor Features 1928–38:
  American Film Institute Feature Film Catalogue, 1921–1930
  JSMPTE (Herbert Kalmus, "Technicolor: Adventures in Cinemaland," Dec. 1938

Television and Color Television Households:
  Television Almanac
  Historical Statistics of the United States

Network Color Broadcasting:
  Broadcasting

1965, although NBC had gradually been increasing its color broadcasting since 1954. NBC's affiliation with RCA in part explains its devotion to color, since RCA was simultaneously promoting color through sales of color sets and color broadcasting. An extremely close competition between all three networks and a disclosure by several ratings companies that color set owners watched more television and preferred color programming[34] raised NBC's overall ratings and stimulated ABC and CBS to adopt color and eliminate NBC's competitive advantage. The switch to color broadcasting from 1965 to 1970 (by which time almost all network and local programming was in color) created a new market for color films. *Variety* estimated in 1967 that a "good" feature could make $1.75 million through television release.[35] In the fall of 1967 *Broadcasting* declared that about 80 percent of the prime time ABC movies were in color.[36] Obviously, television had a tremendous impact upon feature-film conversion to color in the 1960s.

The percentages of color feature films made between 1940 and 1970 reflect the changes which occurred in the economic markets for color features. In 1940, 4 percent of all U.S.-produced feature films were made in Technicolor, compared to 51 percent in 1955. By 1958, only 25 percent of all U.S. produced features were made in color compared to 75 percent in 1967, and in 1970, 94 percent.[37] The economic changes which occurred in the supply, the costs, and, in particular, the markets for color films in comparison to black-and-white greatly influenced the diffusion rate of color feature films.

Color Aesthetics: Preferences for Fantasy and Reality

Aesthetic preferences of producers and consumers of color feature films also affected color feature-film invention, innovation, diffusion, and near total (90 percent +) conversion. Whether it was the aesthetic preferences of producers or those of consumers that determined which properties were made in color is extremely complex and perhaps impossible to know. Regardless of who was ultimately responsible, evidence suggests that color preferences are discernible from the kinds of color films that were made and the kinds of films that were commercially successful and aesthetically acclaimed from the late 1920s to the late 1960s.

In 1929 and 1930, an association developed between two-color Technicolor and musicals. According to The American Film Institute's catalogue of feature films from 1921 to 1930,[38] fourteen of seventeen full color features, and twenty-three of thirty-four black-and-white feature films with color sequences, released in 1929 and 1930, were musicals. The aesthetic factors behind this association are difficult to isolate with precision. It seems clear, for example, that the two-color process was inherently inaccurate, simply because it could not reproduce all colors of the visible spectrum and because it was often difficult to predict precisely how any one color before the camera would finally appear on the screen. For example, flesh tones, the most important index of accuracy and consistency, might be carefully controlled through heavy makeup, but they also affected the overall color appearance of the set or location, which sometimes seemed unnatural or gaudy. Musicals, and other fantasy or escapist fare, could easily exploit the imprecision of the two-color process to effect an atmosphere of unreality.

But it is overly simplistic to suggest that use of the two-color process was determined by its technological limitations. It might be more correct to say that the inherent unreality of two-color films produced and consumed in 1929 and 1930 conformed to the popular mood in American society. As the social film historian Lewis Jacobs has pointed out, the initial reaction of Hollywood and its consumers to the depression was to ignore it.[39] The apparent economic imperviousness of the movies to the early effects of the depression and the widespread belief (officially reinforced by President Hoover) that prosperity was just around the corner did nothing to undermine the proliferation of musicals and other relatively expensive (sound and color) escapist fare. But as it became more and more obvious that the facts belied this wishful thinking, the demands of feature-film producers and consumers radically changed. Musicals, color, and the wide screen were literally abandoned, and were eventually replaced by black-and-white films about gangsters and other social problems that expressed a realism, skepticism, and pessimism more consonant with the mood of depression-ridden Americans.

As mentioned earlier, during the 1950s primary visual sources of information about contemporary events, such as newspapers and magazines, were almost exclusively in black and white; but as color photographs became more and more prevalent in magazines, black-and-white television emerged as a visual news source and helped to perpetuate black-and-white's convention of realism. But when television converted to color—especially after television news began broadcasting in color during 1965–66[40]—previous conventions changed and color acquired its own illusion of reality. The changes in aesthetic preferences which coincide with television's conversion to color are not without exception. In 1968, for example, *In Cold Blood*, a bitterly realistic portrait of two killers, was photographed in black-and-white and had gross distributor receipts of $6 million. In 1972, *The Last Picture Show*, also in black-and-white, had gross distributor receipts in excess of $13 million,[41] and demonstrated that a black-and-white film that effected a nostalgia for a previous era could still be commercially successful. These anomalies suggest that the change in aesthetic preferences was not absolute and make it difficult to determine to what extent economic factors, such as color-television markets for feature films, dictated aesthetic preferences, and to what extent changes in aesthetic preferences were ultimately responsible for feature-film and television conversions to color.

PART FOUR

Regulation and Censorship

Antitrust Policies and the
Motion Picture Industry

Simon N. Whitney

The first decade of picture making was a period of chaotic competition. Entry was easy, since little capital was needed to make or to exhibit the early films of street scenes and similar subjects. Edison's Kinetoscope Company held the camera patents; but many cameras were imported, or patented as "improvements," or made in clear violation of the patent rights. The rights on projectors were in confusion.

Ten leading firms attempted to escape from this chaos at the end of 1908 by forming the Motion Picture Patents Company, to which they assigned any patents they owned.[1] They attempted, through the license provisions used by this pool, through the terms on which pictures made by its members were rented (not sold) to film exchanges, and through an exclusive contract with Eastman Kodak Company, to control the entire business in cameras, film, pictures, and projectors. Royalties and rentals were agreed upon. Exchanges and exhibitors that did not conform were denied films made by the members.

Independents were not minded to give in to the "trust." Patents were violated freely, and contracts of distributors and exhibitors were broken. In 1910 the trust attempted to meet this situation by organizing the General Film Company, which purchased control of sixty-eight film exchanges and many more of all sizes folded up or were driven out of business.[2] The owner of the sole remaining exchange, William Fox, began making his own pictures and purchased theaters to secure an outlet—thereby pioneering the integration pattern of the next four decades. "Outlaw" producers emerged in great numbers and successfully "bootlegged" their films.

The government filed an antitrust suit against the Motion Picture Patents Company in 1912. Three years later District Judge Oliver B. Dickinson declared the defendant a monopoly, holding that its restrictive activities went beyond what the patent law justified.[3] In 1917 while this case was on appeal, a 6–3 majority of the Supreme Court sustained the District and Circuit Courts in rejecting a patent infringement suit brought by the trust.[4] This decision became a precedent for application of Section 3 of the Clayton Act to outlaw control by a patentee of distribution of unpatented articles sold by him and used with patented ones. Justice John H. Clarke wrote the majority opinion and Justice Oliver Wendell Holmes the dissent. The Motion Picture Patents Company and the General Film Company were dissolved; but historians of the industry assert that the trust was already unimportant by 1914, and attribute its failure partly[5] or mainly[6] to the energy of the independents.

Several innovations of the independents in this rivalry were significant. They improved film quality; perfected the feature in contrast to the trust's cheap, simple, one-reel pictures; and produced "programs" instead of a fixed number of feet of routine film weekly. They publicized their star players to take advantage of the growing public interest in film personalities. They moved from New York to Hollywood, partly to escape proximity to the trust and possible subpoenas for contract or patent infringement, but also with the consequence of opening up an area better adapted by climate and scenery to film production.

New Forms of Combination

Theater circuits, and booking combines that represented independent theaters at film exchange centers, became established in the years after 1912. Their most effective bargaining technique was to confront distributors with the choice of selling to all their theaters at their own terms, or to none of them. Some of their more ruthless methods were enjoined by the Federal Trade Commission in 1918:[7] threatening not to patronize producers and film exchanges that did business with certain competing exhibitors; calculatedly showing films just before competing exhibitors were planning to do so; refusing to license exhibitors unless they agreed not to rent films from competitors; and coercing certain exhibitors to pay a penalty of 10 percent of the cost of any films they booked direct.

The first trust had scarcely left the industry when another potentially powerful combine appeared. The new film exchanges were all local or regional, and five of the biggest united in 1914 as Paramount Pictures Corporation, to distribute films made by studios not connected with the

Motion Picture Patents Company. The largest such studio was that of Famous Players Company, headed by Adolph Zukor, the most successful exploiter of the new pattern of stars and features. A merger in July 1916 created the Famous Players–Lasky Corporation, which in 1917 acquired twelve smaller producers and Paramount, thus combining production and distribution. The combination is said to have distributed more features in 1918 than any other company before or since.[8] Its name was changed to Paramount Famous Lasky Corporation in 1927, Paramount Publix Corporation in 1930, and Paramount Pictures, Inc., in 1935.

To protect themselves from dependence on this combination, twenty-seven theater companies formed a distributing organization, First National Exhibitors' Circuit, in April 1917. No fewer than 3,500 theaters were soon counted as franchise holders. They financed independent producers and later built studios of their own, becoming known after 1924 as First National Pictures, Inc. Zukor, whose films were in danger of being left with only "dives" for outlets,[9] purchased control of more than 300 theaters (usually through partnership with the previous owner) between 1919 and 1921.

Loew's, Inc. (theaters), Fox Film Corporation and Universal Pictures Corporation (formerly Universal Film Manufacturing Company) also attained major stature as producers and theater owners during the 1920s through reinvestment of profits and by mergers. Loew's, for example, purchased three firms in the early 1920s to form its famed producing and distributing subsidiary, Metro-Goldwyn-Mayer. As early as 1923 Famous Players–Lasky, First National, Loew's, Fox, and Universal each released between 46 and 63 features. Pathé Exchange released 26; Warner Bros. and United Artists (formed in 1919 by Charles Chaplin, Douglas Fairbanks, D. W. Griffith, Mary Pickford, and others to distribute films made by independents), 11 each. Miscellaneous independent producers supplied 108.[10] The equilibrium was broken after 1926 when Paramount climaxed its rivalry with First National by acquiring that company's strongest circuits, most notable of which was Balaban & Katz (B&K) of Chicago.

☆
Antitrust Suits of the 1920s

In August 1921 the Federal Trade Commission filed a complaint against the Famous Players–Lasky (Paramount) group, charging unfair practices and monopolizing of first-run theaters. Not until July 1927 did this complaint, in amended form, become a cease and desist order against restrictive practices.[11] One practice cited was purchase or coercion of theaters in order to gain customers for Famous Players features. This charged was dropped. Another was *block booking*, or releasing films only in groups. On appeal, the Second Circuit Court ruled that block booking did not have monopolistic effects.[12]

Two points were emphasized by Judge Manton for the circuit court: Although Paramount offered its films in blocks, it opened negotiations on some other basis if it found no takers. "Complete" blocks, of 13 to 104 pictures each, accounted for only about 40 percent of block contracts. A distributor could legally choose his method of selling unless it seemed likely to create a monopoly; and block booking had not had that effect, for between 1919 and 1923 Paramount features decreased from 17 to 12 percent of the total, and between 1919–20 and 1924 its film rentals decreased from 30 to 20 percent. What the first point meant was that the exhibitor who did not like a Paramount block could either wait until all his competitors had rejected it and then bargain again, or turn at once to another distributor—who was probably also selling in blocks. Either course would leave him in about the same position.[13]

In April 1928 the Department of Justice assailed the "Standard Exhibition Contract" which had been developed by the Motion Picture Producers and Distributors of America (known as "The Hays Office" after its president, Will H. Hays) and by exhibitor representatives, with help along the way from a Federal Trade Commission trade practice conference in 1927.[14] First established in April 1923 and revised in March 1926 and February 1928, the contract provided for compulsory arbitration of distributor-exhibitor disputes and for posting of security by exhibitors who had failed to obey awards. Enforcement was largely through the thirty-two local organizations of distributors, known as Film Boards of Trade. Their credit committees collected financial information from purchasers of theaters and required fulfillment of contracts made by previous owners (to avoid transfer of theaters in order to evade debts).

The antitrust suit was heard before District Judge Thomas B. Thacher in New York. In October 1929 he ruled the arbitration clauses of the uniform contract in restraint of trade, since arbitration had been imposed on all exhibitors whether or not they were represented in the negotiations, but sustained the credit work. A year later Justice James C. McReynolds spoke for a unanimous Supreme Court in condemnation of the whole apparatus.[15] Futile attempts by the industry to set up a system of voluntary arbitration followed.[16]

Establishment of the Five Majors

Research into putting sound on film was ready for commercial development in 1925.[17] Warner Bros. decided to risk its future on the Bell Telephone patents after two larger producers had turned them down for fear their existing equipment and inventories of silent pictures would be made obsolete. The success of *The Jazz Singer* in October 1927 signaled audience acceptance of Warner Bros.' Vitaphone process. Fox had signed a contract to use Movietone, another application of the Bell patents, two months after Warner Bros., and exhibited shorts in sound in January 1927. By the time other producers accepted the inevitable, these two had a head start. Warner Bros.' assets were blown up by acquisitions, new issues, write-ups, and profits from $5 million in 1925 to $230 million in 1930.

In their expansion, Warner Bros. and Fox acquired controlling interests in other major producers, with Warner Bros. buying what remained of First National and Fox securing 45 percent of the stock of Loew's, thus creating what promised to be the biggest film combine of the day. When these moves were attacked by the Department of Justice under Section 7 of the Clayton Act, the Fox company agreed, in April 1931, to dispose of the Loew's stock.[18] More critical for William Fox himself was the stock market collapse, which made it impossible for him to refinance his borrowings. The Chase National Bank and associated groups took over his interests, and in 1935 a new organization, Twentieth Century–Fox Film Corporation, emerged. The Clayton Act suit against Warner Bros. dragged on, and was finally dismissed in 1934.[19]

American Telephone and Telegraph Company's exclusive policy with its sound equipment led to the establishment of another big film company, RKO. Radio Corporation of America had developed the Photophone method of sound recording and reproduction, but found the studios bound by ten-year contracts to use the Vitaphone system. In 1928 it combined independents, one of them previously integrated, as Radio-Keith-Orpheum Company, so as to secure an outlet for its method. RKO, which acquired Pathé in 1931, joined Fox, Loew's, Paramount, and Warner Bros. as one of the five "majors." Meanwhile Columbia Pictures Corporation became a national distributor in 1929, ranking with Universal as an important producer of grade B features. These two firms and United Artists made up the so-called "minors," or "little three."

Private suits charging restraint of trade may have been helpful in straightening out the sound-patent tangle. In 1929 the Allied States Association of Motion Picture Exhibitors secured an injunction against refusal of sound-equipment makers to permit interchangeability of equipment. Such restraint, however, was probably "doomed in any event." [20] In 1935 a suit by RCA against American Telephone was settled out of court, and the manufacture of full sound equipment was opened up to both groups. [21]

The depression hit the movie industry late, but hard. In 1933 RKO, Paramount, and Universal's exhibition subsidiary went into receivership. Purchase of theaters at inflated prices in the 1920s was a primary cause, and in the five years 1930–35 the number of theaters owned by major producers was squeezed back from 3,600 to 2,225. [22] Warner Bros.' unprecedented $23 million profit in 1927–30 became a $31-million loss in 1931–34. All the big companies continued to make pictures.

☆
Complaints of Exhibitors

By 1930 the basic structure of the industry had been established, with the eight principal producers and the larger theater circuits acting in harmony to protect their self-interest. [23] There was much bitter complaint from small exhibitors, along three lines:

1. Features made by the eight producers were automatically shown by the *owned theaters* of the five majors for their first runs, or in some smaller towns by the *big independent circuits*. Originally the majors bought theaters indiscriminately, but they found that only first runs were really profitable. Independents with good locations were invited to sell out or become partners, and to enforce the invitation the major might go as far as to decline to supply films, or threaten to build or lease a theater close by. By 1945 the majors leased, or owned in whole or part, 3,137 out of 18,076 theaters. Of these, 214 were jointly owned by two majors and 1,287 by majors and independents. The majors controlled at least 70 percent of first-run theaters in cities of more than 100,000 population and about 60 percent of those in cities of 25,000 to 100,000. [24] Most of the theaters of each major were in separate geographical areas and thus were not in competition with each other.

2. Theaters of the majors and other circuits received advantages which single theaters could not match. These included *franchise agreements*, which extended contracts beyond one season; *formula deals*, by which the circuit could pay film rental as a percentage of its overall receipts from the feature and thus apportion dates and rentals among its theaters according to local competition; or *master agreements* and *blanket deals*,

by which a circuit bought for many or all of its theaters under one contract. In small towns, circuits sometimes engaged in *overbuying*, taking more films than they would otherwise have used, in order to cut off the supply to competitors. In big cities a system called *selective contracts* was substituted, with the circuit taking an option on a producer's entire output, but making its choice among the features at leisure. The *clearance*, or number of days between the end of one run and the beginning of the next (e.g., between the first run of a film and the second), was often unreasonably long—up to sixty or even ninety days. Release of films for subsequent runs was sometimes delayed by *move-overs* from one theater in a circuit to another with no clearance, or by *extended runs* of a film in the first-run theater beyond the date originally set out in the contract.

3. Exhibitors (but not, it was alleged, the big circuits [25]) had to take a distributor's whole set of releases, usually a year's output at once, under *block booking*—though usually with a right to reject 10 percent of the pictures. This also involved *blind buying*, that is, purchase of films without an opportunity to see them. A companion practice was the *forcing of "shorts,"* like newsreels and travelogues, on theaters, whether they wanted them or not. *Designation of play dates* by the distributor—e.g., weekends instead of weekdays for certain pictures—was another grievance. Finally, their rental agreements with the distributors often compelled the small exhibitors, if they wanted to make money, to charge *high admission prices* which they felt drove their regular customers away.

☆

A Defense of Runs and Clearance

The pattern of runs and clearance, which at first codified local conditions, gradually became an unduly rigid one. Without attempting to defend this artificial structure, a good argument can be made for a reasonable system of runs and clearance. Court decisions have approved such a system on many occasions. [26]

Some people are willing to pay for the right to see any sort of show early and in an exciting location—a play in its first season on Broadway, the first run of a new film at a fashionable theater. Others, preferring to save their money, are willing to wait. Two sorts of motion picture theaters will tend to arise in a free market, and patronage will divide between them in reasonably stable proportions. Like other businesses, theaters prosper best when they have regular customers, and regular patronage develops only when customers know they can count on getting the sort of product they want. If clearance is abolished or reduced so low by fiat that downtown, first-run theaters cannot attract enough patrons to support their higher costs, they may be forced to close. Under free market conditions, reasonable clearances are likely to develop; and it would take artificial controls either to maintain unduly long clearances (as in the past) or to abolish them.

Separate runs are a physical necessity, since no producer could afford to make a print for every theater that wants to show a picture when it is first available. Clearance, on the other hand, is attacked by those who maintain it is a mere price-fixing mechanism intended to protect the high admission prices at costly downtown theaters.[27] Although this is its purpose, the small exhibitor himself usually concedes that a reasonable clearance is justified to protect the larger investment made in first-run theaters.[28] If the big theaters closed, and all patrons paid only "neighborhood" prices, there would be insufficient revenue to induce production of expensive features of the sort that draw well at the box office. The situation is analogous to differentiation in railroad freight rates, where the ability of instruments and fine textiles to pay high rates makes it possible for the railroad to charge low rates for lumber and stone—and thus get bulk traffic, without which it could not operate.

Antitrust Suits Against Theater Circuits

The first of a series of proceedings to establish a free market in exhibition of films was begun in 1925. The results were as follows:

1. A big California circuit, which later became a Fox subsidiary, was charged by the Federal Trade Commission in 1925 and by the Department of Justice in 1928 with coercing distributors to give it various preferences. Criminal charges were dismissed, but the circuit accepted a commission order in 1929 and consent decrees in 1930 and 1932.[29] The outcome, according to a member of the industry, was a moderate reduction in clearances after the first run.

2. In December 1928 a group of Oklahoma theaters, through a consent decree, renounced an agreement, and coercion of distributors, to prevent nontheatrical exhibitors from making use of the local film exchange.[30]

3. In 1932 a suit filed in 1928 against Paramount's Chicago circuit, B&K achieved a consent decree enjoining unreasonable clearances, overbuying, exclusive first choice of films and long-term exclusive contracts. In 1940 three defendants were fined for violation.[31]

4. A 1932 suit charging a circuit with monopolizing prior runs in New Orleans was later dismissed without action,[32] and a proposed suit against distributors in Cleveland was withdrawn when they granted a new system of runs and clearance.[33]

5. When Warner Bros. lost control of its three first-run Saint Louis theaters in a reorganization in 1931, it leased two others to show its own films and those of RKO and Paramount. The new owner of the first three theaters, left with "the very last choice of product—foreign pictures and expensive stage shows,"[34] complained. Warner Bros. was acquitted of restraint of trade in a jury trial in 1935, but the government then brought civil actions, first in Missouri—where Judge Molyneaux of the district court informed the defendant that, contrary to its contention, the Sherman Act allowed both civil and criminal actions on the same facts[35]—and then in New York. Warner Bros. having been "hounded enough," yielded in 1936, moved out of Saint Louis, and gave the independent a ten-year contract to show its pictures[36] that was later extended indefinitely.

6. In 1936 the government sued the Interstate and the Texas Consolidated circuits, which had forty-three and sixty-six theaters respectively and were affiliated with Paramount. They handled three quarters of the total dollar business in their Texas–New Mexico localities and nearly all of the first-run business. The offense was a proposal made in 1934 to each of the eight big film distributors and accepted by them: that grade A pictures shown in the circuit at 40 cents admission should not be licensed to subsequent-run theaters that charged less than 25 cents (many were charging 15 cents) or presented double bills. The talking point was that distributors would find their first-run rentals shrinking if patrons could wait to see features two at a time for less than half the cost.

The Supreme Court enjoined this agreement by a 5–3 vote.[37] Chief Justice Harlan F. Stone, speaking for the majority, declared that simultaneous acceptance of the same plan by eight distributors constituted *prima facie* evidence of collusion, which the defendants had not rebutted. The requirement as to admission prices, which "involved a radical departure from the previous business practices of the industry,"[38] was in his opinion obvious price fixing. Justice Owen J. Roberts dissented on a tail-wags-dog theory: if any one distributor accepted the proposition, he maintained, the other seven had to follow to protect their own sales to Interstate. The Court's decision became the foundation stone for the doctrine—destined to reach prominence fifteen years later—that "conscious parallelism of action" is illegal.

The First Paramount Decree

Aften ten years of theater suits, the Department of Justice decided on a broader attack. It filed a petition in the Southern New York District in July 1938, asking among other things for divorcement of production and distribution from exhibition. This remedy had been applied the year before by North Dakota, but only ten theaters were affected.[39] Columbia, Universal, and United Artists, although they owned no theaters, were made defendants along with the five majors because they regularly licensed their films (many of which were grade B products considered suitable to complete a double bill) in the same way as the majors.

In November 1940 the five majors accepted a consent decree.[40] It did not mention divorcement, but contained the following provisions: (1) No more than five films might be sold in a single block. (2) Exhibitors must be allowed "trade showings" of films before sales were negotiated. (3) No shorts, reissues, westerns, newsreels or the like might be forced on exhibitors as a condition of receiving features. (4) Disputes about runs and clearances, and the forcing of features by distributors, were to be subject to arbitration. (5) None of the five majors was to buy any further theaters except to protect earlier investments or "for ordinary purposes of its business."

The exhibitors and the government soon became dissatisfied with the results of the case.[41] They did not like the fact that distributors could still license films to their own theaters on whatever terms they wished. The arbitration was found disappointing in practice and was abandoned. Trade showings were used only by the large circuits and booking combines, for despite complaints against blind buying, most exhibitors preferred to select features on the basis of reviews, advance advertisements, and box office reports. Exhibitors decided that too many of the authorized five-picture blocks contained one popular film and four bad ones.[42] Finally, Fox and Paramount differed with the government over what theater acquisitions were allowed.[43]

Decrees against Three Theater Circuits

In 1939 the Department of Justice had climaxed its antitrust drive in the exhibition field with suits against three independent theater circuits. The two largest in the country, Schine (in New York, Ohio, Kentucky, and Maryland) and Griffith (in the Southwest), had about 150 theaters each and had been associated with Universal's chain, which was dissolved after 1933. The third circuit involved, Crescent (in the South), was about half their size. All were accused of securing the best films, first runs, and strong clearance protection in those few towns where they faced competition by threatening not to show first-rate films in "closed" towns, where they owned the only theaters. If necessary, they could outbid in open towns and make it up by offering low rentals in closed towns. They were charged with using their leverage to buy or force out independents.

These cases all reached the Supreme Court and were settled in favor of the government, with Justice William O. Douglas delivering the opinions. The Crescent decision was by a 5–1 vote in December 1944, with Justice Roberts dissenting without opinion.[44] The Schine[45] and Griffith[46] decisions were in May 1948, with the Court voting, respectively, 7–0 and 6–1 (Justice Felix Frankfurter was the dissenter).

The court orders about buying practices did not go as far as the industry-wide orders issued simultaneously in the second *Paramount* case. A member of the industry states that the decrees opened up a few closed towns to competition. Some smaller associated circuits were separated from Crescent and Griffith, and the main Griffith chain broke up as a result of death. Crescent was charged with noncompliance in 1950, but has added about one theater a year since 1944 (presumably after a showing that it would not reduce competition).[47] Schine found it hard to sell theaters under post-1948 conditions, even "at a substantial loss,"[48] but reduced its holdings from 150 in 1948 to 116 in 1954 and 109 in 1955. Charged with not disposing of enough theaters, it went through a three-month criminal contempt trial in 1955, which ended when the presiding judge died.[49] A new trial was then slated.

These cases are remembered best for the comments on monopolizing in the *Griffith* opinion. Justice Douglas declared that "specific intent" to achieve monopoly need not be proved if monopoly in fact results;[50] that "monopoly power, whether lawfully or unlawfully acquired, may itself constitute an evil and stand condemned under [Section 2 of the Sherman Act] even though it remains unexercised"; that "size is of course an earmark of monopoly power";[51] and that buying for theaters in open and closed towns together constituted "using monopoly power to expand" and made Griffith "chargeable in legal contemplation" with monopolizing.[52] Since the opinion did not dispute the trial court's conclusion that Griffith had not used its monopoly in closed towns as a threat to secure better terms in open towns, this condemnation of buying for both at once implied an attack on any horizontal combination which contained units possessing local monopolies.[53]

The Second Paramount Case

The Department of Justice had found one good result in the first Paramount decree: arbitration brought many complaints by exhibitors out into the open. In August 1944 the department asked the district court to modify the decree by divorcing the production and distributing branches of the defendants from their exhibiting branches. Divorce of production from distribution was not asked—no doubt because of the "overwhelming" efficiency of this type of integration.[54] After a trial at which the government presented briefs and exhibits but not witnesses, the eight defendants were found to have engaged in a nationwide conspiracy in restraint of trade. The Court listed several infractions of the Sherman Act, including the fixing of admission prices at independent theaters as a condition of receiving licenses on defendants' films. Divorcement was held to be irrelevant, since ownership of only one sixth of the theaters was not judged a potent weapon of monopoly. Various other reforms were ordered, including competitive bidding as the fairest way to select the licensee when two or more competing theaters wanted a film on the same "day and date."[55]

On appeal by both parties, the Supreme Court voted 8–0 to uphold the general verdict of the trial court. The opinion, delivered by Justice Douglas on the same day in May 1948 as his *Schine* and *Griffith* opinions, reviewed the whole series of restraints and found them to evidence "a marked proclivity for unlawful conduct" on the part of the defendants.[56] It reasoned that competitive bidding would lead to great difficulties in practice and would play into the hands of the buyer with "the longest purse."[57] It suggested that the district court make "an entirely fresh start" on the question of theater divestiture.[58] Justice Frankfurter dissented on the remedy, arguing that decrees should be framed by the trial court, which could be presumed to be more expert on the facts. As to this expertness, the exhibitors' associations that had joined the appeal to secure a reversal of the competitive bidding order evidently did not agree.

The Consent Decrees

With this threat over their heads, RKO and Paramount began negotiations for consent decrees. The Department of Justice insisted on complete divorcement of theaters. In November 1948 and March 1949, respectively, the district court approved decrees to this effect. The other defendants refused to go along, but in July 1949 Judge Augustus N. Hand delivered another opinion in the government's favor.[59] In the absence of competitive bidding, the Court held that divorcement was the only way of assuring fair dealing between producers and theaters. The Supreme Court having refused another review,[60] the six defendants accepted decrees, the last being Loew's in February 1952. The content of all the decrees ran along the same lines.

The principal prohibitions were the following: (1) tying the sale of one picture to that of another; (2) stipulating admission prices; (3) establishing any fixed system of clearances, any unreasonably long clearances, or any clearance at all between theaters not in substantial competition; and (4) granting to circuits any franchise agreements, formula deals, master agreements or other privileges—in short, any contract at all except theater by theater and picture by picture.

The new exhibition circuits set up by divorcement were RKO Theatres Corporation, United Paramount Theatres Corporation, National Theatres Company, Stanley Warner Corporation, and Loew's Theatres, Inc. There were no interlocking officers or directors with the producing companies. Time limits were set for dominant stockholders to sell their shares in one or the other, and meanwhile they could vote in one only. The new companies were required to end their joint ownership of theaters by either selling their participations or buying out their local partners, and to dispose of one or more theaters in towns where they had no competitors. By the end of 1954 they had sold 1,111 out of the revised number of 1,197 theaters to which the order applied.[61]

By far the largest of these circuits is American Broadcasting–Paramount Theatres, Inc. (successor of United Paramount Theatres), whose seventeen subsidiary corporations operate nearly six hundred theaters. National Theatres has about four hundred, Stanley Warner about three hundred, and RKO less than one hundred. Loew's had made progress toward, but had not completed, its divorcement in 1956.

The first two decrees (Paramount and RKO) did not prohibit the producing company from purchasing theaters or the exhibition company from entering into production. But as of 1956 none of the four companies involved had yet risked trouble by doing so. The later decrees included such prohibitions.

Effects of Divorcement: I. The Exhibitors

Whether the *Paramount* case should be called "probably the government's greatest economic victory in the 60-year history of antitrust enforcement"[62] may be debatable; but certainly a much freer market in films was created.[63] This is clear from the prohibitions listed in the decrees. Even the defendants in the case admit that conditions before 1948 were not healthy.[64]

For exhibitors, whose protection was the primary purpose of the government's action,[65] the consequences were mixed. First of all, there is ample evidence that the major producers, both because of the injunction against discrimination and because they had little reason to favor their former circuits, were trying to deal with all theaters on an equitable basis. The fact that production and theater companies still had some shareholders in common[66] did not seem to interfere.

Part of the gain, it should be noted, was owing to previous antitrust cases. As early as 1932 a suit for injunction against the "Uniform Zoning and Protection Plan for the Omaha Distributing Territory" had been granted,[67] on the precedent of the *Paramount–Famous Lasky* and *First National* decisions of 1930.[68] The injunction in the 1940 *Paramount* decree against theater acquisitions not in the ordinary course of business gave some protection to independents against being forced to sell out.

Even more important were the treble damage suits which began to be filed in the early 1940s. Above all, the *Jackson Park* decision of a unanimous Supreme Court in 1946 (opinion by Chief Justice Stone) had served a strong warning against inequitable runs and clearances.[69] In this case an independent Chicago theater, the *Jackson Park*, had been awarded three times the estimated profits it had lost through its seven-day clearance behind a nearby B&K theater and the latter's gross receipts were used as one measure of its losses. The licensing of a producer's features in its own theaters first—i.e., Paramount films in B&K theaters— would not in itself have been illegal; but the system involved preferences for the other major producers in Paramount's circuit in return for reciprocal preferences elsewhere.

Since the mid-1940s, therefore, any exhibitor who has felt that the location, size, and furnishings of his theater warranted an earlier run than it was receiving could hold over the heads of the distributors a threat of a treble damage suit, in which the jury might interpret uniform refusal to alter runs as conspiracy.

Extent of Exhibitor Gains

Despite the influence of the treble damage suits, most of the gains of exhibitors followed directly from the *Paramount* decision. The producers were at once "deluged" with demands for better runs and clearances, and after careful consideration made "thousands" of alterations in the position of theaters.[70] A 1951 estimate put the additional first-run outlets at 1,500[71]—a figure which must have referred to theaters showing first-run films when they could get them rather than to those showing them steadily. A later report mentions "one or two, or more" new first-run houses in many communities around Los Angeles.[72] Owners of neighborhood theaters especially stepped up their demands, many insisting on a second run (sometimes called first neighborhood run) on "day and date" with each other and often with larger theaters downtown. Some have gone to court to demand first runs, but such plaintiffs have almost always met with a rebuff. On grade B pictures, first runs in neighborhood theaters have always been common.

Of 41 exhibitors replying to a questionnaire sent out to 221 as part of this study, 3 had stepped up their runs.[73] Twelve noted a shortening of clearance between first and second run in their towns, the change, on the average, being from 56 to 33 days. In the remaining twenty-nine towns, this clearance had averaged only 23 days, and was reported unchanged. It is the unduly long clearances that have been reduced. Six respondents noted a shortening of clearance between second and third run.

Exhibitor Grievances: The Product Shortage

Despite these rights assured to independent exhibitors by the *Paramount* decision, only seven of the respondents to the questionnaire praised it, while eleven called the effects bad, three found them both good and bad, and twenty said they themselves were not affected. The adverse opinion was strongly expressed in 1953 by a prominent exhibitor who declared that before 1948 the independent, "whatever the evils [he] endured, enjoyed rights and privileges which made his business more stable, secure and worthy of investment than it is today."[74] An unidentified circuit operator put the issue about the same way in 1956: "We are only now beginning to realize what a huge mistake divorcement really was. Perhaps even the government is beginning to realize that the theatres cannot survive under these conditions."[75]

First, the decree is blamed by many exhibitors for "the product shortage," or reduced flow of feature pictures. A tabulation of features released shows a big drop during World War II, no particular trend for ten years thereafter, and finally a sharp decrease in 1954 and 1955. The number of domestic features approved by the Production Code Administration (the industry's self-censorship agency) showed no trend from 1945 to 1951, then dropped sharply. The drop occurred among both the large members and the small nonmembers of the Motion Picture Association of America (successor to the Hays Office and headed by Eric Johnston). (See table 10.1.)

The shortage had its severest impact on rural and neighborhood houses accustomed to presenting three double bills weekly; but even the circuits with many first-run houses raised objections.[76] Theaters were

Table 10.1. Motion Pictures: Number of Feature Films, 1937–55

Year or Annual Average	New Domestic and Foreign Features Released		New Domestic Features Approved		
	All National Distributors	Eight Largest Companies	Total	Motion Picture Association of America Members	Association Nonmembers
1937–42	476	380	521	355	166
1943–44	418	276	414	270	144
1945	367	270	358	230	128
1946	382	252	397	254	143
1947	381	249	370	229	141
1948	406	248	394	229	165
1949	411	234	361	252	109
1950	423	263	379	272	107
1951	400	320	369	282	87
1952	353	278	317	259	58
1953	377	301	290	241	49
1954	295	225	232	187	45
1955	283	215	241	210	31

Sources: Releases of national distributors from Motion Picture Association of America; those of Columbia, Loew's, Paramount, RKO, Twentieth Century–Fox, United Artists, Universal, and Warner Brothers from *The Film Daily Yearbook* (New York, 1956, p. 105); features approved by Production Code Administration from Motion Picture Association of America, Annual Report, 1951, p. 31; 1955, p. 19.

obliged, much against their will, to fill out their screen time with imports and reissues, and to offer fewer changes of program. Producers complained that despite the talk of shortage many of their best films were rejected by half the theaters,[77] but that line of argument implies that the problem should have been solved by letting exhibitors be satisfied with less freedom of choice.

While theaters felt that they were losing audiences for lack of new films to show to them, producers were achieving a recovery in profits with the rentals from their few, but "spectacular," pictures.[78] RKO, which was subject to erratic management (including a three-month shutdown to make "a hunt for Communists"[79]), was an exception. The six other large publicly held companies earned only $25 million and $22 million in 1952 and 1953, respectively, but $35 million and $34 million in 1954 and 1955. Even this improvement (perhaps owing in part to income from manufacture of phonograph records, oil wells on studio lots, and other sidelines) left earnings far below the peak levels of 1946 and 1947. A general comparison cannot be made because of the theater separations, but Loew's profits in 1955 were one-third of the 1946 figure and one-half of that in 1947.

Causes of the Product Shortage

Some exhibitors attributed the reduction of output to a producer conspiracy to increase the rental on films by curtailing the supply. As early as 1947 and 1949 the same thought had occurred to writers who noticed the decrease in releases since 1943.[80] No proof of this hypothesis has emerged, however, and as shown in table 10.1, the smaller producers also decreased their output.

The explanation of the product shortage most generally advanced by respondents to this study's questionnaire is that the divorce of production and exhibition removed the incentive Hollywood once had to occupy the screen time of affiliated theaters with a steady flow of films. It is argued also that studios felt safer in making films while they were assured of this guaranteed market, in their own theaters and to some extent in those of other integrated companies. Furthermore, abolition of block booking meant that a producer could no longer count on renting a year's output ahead of time. Each picture had to be salable on its own merits, and this condition in turn required that more attention be given to individual pictures.

The argument about divorcement does not receive much support from the figures. In 1953 all the circuits had been divorced except that of Loew's, but the number of both releases and approved features of the majors was still above the level of 1947 and 1948 (table 10.1). The argument also overlooks the fact that the real market for a feature is the public, not the theater, and that a producer who ignores this truth and pours out features just to fill screen time will eventually lose out at the independent theaters and hear protests from his own. Nevertheless, it is hard to believe that divorcement had no effect on integrated companies, and that they did not feel less pressed to produce films because they owned no theaters.

The principal cause of the product shortage surely lay in the economics of demand and cost. Above all, producers recognized that the best way to get people to theaters was to offer them better pictures than they could see on television. Grade B films (for example, Columbia's western and crime serials) were dropped. Also, modern techniques and increasing costs made production so expensive that studios were not averse to making fewer films. Fewer, better pictures became the formula. In the light of these economic causes of the product shortage, divorcement and the abolition of block booking must be considered merely as psychological, supporting factors.

☆
Integration Proposed Again

Since 1953 exhibitors, acting through their two principal trade associations, have sought some remedy for the product shortage. Interestingly, their proposals have all looked in the direction of reversing the principle of separation of production and exhibition that the *Paramount* decree set forth.

The largest association (so far as can be judged, for membership figures are not available) is Theatre Owners of America (TOA). It includes among its members owners of one, two or three theaters, small circuits, and also the divorced circuits. When one of these, National Theatres, proposed to go into picture making to secure a larger supply of films, TOA endorsed the plan. Its fear that some "question of antitrust legalistics" might be involved[81] proved justified, for the Antitrust Division let it be known that enough firms were interested in producing films to make it unnecessary to restore integration.[82] TOA next set out to raise $10 million to finance independent producers, upon whose product the subscribers would expect to have first call. *Variety* announced the venture in one of its characteristic headlines: "TOA: Regret that Divorce. Yen Old Days of Studio Ties."[83]

Allied States Association of Motion Picture Exhibitors was in a more ambiguous position on this issue, since it took and was given credit for inspiring the whole Department of Justice crusade against integration.[84] Allied had been fighting the producers since its first appearance in 1923 and its reorganization at the end of 1928 under Abram F. Myers, who as federal trade commissioner had presided over the industry's trade practice conferences. At its 1953 convention Allied voted unanimously to investigate the possibility (which turned out to be nil) of investing in the shares of producing companies and then electing directors who would both increase studio schedules and replace some of the distribution executives by "men of vision."[85] It next sponsored a plan by which 2,400 theaters would contract with an independent producer to make a low-cost feature each month which they would use—a revival of block booking and blind selling which the Antitrust Division under these circumstances approved.[87] In 1955 Allied came around to endorsing picture production by the three divorced circuits that now proposed to enter the business. Meanwhile Distributors Corporation of America, organized with other exhibitors as shareholders, was already making pictures available to them.[88]

Endorsement came from another quarter. Adolph Zukor, thinking of his own actions nearly forty years before, said it was quite all right and economically desirable for a circuit to make pictures, but he hoped that in fairness the right of a producer to own theaters would again be recognized.[89] The motive which had stimulated William Fox to originate motion picture integration in 1910 in his battle against the patent trust and First National to build studios in 1917 in its fight against Famous Players, was at work once more (as in such prosaic industries as petroleum and steel) to assure a supply of the raw material.

Exhibitor Grievances: Rise in Film Rentals

The second major grievance of exhibitors was the rise in rentals demanded and obtained by distributors. According to Allied's chairman: "Film rentals dominate every other issue in the business."[90] The extent of the increase was uncertain. Sindlinger & Company, a firm that has specialized in motion picture statistics, used exhibitor sources to estimate that film rentals increased steadily from 27.1 percent of box office receipts in

1947 to 33.6 percent in 1955—or from 32.6 to 35.9 percent of receipts, excluding admission taxes. Price Waterhouse & Company, using data supplied by the ten largest distributors, found an upward trend from 1947 to 1953, but a sharp drop in 1954 and 1955, and a lower ratio throughout—26.0 percent in 1947, 35.0 in 1953 and 27.8 in 1955. (See table 10.2.)

Whatever the precise figures, the ratio of rentals to box office receipts has clearly increased. Other Sindlinger estimates show that miscellaneous expenses advanced from 53.8 to 80.4 percent of net box office receipts (exclusive of admission tax) between 1947 and 1953, while income from concessions went from 4.5 to 21.0 percent. The net effect of the rise in rentals and other expenses, as offset by the gain in lobby concessions, was to reduce net income before taxes from 18.1 to 4.6 percent of receipts.[91] Of this decline, as Table 10.2 shows, rentals alone accounted for 3.4 percentage points, or 25 percent.

Table 10.2. *Motion Pictures: Ratio of Film Rentals to Box-Office Receipts, 1947–55 (in percentage)*

Year	Ratio to Total Receipts (Sindlinger)	Ratio to Receipts minus Admissions Tax	
		(Sindlinger)	(Price Waterhouse)
1947	27.1	32.6	26.0
1948	27.7	33.3	27.8
1949	28.0	33.6	28.6
1950	28.2	33.9	29.0
1951	28.5	34.3	30.3
1952	29.2	35.1	32.3
1953	30.0	36.0	35.0
1954	33.3	36.6	31.0
1955	33.6	35.9	27.8

Source: Estimates of Sindlinger & Company, Inc., Independent Analyst, Ridley Park, Pa., as reported by Trueman T. Rembusch, in *Motion-Picture Distribution Trade Practices—1956*, Hearings Before a Subcommittee of the Senate Small Business Committee, 84th Cong., 2d sess., 1956, p. 74; those of Price Waterhouse & Co. as reported by Adolph Schimel, ibid., p. 305 (these figures are derived from a chart, but they are probably accurate within a tenth of a percentage point).

On many types of pictures the rentals have not advanced, but the over-all trend has been shaped by the big features. It was an unprecedented event when *Gone with the Wind*, a film which perhaps outranked all oth-ers in eagerness of public anticipation and whose $33.5 million gross rentals by the end of 1955 (from the United States and Canada) doubled that of any other, came out in 1939 on a "prerelease" or "road show" basis (special run followed by a long wait before the "first" run) at terms of 70 percent of box office receipts. Its regular runs followed at 40 percent. The five pictures next in popularity—*The Robe*, with $17 million in rentals by the end of 1955, and *The Greatest Show on Earth, From Here to Eternity, This Is Cinerama*, and *White Christmas*, with $12 to $13 mil-lion—were released in 1952, 1953, and 1954.[92] Except for *This Is Cin-erama*, to which a theater circuit (Stanley Warner) owns the rights, these all carried a 50 to 70 percent rental. The 70 percent contracts usually guaranteed the theater 10 percent of gross receipts as net profit, but this was of little help to the smallest theaters, for they require more than 10 percent to exist.[93] These smallest outlets (numbering 5,500) are able to pay no more than $12.50 to $50 flat rental for a two- to three-day showing.[94]

A peak, or perhaps the peak, was reached when Samuel Goldwyn in-structed his distributor (Metro-Goldwyn-Mayer) to ask 90 percent for *Guys and Dolls*, while offering to pay all house expenses and promotion costs. This independent producer believed that television had taken over the function of providing cheap mass entertainment, and that the motion picture industry could only survive on a "class" or quality basis, priced accordingly.[95]

The Rise in Rentals

Rentals increased for three main reasons:

1. Most important, the trend toward spectacular pictures raised the price of each film, both because there were fewer being offered and be-cause each cost more to make.

2. Divorcement played a role. Formerly the big companies had not been concerned whether their profits came through production or ex-hibition, and some in the industry say they preferred the latter. Such fig-ures as are available indicate that most of the majors' income came from their theaters.[96] With divorcement, the big producers naturally became sharper bargainers, to the distress of their formerly affiliated circuits as

well as others.[97] This is reflected in occasional identity of rentals charged in country and city, and on first and subsequent runs. Producers also seemed to be less willing to make an adjustment if exhibitors "grossed" less than had been expected.[98]

3. Competitive bidding became the method of licensing films in somewhere between 400 and 750 "situations," involving from 1,000 to more than 2,000 theaters.[99] One who made a sealed bid was tempted to set his offer high, whereas in an open negotiation he might have discovered the seller's final offer before he disclosed his own. Some exhibitors consequently felt they were being forced to bid themselves into insolvency.[100]

Competitive bidding had its origin in the *Paramount* decision, with the resulting increased demand by theaters for films on the same run. Distributors had to find a way of choosing among them without running into a charge of discrimination. In some places schedules were continued as before—as in the "Loew's split" and the "RKO split" in New York City (the former including Loew's, Columbia, Paramount, United Artists, and half of Universal's pictures; the latter, RKO, Fox, Warner Bros., and the other half of Universal's). Friendly exhibitors might have adopted a deliberate product split, dividing the forthcoming features into two lots and letting one of them have first choice, with the roles reversed on the next group. Although such agreements would have violated not only the principle that sales should be made picture by picture but also antitrust principles in general, they were never prosecuted, and according to a Department of Justice official, were not likely to be unless many uniformities were found among supposedly competing theaters. If a split could not be arranged, individual negotiations with the distributors' salesmen might have continued and both date of showing and price determined; but sooner or later a theater would likely feel unfairly treated and ask, or sue, for the right to bid.

The Debate over Bidding and Rentals

Exhibitors made many further complaints against bidding, the validity of which cannot be determined but which at least reflect their state of mind. They claimed, for example, that the system was illogical since bids that proposed different playing times, a single versus a double bill, or a cash offer versus a percentage, could not be precisely compared; that it inconvenienced the exhibitor by forcing him to hold a given date open until he knew whether he would get the film; or that it permitted favoritism by the distributor, which could not be detected since the winning bid was kept secret. Some distributors expressed willingness to make the winner's offer public if he agreed but he usually felt he had nothing to gain by it.[101] United Artists announced in 1952 that it would permit losers to see the winning bid.[102] In 1955 the Electric Theatre of Kansas City, Kansas, on the occasion of winning $1,334,000 in damages for being put behind Kansas City, Missouri, also received by court order the right to inspect bids when opened.[103]

Distributors had their own complaints. They reported that some exhibitors turned the tables by agreeing privately to put in low bids and, if the distributor rejected these and turned to negotiation, continued their agreement to make low offers.[104] Another trick (not applicable in bidding situations) was to sign a contract, run the picture, and then refuse to settle at the terms agreed upon if attendance was poor. This practice was said to result in a lawsuit only "occasionally,"[105] and in fact the practice predated the *Paramount* case. Another dodge of at least a few exhibitors who found their profits squeezed out of existence between high rentals and disappointing receipts was to falsify their box office reports so as to get more of the proceeds.[106] This, too, had a history of several decades. British and Scandinavian producers, not restricted by antitrust laws, prevented these tactics by threat of a boycott; American producers sometimes installed checkers in the theater lobby. For various reasons, some distributors felt that the widespread change since 1948 from flat rentals to percentage contracts had been a mistake as applied to the very small theaters.[107]

In 1952 the Allied representatives finally walked out of long negotiations over establishment of an arbitration system to handle disputes over availabilities, runs, and clearances because the distributors refused to include rentals also in the list of topics to be arbitrated. Allied received no sympathy from the Department of Justice or the Senate Small Business Committee;[108] but TOA later joined it in its stand. Allied next proposed that the industry be made a public utility and that its wholesale price (rentals), although not its retail price (admissions), be regulated by the Federal Trade Commission—a challenge which it hoped could be traded for lower rentals.[109]

☆
Exhibitor Problems: Block Booking

Unlike the complaints against the product shortage and the rise in rentals, protests against the abolition of block booking were by no means universal. Among exhibitors replying to the questionnaire sent out in this study, 29 wanted it restored, while 11 did not, and one did not care. Iowa was evidently a strong anti-block territory, since Senator Guy M. Gillette reported in 1953 that a great many exhibitors had written him against blocks and none in their favor.[110] He did not say whether the letters were written before or after the 1940 and 1948 decrees. Exhibitors in the neighboring state of Minnesota apparently felt differently, for a state law in 1941 ordered the sale of a season's product at one time. The law had to give way to the contrary rule of the consent decree of 1940.[111] One industry member claimed that exhibitors found block booking a convenient scapegoat when parents or reformers criticized them for showing an off-color picture.

Exhibitors favoring block booking argued that it is a quantity method of distribution, and therefore a low-cost one. Some of them pointed out that a theater that showed from four to six features weekly had to buy most of the currently produced films in any case,[112] for its patrons would have become bored with a heavy diet of foreign films. Typical of these attitudes were the remarks that, "Today, buying one picture at a time, it is a killer. If you are an individual operator, you have to be on the roam maybe 5 days a week and then try to run the theatre at night." [113] And, "What is the difference if we buy them one at a time or buy them altogether; we still have to play them all." [114] These difficulties caused many small theaters to turn over their buying functions to booking agencies.[115] Some complained that a theater could no longer advertise and tried to maintain a reputation of always showing certain stars or types of pictures. Even if such advertising were effective, a competing theater might have found it worthwhile to capitalize on it by overbidding on some of these pictures.[116]

In noncompetitive areas during the mid-1950s, distributors still sold blocks of pictures to theaters at their request, allowing cancellation privileges of perhaps 20 percent so that the exhibitor could reject the pictures he deemed offensive or unsalable to his audience.[117] Those who wanted block booking restored would have liked such a cancellation privilege, but some conceded that no exhibitor was obliged to show every picture he received in the package. As late as 1958 about half the theaters leased some of their films in groups [118]—for the labor of buying would otherwise have been impossibly heavy—although they signed an individual contract for each. The real problem was that automatic block booking was not feasible as long as anyone in the competitive area objected. It was also possible that a studio might prefer to license its better pictures one at a time and extract the maximum price for each—even if on other occasions a salesman may, without authorization, have conditioned the license of one picture on that of another.[119]

Exhibitor Problems: Crowded Runs

There was always a problem, from both the exhibitor's and the viewer's standpoint, of too many theaters showing the same feature at the same time. In the late 1950s this problem intensified for several reasons, among them a feeling of some producers and circuits that a citywide or nationwide advertising campaign could best be exploited by issuing the feature simultaneously in as many theaters as possible. But here also the *Paramount* decree was a contributing factor—at least in the view of eighteen theater operators who answered this study's questionnaire, as against only three who thought it had not.

This crowding of runs was believed by many to have cut down total theater attendance considerably. Whereas formerly a big feature built up a reputation by having its name emblazoned in bright lights for weeks at a screen palace in a busy downtown section frequented by shoppers and out-of-towners, in the late 1950s it moved on quickly from this "showcase" to its next run. Or it might have opened at a smaller house at the risk of being "tagged as an inferior picture."[120] Another danger was that a feature might come and go before enough prospective viewers knew of its arrival. Features were formerly played off over a five-month period in the large cities, but by the late 1950s the time was reduced to a few weeks. One circuit stated, "This was graphically illustrated in a survey conducted for us in a large metropolitan area where we have theater interests. The survey found that among the potential audience for *Quo Vadis*, as many as 200,000 people were still waiting for the attraction to play in suburban theatres although it had already played and gone. We believe that this situation is generally typical of the effect of multiple runs everywhere."[121] In *Variety*'s language, "Distribs feel that this has upset the whole system of gradual playoff of pix through various runs—a system on which the success of the industry was built. This trade practice revolution is thought in many circles to be largely responsible for the tough times at the b.o. in recent years."[122] And, "2 Pix for 117 Nabes. Just about every important neighborhood theatre in New York will be tied up with only a total of two pictures this week."[123]

One problem created by this situation was a print shortage, which producers were naturally not always willing to alleviate by making expensive extra prints.[124] Sometimes theaters had to wait their turn, regardless of any court order on clearance.[125]

Informed opinion in the industry was that the enthusiasm of theaters to get on earlier runs would be gradually controlled, and that each theater would find the best run for its long-term advantage. Many viewers (including senators[126]) anticipated being thankful.

☆
Two Senate Investigations

When the Subcommittee on Monopoly of the Senate Small Business Committee held full hearings on exhibitor problems in the spring of 1953, one fact which emerged was that complaints to the Department of Justice were likely to outnumber those following any other antitrust decree.[127] The informal methods used by the Antitrust Division to help exhibitors who were having trouble[128] did not convince the subcommittee, which recommended that the Division enforce the law more vigorously—but without making it clear just how, since "the committee was impressed by the fact that virtually every problem that came to its attention during its extensive hearings disclosed merit on both sides."[129] Its further recommendation was that the industry set up a system of arbitrating disputes.

Three years later another Senate Small Business subcommittee, with one member remaining over from the first, was kinder to the Antitrust Division. Although it reported that "exhibitors presented convincing testimony as to alleged misconduct by the Division," the subcommittee itself was evidently not convinced, for it went on to say that "the judgments in the Paramount case are being conscientiously enforced by able persons."[120] This report contained ten recommendations as against two the time before: voluntary arbitration, government loans to theaters for reequipment, only normal clearance after prereleases or other special handling of big films, replacement of competitive bidding if an alternative could be suggested, fuller notice to competitors when a divorced circuit asked court permission to add a theater, some standard-size prints of all large-film pictures, less showing of features simultaneously in many theaters, no production by the divorced circuits, no federal legislation on rentals or trade practices, and better distributor-exhibitor cooperation generally.[131] About this last point, the subcommittee chided the producers for selling their old films to television—something which another organ of the government, the Department of Justice, had recently brought suit to force them to do. The Senate report was generally regarded as rejecting the exhibitors' claims.[132]

☆
Fundamental Causes of Exhibitor Troubles

Statistics on motion picture exhibition from 1946 to 1955 record about 19,000 theaters which operated each year but show a steady increase in drive-ins at the expense of "four-wall" theaters. Rough estimates also show a decline in theater attendance, from 82 million (59 percent of the population) weekly in 1946 to 46 million (27 percent of the population) in 1955. Although these figures are not to be taken too literally since they are subject to a wide margin of error, the "movie habit" seemed to have been reduced by about half between the peak year of motion picture prosperity, 1946, and 1955. Theater-box-office-plus-concession receipts, exclusive of admissions tax, dropped meanwhile by 16 percent, and declined from 1.0 to 0.5 percent of total consumer expenditures. Exhibitor profits fell from an estimated $325 million to a presumed deficit of $12 million. (See table 10.3.)

Three causes of the plight of the independent exhibitor were fundamental. One was the drive-in theater, which developed as a natural response to the automobile age and the movement of population to suburbs and as an answer to such problems as parking space and baby-sitters. Some exhibitors, perhaps annoyed that drive-ins should be demanding early runs which they themselves expected to receive after the *Paramount* decree, claimed that drive-ins had sometimes been built for their nuisance value, to force competitors to buy them out.[133] Many small circuit operators, however, built their own drive-ins.

Between 1948 and 1954, according to the Census of Business, drive-ins increased from 820 to 3,799, or by 2,979, while closings reduced the number of four-wall theaters by 2,928. During the same span of years the gross receipts of drive-ins increased from $47 million to $229 million, while those of four-wall theaters decreased from $1,567 million to $1,187 million.[134] These figures would imply that 48 percent of the decline in four-wall receipts might have been attributable to the expansion of drive-ins, except that obviously a substantial number of drive-in patrons would never or seldom have gone to regular theaters.

The second and major cause of the exhibitor's troubles was the decline in attendance since 1946. Many factors played a part: a decrease in the proportion of adolescents (the largest moviegoing age group) in the population due to the low birth rates of the 1930s; the great rise in the birth rate which tied down young parents; the preoccupations of suburban life such as gardening, repairing homes and commuting; and new forms of entertainment like night baseball. Beginning in 1949, television became the dominant influence. Sindlinger & Company, by comparing national attendance trends with those in the western areas which were slow in getting television, found that television accounted for 50 percent of the box office decline from 1949 to 1955.[135]

Hollywood resisted the inevitable for a long time, and only new and small companies made films for television. Some exhibitor associations attempted in vain to apply boycotts. One national organization circulated

Table 10.3. *Motion Pictures: Number of Theaters, Attendance, Receipts, and Exhibition Profits, 1946–55*

Year	Active Theaters (in thousands)			Average Weekly Attendance (in millions)	Income (in millions)		
	Total	4-Wall	Drive-in		Net Box Office Receipts	Concession Income	Exhibitor Net Income Before Taxes
1946	19.0	18.7	.3	82	1,500	$ 34	$325
1947	18.6	18.1	.5	75	1,398	63	253
1948	18.4	17.6*	.8*	66	1,245	105	144
1949	18.6	17.4	1.2	63	1,203	128	125
1950	19.1	16.9	2.2	61	1,154	160	111
1951	19.0	16.2	2.8	56	1,103	191	90
1952	18.6	15.3	3.3	51	1,054	201	54
1953	18.0	14.2	3.8	46	1,007	211	46
1954	19.1	15.0*	4.1*	49.2	1,055	220	†
1955	19.2	14.6	4.6	45.8	1,055	230	-12

Source: Estimates of Sindlinger & Company, Inc., Independent Analyst, Ridley Park, Pa.: theaters tabulated in *Motion-Picture Distribution Trade Practices—1956*, Report of Senate Small Business Committee, S. Rept. 2818, 84th Cong., 2d sess., p. 28; other series through 1953 in Sindlinger's *Motion Picture Theatres: 1954*, report to Council of Motion Picture Organizations, Ridley Park, Pa., pp. 88, 90; and 1954–55 attendance in *Motion-Picture Distribution Trade Practices—1956*, Hearings Before a Subcommittee of the Senate Small Business Committee, 84th Cong., 2d sess., 1956, p. 266; and 1955 net income from ibid., p. 311. Gross theater income in 1954–55 is estimated in *Survey of Current Business*, July 1956, p. 21, and concessions are assumed to continue their upward trend.

*The Census of Business gives 17,689 regular theaters and 820 drive-ins for 1948, and 14,761 and 3,799 for 1954 (*Motion Picture Herald*, May 26, 1956, p. 18).

† Not available.

to its members lists of old features made available for television, expecting them to be interested, not in the picture, but in the name of the producer. Visitors to local association offices were shown such lists frankly. Gradually production of films for television came to employ nearly as many people as production of theatrical films, and at times more. In 1955 and 1956 most big producers sold their old film libraries for telecasting. One prominent exhibitor, lamenting that the chance to block this sale had been missed, declared that distributor-exhibitor relations had reached an all-time low.[136]

The third cause was the trend toward fewer, more expensive pictures, which deprived independent exhibitors of the "product" they needed for frequent changes of bill and at the same time raised the amount they paid in rental for every dollar of box office receipts. This influence was significant, but should not be exaggerated. More frequent changes of bill would have meant more frequent theatre visits by some patrons, but the resulting poorer-quality pictures would have kept others away. The idea that the entire decline in attendance, aside from that caused by television, must be due to "product shortage"[137] is disposed of by comparing Tables 10.1 and 10.3. In 1947 and 1948 attendance suffered its sharpest drops of the whole postwar period although the first decline in number of features released occurred in 1951 and 1952. The wartime situation, when walking or taking the streetcar or bus to the movies was often the only convenient way to go out for amusement, vanished quickly when gasoline and then new automobiles became available. As for the rental increase, we have already seen that it accounted for only a quarter, and other expenses for three quarters, of the decrease in profit per dollar of receipts between 1947 and 1953.

Since the principal cause of the trend to fewer, better pictures was the effort to cope with television and other competing demands on the public's leisure time, this trend was not entirely independent. The contribution of the *Paramount* decree to the plight of the exhibitors was thus a limited one.

Effects of Divorcement: II. Independent Producers

One result of the antitrust suits has perhaps been some assistance to independent producers. Theoretically, all theaters can now take an interest in their product, whereas formerly the largest and most profitable theaters were forced to show first the products of affiliated producers. On the other hand, most independently produced pictures have always been released through the national distributors, and the Department of Justice conceded when arguing the *Paramount* case that independent production was not being restrained.[138]

Although divorcement does not seem to have been a major reason, it is true that independent production flourished. Entry appeared to be easier than at any time in thirty years. In 1954 it could be said that "the free-wheelers are probably busier than at any previous time in motion picture history";[139] in 1955 that "seldom has Hollywood been so charged with energy and creativity";[140] and in 1956 two thirds of high-quality films were being made by independents.[141] United Artists emerged from near-failure into renewed activity as a distributor of independent films whose preparation it had sponsored, and the new Allied Artists adopted the same plan. The majors also were distributing fewer of their own productions and more of those independently made than ever before. Except for Universal, they welcomed the chance to cut their fixed costs in this era of high wages and salaries but of fewer new pictures by renting out their available studio space to independents.

The primary object of the modern "independent" was not artistic or economic freedom, but lower taxes. A star, writer, or director in the highest income tax bracket could save money by operating through a corporate structure, especially when his or her share in a picture could be sold to make the profit taxable as capital gains at only 25 percent. "The money reason for becoming an independent producer is the only one that really counts in today's Hollywood."[142] Between such independent productions and the continuing major-produced pictures in which the star received a participation (sometimes up to 10 percent of world gross rentals, or 50 percent of domestic net profits[143]) rather than a salary, the distinction, from the major's point of view, began to blur.

The independents frequently followed a major's advice on methods of operation when they rented its facilities and distributed through it. If one defines independents more narrowly as firms that do not release their films through the national distributors,[144] they still played a relatively small role in the industry.

Effects of Divorcement: III. The Defendants

The defendants, as has often been the case after antitrust defeats, seem not to have suffered seriously. Their earnings dropped sharply after their big years, 1946 and 1947, but television and other substitutes for the movie habit offered a good explanation. Getting rid of theaters just when television was striking was by no means pure loss, nor was the added incentive that divorcement gave them to make salable films.

The most serious effect of the *Paramount* case on the defendant producers was in setting loose the greatest flood of treble damage suits in Sherman Act history. A lawyer's secretary told the writer of letters he had sent to exhibitors suggesting such suits—in veiled language, of course. At what was probably their peak, in 1953, total claims were reported to amount to almost $600 million.[145] Usually all eight antitrust defendants were included in these suits, and all eight ran, at least theoretically, the risk of losing every penny of net assets if they lost many cases. At one time, however, Paramount reported that it had won forty and lost fourteen suits, generally settling for 2 or 3 percent of the damages claimed.[146]

In suits covering the years before 1948 the verdict against the defendants in the *Paramount* decision was (under Section 5 of the Clayton Act) *prima facie* evidence against them in treble damage suits. The plaintiff's usual claim was that his theater had not been given a first run or other privilege, and juries and judges were likely to conclude that rejection by all of the defendants indicated conspiracy. This was especially likely if the motive given for rejection seemed to the court so unbusinesslike that all eight distributors could not have held it separately and sincerely—for example, refusal to take a potential higher bid from a drive-in theater merely because they wanted their films to open in a so-called downtown showcase.[147]

The "Conscious Parallelism" Doctrine

Some brief excerpts will illustrate how judicial opinion formulated this doctrine of "conscious parallelism":

> Plaintiff's evidence shows that there is concert of action in what has been done and that this concert could not possibly be sheer coincidence.[148]
>
> It is elementary that an unlawful conspiracy may be and often is found without simultaneous action or agreement on the part of conspirators.[149]
>
> It is incredible that each [distributor] proceeded in ignorance of how the others were dealing with it. . . . In practical effect, consciously parallel business practices have taken the place of the concept of meeting of the minds which some of the earlier cases emphasized.[150]

The doctrine shocked the traditionally minded,[151] but was welcomed by those who wanted the courts to "create a legal concept analogous to collusive oligopoly" and thus outlaw situations where a few big firms operated on a stable basis without much variation in prices or other policies.[152]

A turning point occurred in January 1954. The Supreme Court voted 7 to 1 (with Justice Black submitting a brief dissent) to uphold the lower courts in the so-called *Crest* case, establishing two major principles in favor of the defendants.[153] First, parallel behavior which could have an individual business explanation and lacked supporting evidence was held not to establish conspiracy. Second, the relevance of the *Paramount* decision to events occurring after 1948 was declared to be slight. As these views reached the lower courts,[154] more suits were settled or dropped.

At the end of 1954 the damages still being asked were estimated at "only" $400 million.[155] New suits in 1955 asked for $61 million as against $55 million asked in 1954, but out-of-court settlements in 1955 canceled out $115 million as against $51 million the year before. Court trials in 1955 resulted in one dismissal, one settlement, one verdict for the defense, and three for the plaintiff—the sums awarded amounting to $1,275,000, $60,000 and $3,000, or 27, 2.5, and 0.3 percent of the damages asked.[156]

There was good reason to believe that the flow of lawsuits would gradually dry up. The action of Congress in standardizing the statute of limitations on private antitrust actions at four years, effective in 1956, tended this way. The distributors said they could not be sure, however, that some of their methods would not later prove illegal and subject them to damages.

☆

The Divorced Circuits

The published reports of the divorced circuits show that they were profitable enterprises (except for RKO Theatres and Stanley Warner, in 1953). They tried to select for sale theaters with the least earning power, and their remaining holdings were largely first-run houses suitable for showing quality pictures for runs of a week or more and therefore less affected by the product shortage than the average independent. They also had the resources to install early the modern projection, sound and screen improvements which made it possible to capitalize on the big, new pictures.[157] Perhaps their ability to exert their buying power was increased by the freedom from producer control brought about by divorcement.[158]

Finally, the circuits made an effort to diversify. Stanley Warner owned the rights to the smash-hit Cinerama process, for which it received a special exemption from the decree (good until 1958 only). The Stanley Warner, National, and Paramount circuits laid plans to enter production if permitted. The best example of diversification was the merger of United Paramount Theatres with the American Broadcasting Company early in 1953. The combination gave each a hedge in the movie-television battle and gave ABC the cash it needed to expand its programs in competition with the NBC and CBS networks. Fears that this merger would reduce competition between the two media[159] were not borne out. Except for the divorce between Paramount Pictures and United Paramount Theatres, the Federal Communications Commission might not have allowed the merger. Paramount Pictures likewise used cash to buy what the FCC held to be a controlling stock interest in Allen B. DuMont Laboratories, Inc.,[160] but the support thus brought to DuMont was not enough to keep it functioning as the fourth television network.

Effects of Divorcement: IV. The Public—Quality of Films

How has the public fared as a result of the *Paramount* decree—in quality of pictures, price, and convenience? The government hoped that quality would improve when bad pictures were no longer floated by block booking, when majors were forced to rent their features in an open market, and when all theaters were opened to independent films. There is a good deal of popular comment to the effect that quality has in fact improved. A poll taken in the course of this study shows that motion picture critics think so, too. Out of thirty-four replying to a questionnaire, thirty-two held that quality has improved, one that it has not, and one that the question was unanswerable. Only three of the thirty-two credited the improvement in large part to divorcement, though eight said this might have been a minor contributing factor. An advance in public taste and sophistication was mentioned, but most credit was given to the improving techniques in color, photography, and production generally, and to the stimulus of competition from television. It is agreed that television dealt a heavy blow to the grade B film, which could be seen at home free (though there was a moderate increase in these "cheapies" in 1956). Thus Monogram Pictures Corporation, whose name had been synonymous with such films, became Allied Artists and invaded the quality field.

The influence of divorcement on the quality of pictures may have been minor, but was probably beneficial. Since major producers no longer had to be concerned with keeping screen time of affiliated theaters occupied, they could turn from making many cheap films to fewer high-grade ones. Since all theaters are free to pick and choose among films offered them, features are unlikely to be sold unless they have at least some merit in the eyes of exhibitors. This influence probably outweighs the opposite effect of the abandonment of block booking—that a producer can no longer venture into an experimental picture trusting to its automatic sale as part of a block.

One indirect influence of divorcement on quality may be interpreted as either negative or constructive according to one's view of censorship and self-censorship. After 1934 all industry members were supposedly subject to a $25,000 fine by the industry's Production Code Administration (then called the "Breen Office") for issuing a picture without its seal. In fear of antitrust consequences, this fine was quietly dropped in 1942 for exhibitors, although they were not so informed until 1946.[161] Divorcement removed the link through which the influence of the Breen Office as well as the (Catholic) Legion of Decency over the studios was passed on automatically to the first-run theaters. In 1953, 7,000 theaters played *The Moon Is Blue* without the seal—a show of independence which both the producer, jubilantly, and an officer of the Legion of Decency, regretfully, attributed to the new freedom of theaters since divorcement.[162]

Price and Convenience

Three factors connected with the decree might have been expected to push up box office prices: (1) Reduction of block booking raised distribution costs, even if not by the 50 to 75 percent expected to follow from its complete abolition.[163] (2) Harder bargaining by producers on rentals forced exhibitors to raise their charges. On their biggest features it was possible for producers to decline to license exhibitors who did not raise prices during the week of exhibition, although they avoided the direct resale-price agreement that the courts condemned in the *Paramount* decisions. (3) Theaters that advanced their runs—as for example from second to first—often raised prices correspondingly. If this third tendency went to its logical limit—which it naturally did not—neighborhood theater prices would have risen and downtown prices would have been forced down by slumping attendance as people could see early runs nearby.[164] This condition reduced the variety of price-plus-product packages available to consumers.

The unpublished Bureau of Labor Statistics index of admission prices, which stood at 60 in 1935–39 and 100 in 1947–49, was 123.6 in March 1956. The increase from 1935–39 to 1947–49 was identical with the rise in the consumer price index, but the ensuing 23.6 percent increase to March 1956 compares with only 14.7 percent for the over-all index. A 10 percent cut in the federal admissions tax in April 1954 might also have been expected to bring the price down. Not only did admission prices increase more than most prices, but it is clear that many and probably most theaters kept the benefit of the tax cut.[165]

The changes induced by the decree benefited some moviegoers and inconvenienced others. The reduction of unreasonable clearances was good for all; but the 16 percent of adult moviegoers who attended or wanted to attend more than once a week felt the product shortage. Those who were able to see pictures on earlier runs than before were better off; but those who wished to deliberate before seeing a feature were inconvenienced by having to see it at once or not at all. It is hard to say where the net balance lay, but the new pattern of operation seemed better suited to an era of quick change in popular taste. There also were signs that the theater pattern (including the newly flourishing art theaters) would make the necessary adjustments to meet the public demand in whatever forms it clearly evidenced itself.

Other Antitrust Suits

The antitrust cases completed between 1948 and 1956 include suits relating to licensing of color processes, pooling theatre operations and profits, contract arrangements of an advertising service firm, and licensing of films for telecasting.

The government charged in 1947 that Eastman Kodak Company had given Technicolor, Inc., exclusive rights to use certain aspects of its color cinematography through a series of license agreements. In 1948 Eastman, and in February 1950 Technicolor, signed consent decrees. Eastman opened thirteen color patents royalty-free and fourteen at a reasonable royalty.[166] Technicolor opened ninety-two royalty-free and twelve (plus all patent applications until November 1953) at a reasonable royalty. Technicolor also dropped its exclusive arrangements with the majors and agreed to furnish technical information to all licensees through 1956.[167] Use of competitive color processes increased, and the price of the Technicolor process declined.[168] Opinion in the industry differed in regard to whether the decrees contributed to these developments or not.

In 1951 six drive-in theaters in the Chicago area were indicted for agreeing on admission prices. Two years later the Seventh Circuit Court sustained the dismissal of the indictment. Denying the government's claim that such an agreement necessarily restrained the flow of films into Illinois, the court commented that it knew of no case where the interstate commerce concept had been stretched so far.[169] On the other hand, a 1952 indictment of two companies in Terre Haute for pooling theater operations and profits eventuated three years later in a consent judgment.[170]

In February 1953 the Supreme Court, by a 7–2 vote, overruled the Circuit Court and sustained a Federal Trade Commission order enjoining exclusive contracts running beyond one year between the Motion Picture Advertising Service Company, a supplier of advertising materials, and a substantial number of exhibitors.[171] The opinion of Justice Douglas pointed to the fact that some competitors had been forced out of business by inability to break through this contract wall. Justice Frankfurter's dissent would not accept, without a clear statement of the criteria the commission was using, the proposition that two- to five-year contracts constituted unfair competition.

The 16-Millimeter Case

An important case was opened in July 1952, with the Department of Justice asking the District Court in Los Angeles to enjoin restrictions put on the release of 16-millimeter films. These films were made by all leading producers except Loew's and Paramount, as duplicates of their standard 35-millimeter films. They were shown at Army camps, schools, hospitals and many similar places, and were used for telecasting. In licensing institutional showings, the distributors protected their regular customers by various restrictions, such as refusal to deal with some of these outlets if they were within ten miles of an established theater. Calling the restrictions collusive, the government asked the court to set a time limit between a picture's release in 35-millimeter form and the time it must be released in 16-millimeter form for all uses, including television. It believed that the industry would have full protection against untoward results if it relied on the court's judgment as regarding "reasonable" clearance.[172]

Three years later, on the eve of trial, Republic Pictures signed a consent decree agreeing to make given percentages of its films available from two to three years after their release to theaters. Its president stated that this was already the company's policy and "method of operation." [173]

The other defendants argued their case before Judge Leon R. Yankwich, who handed down a sweeping ruling in their favor in December 1955.[174] He saw no reason to suspect collusion, since the producers might easily have made up their minds individually not to destroy their most profitable customers by freely licensing nonprofit institutions and television. Any similarity of their actions could be explained by the similarity of the problem facing them. In regard to the facts, some outlets rejected by one producer were accepted by another, and interoffice correspondence showed that decisions were made independently. The court saw a natural motive for Walt Disney to hold back *Snow White and the Seven Dwarfs* for reissue to each new generation of moviegoers. It was impressed also by the fact that *King Kong* had earned $1,569 in 16-millimeter form, $710,653 on its first 35-millimeter issue, and $1,608,000 on the reissue, which sale to television would certainly have prevented. Even though other reissues proved disappointing and reissue was not at all probable for most films,[175] still it would seem that producers should have the right to make this decision for themselves.

Three months after the decision the government announced its intention not to appeal it, largely because sale of old features to television had begun.[176] RKO's sale of its "library" of 740 feature pictures and 1,000 shorts (after a three-year clearance) led off at the end of 1955. The other producers who sold their libraries in 1956 (all except Paramount and Universal) used a 1948 cutoff date because of a union contract adopted in that year. This seven-year interval was considerably longer clearance than the government had been hoping for in its suit, but it was doubtful that it would last. The idea of taking first payment in the form of a partnership in the television interest was being broached. This would give the studios diversification, but the theaters would merely be facing increased competition.

☆
Trend of Concentration

The majors, as we have seen, accounted for a substantially smaller percentage of total production than in the past. The only statistics available, however, relate to distribution.

The eight largest producer-distributors released 65 percent of domestic features in 1932–35, 69 percent in 1942–45 and 79 percent in

1952–55. More of the imported features also are released by the national distributors now than before World War II. Columbia, Universal, and United Artists released more films in the early 1940s and 1950s than in the early 1930s, whereas releases by both the five majors and the independents dropped off. (See table 10.4.) Releases of the national distributors bring in much larger gross receipts than the others, and in 1948 (the latest year tabulated) 93 percent of domestic film rentals were accounted for by the eleven national distributors.[177]

Among the big companies, Paramount and RKO showed the principal declines. Paramount's releases formed 17 percent of the total in 1919 and 12 in 1923,[178] 8 percent in 1939, 6 in 1947 and 5 in 1955.[179]

For twenty-five years until 1954 the pattern of the industry was fixed, with five majors (Loew's, Paramount, RKO, Twentieth Century–Fox and Warner Bros.), two minor producers (Columbia and Universal), and United Artists (distributor for independent producers) as the eighth important unit. Then suddenly RKO faded out of the list; picture successes

Table 10.4. *Motion Pictures: Number of Features Released, Eight Largest Firms and Independents, 1932–55*

Firm	1932–35		1942–45		1952–55	
	Number	Per-cent	Number	Per-cent	Number	Per-cent
Total features released	2,757	100	1,778	100	1,816	100
Eight largest firms*	1,373	50	1,150	65	1,019	56
Loew's, Paramount, RKO, Twentieth Century-Fox, Warner Bros.	1,003	37	651	37	533	29
Columbia, Universal, United Artists	370	13	499	28	486	27
Independents*	1,384	50	628	35	797	44
Domestic features	2,001	100	1,635	100	1,175	100
Eight largest firms*	1,307	65	1,114	69	923	79
Independents*	694	35	521	31	252	21
Imported features	756	100	143	100	641	100
Eight largest firms	66	9	36	25	96	15
Independents	690	91	107	75	545	85

Source: *The Film Daily Year Book*, New York, 1947, p. 53; 1956, pp. 103, 105.
*Included under "eight largest firms" are domestic features produced by independents but distributed by the eight companies.

by Columbia and Universal made them appear as important as the majors, and Allied Artists and Republic loomed as contenders for that title. Evidently good or bad management (and perhaps good or bad luck with public reception of features) meant changes in what had appeared to be a rigid structure.

The Question of Size and Efficiency

The relative merits of different sizes of operation were being tested in the market all the time. Thousands of small neighborhood theaters vanished, but the type seemed likely to continue. The fact that half of all theaters belonged to circuits attested to the economies of combination—although the owners of circuits of six or eight theaters insisted on their right to be called independents.

States-rights (local) exchanges handled 75 percent of releases in 1913, and probably not more than 15 percent thirty years later.[180] However, they still functioned for some types of distribution.

The battle between big and small producers was perhaps more evenly matched. Under conditions created by television, with assistance from the income tax law and possibly the *Paramount* decree, the small producers had made advances, as we have seen. Yet they were still linked to the large producer in many ways. The massive facilities of the majors (large lots with many types of sets, thousands of "stock shots," and the rest) ensured their place in the industry, even if it was somewhat smaller than in the past. One commentator, pointing out that the big companies had not capitalized on one advantage of size in most industries, urged them to devote more money to technical research and development.[181]

Performance of the Industry

Hollywood has to its credit great technical achievements in picture making (including notable developments by independents), as well as success in cultivating the mass market. Every other, or nearly every other, country where motion pictures are made has legislation protecting the home industry from American competition, just because Hollywood has found the secret of appealing to the average man, woman, and child over most of the world. The common view of "intellectuals" that Hollywood productions are financial rather than artistic successes did not prevail among the newspaper critics questioned in a 1956 study by the author: twenty-five thought American films superior to European, 2 thought them inferior, and seven said they could not be compared.

Hollywood is at a disadvantage in achieving quality as compared with other media, such as books, magazines, concerts, and to some extent, plays. These media are designed for smaller, self-selected audiences that are looking for particular qualities. The high cost of film production and distribution calls for audiences in the millions, and mass entertainment forces orientation toward the lowest common denominator of public taste. The general rule in the industry is to offend the smallest number of people, even if this means that intellectual minorities become the so-called "lost audience." The religious, racial, professional, national, and other groups that want to make sure no film casts discredit upon any of their members have a very great cramping influence on Hollywood products.[182] These powerful social forces have been impossible to resist.

Quality seems to have little to do with the competitive situation in the industry. It is true that there are independent producers who put out low-cost productions of artistic merit which cannot hope to win a huge box office return except by an unexpected development in the public's tastes. If the Sherman Act helps preserve their existence it does an important service. But the industry as a whole is geared by its costs to box office success. This is especially true of the small exhibitors. They want to eliminate not only "a lot of low-grossing arty pictures,"[183] but also serious social dramas and renditions of literary classics and historical themes (except those with "outdoor action"). A recent poll showed that the types of stories exhibitors want are, in order of preference: comedy, "family," musical, outdoor action, western, "women's," and mystery.[184] A well-financed producing or exhibiting organization might consider devoting a small part of its funds to experimentation with unusual offerings on a high artistic level, and there are small producers willing to take a "flyer" on a fresh idea; but the smaller exhibitor who expects to stay permanently in business cannot afford to do so very often.[185] Only the art theaters provide a regular outlet for such films, and they have so far established themselves only in cultural centers or large cities.

Summary

1. After a few years of chaotic competition among the pioneers of the movie business, the *Motion Picture Patents Company* was set up in 1908 to settle conflicting patent claims and incidentally to monopolize the in-

dustry. Its failure was owing less to the antitrust actions that it lost than to the greater initiative of its independent competitors.

2. The *Paramount–Famous Players–Lasky interests*, organized in 1916 and 1917 by independents who had fought the trust, next threatened to dominate the industry. The principal theater circuits combined to protect themselves, under the First National title, and established their own studios. The Paramount group, facing loss of its market, bought theaters. Although the group finally overcame First National, competitive equilibrium was maintained as Fox and Loew's also integrated and gained strength.

3. When Warner Bros. and RKO gained established positions at the end of the 1920s through exploitation of talking pictures, the industry came under *domination by five integrated "majors"* and three allies (Columbia, Universal, and United Artists). Together they made nearly all the feature pictures produced, and owned most of the first-run theaters. Large independent theater circuits had special advantages in buying. The independents who (largely because their facilities were not wanted) had not sold out to the majors or accepted them as partners played the pictures only after long "clearances." Clearances which gave reasonable protection to the big investment in downtown, first-run theaters were not generally criticized by the independents.

4. The *first twenty-five years of antitrust action* had only modest results. In 1918 the Federal Trade Commission required a booking combine to drop certain restrictive practices. In 1929–30 the federal courts outlawed compulsory arbitration of distributor-exhibitor disputes and a system of checking the credit of exhibitors. A Fox-Loew's combination was enjoined in 1931. In 1929 and 1935 private suits contributed to opening up sound-film patents. From 1929 to 1936 monopolistic practices of five groups of theaters were enjoined. The first overall suit against the majors resulted in a consent decree in 1940, in which the forcing of films on exhibitors was limited in certain respects.

5. In 1944 and 1948, the Supreme Court upheld the government against the *Crescent, Griffith, and Schine circuits*. They had obtained preferences over competitors in towns where they met competition by facing distributors with the alternative of losing any showings in their "closed" towns. The courts enjoined this practice and directed sale of some of their theaters in closed towns.

6. The Supreme Court's *Paramount decision of 1948* led to a new set of restrictions on the operations of the eight principal companies—abolition of compulsory block booking, of unreasonably long clearances, of deals with circuits on any other basis than picture by picture and theater by theater, and of any discrimination in licensing films. Loew's, Twentieth

Century—Fox, Paramount, RKO, and Warner Bros. were split into production-distribution and exhibition companies. The new theater companies were required to dispose of their interests in about 1,200 theaters.
Whether or not this was, as one writer has called it, the government's
greatest antitrust victory, it definitely established a freer market for films.

7. The *effects on independent exhibitors* were mixed. On the constructive side, exhibitors were freed from the artificial system of runs and
clearance formerly imposed on them. But there were disconcerting consequences as well—two major and two minor ones. (1) Divorce from exhibition removed the incentive to the majors to make enough films to fill
the screen time of their own circuits, and the abolition of block booking
made producers more cautious in deciding whether to make each new
film. These factors probably contributed to the decline in the number of
features produced and thus to the difficulties of exhibitors seeking films
to show. As a result, exhibitors reversed their position and urged renewed integration of production and exhibition. (2) The decline in the
number of films, the sharper bargaining of producers no longer tied to
exhibition, and competitive bidding among several theaters desiring
films on the same run, have all tended to raise the average film rental and
thus to reduce theater profits. (3) The abolition of compulsory block
booking, in itself a real achievement of the *Paramount* decision by giving
theaters more freedom to select films—often to the benefit of independent producers and of the audience—was nevertheless unpopular with a
substantial number of exhibitors who would have preferred to save time
and money by renting films in blocks. (4) So many theaters have stepped
up to prior runs that moviegoers had a shorter period in which to see a
picture, and it is possible that overall attendance was reduced.

8. The main *cause of the exhibitors' troubles* was the decline in attendance caused by television and other distractions and family preoccupations; and for four-wall theaters an important secondary cause was competition of drive-ins. The studios adjusted themselves by making "fewer
but better" films which attract people out of their homes, and by making
films for television, but the exhibitors have found no effective defense.
The impact of interindustry competition and of changes in population,
consumer habits, and technology—as represented by television and the
drive-in—was far more influential then the antitrust decrees.

9. *Independent producers* flourished in Hollywood more than ever before divorcement, but the stimulus through the abolition of block booking and of theater ownership by the majors was minor compared to the
desire of the majors to cut studio fixed charges, not to mention the attraction of the capital gains tax to stars and directors formerly on salary.

10. The *Paramount case defendants* did not seem to have suffered fi-

nancially from the decree, and the producer-distributors may in fact have profited from the splitting off of their theater interests. Although treble damage suits threatened the defendants with fatal financial losses, these suits soon went on the decline and the threat was not fulfilled. "Conscious parallelism" was no longer proof of conspiracy without other evidence. As a result of divorcement, the Federal Communications Commission permitted the American Broadcasting–Paramount Theaters merger, which increased the competitive strength of this network and theater circuit.

11. The *effect on the public* was mixed. The decree has probably had a modest effect in improving the quality of pictures, since a firm could no longer automatically show poor pictures in its own theaters and foist them off on others through block booking. Divorcement perhaps weakened Hollywood's self-censorship, by setting more theaters free from producer control. There was a net rise in admission prices as a result of high film rentals, of higher distribution costs under the picture-by-picture system, and of the stepping up of runs. Although some members of the public were annoyed that so many theaters claimed the right to show the same feature simultaneously, the new pattern of quick changes seemed to suit the times better.

12. *Antitrust cases between 1948 and 1956* perhaps contributed to increased competition in the supply of color film to producers and of advertising material to theaters. The "16-millimeter decision" of federal Judge Yankwich in 1955 denied the government's right to require producers to license their films for telecasting, but within a few months market considerations caused this very development (but with clearances chosen by the producers rather than directed by the courts).

13. Between 1932–35 and 1952–55 the *share of the five majors* in the number of pictures released dropped from 36 to 29 percent, that of Columbia, Universal, and United Artists increased from 14 to 27 percent, and that of the independents decreased from 50 to 44 percent. In the competitive struggle of large and small companies, the little exhibitor and little distributor were on the losing end. The larger producer, while ceding to the independent producer in many respects, continued to furnish many of the latter's production and distribution facilities.

14. The *performance of the industry* has been notable in its creation of a new and almost universal form of mass entertainment. Its chief weakness has sprung from this very fact—that is, the quality of films has been kept down by the necessity of appealing to the lowest common denominator in the potential mass audience.

In brief, attempts by a single company to monopolize the motion picture industry have been defeated by competition, with relatively minor

aid from the antitrust laws; and the effects of the 1948 divorcement decree against the dominant group have been mixed: a rigid pattern of control was abolished and independent theaters won the right to show features sooner; but this plunge into a free market has given them a new
appreciation of the advantages of integration; and the benefits to the public have been uncertain and, at best, moderate.

Hollywood, the National Recovery Administration, and the Question of Monopoly Power

Douglas Gomery

For economic and social historians of the American cinema, one major reference point has been and continues to be the film industry's relationship to the U.S. federal government. By and large we learn of dramatic tales of battle; the industry triumphs on the censorship front and is driven back—in the end—by antitrust warfare. Robert Sklar in his *Movie-Made America* and Garth Jowett in his *Film: The Democratic Art* summarize previous historical research and thus closely follow the dominant trend. Typically, Sklar argues, "Congress, the executive departments and the federal courts had tried persistently over the years to influence the policies and practices of the [film] industry without marked success."[1] Both Sklar and Jowett claim that an important change came with President Franklin D. Roosevelt's National Recovery Administration (NRA) in 1933. According to Sklar, with the NRA the federal government finally asserted control so that, "the code for the motion picture industry ended up strengthening the small [exhibitors] at the expense of the major producer-distributors."[2] For Jowett, previous studies indicate that NRA proved the film industry was in chaos and thus the film industry invited and secured federal interference.[3]

If the NRA indeed signals a significant turning point in film industry–federal government relations, Sklar and Jowett fail to provide a systematic method by which to explain how and why relative power shifted to the federal government. In addition, each relies, almost completely, on one primary source.[4] In this article, after explaining my methodology, I shall argue that with the NRA the "big-five" vertically-integrated movie companies (Fox, RKO, Warners, Loew's, and Paramount) and the three

205

other major producer-distributors (Columbia, United Artists, and Universal) gained monopoly power. By lobbying successfully through their trade association, the Motion Picture Producers and Distributors Association (the MPPDA or Hays Office), these eight firms were able to convince the federal government to sanction their pre-1930 monopolistic trade practices. The small exhibitors, contrary to Sklar's claim, were hurt, not helped, and the monopolists were not in chaos but near the acme of their power. The NRA does mark an important point in the history of the U.S. film industry because for the life of that law, Hollywood legally exercised its monopolistic power.

Confusion about film industry—federal government relations arises because historians rarely make explicit their method for analysis. For economic questions, most film historians implicitly use a framework from neoclassical economics. Simply put, for neoclassical economists the modern capitalist system functions optimally when competition dominates and there exists minimal government interference in the marketplace. To initiate any action, a governmental unit should demonstrate there exists a market failure which only collective action can correct. The working assumption is that unless it can prove interference in the marketplace will make the economy run more efficiently or the distribution of income more equitable, governmental action causes harm. Thus for questions of monopoly behavior for one single corporation, the government and that particular business become foes, with the government trying to prove antitrust action will be beneficial, and the corporation (or corporations) arguing that such intervention will only be harmful. Such antitrust suits for writers who follow the neoclassical method become dramatic, hard fought battles with conservative historians usually portraying the government as evil, and liberal historians arguing that government intervention is necessary.[5]

The neoclassical model assumes a world of competition and thus fails to provide a suitable method for the analysis of a market dominated by large corporations, for example the U.S. film industry in 1933. I shall assume that for the questions raised in this article, the Marxist economic model provides a more appropriate method for analysis. Although Marx did not work out an explicit theory of the state, Paul Sweezy and James O'Connor have provided an initial framework to explain how the state and industry function in advanced capitalism. Sweezy and O'Connor assert that the class which occupies the most powerful positions in the process of production fashions a state to enforce that set of property relations which will act in that class's own best interest. Thus unlike the neoclassical model in which government and industry are foes, in the Marxist model the government is an ally to big business. Governmental regulation of industry can only be acceptable if it helps the monopoly capitalists. In this model one assumes, despite what seems to appear on the surface, that government activity benefits monopoly capitalists. There can be struggle, or even short-term setbacks, but in the long run the monopoly capitalists and government work in tandem, not as enemies. Thus I assume that the NRA should have helped, not hurt, the Hollywood monopolists. Minimal evidence suggests that was the case, since all the movie monopolists survived the Great Depression and surged to large profits during the late 1930s and into the 1940s.[6]

Before I analyze how the Hollywood monopolists benefited from the NRA, I think it is necessary to describe the mechanism, a trade association, they used to pressure for and secure favorable state action. Generally, a trade association is an organization of large firms in one field that band together to further monopoly power. The association compiles data, initiates public relations, handles labor difficulties, and pressures for favorable governmental conduct. As a few large corporations began to dominate the U.S. film industry, they recognized the need for such an organization. In 1916, the large producer-distributors and exhibitor chains formed the National Association of the Motion Picture Industry. This association proved unworkable, especially in the area of censorship, so in 1922, the now vertically-integrated combines formed the Motion Picture Producers and Distributors Association. The immediate goal of the MPPDA was to ward off state or federal censorship laws or both; after success in that area, the long-run concern became the preservation of world-wide monopolistic trade practices. The Hollywood monopolists hired Will Hays, former Republican national chairman, and paid him nearly one hundred thousand dollars annually to use his political connections to lobby. To the general public, the Hays Office seemed primarily a censorship organ; for member companies, more important were efforts to minimize taxes and antitrust interference and to provide a business climate to maximize monopoly (surplus) profits.[7]

The 1920s were an era of vast growth of monopolies and also a period when trade associations multiplied and expanded. Intraindustry cooperation had existed before World War I, but during that war the federal government openly promoted the establishment of trade associations. The Republican administrations of the 1920s, boosted by monopoly capitalists, continued to encourage trade associations. During the "New Era" business (read *monopolists'*) interests became overtly equated with the national interest. The Department of Justice nearly ceased antitrust activity; the Department of Commerce and the Federal Trade Commission assisted trade associations to expand, formulate codes for "fair" practices (read *maintain the status quo*), and generally remove price competition. At the outset of the Great Depression, it seemed that harmony might be difficult to maintain. Quickly, however, monopoly capitalists rallied around the idea of government-supported cartels to eliminate "unfair" price-cutting, promote stability and, so the argument went, return the country to the prosperity of the 1920s. Trade association spokespersons first pushed for repeal or modification of the antitrust laws. Soon the U.S. Chamber of Commerce and the American Bar Association joined the call and offered proposals to Congress to prohibit pricing below the competition and to reestablish Federal Trade Commission industry conferences to promote cooperation. President Hoover opposed such direct measures. When Franklin Roosevelt and the new Congress took over in March 1933, trade associationists took the day and helped write a law, the National Industrial Recovery Act (NIRA). Each industry would have self-government with an industrial code, supervised by the dominant trade association, with government sanction, not supervision.[8]

The National Industrial Recovery Act became law on 16 June 1933. Title I established the National Recovery Administration (NRA) to institute and supervise the codes for "fair competition" for all U.S. industries. The law assumed that the industry's dominant trade association would write the code; if not, President Roosevelt could impose a government-authored code. In exchange for the acceptance of a code, the industry became exempt from any prosecution under existing antitrust laws. For labor, under NIRA section 7, each code had to permit employees to organize and bargain collectively, outlaw company unions, and stipulate, explicitly, maximum hours, and minimum wages, and working conditions. Under Hugh Johnson, the NRA first attempted to compel the ten largest industries to institute codes, and then, so the logic went, smaller industries would jump on the bandwagon. The ten were: textiles, coal, petroleum, steel, automobiles, lumber, garments, wholesale trade, retail trade, and construction. Conspicuously absent was the U.S. film industry, which since the late 1920s had heralded itself as the United States' fourth largest industry; more accurate estimates ranked the film industry about fortieth.[9] Johnson's strategy failed; only the textile industry would agree to a code. Thus in July 1933 Johnson began to try to make the NRA a mass movement, complete with the Blue Eagle as logo. Within a month, Johnson signed up two million firms. By 18 September 1933, all of the top-ten industries had codes. From then until 16 June 1935, when the NIRA expired, Johnson and his staff formulated and administered more than 500 codes.[10]

The monopolists of the U.S. film industry quickly embraced the NIRA. In fact, ten days before Congress even passed the legislation, representatives of the Hays group had formulated a proposal: pool all production and distribution under a single government commissioner. Such a plan would maximize monopoly profits, yet cause insurmountable problems for dividing up the surplus.[11] By mid-June, the Hays group had modified its plan to a simple restatement of the monopolistic practices used just before the Great Depression, during the salad days of 1929–30. Opposing the monopolists were the small, unaffiliated exhibitors, represented through their trade association, the Allied States Association of Motion Picture Exhibitors (Allied States). Former Federal Trade Commissioner F. Abram Meyers spoke for the Allied States' interests. As soon as Hays had made public the MPPDA plans, Meyers petitioned to Hugh Johnson to deny the Hay's group's proposal and accept one more sympathetic to the small exhibitor. In brief, the Allied States recommended that all current and proposed monopolistic behavior be outlawed. Early in July 1933, Johnson ruled that only one code would be accepted, and it had to be "truly representative." There was little doubt Johnson would eventually accept the Hays group's version, but how were Allied States' demands to be resolved without adverse publicity? Censorship difficulties forced the Hays group to tread lightly.[12]

In July 1933 Hugh Johnson appointed Solomon A. Rosenblatt, a New York lawyer sympathetic to the Hays group, deputy administrator in charge of drawing up the motion-picture-industry code. Still, after Rosenblatt could not quiet Allied States' protests he held public meetings in Washington, D.C., on 12, 13, and 14 September 1933. Despite extensive press coverage, the publicity proved not as injurious as the Hays group had anticipated. Deep in a depression, the public and politicians at the time seemed to care little about squabbles in the film industry. After yet another month of private negotiations, Allied States gave in on all issues except one: it would permit double features to be banned under the motion picture code. The Hays group agreed, and the two-for-one exhibition policy became the only nonmonopolistic competitive strategy not outlawed in the code. On 28 October 1928 Rosenblatt forwarded the code to Johnson; one month later President Roosevelt signed it into law. However, one issue remained to be resolved. One section of the executive order which accompanied Roosevelt's signing of the code empowered Johnson to modify the code if major difficulties arose. The Hays group feared Johnson might take this as a cue to begin to interfere directly with industry affairs. Thus on 8 December 1933 Will Hays and representatives from Loew's and Paramount called on President Roosevelt personally and obtained a directive by which Roosevelt ordered Hugh Johnson to stay out of the movie business. The motion picture code was now set: the Hays group had used the NRA to sanction officially the monopoly behavior of the pre-Depression industry.[13]

The motion picture code spelled out in detail trade practices for all branches of the industry and even specifically named the ten-code authority commissioners who could ultimately arbitrate disputes. Of the code authority's ten members, nine were affiliated with the Hays group. The code authority acted as the supreme court for industry appeals; sixty-two local boards handled any disputes initially. Each local board consisted of seven members, four of whom came from the Hays group, thus guaranteeing that only the most important problems were ever placed before the national code authority. The bulk of the code covered noncontroversial issues. For example, companies were prohibited from defaming competitors and disparaging the quality of other firms' movies. Very few provisions helped Allied States' members. The code required a standard contract between distributor and exhibitor; this basic contract is still used today. An exhibitor could cancel 10 percent of the films he or she booked in a block. The 10 percent figure was a compromise between the Allied States' proposed 100 percent and the Hays group 5 percent (5-5-5 system).[14] The vast majority of the code guaranteed that the Hays group could continue monopolistic behavior and, indeed, a few provisions severely curtailed the current behavior of independent exhibitors. Thus except for double features, the code eliminated all the forms of nonprice competition, which had been lifesavers to small exhibitors during the severe economic downturn. Since these exhibitors usually secured films during the fourth, fifth, or subsequent run, they offered games, such as bank night, race night, or screeno, or premiums, such as free dishware, to attract customers away from the first-run houses owned by the Hays group.[15] The code specifically outlawed all games or premiums because they were "unfair" competition, and even went so far as to prohibit the giving away of free parking as a premium.[16]

The provisions in the motion picture code for labor, required under section 7, at first did not seem controversial or innovative. Motion picture unions lacked strength and were divided; there were 140 separate labor groups that signed the code. Because of their weakness, these unions readily agreed to federally imposed boundaries for maximum hours and minimum wages. The immediate, short-run problem for the Hays groups was not the threat of growing unions, but the stigma generated by the industry's extremely high salaries. How could stars and industry executives be paid several hundred thousand dollars yearly while millions starved and went unemployed? The Hays group, in order to minimize publicity, agreed to a federal study of the issue, and in his executive decree signing the code, President Roosevelt did order an investigation of this problem and thus suspended any immediate action. The report, issued 7 July 1934, documented that some executives and stars had taken cuts in salary (for example, from $10,000 per week in the early 1930s to $500 per week), but most remained among the highest paid individuals in the United States. No action by the NRA was forthcoming, and by 1935 salaries were returning to pre-Depression levels. Sklar suggests that the salary investigation was yet another setback for the Hays group. I argue the opposite. Again, the Hollywood monopolists defused one more potentially explosive issue and returned conditions to the status quo.[17]

The greatest change for labor came in the long run. Although a complete analysis lies beyond the scope of this article, I argue that section 7 of the NIRA provided the first major impetus toward the growth of strong unions in Hollywood. The full effects would not be worked out until a decade after the NIRA expired. During the life of the NRA, numerous Hollywood unions began to organize, institute collective action, and gather strength; only the Screen Actors Guild (SAG) made significant progress. The Hays group maintained the Academy of Motion Picture Arts and Sciences as a company union in order to counter all unionizing efforts. The powerful, New York-based Actors Equity had tried to organize performers in the new sound movies in 1929 and failed. By 1933 most actors and actresses made no more than one thousand dollars per year while an estimated fifty elite stars earned fabulous six-figure salaries. Because many stars felt threatened by the salary cuts implied by the NRA study, a group led by Actors Equity members formed the Screen Actors Guild. The new union's first action was to oppose any federally enforced ceiling on actors' or actresses' salaries. Since the Hays group agreed with the position, SAG efforts proved successful. All other SAG demands, for the life of the NRA, went ignored; the studios still controlled the actors' or actresses' ability to move, working hours, salary, and all other conditions of labor. In fact, the Hays group would not even recognize the SAG until 1937. Only after the passage of the Wagner Act of 1935 could Hollywood unions become strong enough to obtain recognition and a modicum of demands.[18]

Allied States and the struggling Hollywood unions constantly proclaimed that the NRA favored the Hays' group. All of America's liberal and radical organizations hurled similar charges and accusations at the NRA's codes. Consequently in March 1934 Hugh Johnson created the National Recovery Review Board (Review Board), and appointed Clarence Darrow as its head. During the spring of 1934 Darrow and his staff held hearings, considered complaints, and issued reports. In sum the review board found that the steel and motion-picture-industry trade associations had engineered the most oppressive codes. Since Hugh Johnson, Franklin Roosevelt, and the U.S. Congress completely ignored the review board's suggestions for change, their findings proved only to be well-documented complements for the Hays group and a further reminder to the Allied States' members of their powerlessness. Moreover, despite the publicity generated by the review board, the NIRA remained a popular program.[19]

On 27 May 1935, the U.S. Supreme Court found the NIRA unconstitutional. The immediate effect on the motion picture industry was slight. Since the Hays group had authored the code and continued to control the industry, only federal sanction was eliminated. There were some minor changes. Immediately, small exhibitors reinstituted premiums: the end of the NRA signaled the beginning of those famous dish giveaways of the 1930s. Massive nonprice competition would only cease with the restrictions of World War II. In the longer run, the publicity generated and information gathered during the NRA concerning the motion picture industry, coupled with change in the Roosevelt administration's strategy to combat hard times, led to antitrust action against the film industry's monopoly capitalists. The Hays Office fought the charges and on 20 November 1940, the Department of Justice and the defendants signed a consent decree very favorable to the film industry. In exchange for dropping the case, the film industry agreed to set up a system to settle disputes almost identical to that which had been operative under the NRA's motion picture code. In place of the sixty-two local grievance boards under the code, the consent decree called for thirty-one independent arbitration tribunals administered by the American Arbitration Association. The Hays group continued to dominate until 1944, when the Department of Justice reopened the case.[20]

In conclusion I have argued that indeed the NRA did signal a change in film industry–federal government relations, but not for the reasons suggested by previous historians. By using a Marxist model, I have found that with the NRA the federal government first openly sanctioned the behavior of the Hollywood monopolists. Instead of the informal collusion that had existed since the mid-1920s, open and explicit collusion and exploitation took place, free from the threat of antitrust action. This certainly guaranteed the survival of the Hays group during America's worst economic downturn by increasing profits and maintaining strict barriers to entry. Although the NIRA expired in May 1935, the Hays group continued to dominate until 1944. The NRA had set important precedents. Yet imbedded within this process of film industry/federal government interaction was one element that would hurt the monopolists' defense of this antitrust case and indirectly assist with the opening and reopening of that case. Before the NRA there existed little accurate data concerning film-industry monopolistic behavior. The various public hearings and the review board's report revealed that Hollywood was an evil monopoly.[21]

Like many large federal government programs, the NRA failed in its appointed task—helping the United States emerge from a major depression—but it did have important secondary effects. For the film industry, the NRA fostered the growth of B-genre films. Firms like Monogram and Republic grew and prospered despite a severe depression. During the 1920s, only a few theaters offered double features, but in bad times the two-for-one exhibition strategy became an important competitive tool for the subsequent-run exhibitor. Since Allied States was able to prevent the Hays group from banning double features under the NRA code, the two-for-one policy became the principle means by which small, independent theaters competed from 1933 to 1935. Small producers responded to this increase in demand, and B-grade production flourished. By May 1935 double features had become the dominant form of U.S. film exhibition. The rise of the double feature was not completely owing to the NRA motion picture code, but without the code's restrictions the policy certainly would not have become as widespread as it did.

Afterword

Based on research conducted while I was still a graduate student (see Tino Balio, *United Artists* [Madison: Univ. of Wisconsin Pr., 1976, p. 298]), this essay represents my initial effort at what economists categorize as public policy analysis. Any discussion of relations between government and business requires a powerful methodology. Therefore, upon rereading my article, I was struck with how cavalierly I handled fundamental theoretical questions. I must thank the editor for allowing me to produce a needed auto-critique.

As it presently stands this case study of the NRA and the U.S. film industry relies upon a relatively simplistic understanding of Marxist economics. I blithely assumed that for the questions I raised, a Marxist model provided the only appropriate methodology. I also resorted to knocking down a "strawman" in order to justify my efforts. In 1981 I believe I oversimplified both the Marxist and the neoclassical positions, so much so that I reduced the value of each. One does not need Marxist economics to produce a framework for how and why American big businesses of any genre might desire government subsidies or sanctions. Simply put, neo-classical economics does offer a much more subtle framework for economic analysis than I realized at the time.

And to compound my problem, I created a rather simplistic tale of the evil movie monopolists (supported by the U.S. federal government) exploiting a nation of benign moviegoers. A classic tale: David versus Goliath! But is such storytelling any more valid than the neoclassically based struggles of competition? I doubt it. In defense of my reading of Sweezy and O'Connor, they do demand that neoclassical economists confront difficult questions of how to analyze properly the role of government in business. My study of the NRA stands as positive initial effort. Much remains to be done. In future studies I plan to think more about an appropriate methodology, and how logically to defend my chosen approach.

Secondly, I would like to respond to the placement of my article in the special issue of the *Journal of the University Film Association*. As indicated above, I did not clearly establish a comparison among or between models of economic analysis. I wish I had. If I had done so, the article would have been much stronger. I did add to accumulated knowledge of the relations between the government and a big business. But I never argued the federal government openly sanctioned the film industry's monopoly position. Backing came about as a secondary effect. In contrast, the Webb-Pomerane Act, passed in 1918, openly advocated the internationalization of U.S. business during World War I.

The reader should be aware that I later incorporated my work on the NRA into an overall analysis of the Great Depression on the U.S. film industry. See "Rethinking American Film History: The Depression Decade and Monopoly Control," *Film and History* 10, no. 2 (May 1980), pp. 32–38. In the future I plan to extend my work on chain theaters to link up with the NRA period.

Finally, obvious extensions of this work should be identified. For example, Mary Beth Haralovich has positioned the role of double features (a direct NRA effect I argue) squarely in the history of the detective genre. See her "Sherlock Holmes: Genre and Industrial Practice," *Journal of the University Film Association* 31, no. 2 (Spring 1979), pp. 53–58. I would go in yet another direction. If during the NRA period, the Roosevelt administration supported the film industry, why the reversal of policy in 1937? We must look beyond the simple causality provided because of "blacklisting," and focus upon broader questions of film, industrial practice, politics, and social change.

Self-Censorship in the Movie Industry:
A Historical Perspective on Law
and Social Change

Douglas Ayer, Roy E. Bates, Peter J. Herman

Everyone recognizes that the movies have grown up. But not everyone agrees about the causes of this phenomenon. Often as not, the credit, or blame, is assigned to law and, specifically, to the "leniency" of the courts. The popularity of this explanation probably stems from the fact that the issue of movie content usually arises in a debate over public policy. If the question is what government can do to control what we see at the movies, the attitude of the courts toward censorship laws is of course central. The context of the debate, however, obscures the social setting within which movie content is determined.

Much more important than the role of public agencies in deciding what will or will not be seen by movie audiences is the role of private decision-makers within the movie industry. Far more pervasive than any scheme of public regulation is the industry's own system of private control. Self-regulation has always been instituted out of fear of governmental censorship, and we shall give attention to the latter insofar as it is necessary to explain the former. But our focus will be primarily on the industry's self-censorship efforts. We shall call this sort of regulation private ordering or private lawmaking, as distinguished from governmental regulation or public ordering.

Even those who recognize the important role of private ordering still tend to give undue credit to law in accounting for the weakness that this nongovernmental form of censorship has exhibited in controlling movie content. The destruction of economic power concentrations within the industry, attributed to an antitrust decision in the early 1950s, made possible the freer expression which the forces of censorship find so offensive. While a sequential relationship exists between the antitrust decision and economic deconcentration, it seems doubtful that the former was chiefly responsible for the latter. If one primary cause for the breakup in economic concentration must be identified, it would surely be television. Moreover, it was the combined impact of television and foreign films (nonlegal phenomena) which caused this breakup to result in the making of more sophisticated movies. Thus while this study portrays a process of private legislation—the formation of the new rating system—its purpose is to show this process in its social setting. Any narrower focus would give a distorted picture of law's role in effecting social change, especially change in the direction of freedom.

We shall start by describing the old code which effectively governed movie content until the 1950s and lingered on until it was replaced by the new rating system in 1968. We shall then examine the forces that brought about change and the reactions to that change, note the occasion for a new code and describe its formulation. We shall conclude with an account of the factors that will determine the actual impact of the rating system on what all of us may see at the movies.

☆

I. The Old Order

A. The Old Code

The motion picture industry has always been under pressure to keep its films "clean."[1] Perhaps this was to be expected since many Americans came to regard Hollywood as second only to the Garden of Eden as the birthplace of sin. Citizens of that persuasion succeeded during the period of 1911 to 1922 in getting several of their state legislatures to establish such powerful movie censorship boards as those in Kansas, Maryland, and New York, which were still functioning in the sixties.[2] These boards withstood constitutional challenge in *Mutual Film Corp.* v. *Ohio,*[3] the only motion picture censorship case decided by the Supreme Court before 1952. In the Court's first encounter with movie censorship, it denied motion pictures the protection of the first amendment on the ground that the industry was "a business, pure and simple."

By 1922, another two dozen legislatures were considering censorship bills, and the industry feared the economic effect of them.[4] Films were viewed by each censorship board in advance of exhibition and money was lost while the films lined up to be "scrutinized." The plethora of boards meant that different standards would be applied across the country, and producers could not know in advance how the original version of a film would fare before these various boards. If a film were cut to a fraction of its original version, it would be too late to reshoot scenes, and the producers would have to swallow the loss.

The industry's solution to these problems was to try to ease public pressures by keeping industry censorship a step ahead of the governmental censorship boards and by improving the industry's public relations. Former Postmaster General Will Hays was appointed as President of the newly constituted trade association, the Motion Picture Producers and Distributors of America (MPPDA). Throughout the next eight years the organization tried various experiments with self-censorship[5] before hitting upon the code in 1930. The Production Code Administration (PCA) was established to administer the standards for production adopted by the MPPDA. Eric Johnston, president of the Chamber of Commerce of the United States, replaced Will Hays, the first president of the MPPDA, in 1945, and changed the name to the Motion Picture Association of America (MPAA). Jack Valenti, former assistant to President Lyndon Johnson, became head in 1966.

The code worked. Producers had to submit scripts in advance of production and were advised about what cuts were needed in order to win the code seal—the badge of compliance. Appeal could be made to a specially composed board, but was rarely granted. The PCA was composed of approximately ten censors, with appeal available to the MPAA Motion Picture Code Board composed of industry representatives.[6] The standards of the code involved twelve areas: crimes, sex, vulgarity, obscenity, profanity, costume, dances, religion, locations (e.g., bedrooms), national feelings, titles, and repellent subjects (e.g., torture). No Hollywood film without a seal played the nation's theaters until 1953, and it is now known that extensive changes were required on numerous occasions.[7] Information rarely reached the public concerning deletions or rejections made in films before exhibition, thus depriving free speech advocates of ammunition. Various examples that have subsequently come to light will serve to illustrate the rigidness of the restrictions imposed upon producers. A scene in a 1940 production was found objectionable for no other reason than it showed a couple embracing while lying on the ground. The expression "Thank the Lord" was not permitted. Such words as *alley-cat* (applied to a woman), *S.O.B.*, *whore*, and *hot* (applied to a woman) were of course *verboten* and resulted in denial of the seal.[8]

Failure to heed the standards and rules of the code supposedly resulted in a $25,000 fine, but this was never imposed, since compliance was obtained in other ways. An important one was through the power of the Catholic church which, in 1934, organized the Legion of Decency to combat evil films. It told the MPPDA to enforce its code, which had been weakly administered during the first four years of its existence, or else prepare for a boycott of Hollywood films by millions of Catholics as well as members of other faiths. Under this stimulus, the movie industry began seriously to police the content of its product—a restraint on free expression that was to reign unchecked until the fifties, when the forces of television and foreign films brought down the commandments of Will Hays.

B. *The Economics of the Motion Picture Industry: Cartelization and Overinflation*

The success of the movie industry's program of self-regulation before the 1950s can be attributed largely to the cartelized structure of the production-distribution-exhibition process. Early in its history, the industry took the form of an oligopoly, with studio mergers and consolidation resulting in the emergence of five major and three minor companies. Vertical and horizontal combinations and arrangements were commonplace. Each of the five majors—Warner Bros., RKO, Paramount, Twentieth Century–Fox, Loew's (MGM)—was involved in exhibiting films, as well as producing and distributing them. Seventy percent of all first-run theaters in cities with a population over 100,000 were owned by the majors, separately or jointly, putting them in a position to guarantee the failure of any picture deemed unacceptable by them as a group.

The Production Code Administration served as the official machinery through which the majors, joined by the three "minor" studios (United Artists, Universal, Columbia), determined the standards of acceptability for motion picture content. Once that determination was made, enforcement was relatively easy. Nonseal movies, by common understanding among the majors and the theater circuits, were simply not exhibited. For a motion picture to have any chance for financial success, it was forced to comply with code standards.

The use of power gained by combination was not limited to controlling the content and supply of Hollywood films. Independent exhibitors, who might be expected to provide outlets for some independent productions, were often forced by MPAA members to accept onerous contract provisions as a condition for access to Hollywood movies. Commonplace trade practices included block booking (tying the rental of a good movie to acceptance of several mediocre and poor quality films), clauses fixing minimum admissions prices, unreasonable runs and clearances (allowing first-run theaters to exhibit a film for as long as it was profitable and agreeing not to release the film to second-run houses for several weeks thereafter), and clauses committing the exhibitor to a policy of not exhibiting foreign films. An exhibitor refusing to abide by these conditions might be boycotted by his primary source of films, the Hollywood studios.[9]

Through this complex arrangement of vertical integrations and horizontal agreements, a relatively small number of companies were able effectively to control production, distribution, and exhibition of movies throughout 1930–50, despite numerous private antitrust suits.[10] The tightly integrated, oligopolistic structure of the industry ended in the early 1950s, pursuant to decrees issued under the Supreme Court's *Paramount* decision.[11]

An economic aspect of the motion picture industry not recognized as particularly dangerous until the 1950s was overinflation. The majors acquired huge studio facilities and had long lists of actors and directors under long-term contracts at outlandish salaries, matched only by the compensation given to studio executives. Since spiraling production costs— e.g., a 300-percent increase during the 1940s alone—were matched by booming profits, Hollywood did not concern itself with budget watching.[12] The dangers of overinflation came to fruition in the post-World War II period, when a combination of events, led by the entrance of television into the entertainment business, hit the industry all at once. The effects of inflation can be seen in the higher operating costs for the studios. For example, Paramount Pictures' theater receipts, film rentals, etcetera, went from a 1946 high of $193 million to a 1949 figure of $162 million, while net income dropped drastically from $39 million to $20 million.[13] Similarly, Loew's, parent of MGM, saw its total operating revenues drop little from 1946 to 1949 ($165 million to $160 million), but its gross income went from $33 million to $12 million in this period.[14] Movie audiences declined drastically, causing profits to disappear without a commensurate decrease in costs. Studios halted production, but found themselves with inventories of unreleased features made at inflated costs and facing a crumbling market. Stars were "released" from contract; executives' salaries were cut in half. Despite desperate attempts to reduce overhead, production financing became difficult, with institutional lenders no longer anxious to extend credit to the studios.[15]

II. The Forces of Change

A. The Advent of Television

After a record-breaking decade in the 1940s, the motion picture industry looked forward with understandable anticipation to a postwar era of high consumer spending and leisure time. Average weekly attendance at movie theaters reached an all-time high of 80 million in 1948, with box office (i.e., the industry's gross receipts) reaching $1,692,000,000. The future looked bright.[16]

Within five years, however, Hollywood found itself at the brink of disaster. Movie attendance had fallen by 50 percent, and thousands of theaters were closing. A survey by Sindlinger & Co. indicated that the average American household spent $47.12 on movies in 1946, but only $27.82 in 1952, a 41 percent decrease.[17] Attendance declined steadily in the decade after 1946, from the annual high of 4,127,000 in 1946 to 1,961,000 in 1957. The basic cause of the movie industry's problems was not difficult to spot: the rise in popularity of television paralleled closely the decline of motion pictures. A Stanford Research Institute study estimated that 50 to 70 percent of the drop in admissions was owing to television rivalry.[18]

Immediate effects on the industry were highly visible. Output of films declined significantly; when the full impact of television was felt at mid-decade, features released in the United States market had fallen from 654 in 1951 to 392 in 1955.[19] Studios began releasing actors and directors under long-term contracts in order to cut overhead. For example, contract stars, 806 strong in 1944, were reduced to 216 by 1954.[20] Industry employment dropped alarmingly, from 204,000 in 1948 to only 146,900 in 1956.[21]

Undisguised panic gripped Hollywood. Predictions of disaster abounded: what movies had done to vaudeville, television would do to movies. Charles Skouras, head of Twentieth Century–Fox's newly independent theater chain, expected that 40 percent of U.S. motion picture theaters would close in the five to seven years following 1951.[22] Theater owners considered this estimate conservative as they felt the effects of declining movie attendance. Pessimists could see a singular fate awaiting the film industry, a quick death, unless important corrective factors intervened immediately.[23]

Perhaps the most significant effect of television on the movies, however, was not simply its direct relation to a drop in attendance figures, but its indirect influence on the quality of motion pictures shown in this country. Television's repercussions destroyed the big-studio system. Before television, movies were entirely a studio product: on a Paramount sound stage a Paramount director supervised Paramount stars, supporting cast, and extras as they acted out a script written by Paramount writers to produce a movie that would be marketed by Paramount sales and advertising forces and, until the *Paramount* decision, exhibited in Paramount theaters. The retrenchment forced by television hit hardest in production. Contract performers, writers, and directors were eliminated as sound stages were sold off or rented out to reduce overhead. This forced retirement from production opened the field to independent producers.[24] Eventually, this change was to result in a freer medium.

Attempts to attribute causation to one phenomenon, rather than another, when both occurred concurrently are always difficult. But the frequent crediting of the *Paramount* decision with the maturation of movies calls for careful scrutiny. The effect of *Paramount*, which is cited to support this contention, was the divorcement of exhibition from production and distribution. But it was production, not ownership of theaters, which gave Hollywood its commanding power. The most important barrier to entry was not lack of access to the theaters but Hollywood's control over the means of production. Stars, directors, and writers were almost all under contract with the majors and without these a successful movie could not be made. Without the advent of television, Hollywood would have continued to be the predominant supplier of films to the nation's theaters, regardless of who owned them. Had there been no antitrust decree, the studios would still have cut back on production because the market for family films had been substantially curtailed by television. And it was retrenchment in production that made way for foreign films and pictures by independent American producers.

Since television now offered Americans a free alternative to movies, mediocre films could no longer attract paying audiences. The entire audience for B-movies virtually disappeared at once, and their stars, such as Roy Rogers and William Boyd, turned to television in search of a substitute.[25] To get people out of their TV-equipped homes, Hollywood had to offer a product distinguishable from the mediocrity flickering on the silver screen.

Hollywood's first experiments at product differentiation were strictly technical gimmicks such as 3-D, Cinerama, Cinemascope, and Todd-AO. Another bright hope was for some type of cooperative effort with the new medium. Large-screen theater television was tried with events like the Joe Louis–Lee Savold boxing match, and subscription TV was discussed. These innovations proved initially successful, but lacked staying power in luring television viewers away from their sets.[26] Indications were clear that an improvement in content quality would be necessary. Sam Goldwyn predicted: "We are at the beginning of a new era where quality is replacing quantity. . . . Television helped some in keeping people away from the box office. . . . But that wasn't all. It was the continuous flow of pictures that didn't measure up to what the public expected that turned them to other forms of entertainment."[27]

Motion picture theme, content, and treatment corresponded less and less to the substantive requirements of a "mass medium." No longer did each film try to reach the broadest possible audience, without regard for differences in age, education, or taste. Selective audiences, unlikely to be satisfied by the bland entertainment of television programs, were identified. The movies, as *Variety* observed, were attracting the "highbrows." [28] The need to eschew controversial subjects which the movie makers felt when theirs was the mass medium in the area of visual entertainment, gave way to a need to deal with subjects that this differentiated audience would find interesting. Consequently, themes that were strictly taboo on television made frequent appearances on the movie-screen—dope, politics, race, and especially, sex.

Not only was the content of movies more varied than that of television programs but the quality of the former generally out-distanced the latter. This also was the result of television replacing the movies as the mass medium in the area of visual entertainment. As has been noted by John Kenneth Galbraith, the industrial system, which depends on organization and committee decision making, is fundamentally in conflict with aesthetics, which depend on the work of individual artists. [29] The movie industry was following the pattern of development outlined by Galbraith—from entrepreneurial corporations dominated by commanding individuals to mature corporations dominated by a technostructure. [30] The studio system, however, was the closest that the movie industry came to Galbraith's mature corporation in the area of production (as distinguished from distribution). Television interrupted this development by capturing the mass market, which is the one that a mature corporation can serve, thereby leaving movie production to artistic entrepreneurs. [31] Consequently, television became the medium of mediocrity. [32]

Young people played an important part in the changing character and quality of movie content. Television tended to keep older persons at home, so movie audiences became younger. Thus, by 1957, persons in their twenties and late teens made up 41 percent of movie audiences. [33] In 1968, people from sixteen to twenty-four alone accounted for an estimated 48 percent of the box office. [34] By the late sixties, movies had attained a new popularity as a youth-oriented medium. Films such as *The Graduate*, *Easy Rider*, and *Midnight Cowboy* captured the attention of moviegoers who, whatever their ages, identified with the attitudes and outlook of youth. In contrast, childish family fare continued to dominate the television screen.

B. Foreign Films

While television was usurping movie supremacy in the area of family entertainment, foreign films began to divert from Hollywood some of the remaining customers, especially young adults and moviegoers in their late teens. Foreign films have been exhibited in the United States for sixty years, but it was only after World War II that these films made a significant impact on the American market. Whereas imported films made up only 20 percent of the total releases in the United States in 1946, they comprised 40 percent by the early fifties and jumped to over half by 1958.[35] The increasing popularity of foreign films gave rise to the only sustained building boom in movie theaters. While the number of movie "palaces" (four-wall theaters playing chiefly Hollywood offerings) steadily declined after 1950 and the number of drive-ins in 1966 was about the same as in 1952,[36] the number of "art" theaters (traditionally the major outlet for foreign films) climbed ever upward. Art theaters often seat fewer than 400 patrons, and by the late sixties, they accounted for less than 10 percent of all tickets sold.[37] But their number had grown. In 1950, there were only 83; by 1966, there were 644.[38] Moreover, in the 1960s, the major studios began financing and distributing foreign films, thereby giving them a play in the "palaces" and the drive-ins.

What attracted American capital to foreign films was their combination of low production costs and at least modest returns. The prospect was for a good profit margin, despite the fact that the "grosses" for the most popular foreign films have remained small in comparison with Hollywood spectaculars. For example, *La Dolce Vita* and *I Am Curious (Yellow)* had grossed approximately $7.5 and $8.6 million respectively by April 1970, while the lowest of the all-time top ten grossing Hollywood films, *Cleopatra* grossed $26 million, and the all-time champ, *Sound of Music*, $72 million.[39]

Unlike the Hollywood product of the thirties and forties, the foreign films which won acclaim in the United States were often the personal statement of the director. Men such as Truffaut, Bergman, and Kurosawa had such complete artistic control of their films that moviegoers came to associate distinct styles with individual directors. The cult of the director overshadowed the star system, and with it came an increase in both realism and symbolism. The search for subject matter appropriate to artistic treatment propelled the foreign directors to themes that Hollywood considered untouchable. The two and one-half decades following World War II saw such directors as Fellini, Bunuel, Antonioni, and Richardson turn their cameras on decadence, sex, religion, ennui, and angry young men.

The movies were on their way to being considered as a serious art form. The new ferment from abroad was given a hearty welcome by the critics. But the legal reception that awaited these films in the United States was something else again. It was the fate of foreign films not only to lead the way to more artistic expression but also simply to freer expression, especially concerning sex. The landmark cases on censorship and obscenity almost invariably involved books rather than films. But where films were involved, they were, more often than not, foreign ones. American films played a supporting role. Until the 1960s, most major studios played little or no part in the court battles over censorship. The Hollywood big-budget film has rarely been the subject of litigation because too much money is tied up in it. Until recently, the film could not be shown while involved in litigation and interest payments on the money borrowed to finance the film had to be made. Since Hollywood had more to lose, it exercised more self-restraint in producing its films initially. The most likely litigant in a significant censorship case has been the middle-sized distributor exhibiting a relatively inexpensive and often artistic film.[40] Such distributors are more likely to be involved in litigation not only for economic reasons, but also to preserve artistic integrity. One deleted scene can ruin a whole film. Of course, preserving artistic integrity is not unrelated to economic considerations. The middle-sized distributor lacks Hollywood's publicity machinery and thus is more dependent upon such gratuitous forms of publicity as good reviews and even the notoriety of battling with the censors. The result has been famous censorship cases involving, for example, *The Miracle*, *Lady Chatterly's Lover*, *The Lovers*, and *I Am Curious (Yellow)*.

The impact of foreign films on American movies, then, was greatly strengthened by the devastating effects of television. Having lost its mass market, Hollywood was undoubtedly quicker to follow the lead of foreign films. But were it not for foreign films, American moviegoers might have had to wait a while longer before American movie producers perceived the selective audience that would support films displaying greater artistic quality and more sophisticated subject matter.

C. The Paramount Decision

Reinforcing television's disruptive impact on the movie industry in the early 1950s was the culmination in the *Paramount* case of the federal government's antitrust action against the tightly-integrated structure of the production, distribution, and exhibition aspects of the motion picture field. Of particular importance for the purpose of this study were the divestiture and divorcement decrees, which required the major studios to divorce production and distribution from exhibition by relinquishing their theaters and forced the circuits (theater chains) to divest themselves of enough theaters to increase competition in the exhibition field.

It was hoped that these remedies would open up the industry to independent producers by removing, or at least weakening, illegal barriers to film marketing. Some observers think *Paramount* brought about the demise of self-censorship as well. Michael Conant,[41] for example, sees the antitrust case as solely responsible for a weakened PCA. Richard Randall is more balanced: "the antitrust decision, however, was only one factor in the erosion of the Code's authority. Changes in the constitutional status of movies and a narrowing of the legal concept of obscenity, on the one hand, and stiff competition from television and foreign films, on the other, all added to the decline of self-regulation."[42] Jack Valenti dates the decline of the code seal from the *Paramount* case.[43] *Daily Variety*[44] appears to agree. It also asserts that the $25,000 fine was of great importance in gaining code compliance, although it fails to note that the fine was never used. Ironically, during the New Deal period, local "morality groups" wanted to break up the monopoly of the majors in order to increase censorship.

The antitrust action may have hastened the greater freedom of expression that was being caused by television and foreign films. Without the structural changes forced by *Paramount*, improvement in American movies might have been delayed, and the process surely would have been difficult. The major studios would probably have retained for a while longer their power to exclude independent producers, who are generally credited with bringing the real vitality to American movies by, among other things, challenging the Hollywood policy of avoiding all material considered potentially controversial or objectionable. Since exhibitors were no longer tied directly or indirectly to the major producers, they were undoubtedly more willing to deal with independent producers, and the majors' tight grip on film content through the Production Code Administration was considerably loosened. But this increased willingness was probably owing more to the product shortage created by the majors' retrenchment in production as a result of competition from television than to the *Paramount* decision.

The contention that the *Paramount* decision was the major cause of the disintegration of the industry's structure and the consequent entry of independents into the production field does not fully explain what happened. The improved quality of movies was primarily the result of competition from TV and foreign films. Television eliminated the market for mediocre films and forced an economic retrenchment in the movie industry that was more substantial than anything an antitrust action could hope to accomplish. Meanwhile, the success of several movies that were unconventional by Hollywood standards forced Hollywood to reevaluate the quality of its offering to the American public. The undeniable changes in social attitudes that manifested themselves in postwar America by increased permissiveness in all areas of American life could not be ignored by Hollywood indefinitely, especially when they were manifested explicitly and successfully in foreign films.

The importance of the *Paramount* decision to free expansion in the movie industry came more from dictum in the Supreme Court's opinion than from the case's complex holding. Writing for the Court, Mr. Justice Douglas announced: "We have no doubt that movie pictures, like newspapers and radio, are included in the press whose freedom is guaranteed by the First Amendment."[45] With the overturning of *Mutual Film Corp.* thus foreshadowed, the movies were about to take some major steps toward maturity.

III. Breakthrough

Censorship, as we have seen, can result from governmental decrees, from the pressures of powerful organizations (such as the Catholic church) and from private arrangements (such as the MPAA Code). Whatever the source, censorship is an attempt to order men's affairs, to control their behavior—in this case, to regulate what they can see at the movies. To the moviegoer, the source of the regulation, whether it is public or private, makes no difference. If he cannot see what he would like to see, it matters not at all whether the reason is that movie producers are complying with standards formulated and administered by the movie industry under pressure from the Catholic church (an example of private ordering), or with standards formulated and administered by, e.g., the New York Board of Regents, which may likewise be under pressure from the Catholic church (an example of public ordering). The form which the censorship takes is also unimportant to those who do not want the moviegoer to see what they deem offensive.

But the difference is important to some. Hollywood has good economic reasons, previously noted, for preferring censorship by an industry tribunal to censorship by a plethora of state and municipal boards. Moreover, our political heritage has conditioned us to feel a greater sense of alarm when a governmental agency orders the suppression of expression than we feel when a private institution does the same thing. And this distinction is, for the most part, firmly embedded in our law.[46] It is probably for this reason that the amount of attention focused upon *The Miracle*, an obscure movie which became the occasion for the breakthrough in public ordering, has been disproportionate to that given *The Moon Is Blue* and *The Man with the Golden Arm*, which led the breakthroughs in private ordering.

A. The Miracle *Decision—Breakthrough in Public Ordering*

In 1952, four years after the *Paramount* decision, the Supreme Court in *Burstyn* v. *Wilson*,[47] the first censorship case to reach the Court since 1915, held what had been dictum in the antitrust case. The Court announced that it now considered motion pictures a significant medium for the communication of ideas.[48] This perception, of course, entitled the movies to the protection of the First Amendment. The case is rightly regarded as a landmark, but its impact is easily overemphasized. Governmental censorship boards were by no means dealt a fatal blow. Prior restraint, such as these boards characteristically practiced in exercise of their licensing powers, was not entirely eliminated, though it was limited to exceptional cases, which came to mean those involving "obscenity" and those alone. Five more years would elapse before the Court gave "obscenity" a narrow definition in *Roth* v. *United States*. The amount of ink spilled over the meaning of *Roth* is overwhelming and not a little appalling. No contribution could be made here by adding to the verbiage. Suffice to quote the *Roth* test as most recently formulated by the Supreme Court: "(T)hree elements must coalesce: it must be established that (a) the dominant theme of the material taken as a whole appeals to a prurient interest in sex; (b) the material is patently offensive because it affronts contemporary community standards relating to the description or representation of sexual matters; and (c) the material is utterly without redeeming social value."[49] It took still more time before the Supreme Court circumscribed the four state boards and the handful of municipal boards that remained active in 1965 by requiring these boards to observe the requisites of procedural due process. The burden is now upon the censor to prove that the film is obscene, judicial review of the decision is available, and prompt action by both censor and court is guaranteed.[50]

Still, the legal impact was quite striking when compared to the rather slight difference that *Burstyn* made to the average moviegoer. The circumstances which gave rise to the case indicate why the immediate effect of the case would not be great so far as movie audiences were concerned. Plaintiff Burstyn, a noted distributor of foreign films, acquired the distribution rights to Roberto Rosselini's *The Miracle*, part of a trilogy entitled the "Ways of Love." Burstyn sought and received a license from the New York Board of Regents through the Motion Picture Division of its Education Department, whose commissioner was Wilson. The film played for two months in a New York City art theater until pressures from Cardinal Francis Spellman and the Catholic church resulted in the rescission of the license by the Board of Regents. The board found that the film was "sacrilegious," one of the grounds set out by the New York censorship statute for denial of a license.[51] Although the New York courts upheld the board, Burstyn triumphed in the Supreme Court. Censorship of a film because it was "sacrilegious" was not permitted by the Court because the censor would find it impossible to avoid favoring one religion over another, and would be "set adrift upon a boundless sea amid a myriad of conflicting currents of religious views, with no charts but those provided by the most vocal and powerful orthodoxies."[52] Thus the cardinal's attempt to keep New Yorkers from seeing a rather obscure Italian movie that was plainly disrespectful to the church ultimately failed. But it would be some time before films such as *The Miracle* would obtain any wide distribution outside Manhattan. In 1952, when the Supreme Court decided *Burstyn*, there were only slightly more than 100 first-run art theaters in the entire country, most of which were quite small and many of which were in New York. If movie audiences generally were to be exposed to greater film sophistication, the code—the industry's self-imposed form of prior restraint—had to be defied, and defied successfully. As it turned out, the breakthroughs in private ordering were just around the corner.

B. The Moon Is Blue *and* The Man with the Golden Arm— *Breakthrough in Private Ordering*

While a measure of freedom from governmental censorship was gained as the result of a dramatic courtroom battle,[53] the industry's own censorship scheme was weakened when United Artists released two Otto Preminger productions without that badge of code compliance, the seal. *The Moon Is Blue* was denied a seal because it dealt with adulterous conduct, while *The Man with the Golden Arm* was disapproved because of its treatment of drug addiction.

That both films proved financially successful does not detract from the foresight and courage shown in producing and releasing them. True, the cutback in movie production occasioned by the onslaught of television had created a product shortage that assured any Hollywood film of a fair run, seal or no seal. Exhibitors, no longer under the iron grip of the majors as a result of the movie industry's economic difficulties and the *Paramount* divorcement decree, were anxious for films that would lure TV viewers back to the theaters, and both Preminger films provided fare that could not be seen at home. But in the early fifties when *The Moon Is Blue* and *The Man with the Golden Arm* appeared, no one had acted upon the perception, if indeed the perception had occurred, that the seal might no longer be a prerequisite for the exhibition of Hollywood films on a nationwide basis. The success of these films made clear that such a situation existed.

The code would be defied again and again: foreign films like *Room at the Top* and *Never on Sunday* would triumph at the box office sans seal, and in the 1960s, the majors released films through their subsidiaries that did not possess the once-important seal. Profit-motivated producers and exhibitors were overcoming their hesitations about pictures denied seals. The seal has never recovered the prominence it once knew under the old code.[54]

In summary, the denouement of the old code came about chiefly because Hollywood faced new competition after World War II. Television preempted the "family" entertainment market, while foreign films pointed the way to retention at the box office of support from moviegoers who were teenagers and young adults. Law can take little credit for the maturation of movies. Without these new competitive forces, it is unlikely that the government's antitrust action could have contributed in any way to greater freedom of expression in the movies. Given these forces, the *Paramount* decision was hardly more than the frosting on the cake that the new competition would have eventually produced in any event.

The principal causes of increasingly sophisticated motion pictures, then, were economic, not legal. Legal institutions, whether public or private, played no positive role in bringing about this social change in the direction of greater freedom. They did perform part of a necessary clearing operation. Law, both public and private ordering, has perhaps its greatest social impact as an instrument of repression, and law was used extensively in this fashion in connection with the movie industry. Law is perhaps most valued not as an instrument of social change but as a technique for facilitating social activity. But when law is used in this fashion it does little to shape social change. Instead, if it is working well, it reflects it. Roadblocks had been put up which had to be broken through before the causative forces of freedom could prevail. Legal institutions (the courts) did play a role in this negative task of removing these roadblocks. But it was a partial role. In a series of First Amendment decisions, starting with *Burstyn*, some of the roadblocks that had been erected by governmental officials were overcome. This was the extent of the law's contribution. The roadblock erected by private lawmakers, the code, was brought down not by court decisions but by the economic forces noted above. And it was these forces that account for the movie industry's taking advantage of the protection of the First Amendment to make sophisticated entertainment so widely available.

IV. Reactions

The increasing opportunity to enjoy mature entertainment at the movie theater did not go unnoticed, and not all liked what they saw. Concern was concentrated primarily on excessive nudity and eroticism on the screen, with comparatively little objection to obsessive violence and brutality. Censorship pressure had traditionally manifested itself in the restrictive attitudes of state and local boards, but with the demise of most of the licensing boards and the narrow field of discretion which the courts left to those few boards that did survive, the pressure was felt most acutely in the legislatures. In the late 1960s a rash of legislative proposals emerged, mainly in the form of obscenity statutes designed to protect children. But neither boards nor legislatures are completely self-starting. Oftentimes their actions are responsive to the pressures of private organizations, although these organizations have not confined their efforts to pressing public officials for decisions favorable to their cause. It is to these groups that we must now turn our attention.

A. Guardians of the Public Taste: Private Pressure

A major development of the postwar period has been the proliferation of private groups determined to obtain the removal from public view of material they regard as offensive.[55] While some of these groups are ad hoc citizens' committees, many are established, nationwide organizations, such as the Parents-Teachers Association (PTA) and Veterans of Foreign Wars (VFW), not organized primarily to fight pornography. Such groups have made their impact through direct methods, such as boycotts of particular films and theaters, as well as through indirect methods, such as lobbying for official action. Indeed, the former may well be the more coercive. Richard Randall reports that the real war for freedom of expression in films today is less one of a conventional, set-piece struggle against governmental censors than one of an "anti-guerrilla campaign against scattered, frequently unseen, but often highly effective opposition."[56]

1. Legion of Decency. Unquestionably, the oldest private pressure group and the one that once was most effective in influencing the content of motion pictures is the Legion of Decency, which was organized in 1934 to pressure the film industry into enforcing its own Code of Self-regulation. The legion had a close relationship with the Production Code Administration, as evidenced by the high correlation between those pictures condemned by the legion and those denied seals of approval by the PCA.[57]

The legion, now called the National Catholic Office for Motion Pictures, operates its own rating system designed to judge the suitability of various films for Catholic viewers.[58] The name was changed in 1965. Ratings as of 1970 were A-I (morally unobjectionable for general patronage); A-II (morally unobjectionable for adults and adolescents); A-III (morally unobjectionable for adults); A-IV (morally unobjectionable for adults, with reservations); B (morally objectionable in part for all); C (condemned). Its strength rests in numbers and in its willingness—often demonstrated in the past—to mobilize Catholics against movies it finds particularly objectionable. Implementation of its rating system in past years has taken several forms: encouragement to observe the ratings through pledges and admonitions from the pulpit, pressure on public officials to take action against exhibitors showing condemned films, and direct action against exhibitors in the form of letters, committee calls, boycotts and picketing.

Perhaps the most notorious example of the organization's tactics centered around *The Miracle* in 1951. Cardinal Spellman spoke from the pulpit and urged every Roman Catholic to boycott the film. The Catholic Welfare Conference of New York demanded stronger censorship laws, while the Catholic War Veterans and the Holy Name Society picketed the New York theater.[59] The New York censorship board yielded to the pressure and withdrew its previously issued license, an act which, as noted above, led to *Burstyn*. Of course, the effectiveness of Catholic activity in any area depended on the proportion of Catholics in the community, so that exhibitors in cities with large Catholic populations (e.g. St. Paul and Albuquerque), carefully followed legion advice.[60]

Recently, the legion has mellowed somewhat. The rise of the "new movies" influenced the organization to show increasing tolerance for sophisticated treatment of sex and nudity in films. Catholics had begun to criticize the legion as lagging behind the times, and Protestant derision was not unknown. The legion amended its regulations in 1957 and 1963 to permit a special class for adult movies with artistic merit.[61] In addition, the power of the legion within the movie industry has declined. Movie producers are far less worried today about the effect of receiving a condemnation from the legion, and consequently most producers do not even bother to check with it, a common practice for many years.[62]

2. Citizens for Decent Literature. Although many local ad hoc citizens' groups form occasionally to combat objectionable literature and films, the only permanent national organization devoted exclusively to censorship in the arts is the Citizens for Decent Literature (CDL). The CDL, a nonsectarian nonprofit group which "opposes pornography by informing the public and by assisting law enforcement,"[63] has strong support in major religious faiths, veterans' organizations, and women's clubs. Through its bimonthly newsletter, the *National Decency Reporter*, the CDL encourages the formation of local citizens' groups to combat eroticism and nudity in movies and literature. It is quick to point out that almost all arrests of movie exhibitors on obscenity charges result from citizens' complaints.[64] Although such local groups find it difficult to maintain a high level of activity over a long period of time,[65] several have been notably successful. For example, the success of the Roseville Cinema Groups in forcing exhibitors in Roseville, Minnesota, to submit advance lists of coming attractions to the group for approval has encouraged talk of expansion into Minneapolis–Saint Paul.[66] Christians United for Responsible Entertainment (CURE), formed by parents in Knoxville, Tennessee, to marshall protests against unsuitable entertainment for children, quickly spread to New Orleans.[67] And the Dallas Citizens Committee for Decent Movies was instrumental in stirring up the ferment that eventually led to a municipal ordinance requiring licensing of movies for children.[68]

3. Various Religious, Ethnic, and Professional Groups. Pressure from Protestant church groups differs from Catholic pressure in degree and strength, in the manner of application, and in the points at which the pressure is applied. While the National Council of Churches issued a forceful attack on movies' "pathological preoccupation with sex and violence" in 1960, the group reiterated its staunch opposition to church censorship in the form of coercive ratings and boycott tactics. The Protestant Film Council did rate films, but only as a guide to parents.[69] In practical effect, these Protestant groups exerted little influence at the production level and rarely marshall effective action at the exhibition level.

Established national organizations often operate in the motion picture production and exhibition field as a complement to their primary objectives. The most effective of the groups has been the American Legion, whose main concern has been alleged Communist influence in the movie industry; that organization once prevented distribution of Charlie Chaplin's *Limelight* because of the actor's leftist activities.[70] The General Federation of Women's Clubs, with 800,000 members, recently withdrew its traditional support for motion picture industry efforts at self-regulation, criticizing the industry's new classification system as an "exercise in public deception" which failed to prevent excessive sex and violence in movies.[71] Until late in 1969, the federation, along with eleven other groups, such as the DAR and PTA (with financial support from the MPAA), had published *The Green Sheet*, a service which rated all films according to their suitability for various audiences.[72]

Various organizations also attempt to affect motion picture content at the production stage. Prominent among those exerting such influence on the industry are professional organizations, which object to the presentation of persons like doctors and lawyers as incompetent; public officials who are sensitive to portrayals of corruption in public life; and various ethnic groups, which desire to have their members treated sympathetically. Particularly active in the latter category has been the National Association for the Advancement of Colored People (NAACP), which in 1963 threw the full strength of its national organization into the fight against racial bias in movies with threats of mass demonstrations and economic and legal offensives. Several Jewish organizations, which object to films showing Jews in an unfavorable light, have been effective; a British version of *Oliver Twist* had few showings in this country because of its unflattering portrayal of Fagin, a Jew.[73]

Recently a noticeable upsurge of censorship campaigns has appeared on the local level. Usually, ad hoc citizens groups and local chapters of national organizations provide the backbone of such activities. While rarely successful in large cities,[74] these "decency drives" can seriously affect the fortunes of individual movies and exhibitors in small and medium-size localities.

In the opinion of author Murray Schumach, censorship would be neither created nor sustained without these private pressure groups.[75] They constitute a form of inhibition on expression more dangerous in some ways than governmental restrictions or industry self-regulation because they can operate without public scrutiny under rules of their own making.

B. Guardians of the Public Taste: Official Pressure

On the other hand, the official guardians of the public taste can be called to a judicial reckoning for at least some of their actions and in those cases that have come before them, the courts have proved themselves to be sensitive to the value of free expression. The happy result has been to hamper official censors in their justifiable activities, although the unfortunate by-product has been a resort to extralegal forms of censorship.

1. Censorship Boards. When significant changes began taking place in the movie industry in the early 1950s, eight states and numerous (perhaps 90) cities had licensing boards that reviewed all motion pictures exhibited in their jurisdiction. The demise of the whole procedure of prior restraint of movies, which began in 1952, was complete by the mid-1960s, when all but a handful of the boards had been invalidated because of their unconstitutional standards or effectively destroyed because of procedural defects.[76]

While in operation, the boards had exerted a powerful influence over the industry. The impact of those in New York, Maryland, Ohio, and Illinois radiated beyond their territorial jurisdiction. From an early concern with violence and brutality in the 1920s,[77] government censors had undergone a transformation by the 1950s to almost a total preoccupation with nudity and sex,[78] although censorship of political and religious material was still not unknown. Court decisions had eliminated many standards once employed for denying the public access to sophisticated motion pictures, until obscenity, as narrowly defined by the courts, was practically the only criterion. As Richard Randall noted, however, this court requirement of obscenity often meant only that the censors shifted their terminology and hid other standards behind the label of "obscenity."[79] There was nothing in the training or experience of the censors that could be taken as qualifying them to judge the merits of films or to apply legal standards; for example, the Chicago board, which was under the supervision of the police department, was composed entirely of the widows of policemen.

Most of the decisions made by the boards were highly subjective. Ira Carmen concluded from an extensive study of board members that decisions were based mainly on personal reactions and impulses and the inherent prejudices of individual censors.[80] Their judgments were rarely sustained in court tests of their decisions, and the boards generally ignored court rejections of their efforts.[81] As the Chicago police censorship overseer stated, "Courts don't lay down guidelines for us."[82] Such attitudes flourished because resistance to censorship orders rarely reached the court level for judicial examination.

While the major reaction of state and local governments to this judicial emasculation of prior-restraint activities has been a shift to reliance on obscenity prosecutions and extralegal harassment, a few public officials have attempted to retain a vestige of prior restraint of movies by implementing age classification systems. The Supreme Court in *Interstate Cir-*

cuit v. *Dallas* [83] invalidated the first such attempt by Dallas because of the vagueness of the classification standards, but left the path clear for future attempts by hinting that age classification systems with more tightly-drawn standards might survive application of constitutional tests.[84]

Even without prior censorship, movies would still be subject to efforts at suppression stemming from obscenity prosecutions and extralegal actions by public officials, not to mention private actions of various kinds. These alternative forms of censorship, which are often more restrictive and effective, may be increasingly practiced for the very reason that prior restraint itself has become less effective.[85]

2. Obscenity Prosecutions. Major governmental reliance for controlling the dissemination of objectionable motion pictures today is placed in prosecutions under obscenity laws. The movie industry prefers this method of control over prior restraint for several reasons. First, procedural safeguards, such as the presumption of innocence, heavier burden of proof on the government, and the choice of trial by jury or by judge, are normally available in a criminal prosecution. Second, the film will have entered the market before confiscation and may possibly be allowed to play during adjudication of the obscenity issue. Several courts have ruled recently that before a film may be seized, an adversary hearing must be held.[86] Third, all films need not be submitted and examined when relatively few are objectionable. Fourth, given the strict judicial definition of obscenity, which includes the criterion of a lack of all redeeming social value, the probabilities for successful prosecution on obscenity grounds are quite low.

Of course, several disadvantages to the method of criminal obscenity prosecutions are evident: the exhibitor, who has the fewest resources with which to defend himself and who depends largely on the good will of the community for his livelihood, is the one who faces the brunt of the attack, rather than the producer or distributor; some public officials who hesitate to use the criminal process because of the liberal doctrine prevailing in the courtroom may see the use of extralegal action, such as threats and harassment, as the only alternative for policing the content of motion pictures.

3. Extralegal Actions of Public Officials. With prior censorship and obscenity prosecutions losing their effectiveness, some public officials have turned to forms of pressure which rarely result in interference by the courts. Responding to community pressures, officials communicate their desire to exhibitors through a variety of extralegal actions, e.g., threats of or attempts at interference with theater property, with exhibitors' personal reputations, with the convenience of customers and employees, and even with exhibitors' personal liberty.

The most blatant extralegal tactic is the incipient use of the criminal process—arrests and confiscations as harassing techniques. Often employees are arrested along with the exhibitor, and occasionally even patrons have been taken into custody.[87] In many cases the police know that an obscenity prosecution would be unsuccessful, and soon dismiss the charges. Alternatively, "disorderly house" laws have become popular weapons in campaigns against exhibitors, and seizure of films is a commonplace harassment procedure.[88]

Exhibitors who are willing to go to court can usually obtain judicial relief in the form of an injunction against these types of tactics by public officials. Several such injunctions have been issued within the past year in Phoenix, Pittsburgh, New Orleans, and San Francisco, cities where government harassment has been particularly active.[89] But in isolated instances of police harassment, exhibitors are generally unwilling to seek redress in the courts.

City councils use their powers to issue theater licenses and building permits to "encourage" film exhibitors not to show objectionable movies. For example, the city council of a Los Angeles suburb after a five-month delay approved construction of a theater complex upon receiving assurance that no movies rated X by the MPAA would be exhibited there.[90] A Florida city shut off the electricity and water to a theater a few minutes before *Fanny Hill Meets Lady Chatterly* was to be exhibited and then employed a technicality regarding the ownership of the building to, in effect, revoke the theater license and refuse to issue a new one.[91]

Many other effective methods of obtaining exhibitor cooperation are available. Threats to send inspectors are effective in cities with complicated and strict health and safety codes; visits from fire safety inspectors often serve as a reminder to exhibitors that they could be closed at any time for some technical violation of the ordinance. Drive-ins can be especially affected by zoning and public nuisance laws. The district attorney of Oklahoma City chose the approach of simply writing a letter to all theater owners warning them to act as their own censors because obscenity statutes would be strictly enforced: "Bear in mind, but do not entirely depend on the current Supreme Court guidelines. . . . Your choice of movies will be made at your own risk. . . . Be a real city 'Dad'."[92] District attorneys often give "informal advice" on the nature of particular films. In a Boston suburb, uniformed policemen were sent to a theater to turn back all children under sixteen trying to attend *Bullit*, an M-rated movie, and the exhibitor was informed that he would have to pay the wages of the two policemen.[93] *Succubus* was canceled in one city the day after the city council voted to have the city attorney investigate the general question of obscene movies.[94]

The popularity of these extralegal devices is attributable to their effectiveness. Most exhibitors inevitably yield rather than seek relief in the courts. The procedures are objectionable because the substantive standards for such informal censorship are far broader and more subjective than would be the case in an obscenity prosecution; because procedural due process is lacking; because the informal censor attacks the motion picture at its weakest point, the small exhibitor; and because any court action will not lead to a determination of the character of the film so as to hinder future harassment efforts.

A unique form of censorship occurs when the subject matter of a motion picture revolves around a governmental agency, such as the armed forces or the FBI. These films require considerable cooperation from the agency concerned, which normally requests the power to censor the script. Examples of this type of censorship are numerous: to please the army, the script of *The Young Lions* had to be changed to tone down anti-Semitism among the officers; MGM and Twentieth Century–Fox both lost interest in filming *The Caine Mutiny* when the navy refused to cooperate—the navy feared that the movie might hurt recruitment and upset parents. Eventually, the navy did help after Stanley Kramer appealed to the secretary of the navy.[95]

C. The Dallas Decision

By the late 1960s, the institutions for movie censorship, both public and private, were in substantial retreat. The old morality that made open treatment of sexual themes taboo, continued to reign supreme over television, but in large part because of television, it had long since been vanquished as far as movies were concerned. None of the orderly ways of censorship was working: the code was virtually defunct, owing to its ineffectiveness in controlling movie content, and both prior restraint and obscenity prosecutions were out of favor in the courts. The proponents of censorship had to turn to extralegal techniques, such as economic boycotts and harassment.

Continuation of the war for institutional censorship required a shift in strategy: the guardians of the public taste no longer talked loudly about saving all the world; now they proclaimed that their principal interest was in preventing the corruption of the nation's youth. As it turned out, the scene of battle was to be Dallas, Texas.

There a board had been established in 1965 to determine which films were "not suitable for young persons." "Not suitable for young persons" means:

> (1) Describing or portraying brutality, criminal violence or depravity in such a manner as to be, in the judgment of the Board, likely to incite or encourage crime or delinquency on the part of young persons; or
>
> (2) Describing or portraying nudity beyond the customary limits of candor in the community, or sexual promiscuity or extramarital or abnormal sexual relations in such a manner as to be, in the judgment of the Board, likely to incite or encourage delinquency or sexual promiscuity on the part of young persons or to appeal to their prurient interest.
>
> A film shall be considered "likely to incite or encourage" crime delinquency or sexual promiscuity on the part of young persons, if, in the judgment of the Board, there is a substantial probability that it will create the impression on young persons that such conduct is profitable, desirable, acceptable, respectable, praiseworthy, or commonly accepted. A film shall be considered as appealing to "prurient interest" of young persons, if in the judgment of the Board, its calculated or dominant effect on young persons is substantially to arouse sexual desire. In determining whether a film is "not suitable for young persons," the Board shall consider the films as a whole, rather than isolated portions, and shall determine whether its harmful effects outweigh artistic or educational values such film may have for young persons.[96]

Persons under sixteen years of age were proscribed from seeing movies so classified. Almost immediately, Interstate Circuit, a major theater chain in the Southwest, began a series of assaults upon the ordinance.[97] Eventually the Dallas board found that *Viva Maria*, a United Artists picture starring Brigitte Bardot and Jeanne Moreau, was "not suitable for young persons." Interstate, the exhibitor of the picture, deliberately staged a confrontation by showing the film without imposing age restrictions on its audiences, as the ordinance required. When the Supreme Court declared the law unconstitutional,[98] another victory against movie censorship had been won.

The victory, however, was a Pyrrhic one, which, as we shall see, led to a renewed attempt at censorship by private ordering. The ground on which the Court faulted the Dallas ordinance was its vagueness. The Court was careful to note, however, that its ruling would not preclude a more carefully drafted classification scheme. It pointed to *Ginsberg* v.

New York,[99] decided the same day as *Dallas*, wherein the Court had upheld a New York statute that prohibited the sale to minors of material that young people would find obscene, though the same material could not be considered obscene if adults were to read it.

The Court based its decision on the concept of "variable obscenity" which is adequately defined as follows:

> (M)aterial which is protected for distribution to adults is not necessarily constitutionally protected from restriction upon its dissemination to children. In other words, the concept of obscenity or of unprotected matter may vary according to the group to whom the questionable material is directed or from whom it is quarantined. Because of the state's exigent interest in preventing distribution to children of objectionable material, it can exercise its power to protect the health, safety, welfare and morals of its community by barring the distribution to children of books recognized to be suitable for adults.[100]

The Roth rule "was to be applied, but to be discounted by youthful immaturity. . . . (A)ll New York had done was to adjust the definition of obscenity to the empirical realities of the target audience."[101] Thus, the *Dallas* case, when read in conjunction with *Ginsberg*, invited cities and states to try to control movie content through more tightly-drawn classification laws.

V. From Big D to Circle X

The Supreme Court rendered the *Dallas* decision on 22 April 1968. Within the next five months, the private lawmakers of the motion picture industry had hammered out their own system for classifying films. How they did this and to what purposes is the core of our story. But we must first identify the cast of characters. Who were these private orderers?

A. The Private Orderers

The most important industry organization is the Motion Picture Association of America (MPAA), which has offices in New York, Washington, D.C., and Hollywood, and numbers among its members the major companies, including Allied Artists, Avco—Embassy Pictures Corporation, Columbia, MGM, The Mirisch Corporation, Paramount, Twentieth Century—Fox, United Artists, Universal, and Warner Bros.[102] Its current president is Jack Valenti, former assistant to President Johnson, and its general counsel is Louis Nizer, a renowned attorney who represented United Artists in the *Dallas* case. Communication is easy and decision-making can be done informally in the MPAA because the organization's board of directors is comprised of the top officials of the majors, as are the important committees through which the MPAA operates. Rarely do all the directors of the Association meet together. Valenti apparently coordinates the decision-making process by having private discussions with the various individuals, thereby formulating a consensus. Sometimes matters are formally approved by a vote, but this does not seem the norm.

The association has remained strong ever since its beginnings but the advent of new film companies, such as CBS's Cinema Center, ABC Pictures, and National General, none of whom are members, may portend a diminution of MPAA's ability to speak for the nation's moviemakers. At present it is the organization representing the industry.

The second prominent actor in our story is the National Association of Theatre Owners (NATO), which was formed a few years ago as the result of the merger of two exhibitor organizations, Allied States and Theatre Owners of America. It represents exhibitors who own over 13,000 of the approximately 18,000 hard-top and drive-in theaters in the United States.[103] The headquarters of NATO is in New York and the president and the chairman of its board of directors were, during formulation of the new code, Julian Rifkin and Sherrill Corwin, respectively. Its state and regional affiliates number approximately forty-five and annual conventions are held at both the national and regional levels. Exhibitors must be members of local, state, or regional associations (except where there are none) before being granted NATO membership.[104]

The decision-making apparatus of NATO is much more formal than that of MPAA. Article III of the NATO constitution vests the supreme authority of the association in the board of directors. The board consists of one representative from each affiliate, as well as past presidents of TOA, Allied States, members of the executive committee, officers of NATO, and directors at large elected by the board of directors. At least three meetings must be held annually, one of which must be held at the yearly convention. Subject to the approval of the rather large and diverse group that constitutes the board of directors, the executive committee has the power to conduct the general affairs of NATO. The executive committee consists of 21 members elected by the board, including the incumbent chairman of the board of directors, the finance committee chairman, the president, and all past presidents and chairmen of the board. The incumbent president is chairman of this committee.

The organization chiefly concerned with foreign films is the International Film Importers and Distributors of America, Inc. (IFIDA). Independent distributors predominate in IFIDA, although a few of the larger companies are members. Its members include, among others, Allied Artists Pictures, Inc., American International Pictures Export Company, Avco–Embassy, Brandon Films, Inc., Joseph Burstyn, Inc., Cinecom Corporation, Cinema 5, Ltd., Grove Press Films, Janus Films, Paramount, Pathé Contemporary Films, Walter Reade organization, Sherpix, Sigma III, Times Film Corporation, and Toho International (USA), Inc. Since most foreign films are imported through and first exhibited in New York, the principal office of IFIDA (and of most of its members) is in New York. IFIDA's governing committee was composed, at the time of code formulation, of Munio Podhorzer, Leonard Gruenberg, and Eugene Picker. Its board of directors consists of one designee from each member company. Podhorzer was the spokesman for IFIDA. The organization was unable to command support for the code from all members, the most conspicuous dissenter being Walter Reade's organization, Continental Distributing, Inc. Reade has been one of the top seventy-five exhibitors in the country, owning over sixty theaters in the major markets.[106]

B. Expressions of Concern

The first reported response of the movie industry to the *Dallas* decision was one of elation. The day after the decision Valenti rejoiced that the question of offensiveness in films would be decided by obscenity prosecutions.[107] Undoubtedly, Valenti had in mind the strict standards of due process, applicable in all criminal prosecutions, which would assure that the industry would rarely lose such a test. Second thoughts were aired a week later by *Variety* concerning the results of the *Dallas* decision. The trade journal considered that case in conjunction with *Ginsberg* and saw the Court as giving the "green light" to classification systems that did not violate constitutional standards of vagueness.

By mid-May, Valenti had reversed his position. By then, Nizer had had time to advise Valenti about the correct interpretation of the *Dallas-Ginsberg* decisions, and, if that were not enough, Valenti could have seen the writing on the wall as California considered a classification bill. Dallas began rewording its code in order to comply with Supreme Court standards, and New York began a test case against a motion picture under the *Ginsberg* law. Valenti, at least by mid-May and probably within two weeks after *Dallas*, saw that some voluntary classification scheme was necessary to fend off governmental classification.[108]

While Valenti may have derived some momentary pleasure at the thought of battling the obscenity issues through criminal prosecutions

rather than administrative proceedings, the members of NATO were unlikely to share in the delight. Valenti's favorite method of censorship
meant that the target would no longer be the distributor or producer but
the theater owner, and even the projectionist. The *Ginsberg* decision
gave warning that criminal prosecutions were by no means a thing of the
past. In addition, the reasoning in *Dallas* indicated that theater owners
could look forward to new governmental classification schemes as well.

Not only was the concern with censorship efforts more immediate
among NATO members, but the atomistic structure of the organization,
with affiliates stretched from coast to coast, precluded the close coordination of a defensive strategy. While Valenti could easily confer in private
with his members, NATO president Julian Rifkin could only reach his
membership by speaking out publicly. And speak out he did. At the Carolinas' regional convention in mid-May, Rifkin became the first industry
spokesman to state publicly the possible implications of *Dallas*. It might,
he said, result in the classification of about one-half of the films being
shown today as not suitable for young people. This would not be limited
to "nudies" but would include such critically acclaimed productions as
Bonnie and Clyde and *The Graduate*. On the same day that Rifkin was
addressing the Carolinas' convention, NATO of Florida provided further
evidence of exhibitors' concern by decrying the production of too many
adult films and calling on the state legislature to adopt more specific age
guidelines.[109]

C. Valenti Seeks a New Code

For the past two years the MPAA had been designating some films as "suggested for mature audiences" (SMA), and in his statement on 21 May Valenti insisted that parents should not let their children see SMA films.
Informed parental discretion was the banner under which Valenti set out
in search of a new code. The most the movie industry should do, according to Valenti, was provide parents with information to facilitate the exercise of their discretion concerning which films their children should or
should not see. The responsibility was theirs alone to police their children's movie attendance. At least this was Valenti's position at the start
and he would continue to maintain it to justify the new system of self-
regulation, even though certain features of the new scheme were incon-
sistent with this "facilitative" rationale.[110]

Valenti began his search for a new code a few days before his 21 May
statement. After a series of individual conferences with company executives and studio heads, Valenti and Nizer met with the MPAA board in
secret. On the twenty-first, Valenti stated that he had to talk with one

hundred key people to obtain the support that would be needed for a new code, not only from MPAA members, but from independent producers, distributors, and exhibitors.[111] Apparently, a combination of legal advice from Nizer concerning the effect of *Dallas*, Rifkin's and NATO's concern, and actions in state legislatures and in Dallas had persuaded Valenti that the MPAA had better move fast to an industry rating system.

Tentative agreement to the principle of an industry rating system was obtained by Valenti at a closed meeting with the NATO board of directors in Scottsdale, Arizona, on 22 May.[112] It is not clear whether specific ratings had been proposed at this point. But it seems certain that the most severe rating would have done no more than preclude persons under sixteen unaccompanied by their parent from attending the films in this category. No one had yet considered challenging the autonomy of parental control by banning young people from films, which was later to be done by the emergence of the *X* rating.

D. The Emergence of the X

The Scottsdale agreement did not quiet Rifkin's fears that governmental censorship via age classification schemes would occur on a wide scale. However, he did appoint a special committee to represent NATO in negotiations with MPAA over the details of the new code, and meetings began on 4 June.[113] But Rifkin's pessimism was still very much in evidence the following week when he addressed the Cinematography Exhibitors Association in Edinburg, Scotland. The Supreme Court had opened the door to governmental regulation of movie content by permitting the classification of films as not suitable for persons under a certain age, he told his audience, and he direly predicted that giving such power to public tribunals would sharply restrict both the quantity and the quality of films.[114]

The spectre of governmental censorship that captivated the NATO high command led them to press for a partial abandonment of Valenti's facilitative approach to industry classification. Whereas the new code Valenti sought would simply have made easier the task of parents in controlling their children's movie attendance, the code that NATO sought, and successfully, would proscribe the attendance of young people at certain movies even if their parents were willing to accompany them. Apparently, the motivating belief behind the *X* rating was that a certain toughness was necessary to forestall governmental classification schemes and to protect theater owners from criminal prosecutions. The extremity of the toughness is suggested by the fact that the Dallas ordinance did not proscribe the attendance of young people accompanied by their parents.[115] The device for accomplishing this proscriptive purpose was the *X* rating.

News that agreement had been reached on a rating system that included an *X* category reached the public on 19 June. *Variety* headlined, "'X' Marks the Taboo Film Plot, under-16 Ban For First Time." A document embodying the new code before the MPAA board listed these ratings: *G* (General Audience, open to all audiences), *P* (Parents' Discretion, open to all audiences with a warning to parents like the old SMA moniker), *R* (Restricted, no one under sixteen admitted unless accompanied by a parent), and *X* (no one under sixteen admitted under any circumstances). *X* films would not receive a seal, and all majors would be pledged to submit all films. An appeals board was provided for, and all advertising for *G*, *P*, and *R* films had to be approved.[116] Not only was agreement reached between MPAA and NATO, but on 17 June IFIDA acceded to the rating system. The support of this group of independent distributors may have been won as a result of their impression that the new code was not intended to condemn film content but only to provide easily attainable information about the suitability of movies for young people.[117]

Various hypotheses concerning the emergence of the *X* can be put forth; the three most plausible are that the *X* emerged because of pressures by NATO, or IFIDA, or a combination of both. (1) NATO was worried about exhibitors being prosecuted under *Ginsberg* laws and feared governmental classification. Valenti needed NATO's cooperation in order to put the code into operation. IFIDA showed its films at NATO theaters, and thus could be convinced to cooperate. (2) It is possible that IFIDA proposed the *X* rating. That organization may have demanded the *X* as its price of approval. The IFIDA was the fringe of the industry; low-budget foreign films were the staples of IFIDA members, and many of these films had been involved in court cases over the last two decades. The MPAA, in order to achieve consensus, without which the code would be unworkable, had to have IFIDA approval. Many pictures from the IFIDA contained sex and the *X* could be used as a come-on to attract customers.[118] While the IFIDA had little to gain or lose from a system whose most restrictive rating was *R*, it would be worthwhile to have films rated or self-rated when a rating was included which actually banned children, who rarely saw subtitled, sexy films anyway, and had the connotation that the letter *X* carried. Moreover, if a film was rated *X*, or if the producer self-rated his film *X*, the fee to the PCA would be nominal, or none at all.[119] (3) The third possible hypothesis is that Valenti was caught in a squeeze between the two groups.

Subsequent events have led the authors to the conclusion that the first hypothesis is the correct one. As just noted an *X* rating meant that persons under sixteen precluded from seeing films so classified probably did not bother the IFIDA people, since the most likely market for films distributed by IFIDA members is that of young adults. What would have bothered IFIDA was any understanding that self-rated *X* movies should not be allowed to play in theaters that typically exhibit films produced or distributed by MPAA members. That such an understanding may have existed has recently been suggested by the *Stitch* incident.

A Danish film entitled *Without a Stitch* opened in January 1970 at one of the nation's finest movie houses, Loew's State I at 45th and Broadway in New York City. Playing at the twin Loew's State II was *Paint Your Wagon*, a Paramount production costing 15 times as much as *Stitch*. *Stitch* cost under $1,000,000 and *Wagon* approximately $15,000,000.[120] As *Stitch* proceeded to outgross *Wagon*,[121] Valenti denounced the Danish film as "trash," "pornographic," and "unfit for major showcase exposure."[122] Loew's canceled the *Stitch* engagement at its Cine Theatre in New York City, where the controversial movie had been playing in addition to its run at Loew's State I.[123] The film's American distributor, Tonylyn Productions, sued, alleging antitrust law violations, interference with business opportunities, and trade libels.

The complaint was filed in the U.S. District Court, Central District of California, on 9 February 1970. Plaintiff Tonylyn Productions was represented by attorney Stanley Fleishman, who successfully defended the film when it was seized by customs upon entry into this country through the port of Los Angeles. Defendants named were MPAA, NATO, Gulf & Western Industries (parent of Paramount), Valenti, Picker, and Charles G. Bludhorn, head of G&W. Paramount's alleged threat is found in paragraph XI of the complaint. An answer was filed by Paramount and the MPAA, but no discovery had been taken at the time this was written. According to the complaint, Paramount threatened to withhold its productions from Loew's, and Valenti, on behalf of MPAA, urged a boycott of *Stitch* by first-run theaters.[124] The current president of NATO, Eugene Picker, allegedly entered the fracas to announce that Loew's had abandoned a "gentlemen's agreement" between NATO and MPAA to boycott *X* films not produced or distributed by MPAA members. Since MPAA members produced most of the largest grossing films, NATO members could scarcely avoid *X*-rated films like *Midnight Cowboy*, but could easily "boycott" *X*-rated films of independent producers. *Stitch* had been self-rated X by the distributor.

E. Formal Consensus

As of 3 July 1968 the MPAA would still not say that the code was set.[125] Numerous formal votes were needed, and early fall was the target date for beginning operation. It was rumored that Twentieth Century–Fox was opposed to the *X* and this might prove troublesome for Valenti.[126]

Apparently all wrinkles were ironed out because on the eighteenth of September, the MPAA directors met to approve the code. Rifkin assured Valenti that under sixteens would be refused admission and in some cases the bars would be raised to under eighteens. The feelings of the industry were described as, "The American majors, on the overall basis, are acquiescent, but the U.S. and foreign independents (IFIDA) could be a problem which is where the theatre owners are an important ally. They provide the teeth because, on local level, they are the targets of the gendarmerie, parents-teachers associations, civic groups, and the like." [127] The IFIDA had already approved it on the twelfth, and NATO acquiescence had been achieved previous to the MPAA meeting. It was hoped to have the code in operation by 8 October so that there would be three months before state legislatures met in January, in order to prove that industry self-regulation could work.[128] On 7 October, the plan was officially revealed. On the platform with Valenti were Rifkin and Podhorzer. By cooperating, the IFIDA, NATO, and the MPAA had promulgated a new code, with an estimated 85 percent of the exhibitors, the key link, cooperating.

The code was to rate all pictures to be released in the United States after 1 November. NATO agreed to enforce ratings by playing pictures in accordance with the ratings, by enforcing ratings, by restricting audiences, and by publicizing ratings at the box office.[129] The ratings were *G-M-R-X*; the first signified general audience films, open to all; the second, those recommended for mature audiences; the third, those restricted to under sixteens unless accompanied by a parent; and the last, those banned to all under sixteen. Early in 1970, the *M* was changed to *PG* (All Ages Admitted, Parental Guidance Suggested). The M had tended to be confusing. The *R* and *X* age limits were upped to seventeen, i.e., those under seventeen were banned from *X* films and had to be accompanied by a parent to *R* films. The *PG*, in some instances, was seen as the kiss of death. One production company was advised by exhibitors to restore cuts suggested by the CRA and regain its *R* rating, rather than *PG*. Otherwise, exhibitors said, the film would be classed as a "family" product, and flop at the box office.[130]

VI. The Rating System in Operation

Law permits at least two distinct approaches toward the ordering of man's social activities. We most commonly think of law as controlling human behavior by proscribing certain conduct, and the criminal law furnishes a clear example of the "proscriptive" approach. But law can also aim at facilitating man's behavior. A good deal of our contract law is of this type. It may specify the consequences which attach to the use of a certain term, but leave it to the discretion of the contracting parties whether or not to use it. If the parties should use the term, they are spared the need of spelling out the attending consequences in their agreement because the law has done it for them. Similarly, through trade associations or governmental agencies, an elaborate system of classification may be developed to help those making decisions to make them more intelligently. For example, much of the country's agricultural produce is graded to assist the consumer.

The formulation of the movie industry's new rating system represented a compromise between these two approaches. Whether the purpose of the code formulators, the private lawmakers, was to proscribe or facilitate, it attempted to deal with a phenomenon, young audiences seeing mature films, which influential groups in our society regard as a problem. The champions of both approaches were also agreed in seeking to preclude certain solutions to this problem that they feared might be attempted by governmental agencies.[131] The difference was that the facilitative approach would totally redefine the "problem" in terms of a young person's attendance at a movie which his parents would not want him to see. Were this the problem there would be no reason why the movie industry would have to rate its films if parents would expend the time necessary for the proper exercise of their police function. While it is perhaps asking too much to expect them to preview every film that their children might wish to see, it does not seem unrealistic to expect them to use such usual sources of information about films as advertising, critical reviews, and gossip. But in this busy world with all the other problems that concern teenagers and their parents (e.g., drugs, the draft), garnering sufficient information from these sources is too onerous a task to place on parents, or so the argument for a facilitative rating system would go. Easily understandable, easily communicable, standardized categories were necessary to remedy the preexisting communications gap.

That this gap exists is evidenced by a study conducted for the MPAA by Opinion Research Corporation in August–September 1969. Revealing statistics are: 77 percent of all moviegoers, and 58 percent of the public knew of the existence of the code, although the study reported that "few people have a clear understanding of the specific admission policies embodied in the rating system." Among moviegoers, fewer than 20 percent were able to demonstrate accurate knowledge of the meaning of any rating symbol. The best understood concerned the symbol X, and that was accurately defined by only 25 percent.[132]

In contrast, the "proscriptive" approach taken by NATO in connection with the X category would not redefine the young audience—mature film problem in terms of parental discretion, at least regarding a certain class of pictures. The purpose of this approach was to forbid young people from seeing mature films, since their mere presence at such a movie is of significant social concern. As we have seen, NATO was successful in obtaining an X rating, thus making the rating system partially proscriptive from the start.

With respect to the young audience—mature film problem, however, the distinction between these approaches may not be important, so long as the touchstone of a facilitative approach is parental discretion. Neither approach would permit young people to see films that their parents deem unsuitable. This is the result of the R rating, which even insists that a parent evidence his consent by accompanying his child to the movie. Without the evidence of accompaniment, no person under seventeen will be admitted to an R movie, whatever the actual wishes of his parent. The difference between the approaches comes only when parents would permit their children to attend a film which the movie industry considers unsuitable. But such instances would seem rare. Parents can take their children to movies rated R, but the exercise of this privilege has not been overwhelming. Because few teenagers attend movies with their parents, an R rating is essentially an X rating for all practical purposes.[133] Those parents who would object to the exclusion of their children from theaters playing X pictures are not likely to be numerous in present American society. Were the proscriptive effects of the new code limited to the exclusion of young people from X films and R films when unaccompanied by their parents, the departure from a facilitative approach would be slight indeed.

But the proscriptive effects are not so confined. In actual operation, it seems doubtful that they could be, however faithful was the rating system in design to the facilitative approach. To assume that the censorship forces are concerned only with youthful audiences who see mature films is to take them at their word, given only when pressed in a debate over institutional censorship necessary and the type which can still be done through public and private ordering. But it is not hard to find indications that what is wanted is a curtailment of what the various guardians of the public taste find not to their liking. An example from the realm of official action is the Las Vegas district attorney who, in announcing a new "get-tough" campaign against obscenity, stated that his hopes, along with those of many Nevada legislators, for self-regulation by the movie industry had gone "down the drain in a deluge of pornographic promiscuity." [124] The Texas legislature failed by a narrow margin to enact a bill that would have placed an admissions tax on tickets to all X-rated movies, and several states and cities are considering similar "smut tax" proposals. [135] Private attempts to use the rating system proscriptively can also be found. An example of this effort is the news and advertising blackout effected against X movies by a goodly number of newspapers and television and radio stations. As a matter of policy, they refuse to print or broadcast advertisements for, reviews of, or stories about such films. [136] Moreover, a NATO survey indicated that almost half of NATO members would refuse to play any X film. [137] What the rating system may facilitate is not parental control so much as sniping attacks against more easily identifiable targets. In an editorial *Variety* noted "the strange tendency all over the nation to translate the X-rating from warning signal into a sort of "confession of guilt" and to set up punishments to shut out such releases from the market." [138]

The extent, then, to which the rating system will be proscriptive in operation will not be determined by the intent of the private lawmakers who designed it but by the balance of social forces. *Variety* pointed out that the tendency it identified was unintended by the new code's formulators. It concluded: "It is perhaps an instance of the common impression in the film business that 'public indignation' has been shy of practical strategems." [139] A crucial factor is the willingness of movie producers to stand by their sense of what their movies should include. Examples abound indicating that such fortitude is not the most common quality among moviemakers. *Last Summer* was re-rated *R* after cutting a few words; [140] *If It's Tuesday, It Must Be Belgium* dropped a bedroom scene and upped itself from *M* to *G*; [141] *Zabriskie Point*, the controversial Antonioni film, was rated *R* after a skywriting scene with explicit language was edited. [142] Still, resistance to the MPAA raters is not unknown. The producer of *Honeymoon Killers* refused to eliminate the sound of urination which accompanied a conversation that the leading character carried on from the bathroom. Despite a warning that retention of the sound would result in an *X*, the movie was given an *R*. [143] And Paramount became the first major studio to defy the new code by refusing to advertise the *M* rating of *Paint Your Wagon*. Paramount claimed that films containing more adult material, such as *Sweet Charity* and *Pepi*, had received *G* ratings. Paramount had appealed the *M* rating but lost 10–9. On rehearing, with new evidence to present, the vote went against them by 13–9.[144] There are over a dozen appeals. Few producer-distributors have yet prevailed. And the Academy Award victory, as well as the box office success, of *X*-rated *Midnight Cowboy* surely does not discourage production independence.

Ultimately, however, producers will give the public the kind of movies that sell. If a strong demand exists for mature pictures, the fact that such films are rated *R* or *X* will not deter their production and distribution. Indications of the continued presence of such a demand can be spotted. For one thing, self-rated *X* pictures from abroad have begun to play the movie palaces.[145] For another, the raters seem to be easing up on the requirements for an *R*. *Boys in the Band*, Fellini's *Satyricon*, and *The Magic Garden of Stanley Sweetheard*, films that one would have expected to be *X*ed, were given *R*'s.[146] The attempt of the new code administrators may be to reconcile the rating system with market realities by getting the *X* equated in the public mind with trash, i.e., stag films and nudies, and the *R* with artistically respectable productions which frankly present sexual matter. If so, the distinction will be blurred by *X* pictures like the film adaptation of Henry Miller's *The Tropic of Cancer* and Visconti's *The Damned*.

The economic forces that brought down the old code, the new competition from television and foreign films, brought into being a new sort of movie audience, comprised of young adults sophisticated in their likings. They became the steady customers of the movie theaters because they were least enthralled with television entertainment and were attracted by the maturity they found first in foreign films and eventually in ones from Hollywood. They grew up with the movies. It is late in the day to deny this audience films that suit their tastes. The new rating system may yet avoid unduly proscriptive effects.

Films Which Served as Sources of Litigation Related to Censorship

Foreign Films

1. *A Stranger Knocks*   Trans-Lux Distributing Corp. v. Board of Regents, 380 U.S. 259 (1965)

2. *And God Created Woman*   Kingsley International Pictures Corp. v. City of Providence, 166 F.Supp. 456 (D.R.I. 1958)

3. *Dirty Girls*	Leighton v. Maryland State Board of Censors, 242 Md. 705, 218 A.2d 179 (1966)
4. *Don Juan*	Times Film Corp. v. Chicago, 365 U.S. 43 (1961)
5. *491*	United States v. One Carton Positive Motion Picture Film Entitled "491," 367 F.2d 889 (2d Cir. 1966)
6. *Game of Love*	Times Film Corp. v. Chicago, 355 U.S. 35 (1957)
7. *I, Am Woman*	Variety, Feb. 26, 1969, at 26, col. 5.
8. *I Am Curious (Yellow)*	United States v. A Motion Picture Film Entitled "I Am Curious (Yellow)," 404 F.2d 196 (2d Cir. 1968)
9. *Lady Chatterly's Lover*	Kingsley International Pictures Corp. v. Regents, 360 U.S. 684 (1959)
10. *La Ronde*	Commercial Pictures Corp. v. Board of Regents, 346 U.S. 587 (1954)
11. *Lovers*	Jacobellis vs. Ohio, 378 U.S. 184 (1964)
12. *M*	Superior Films v. Dept of Education, 346 U.S. 587 (1954)
13. *The Miracle*	Burstyn v. Wilson, 343 U.S. 495 (1952)
14. *Miss Julie*	Brattle Films, Inc. v. Commissioner of Public Safety, 333 Mass. 58, 127 N.E.2d 891 (1955)
15. *Naked Amazon*	Maryland State Board of Motion Picture Censors v. Times Film Corp., 212 Md 454, 129 A.2d 833 (1957)
16. *Never on Sunday*	Atlanta v. Lopert Pictures Corp., 217 Ga. 432, 122 S.E2d 916 (1961)
17. *Revenge at Daybreak*	Freedman v. Maryland, 380 U.S. 51 (1965)
18. *Twilight Girls*	Metzger v. Couper, 15 Y.Y.2d 802, 205 N.E.2d 694, 257 N.Y.S.2d 599 (1965)
19. *Un Chant D'Amour*	Landau v. Fording, 388 U.S. 456 (1967)

20. *The Unsatisfied*	Cambist Films, Inc. v. Board of Regents, 46 Misc.2d 513, 260 N.Y.S.2d 804 (Sup. Ct. 1965)
21. *Virgin Spring*	Janus Films, Inc. v. Fort Worth, 163 Tex. 616, 358 S.W.2d 589 (1962)
22. *Viva Maria*	Interstate Circuit v. Dallas, 390 U.S. 676 (1968)
23. *Women of the World*	Embassy Pictures Corp. vs. Hudson, 242 F. Supp. 975 (W.D. Tenn. 1965)

American Films

1. *Anatomy of a Murder*	Columbia Pictures v. Chicago, 184 F.Supp. 817 (N.D. Ill. 1959)
2. *The Bedford Incident*	State ex rel. Londerholem v. Columbia Pictures Corp., 197 Kan. 448, 417 P.2d 255 (1966)
3. *Blue Movie*	Variety, Aug. 6, 1969, at 26, col. 2.
4. *Body of a Female*	Teitel Film Corp. v. Cusack, 390 U.S. 139 (1968)
5. *Bunny Lake Is Missing*	Same as 2.
6. *Candy*	Variety, March 5, 1969, at 22, col. 1
7. *The Connection*	Connection Co. v. Board of Regents, 17 App; Div. 2d 671, 230 N.Y.S.2d 103 (1962)
8. *The Devil's Weed* (later revised to *She Should'a Said No!*)	Hallmark Productions v. Carroll, 384 Pa. 348, 121 A.2d 584 (1956)
9. *The French Line*	RKO Radio Pictures v. Dept of Education 162 Ohio St. 263, 122 N.E.2d 769 (1954)
10. *Garden of Eden*	Excelsior Pictures Corp. v. Chicago, 182 F.Supp. 400 (N.D. Ill. 1960)
11. *Have Figure, Will Travel*	Fanfare Films, Inc. v. Motion Picture Censor Board, 234 Md. 10, 197 A.2d 839 (1964)

12. *The Killing of Sister George*   Variety, March 5, 1969, at 22, col. 4

13. *Man with the Golden Arm*   United Artists Corp. v. Maryland State Board of Censors, 210 Md. 586, 124 A.2d 292 (1956)

14. *Mom and Dad*   Capitol Enterprises v. Board of Regents, 1 App. Div. 2d 990, 149 N.Y.S.2d 920 (1956)

15. *The Moon Is Blue*   Holmby Productions v. Vaugh, 350 U.S. 870 (1955)

16. *Native Son*   Same as 12-Foreign

17. *Pinky*   Gelling v. Texas, 343 U.S. 960 (1952)

18. *Rent-a-Girl*   Same as 4

19. *Teenage Menace*   Broadway Angels v. Wilson, 282 App. Div. 643, 125 N.Y.S.2d 546 (1953)

20. *This Picture Is Censored*   Hewitt v. Maryland State Board of Censors, 243 Md. 574, 221 A.2d 894 (1966)

21. *Vixen*   Variety, March 26, 1969, at 22, col. 1

PART FIVE

Media Interaction:
Television and Film

The Effects of Television
on the Motion Picture Industry:
1948–1960

Fredric Stuart

The motion picture industry entered upon a period of severe decline beginning about 1947. Table 13.1 and figure 13.1 illustrate the nature and extent of this recession. Between 1946 and 1956 the industry lost almost half of its customers, with the average weekly attendance at theaters declining from 90 million to 46 million (table 13.1, col. 4). This estimate is corroborated by Department of Commerce data on personal consumer expenditures on motion picture admissions which, deflated by the index of admission prices, show a reduction of 42 percent for the period (col. 2). This defection on the part of consumers occurred during a period of rising expenditures on most other goods and services, so that the industry's share of total consumer purchases was reduced from 1.15 percent to 0.49 percent in ten years (col. 3).

Though the reduction in attendance has been continuous since 1946, the profits of motion picture production companies reached a low turning point in 1952, having been reduced by over 80 percent as measured by the experience of the seven leading firms (col. 5).[1] The readjustments which permitted increased profits after 1952 will be discussed later.

Have any factors other than reduced attendance at theaters contributed to the decline in profits of the large studios? One factor which has been suggested is the divorcement of motion picture theaters from production companies pursuant to a 1948 Supreme Court decision on federal antitrust action which had commenced in 1938. By consent decree the combined production-exhibition companies were dissolved and reformed as indicated in table 13.2. The profit figures presented in table 13.1 include net profits of both production and exhibition companies,

257

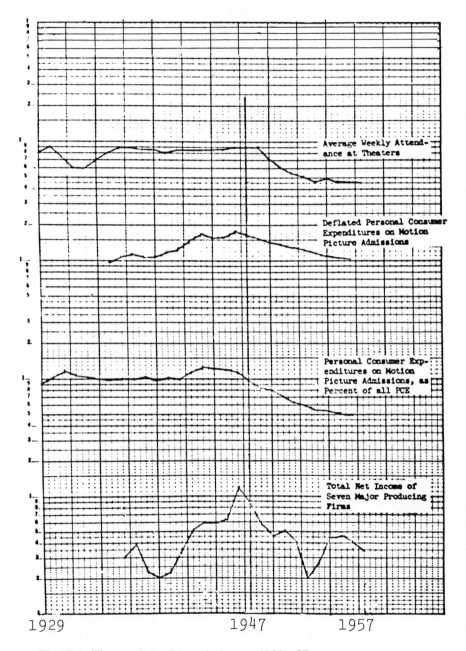

Fig. 13.1. *The motion picture industry, 1929–57*
Sources: See table 13.1.

Table 13.1. *The Motion Picture Industry, 1929–1957*

Year	Personal Consumer Expenditures On Motion Picture Admissions (1) Absolute* ($ millions)	(2) Deflated By Admission Price Index†	(3) As Percent of all PCE	(4) Average Weekly Motion Picture Attendance* ($ millions)	(5) Total Net Income of 7 Major Firms§ ($ millions)
1929	720		0.91	80	
1930	732		1.03	90	
1931	719		1.17	75	
1932	527		1.07	60	
1933	482		1.04	60	
1934	518		1.00	70	
1935	556	974	0.99	80	
1936	626	1,074	1.00	88	30
1937	676	1,119	1.00	88	39
1938	663	1,075	1.03	85	23
1939	659	1,084	0.97	85	20
1940	735	1,182	1.02	80	22
1941	809	1,235	0.99	85	35
1942	1,022	1,481	1.14	85	51
1943	1,275	1,695	1.27	85	60
1944	1,341	1,543	1.22	85	59
1945	1,450	1,586	1.20	85	65
1946	1,692	1,798	1.15	90	119
1947	1,594	1,620	0.97	90	86
1948	1,506	1,514	0.85	90	56
1949	1,468	1,439	0.81	70	45
1950	1,394	1,372	0.72	60	50
1951	1,338	1,298	0.64	54	41
1952	1,284	1,235	0.59	51	20
1953	1,252	1,149	0.54	46	28
1954	1,275	1,099	0.54	49	44
1955	1,286	1,055	0.51	46	46
1956	1,298	1,041	0.49	45	41
1957				45	34

Sources:
*U.S. Department of Commerce, *National Income Supplement to the Survey of Current*

subsequent to the divorcements. However, it may be argued that the new total profits would tend to be lower than the former income of the parent company, even in the absence of any decline in motion picture attendance. Indeed, this is an implicit purpose of antitrust proceedings, which if successful presumably eliminate some monopoly profits. In the present case, a redistribution of income between the seven major companies and all other production and exhibition companies would be an expected result of the divorcement. In 1946 the five companies listed in table 13.2 controlled 16 percent of the nation's theaters.[2] Since these theaters were assured of first-run bookings of the best feature pictures, they probably received a larger share of total theater receipts before than after the reorganization. On the production side, the "major" companies lost a guaranteed market for feature films of inferior grade after the divorcement, so that a larger share of rental receipts has accrued to independent production companies after the court decision. Competition from smaller producers was encouraged by the Court when it outlawed the specific restrictive practice of "block booking," the industry version of the tie-in sale. By forcing theaters to rent pictures in large lots, the major companies had been able to dispose of low-cost, low-quality pictures, and effectively block the formation of independent production companies.

Thus the profit problems of the major production firms between 1948 and 1952 were not wholly attributable to the decline in motion picture attendance. On the other hand, this decline was so large that it appears as the most important part of the problem, even with the most exaggerated estimates of profits from coercive practices before the court order. The point will be made later that some of the producers' reactions to television competition were suggested or facilitated by the coincidental timing (relative to television) of the Supreme Court decision.

Was the decline in attendance and box-office receipts directly and solely attributable to television? The data examined thus far indicate that the motion picture and television industries moved sharply in opposite directions during the 1950s. While television grew to major-industry di-

Business (Washington, D.C., 1954), and "Personal Consumption Expenditures by type of product, 1952–56," *Survey of Current Business*, July 1957, p. 21.

[†] Index from U.S. Bureau of Labor Statistics, "Consumer Price Index: Price Indexes for Selected Items and Groups." (Annual indexes for 1935–55 published in the July 1956 number, subsequent data from monthy bulletins thereafter).

[‡] Wid's Films and Film Folks, Inc., *Film Daily Yearbook: 1957* (New York, 1957).

[§] Moody's Investors' Service, *Moody's Industrial Manual—1958* (New York, 1958). The firms included were Loew's, Paramount, Twentieth Century–Fox, Warner Brothers, Columbia, Radio-Keith-Orpheum, and Universal. Income of the new theater-owning companies, formed subsequent to the divorcement of production and exhibition by consent decree, has been added for 1949–57.

Table 13.2. *Divorcement of Motion Picture Production and Exhibition Companies*

Old Company	New Companies a. Production b. Exhibition	Date Accomplished
Paramount Pictures, Inc.	a. Paramount Pictures Corp.	
	b. United Paramount Theaters, Inc.	1949
Radio-Keith-Orpheum Corp.	a. RKO Pictures, Inc.	
	b. RKO Theaters Corp.	1950
Twentieth Century–Fox	a. Twentieth Century–Fox	
	b. National Theaters Corp.	1951
Warner Bros.	a. Warner Bros. Pictures	
	b. Stanley Warner Corp.	1953
Loew's, Inc.	a. Metro-Goldwyn-Mayer Corp.	ordered in 1954, not yet
	b. Loew's Theaters, Inc.	accomplished

mensions, the motion picture business was transformed from a highly prosperous to a distinctly declining industry. To what extent are the two developments related?

The fact of simultaneous occurrence, while suggestive, is not acceptable as conclusive evidence of a causal relation—no more than the secular increase of cancer incidence and cigarette consumption can be accepted as proof that cigarettes cause cancer, or the rise in the number of working economists and the lessening severity of business contractions as proof that economists cure depressions. This well-known injunction against hasty conclusions based on correlation through time is tempered in the present case, however, by a strong *a priori* presumption that television and motion pictures are competing industries. The concurrent rise of one and decline of the other is hardly likely to be entirely coincidental.

Most analysts of the decline in theater attendance list television as a major cause, but there has been disagreement about the relative importance of this and other factors operating during the same period. Some other suggested explanations of motion picture decline (not listed in the order of their popularity) are:

1. Consumers, experiencing rising incomes and shortages of tangible goods during World War II, diverted more than the "normal" share of their expenditures to the motion picture industry, which became overexpanded. This behavior was reversed after the war. With a backlog of unsatisfied demand for consumer goods, the lifting of wartime market restrictions led to diminishing expenditures on motion picture admissions (and other amusements), both in absolute terms and relative to total consumer expenditures.

2. The movement to the suburbs also adversely affected the motion picture industry in several ways:

a. Since most theaters are located in downtown areas of large cities, transportation problems (in terms of additional cost and inconvenience) come between the suburbanite and his motion picture habit.

b. Alternative activities not indigenous to large cities are available in suburbs, e.g., the basement workshop or playroom, participation sports, and lawn-mowing.

c. Baby-sitters are more necessary, more expensive, more difficult to find even at higher rates, and employed for longer hours (when motion pictures are attended), in the suburbs than in cities.

3. Attendance at regular motion picture theaters was reduced by competition from an increasing number of drive-in theaters, which resulted in an overall decline in receipts, since the admission price per person is less at drive-in theaters.

4. Increased traffic congestion in the downtown areas of large cities, reflected in rising transit and car-parking rates, discouraged attendance at the large, first-run houses, which had traditionally been the industry's best sources of revenue. As in the case of drive-in theaters, the lower neighborhood prices resulted in an overall decline in receipts when consumers shifted from first-run to second-run theaters.

5. The quality of motion pictures has deteriorated.

The strongest argument against any of these explanations consists of statistical evidence (to be presented shortly) of the importance of television as primary cause of the motion picture decline. However, let us first consider briefly the merit of each.

1. Postwar reallocation of consumer expenditures. The argument re-

garding deferred demand for physical goods seems reasonable as an explanation of the decline in attendance and receipts during 1948 and 1949, but not for the continuation and deepening of the decline in subsequent years. Consumer expenditures on motion picture admissions rose during 1942–46 from a thirteen-year prewar average of 1.02 percent of total consumer expenditures to 1.20 percent (table 13.2). The return to 0.97 percent in 1947, and even the decline to 0.85 percent in 1948, might be interpreted as an inevitable postwar reaction. But by 1956 consumers were spending only 0.49 percent of their money on theater admissions, and the average from 1947 to 1956 was 0.67 percent. By way of contrast, the percent expended for legitimate theater and opera (which should be subject to the same arguments) was 0.10 before the war, 0.12 during the war years, and returned to 0.09 during 1947–56.[3]

2. Movement to the suburbs. The suburban movement involves too small a fraction of the population to account for much of the 49 percent drop in motion picture attendance, even if all the new suburbanites had shunned the theaters entirely. Further, in the absence of other depressing factors, one would expect exhibitors to follow the migrating audience by opening suburban theaters. Transportation difficulties would then provide only a temporary impediment to continued attendance.

While the suburbs provide some unique alternative amusements, others are absent there but available in large cities; such as night clubs, professional sports events, and legitimate theater.

The baby-sitting problem may be solved by attendance at drive-in theaters, more common in suburban than urban areas (for this very reason, among others). Moreover, since admission prices are lower in suburban areas, the total cost of indoor movie plus baby-sitter often approximates that in the city.

3. Drive-in theaters. The number of drive-in theaters increased rapidly, from 300 in 1946 to 4,500 in 1956. During the same period approximately 4,200 indoor theaters were closed.[4] Since the price per person is lower at drive-in theaters, one is tempted to conclude that there has been no attendance decline at all, but only a shift of consumer preference between theater types. This hypothesis will be tested later, after the background for a statistical approach to the problem has been established.

4. Traffic congestion. The motion picture decline has by no means been confined to large cities and their environs. Census of business data for 1948 and 1954, reproduced in table 13.3, show a significant reduction in motion picture receipts in cities of all sizes, as well as in rural areas. While the largest declines occurred in cities with over 500,000 people, in which traffic congestion is most acute, we shall see presently that these are also the cities with heaviest television penetration. It will be

demonstrated that the apparent correlation between population and motion picture decline is in reality a reflection of a marked correlation between population and television density.

5. Picture quality. The thesis that motion pictures have deteriorated in quality is as incapable of proof (disproof) as the opposite claim made in self-defense by the studios: "Movies are better than ever." Even if true, it could account for only a small fraction of the lost audience. For example, in a 1956 consumer survey[5] 15 percent of respondents in the New York metropolitan area expressed the opinion that picture quality had diminished, and 61 percent stated that their personal attendance had diminished.

The technology of motion picture production and exhibition has improved since 1946. The development of wide-screen projection systems, stereophonic recording systems, and other innovations will be discussed farther on, since their appearance during this period is demonstrably a reaction to television competition. In the more difficult area of picture content there is also objective evidence of improvement rather than deterioration in quality. For example, the number (and the proportion) of films based on novels, short stories, and plays of recognized literary quality increased.

On the other hand, since quality may best be judged by comparison with available alternatives, the appearance of television "reduced" the quality of motion pictures. For television is the first close substitute for

Table 13.3. *Change in Motion Picture Receipts, 1948–54 (by city size)*

City Size	Receipts $(millions)		% Change
	1948	1954	
500,000 and over	399	337	−16
250,000–500,000	97	95	−2
100,000–250,000	136	117	−14
50,000–100,000	115	98	−15
25,000– 50,000	118	111	−6
10,000– 25,000	152	140	−8
5,000– 10,000	98	90	−8
2,500– 5,000	67	65	−4
Remainder of Area	129	127	−2
U.S., Total	1,311	1,180	−10

Source: U.S. Bureau of the Census, *U.S. Census of Business: 1948* (Washington, D.C., 1951), vol. 6, and *U.S. Census of Business: 1954* (Washington, D.C., 1956), vol. 5.

motion pictures to appear since the beginnings of the industry. Until 1946 the cinema was a unique entertainment, towering over competitors (such as radio) by a margin sufficient to escape quality judgements by default. A large majority of the pretelevision movie audience had never been exposed to any other form of visual entertainment.

☆
Statistical Evidence

The fact that the rate of television penetration varied considerably in different geographical areas of the United States provides useful statistical evidence of the impact of television on motion picture attendance. In general, television development has been most rapid in the northeast and north central states, and least rapid in the West and South. By 1956 over 80 percent of households in the New England and mid-Atlantic states were equipped with one or more television sets, while the figure for many western and southern states (e.g., Mississippi, Montana, Wyoming) was between 30 and 40 percent.[6] These estimates are based on a television supplement to the Current Population Survey of February 1956, conducted by the U.S. Bureau of the Census. The census bureau has undertaken five such surveys since 1955, the results of which are presented in table 13.4.

In the census surveys a probability sample of households in 435 counties is designed to yield reliable estimates of the percentage of households with television sets for the United States as a whole and for four geographic regions. For June 1955 and February 1956 Advertising Research Foundation derived estimates for all U.S. counties and for states, by combining the census data with independent county estimates.[7] A comparison of this information with geographic data on the motion picture industry will enable us to determine the extent to which the drop in motion picture receipts may be explained by competition from television receivers.

The best area breakdowns of motion picture data are obtained from the *U.S. Census of Business*, conducted in 1948 and 1954. This seven year period is a good one for the present purpose, since television did not offer potent competition until early 1949, when the networks had commenced operations and set ownership passed the million mark.

The census figures showed a decline in admissions receipts of 13 percent for the United States as a whole between 1948 and 1954, from $1,614,000,000 to $1,407,000,000. On a per-capita basis this was a 21

Table 13.4. *Percent of Households with Television Sets, 1955–58 (by area)*

Area	June 1955	Feb. 1956	Aug. 1956	Apr. 1957	Jan. 1958
United States	67	73	76	80	83
Northeast	80	82	85	88	90
North Central	72	79	79	85	87
South	53	62	65	71	74
West	62	66	75	77	82

Source: U.S. Bureau of the Census, *Housing and Construction Reports*, series H-121, nos. 1–5. (Washington, D.C., 1955–58)

percent reduction, from $11.05 to $8.73. There was great variation, however, in the experience of theater operators in different areas. Whereas per-capita receipts fell by more than 20 percent in most New England states, states in the West showed *increases* of up to 44 percent! Indeed, thirty states registered increases in per-capita motion picture receipts during this period. In these states the (unweighted) average percentage of households with television in 1955 was 48 percent, while in the eighteen states showing a decline in per-capita receipts average television density was 75 percent.[8] The motion picture data for states appears in table 13.5.

The best available television data with which to compare these changes in motion picture receipts comes from the June 1955 census bureau sample projected for state and county breakdowns by Advertising Research Foundation.[9]

The scatter diagram (fig. 13.2) clearly indicates a negative linear relationship between the percentage of households with television sets (the independent variable) and the percentage change in per-capita motion picture receipts. Table 13.6 shows the results of a least-squares correlation analysis. The coefficient of correlation (0.91) is of significant size, at the 0.01 level of confidence.[10]

Eighty-two percent of the variance in the motion picture data is explained by the relation to television density. Television thus appears to have been a major cause of the overall decline in motion picture receipts during this period. Indeed, the evidence suggests that in the absence of television competition there might have been a substantial increase in motion picture revenues between 1948 and 1954. This does not eliminate the other explanations offered above for the movies' difficulties,

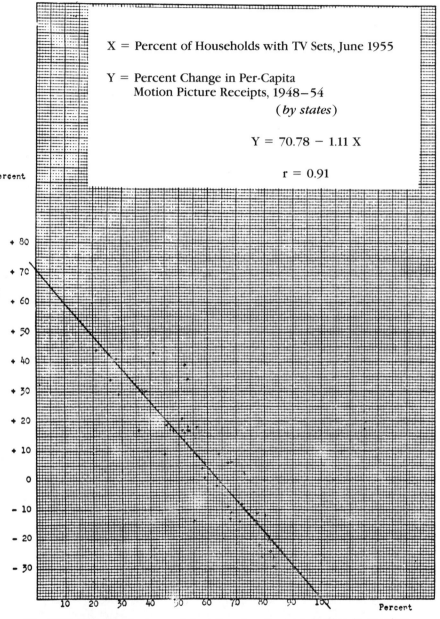

Fig. 13.2. *Relation between television density and decline in motion picture receipts*
Sources: See table 13.6.

Table 13.5. Change in Per-Capita Motion Picture Receipts, 1948–54 (by states)

State	Motion Picture Receipts $ (000)		Per-Capita Receipts ($)		Percent Change	
	1948	1954	1948	1954	+	−
Maine	7,655	8,565	8.72	9.51	9.06	
New Hampshire	4,599	4,260	8.84	7.72		12.67
Vermont	2,681	3,269	7.47	8.74	17.00	
Massachusetts	49,138	39,629	10.30	8.21		20.29
Rhode Island	8,299	6,087	10.55	7.54		28.53
Connecticut	19,641	18,586	9.75	8.54		12.41
New York	199,991	176,807	13.80	11.17		19.06
New Jersey	51,624	41,966	10.81	8.04		25.62
Pennsylvania	94,248	77,626	9.16	7.15		21.94
Ohio	67,311	57,266	8.55	6.48		24.21
Indiana	33,491	33,654	8.64	7.94		8.10
Illinois	94,488	86,420	11.05	9.44		14.57
Michigan	56,080	55,199	9.03	7.80		13.62
Wisconsin	26,176	25,937	7.90	7.15		9.49
Minnesota	21,524	23,017	7.50	7.35		2.00
Iowa	19,503	18,242	7.67	6.84		10.82
Missouri	30,296	34,441	7.88	8.35	5.96	
N. Dakota	3,937	5,612	6.79	8.82	29.90	
S. Dakota	4,171	5,911	6.82	8.78	28.74	
Nebraska	10,471	11,897	8.28	8.76	5.80	
Kansas	14,649	21,822	7.74	10.79	39.41	
Delaware	2,962	2,608	9.49	7.07		25.50
Maryland	18,366	18,712	8.09	7.18		11.25

N. Carolina	23,092	30,806	6.02	7.29	21.10
S. Carolina	9,898	13,095	4.96	5.78	16.53
Georgia	19,196	28,669	5.89	7.90	34.13
Florida	27,354	41,877	10.61	12.36	16.49
Kentucky	15,888	19,718	5.64	6.59	16.84
Tennessee	18,720	23,046	5.82	6.85	17.70
Alabama	15,317	19,887	5.16	6.15	19.19
Mississippi	8,493	12,314	4.09	5.78	41.32
Arkansas	9,866	11,476	5.41	6.35	17.38
Louisiana	18,401	23,959	7.09	8.30	17.07
Oklahoma	17,696	19,204	8.47	8.78	3.66
Texas	65,684	86,329	8.61	10.20	18.47
Montana	4,931	7,527	9.10	12.16	33.63
Idaho	5,325	6,824	9.66	11.51	19.15
Wyoming	2,938	4,693	10.92	15.75	44.23
Colorado	12,126	16,788	9.60	11.25	17.19
New Mexico	5,615	9,269	9.30	12.05	29.57
Arizona	6,896	10,438	9.99	11.22	12.31
Utah	7,279	9,978	11.15	11.78	5.65
Nevada	2,157	4,184	13.83	19.74	42.73
Washington	20,027	22,789	8.88	9.02	1.58
Oregon	13,488	17,306	9.60	10.50	9.38
California	133,710	142,446	13.29	11.39	14.30

Source: U.S. Bureau of the Census, *U.S. Census of Business: 1948* (Washington, D.C., 1951), vol. 6, and *U.S. Census of Business: 1954* (Washington, D.C. 1956), vol. 5. (Editor's Note: According to Henry Williams, the amounts given for "Motion Picture Receipts" are invalid because they include more than admissions. But if the percentage of these figures devoted to concessions, etc., are about the same in each state, this complication does not invalidate Stuart's analysis. See Henry Williams, "Economic Changes in the Motion Picture Industry as Affected by Television and Other Factors," Ph.D. diss., University of Indiana, 1968.)

Table 13.6. *Correlation of Television Density and Relative Change in Per-Capita Motion Picture Receipts, 1948–54 (by states)*

State	Percent of Households with Television Sets, 1955 (X)	Percent Change In Per-Capita Motion Picture Receipts, 1948–54 (Y)	
Maine	64	9.06	
New Hampshire	68	−12.67	
Vermont	53	17.00	
Massachusetts	81	−20.29	
Rhode Island	83	−28.53	
Connecticut	80	−12.41	
New York	81	−19.06	
New Jersey	83	−25.62	
Pennsylvania	78	−21.94	
Ohio	82	−24.21	
Indiana	72	−8.10	
Illinois	77	−14.57	
Michigan	77	−13.62	
Wisconsin	67	−9.49	
Minnesota	63	−2.00	
Iowa	68	−10.82	
Missouri	67	5.96	
N. Dakota	37	29.90	
S. Dakota	29	28.74	
Nebraska	59	5.80	
Kansas	52	39.41	
Delaware	79	−25.50	
Maryland	77	−11.25	$Y = 70.78-1.11x$
Virginia	59	1.29	(.08)
W. Virginia	55	−14.14	
N. Carolina	51	21.10	$r = 0.91$
S. Carolina	48	16.53	
Georgia	53	34.13	$r^2 = 0.82$
Florida	52	16.49	
Kentucky	47	16.84	
Tennessee	53	17.70	
Alabama	45	19.19	

Table 13.6. (*Cont.*)

State	Percent of Households with Television Sets, 1955 (X)	Percent Change In Per-Capita Motion Picture Receipts, 1948–54 (Y)
Mississippi	28	41.32
Arkansas	36	17.38
Louisiana	51	17.07
Oklahoma	58	3.66
Texas	56	18.47
Montana	26	33.63
Idaho	45	19.15
Wyoming	21	44.23
Colorado	53	17.19
New Mexico	38	29.57
Arizona	50	12.31
Utah	68	5.65
Nevada	41	42.73
Washington	60	1.58
Oregon	45	9.38
California	71	−14.30

Sources: Television data, Advertising Research Foundation, Inc., *U.S. Television Households by Region, State, and County, June 1955* (New York, 1955). Motion Picture data, from table 13.5.

since factors, such as the suburban movement and growing traffic congestion, have certainly acted as contributory causes of the decline in motion picture attendance, in particular areas.

The importance of television density in the determination of motion picture revenues in a given period may be measured by applying the correlation procedure to state data for each year in turn. In 1948, with television an insignificant factor, per-capita motion picture receipts were substantially predictable on the basis of per-capita personal income. Figure 13.3 and table 13.7 indicate a linear relationship, with correlation coefficient of 0.77. The interference of television with this relationship is evident from the decline of the correlation coefficient to 0.38 when the same two-variable analysis is applied to 1954 data. In the latter year, a

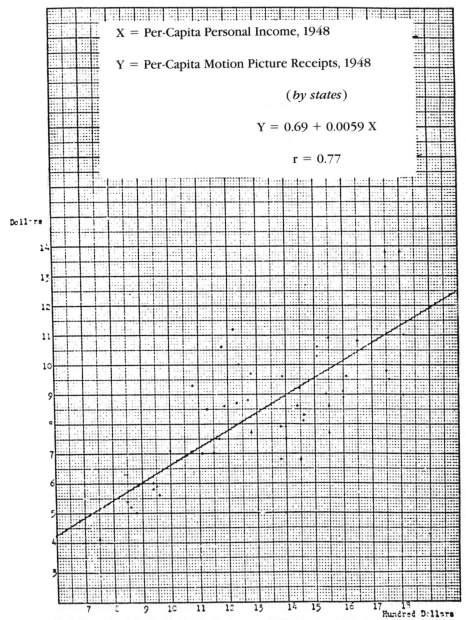

Fig. 13.3. *Relation between personal income and motion picture receipts*

Sources: See table 13.7.

Table 13.7. *Correlation of Per-Capita Personal Income and Per-Capita Motion Picture Receipts, 1948 (by states)*

State	Per-Capita Personal Income ($) (X)	Per-Capita Motion Picture Receipts ($) (Y)	
Maine	1,229	8.72	
New Hampshire	1,269	8.84	
Vermont	1,170	7.47	
Massachusetts	1,513	10.30	
Rhode Island	1,513	10.55	
Connecticut	1,751	9.75	
New York	1,798	13.80	
New Jersey	1,650	10.81	
Pennsylvania	1,446	9.16	
Ohio	1,552	8.55	
Indiana	1,440	8.64	
Illinois	1,809	11.05	
Michigan	1,542	9.03	
Wisconsin	1,402	7.90	
Minnesota	1,404	7.50	
Iowa	1,547	7.67	
Missouri	1,384	7.88	
N. Dakota	1,383	6.79	
S. Dakota	1,451	6.82	
Nebraska	1,463	8.38	
Kansas	1,276	7.54	
Delaware	1,763	9.49	
Maryland	1,457	8.09	
Virginia	1,112	6.98	
W. Virginia	1,146	7.00	$Y = 0.69 + 0.0059x$
N. Carolina	943	6.02	(.0007)
S. Carolina	879	4.96	
Georgia	948	5.89	$r = 0.77$
Florida	1,184	10.61	
Kentucky	965	5.64	$r^2 = 0.59$
Tennessee	935	5.82	
Alabama	856	5.16	
Mississippi	753	4.09	
Arkansas	846	5.41	

Table 13.7. (*Cont.*)

State	Per-Capita Personal Income ($) (X)	Per-Capita Motion Picture Receipts ($) (Y)
Louisiana	1,002	7.09
Oklahoma	1,129	8.47
Texas	1,187	8.61
Montana	1,596	9.10
Idaho	1,281	9.66
Wyoming	1,554	10.92
Colorado	1,394	9.60
New Mexico	1,075	9.30
Arizona	1,242	9.99
Utah	1,219	11.15
Nevada	1,750	13.83
Washington	1,600	8.88
Oregon	1,609	9.60
California	1,750	13.29

Source: Income data, U.S. Department of Commerce, *Personal Income by States since 1929*, (Washington, D.C., 1956): Motion Picture data, from table 13.5.

multiple correlation procedure using both per-capita personal income and percentage of households with television sets as independent variable brings estimates of per-capita motion picture receipts up to the 1948 level of accuracy (table 13.8). The multiple correlation coefficient ($R_{1.23}$) is 0.78. The partial coefficients are 0.76 ($r_{12.3}$, effect of per-capita income, television held constant) and -0.75 ($r_{13.2}$, effect of television density, per-capita income held constant).

Economic analysis of the substitution relationship between commodities usually centers on the measurement of cross-elasticity of demand. Since television service is delivered "free" to the consumer, change in motion picture expenditures / change in television price cannot be measured. The analysis just completed provides change in motion picture expenditures / change in television ownership as the most convenient available measure of the extent of substitution by consumers. The price of television sets is not a relevant variable here, since the consumer choice between consumption of motion picture and television entertainment is a continuous one, taking place in time periods subsequent to the set purchase. The consumer may not be expected to take the historical cost of the television set into account when deciding whether to attend a motion picture theater, though his ownership or nonownership of the television set is certainly pertinent.

The introduction of pay-television systems, discussed later, would make possible the conventional measurement of cross-elasticity of demand for motion pictures and television.

Motion Picture Theaters

Between 1948 and 1954 the number of motion picture theaters operating in the United States diminished from 18,631 to 18,491. This is a large decline, when the increase in population during the period is considered.[11] On a per-capita basis, the number of operating theaters dropped by 10 percent.

This reduction in establishments is a natural result of the decline in motion picture receipts, and therefore is attributable to television competition. To demonstrate this fact we have fitted linear regression equations to data for states, again using Census of Business information. Table 13.9 shows the relation between relative change in receipts and relative change in the number of theaters, on a per-capita basis. The least-squares regression equation

$$Y = -7.30 + 0.35 \, X$$

indicates that a 10 percent decline in per-capita receipts was associated with a 3.5 percent reduction in per-capita establishments.

Having already established a relation between television density and changes in motion picture receipts for the same period, we may now combine the two equations to establish a relation between television density and changes in the number of operating theaters:

Let R = percentage change in per-capita motion picture receipts, 1948–54

T = percentage of households with television sets, 1955

E = percentage change in per-capita motion picture theaters, 1948–54

We have

(1) $R = 70.78 - 1.11 \, T$
(2) $E = -7.30 + 0.35 \, R$

Table 13.8. *Multiple Correlation: Per-Capita Motion Picture Receipts, Per-Capita Personal Income, and Percent of Households with Television Sets, 1954 (by states)*

State	Per-Capita Motion Picture Receipts (X_1)	Per-Capita Personal Income (X_2)	Percent of House-holds with Television Sets (X_3)
Maine	9.51	1,447	64
New Hampshire	7.72	1,620	68
Vermont	8.74	1,443	53
Massachusetts	8.21	1,957	81
Rhode Island	7.54	1,886	83
Connecticut	8.54	2,368	80
New York	11.17	2,159	81
New Jersey	8.04	2,227	83
Pennsylvania	7.15	1,810	78
Ohio	6.48	1,947	82
Indiana	7.94	1,797	72
Illinois	9.44	2,162	77
Michigan	7.80	2,003	77
Wisconsin	7.15	1,771	67
Minnesota	7.35	1,651	63
Iowa	6.84	1,669	68
Missouri	8.35	1,713	67
N. Dakota	8.82	1,195	37
S. Dakota	8.78	1,339	29
Nebraska	8.76	1,645	59
Kansas	10.79	1,686	52

	Motion Picture Receipts	Income	Television
Virginia	7.07	1,483	59
W. Virginia	6.01	1,215	55
N. Carolina	7.29	1,173	51
S. Carolina	5.78	1,055	48
Georgia	7.90	1,217	53
Florida	12.36	1,576	52
Kentucky	6.59	1,200	47
Tennessee	6.85	1,200	53
Alabama	6.15	1,054	45
Mississippi	5.78	850	28
Arkansas	6.35	986	36
Louisiana	8.30	1,296	51
Oklahoma	8.78	1,445	58
Texas	10.20	1,572	56
Montana	12.16	1,735	26
Idaho	11.51	1,440	45
Wyoming	15.75	1,799	21
Colorado	11.25	1,688	53
New Mexico	12.05	1,401	38
Arizona	11.22	1,598	50
Utah	11.78	1,504	68
Nevada	19.74	2,387	41
Washington	9.02	1,964	60
Oregon	10.50	1,762	45
California	11.39	2,170	71

(.0008) (.002)

$R_{1.23} = 0.78$

$r_{12} = 0.38$

$r_{12.3} = 0.76$

$r_{13.2} = 0.75$

$R^2_{1.23} = 0.62$

$r^2_{12} = 0.14$

$r^2_{12.3} = 0.58$

$r^2_{13.2} = 0.56$

Sources: Motion Picture Receipts, from table 13.5.
Income data, U.S. Department of Commerce, *Personal Income by States Since 1929* (Washington, D.C., 1956). Television data, from table 13.6.

Table 13.9 *Correlation of Relative Change in Per-Capita Motion Picture Receipts and Relative Change in Per-Capita Motion Picture Theaters, 1948–1954 (by states)*

State	Number of Theaters		Percent Change in Per-Capita Theaters (Y)	Percent Change in Per-Capita Motion Picture Receipts (X)
	1948	1954		
Maine	135	173	+25	+9
New Hampshire	79	92	+10	-13
Vermont	59	77	+25	+17
Massachusetts	393	355	-13	-20
Rhode Island	63	48	-26	-29
Connecticut	183	195	-1	-12
New York	1,275	1,159	-17	-19
New Jersey	400	320	-27	-56
Pennsylvania	1,195	941	-24	-22
Ohio	887	763	-23	-24
Indiana	471	469	-9	-8
Illinois	930	785	-21	-15
Michigan	663	601	-20	-14
Wisconsin	415	433	-5	-9
Minnesota	451	444	-10	-2
Iowa	484	450	-11	-11
Missouri	571	557	-9	+6
N. Dakota	157	173	+1	+30
S. Dakota	174	165	-14	+29
Nebraska	286	286	-7	+6

State					
Maryland	241	227	−18		−11
Virginia	378	422	+ 2	+ 1	−14
W. Virginia	323	303	−11		
N. Carolina	516	579	+ 2	+21	
S. Carolina	240	289	+ 6	+17	
Georgia	377	466	+11	+34	
Florida	363	461	− 3	+16	
Kentucky	317	353	+ 5	+17	
Tennessee	353	403	+ 9	+18	
Alabama	335	333	− 4	+19	
Mississippi	313	316	− 1	+41	
Arkansas	354	296	−16	+17	
Louisiana	398	393	−11	+17	
Oklahoma	513	459	−15	+ 4	
Texas	1,319	1,426	− 3	+18	
Montana	142	156	− 4	+34	
Idaho	149	151	− 7	+19	
Wyoming	58	84	+31	+44	
Colorado	201	231	− 3	+17	
New Mexico	109	140	+ 1	+30	
Arizona	92	114	− 9	+12	
Utah	134	142	− 9	+ 6	
Nevada	41	48	−14	+43	
Washington	292	314	− 4	+ 2	
Oregon	232	302	+11	+ 9	
California	1,105	1,084	−21	−14	

$$Y = 7.30 + 0.35X$$
$$(.07)$$

$$r = 0.59$$

$$r^2 = 0.35$$

Source: U.S. Bureau of the Census, *U.S. Census of Business: 1948* (Washington, D.C., 1951), Vol. 6, and *U.S. Census of Business: 1954* (Washington, D.C., 1956), vol. 5.

Table 13.10. *Correlation of Television Density and Relative Change in Per-Capita Motion Picture Theaters, 1948–54 (by states)*

State	Percent of Households with Television Sets, 1955 (X)	Percent Change in Per-Capita Motion Picture Theaters, 1948–1954 (Y)	
Maine	64	+25	
New Hampshire	68	+10	
Vermont	53	+25	
Massachusetts	81	−13	
Rhode Island	83	−26	
Connecticut	80	− 1	
New York	81	−17	
New Jersey	83	−27	
Pennsylvania	78	−24	
Ohio	82	−23	
Indiana	72	− 9	
Illinois	77	−21	
Michigan	77	−20	
Wisconsin	67	− 5	
Minnesota	63	−10	
Iowa	68	−11	
Missouri	67	− 9	
N. Dakota	37	+ 1	
S. Dakota	29	−14	
Nebraska	59	− 7	
Kansas	52	+ 7	
Delaware	79	−11	
Maryland	77	−18	
Virginia	59	+ 2	
W. Virginia	55	−11	
N. Carolina	51	+ 2	$Y = 17.67 = 0.40X$
S. Carolina	48	+ 6	(0.10)
Georgia	53	+11	
Florida	52	− 3	
Kentucky	47	+ 5	$r = 0.51$
Tennessee	53	+ 9	
Alabama	45	− 4	$r^2 = 0.26$
Mississippi	28	− 2	

Table 13.10. (*Cont.*)

State	Percent of Households with Television Sets, 1955 (X)	Percent Change in Per-Capita Motion Picture Theaters, 1948–1954 (Y)
Arkansas	36	−16
Louisiana	51	−11
Oklahoma	58	−15
Texas	56	− 3
Montana	26	− 4
Idaho	45	− 7
Wyoming	21	+31
Colorado	53	− 3
New Mexico	38	+ 1
Arizona	50	− 9
Utah	68	− 9
Nevada	41	−14
Washington	60	− 4
Oregon	45	+11
California	71	−21

Sources: Television data, from table 13.6.
Motion Picture data, from table 13.9.

Substituting in equation (2),

$$(3)\ E = -7.30 + 0.35(70.78 - 1.11\ T)$$
$$E = 17.47 - 0.39\ T$$

The consistency of this model may be verified by the fitting of a least-squares regression equation directly to the data on television density and percentage change in per-capita theaters. This is done in table 13.10 with the resulting equation:

$$(4)\ E = 17.67 - 0.40\ T$$

The correspondence of equations (3) and (4) indicates that the three regression equations are mutually consistent.

In this analysis we have treated the change in the number of operating theaters without reference to theater type. We may now consider a question deferred earlier, the relation of the rise of the drive-in theater to these other developments.

The net decrease of 140 theaters between 1948 and 1954, which has been discussed, was actually composed of a net increase of 2,955 drive-in theaters (from 820 to 3,775) and a net decrease of 3,095 indoor theaters. These data suggest that the closing of indoor theaters may be explained by competition from drive-in theaters (50 percent of which were open all year round)[12] rather than by television competition. But a comparison of locations of the new drive-in theaters and the closed indoor theaters does not support such a conclusion. The net changes in both theater types are correlated, by state, in table 13.11. No significant correlation exists, when the influence of population is eliminated. (The coefficient of partial correlation is 0.14). This indicates that drive-in theaters have *not* appeared as direct replacements for closed indoor theaters.

We have seen that the change in the total number of exhibiting theaters during this period was largely a function of the degree of television penetration in each area. The choice between drive-in and indoor theaters in new construction was dependent on other factors, principally weather and degree of population concentration. Drive-in theaters are most popular, relative to indoor theaters, in warm climates and in rural areas. These relationships are demonstrated in table 13.12, which shows the 1954 ratio of drive-ins to total theaters (in each state) to be a positive function of mean January temperature and a negative function of the percentage of the population residing in urban areas ($R_{1.23} = 0.66$).

The evidence thus far examined indicates that the appearance of television sets in an area reduces consumers' demand for motion picture entertainment, producing the short-run effect of decline in theater receipts and the long-run effect of reduction in the number of operating theaters. (Effects on motion picture production companies and on industry organization will be discussed later.) Since television viewing by set-owners shows pronounced seasonality, further evidence may be obtained by studying changes in the seasonal variation in motion picture receipts.

The seasonal variation in television viewing may be measured from estimates of average viewing time per day, per television home, compiled by the A. C. Nielsen Company since March 1950.[13] The ratio-to-moving average method is applied to this data for 1952–57 in table 13.13, producing the quarterly seasonal indexes:

| | Quarter | | | |
	I	II	III	IV
Seasonal Index	117	92	83	108

Table 13.11. *Correlation of Net Decrease in Indoor Theaters and Net Increase in Drive-in Theaters, 1948–54 (by states)*

State	Net Decrease in Indoor Theaters 1948–1954 (X_1)	Net Increase in Drive-in Theaters 1948–1954 (X_2)	Population 1954 (000) (X_3)	
Maine	− 4	34	901	
New Hampshire	5	18	552	
Vermont	3	21	374	
Massachusetts	75	37	4,828	
Rhode Island	23	8	807	
Connecticut	9	21	2,177	
New York	209	93	15,828	
New Jersey	104	24	5,218	
Pennsylvania	360	106	10,856	
Ohio	200	76	8,844	
Indiana	85	83	4,241	
Illinois	226	81	9,151	
Michigan	121	59	7,076	
Wisconsin	39	57	3,630	
Minnesota	46	39	3,131	
Iowa	55	61	2,666	$X_1 = 2.68 + 0.14X_2$
Missouri	122	108	4,124	(0.14)
N. Dakota	0	16	636	
S. Dakota	27	18	673	$+ 0.02X_3$
Nebraska	38	38	1,359	(.002)
Kansas	43	96	2,023	
Delaware	7	9	369	$r_{12.3} = 0.14$
Maryland	42	28	2,606	
Virginia	48	92	3,501	
W. Virginia	77	58	1,991	$r^2_{12.3} = 0.02$
N. Carolina	77	140	4,226	
S. Carolina	14	63	2,266	
Georgia	26	115	3,630	
Florida	38	136	3,389	
Kentucky	53	89	2,994	
Tennessee	42	92	3,364	
Alabama	82	80	3,073	
Mississippi	57	60	2,131	

Table 13.11. (*Cont.*)

State	Net Decrease in Indoor Theaters 1948– 1954 (X₁)	Net Increase in Drive-in Theaters 1948– 1954 (X₂)	Population 1954 (000) (X₃)
Arkansas	109	51	1,807
Louisiana	63	58	2,888
Oklahoma	120	66	2,186
Texas	193	300	8,462
Montana	11	25	619
Idaho	22	24	598
Wyoming	5	21	298
Colorado	9	39	1,492
New Mexico	11	42	769
Arizona	4	25	930
Utah	16	24	762
Nevada	− 2	5	212
Washington	18	40	2,527
Oregon	− 6	64	1,648
California	136	115	12,508

Sources: Theaters, from U.S. Bureau of the Census, *U.S. Census of Business: 1948* (Washington, D.C., 1951), vol. 6, and *U.S. Census of Business: 1954* (Washington, D.C., 1956), vol. 5.
Population, from U.S. Bureau of the Census, *Statistical Abstract of the United States: 1957* (Washington, D.C., 1957), p. 10.

Consumers spend more time at their television sets during the winter months than in any other period, and the least time during the summer.[14]

Data for the seasonal analysis of motion picture receipts have been taken from *Variety*. The paper prints weekly reports of the total receipts (net of taxes) of 200 first-run theaters located in large cities, based on wire and letter reports from the individual theaters. The sample is thus restricted to areas of high television penetration, since large cities were early centers of set concentration.[15] Quarterly seasonal indexes have been calculated for two five-year periods, 1943–48 and 1952–57, for comparison of the pre- and post-television patterns (tables 13.14 and 13.15). The results were:

Table 13.12. *Influence of Weather and Population Concentration on Construction of Drive-in Theaters*

State	Drive-in Theaters As Percent of Total Theaters, 1954 (X_1)	Mean January Temperature (1921–1950) (X_2)	Urban Population As Percent of Total Population, 1950 (X^3)	
Maine	20.8	21	52	
New Hampshire	21.7	20	58	
Vermont	28.6	18	36	
Massachusetts	16.3	29	84	
Rhode Island	18.8	30	84	
Connecticut	13.8	27	78	
New York	10.9	28	86	
New Jersey	9.7	36	87	
Pennsylvania	17.5	34	71	
Ohio	21.5	31	70	
Indiana	23.7	31	60	
Illinois	13.5	25	78	
Michigan	14.5	20	71	
Wisconsin	13.9	23	58	
Minnesota	10.4	12	54	
Iowa	15.1	23	48	$X_1 = 20.47 + 0.30X_2$
Missouri	22.3	32	62	$(.07)$
N. Dakota	9.2	9	27	
S. Dakota	13.9	14	33	$-0.17X_3$
Nebraska	14.3	23	47	$(.05)$
Kansas	25.8	32	52	
Delaware	23.1	33	63	
Maryland	24.5	37	69	$R_{1.23} = 0.66$
Virginia	28.0	41	47	
W. Virginia	25.1	36	35	
N. Carolina	35.6	42	34	$R^2_{1.23} = 0.44$
S. Carolina	34.3	48	37	
Georgia	27.5	45	45	
Florida	34.3	63	65	
Kentucky	29.7	36	37	
Tennessee	26.6	41	44	
Alabama	27.9	53	44	

Table 13.12. (*Cont.*)

State	Drive-in Theaters As Percent of Total Theaters, 1954 (X_1)	Mean January Tempera- ture (1921– 1950) (X_2)	Urban Population As Percent of Total Population, 1950 (X^3)
Mississippi	20.6	48	28
Arkansas	18.9	42	33
Louisiana	17.0	56	55
Oklahoma	20.7	38	51
Texas	27.2	48	63
Montana	17.3	14	50
Idaho	21.2	27	63
Wyoming	25.0	26	44
Colorado	20.8	31	43
New Mexico	32.1	34	50
Arizona	25.4	51	55
Utah	23.9	26	65
Nevada	14.6	31	58
Washington	17.8	33	63
Oregon	22.2	40	54
California	14.7	50	81

Source: Theaters, U.S. Bureau of the Census, *U.S. Census of Business: 1954* (Washington, D.C., 1956), Vol. 5.

Temperatures, U.S. Bureau of the Census, *Statistical Abstract of the United States: 1957* (Washington, D.C. 1957), p. 165.

Population, U.S. Bureau of the Census, *Statistical Abstract of the United States: 1958* (Washington, D.C., 1958), p. 23.

	I	II	III	IV
Seasonal Index, 1943–48	102	95	102	101
Seasonal Index, 1952–57	99	92	107	102

The change in seasonal pattern is pictured in figure 13.4. Quarterly variation has become more pronounced, as the result of relative increases in the third and fourth quarters and relative declines in the first and second quarters. The summer increase is not attributable to drive-in theaters,

Table 13.13. *Seasonal Variation in Average Television Viewing Time per Television Home per Day, 1952–1957*

Quarter		Average Daily Viewing Time	Moving Average	Seasonal Relative
1952	III	3.58		
	IV	5.19		
1953	I	5.51	4.73	116.49
	II	4.29	4.70	91.28
	III	3.90	4.66	83.69
	IV	4.98	4.67	106.64
1954	I	5.44	4.70	115.74
	II	4.45	4.74	93.88
	III	3.99	4.79	93.30
	IV	5.17	4.82	107.26
1955	I	5.65	4.82	117.22
	II	4.47	4.83	92.55
	III	3.96	4.88	81.15
	IV	5.32	4.92	108.13
1956	I	5.87	4.96	118.35
	II	4.61	5.00	92.20
	III	4.12	5.00	82.40
	IV	5.44	5.02	108.37
1957	I	5.80		
	II	4.85		

Quarterly Indexes

	I	*II*	*III*	*IV*
1953	116.49	91.28	83.69	106.64
1954	115.74	93.88	83.30	107.26
1955	117.22	92.55	81.15	108.13
1956	118.35	92.20	82.40	108.37
Average	117	92	83	108

Source: A. C. Nielson Company, "National Television-Radio Audience Trends," *Nielson Television Index* (New York City, monthly to subscribers).

since none are included in the *Variety* sample. Neither is it attributable to the increased use of air-conditioning in theaters, since the sample is restricted to first-run theaters in large cities, most of which were air-conditioned by 1948.[16]

The seasonal shift is consistent with the hypothesis that television is the major cause of recent changes in motion picture attendance. A *pri-*

Media Interaction

Table 13.14. *Seasonal Variation in Receipts of First-Run Theaters in Large Cities, 1943–48*

Quarter		Total Receipts* $ (000)	Moving Average	Seasonal Relative
1943	III	35,618		
	IV	36,481		
1944	I	37,888	36,950	102.54
	II	35,893	37,496	95.72
	III	39,454	37,600	104.93
	IV	37,015	37,634	98.36
1945	I	38,189	37,899	100.77
	II	35,863	39,952	92.07
	III	41,606	40,427	102.92
	IV	43,285	41,676	103.86
1946	I	43,719	42,299	103.36
	II	40,231	43,033	95.93
	III	42,139	41,224	102.22
	IV	40,621	40,238	100.95
1947	I	39,913	38,965	102.43
	II	36,241	37,442	96.79
	III	36,031	36,029	100.01
	IV	34,547	34,825	99.20
1948	I	34,682		
	II	31,841		

	Quarterly Indexes			
	I	*II*	*III*	*IV*
1944	102.54	90.72	104.93	98.36
1945	100.77	92.07	102.92	103.86
1946	103.36	95.93	102.22	100.95
1947	102.43	96.79	100.01	99.20
Average	102	95	102	101

*190 Theaters.
Source: "Picture grosses," *Variety*, weekly from July 1943 to June 1948.

ori, the choice between entertainment at home and out of doors is influenced by weather conditions, so that competition from television is most damaging to theaters during winter months, and least effective during summer months. In addition, consumers are frequently away from home (and television set) during the warm-weather vacation periods. The mo-

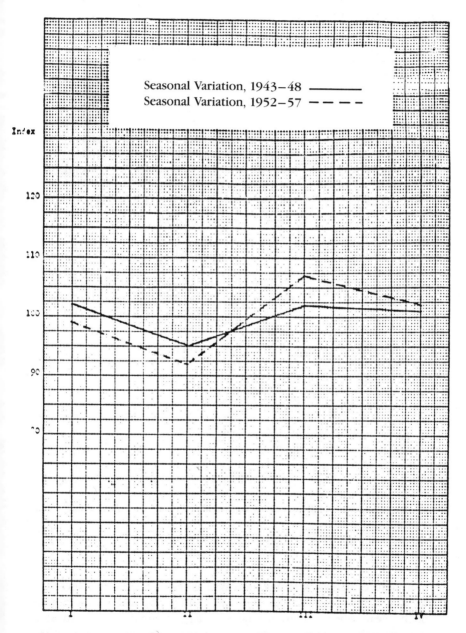

Fig. 13.4. *The changing seasonal pattern of motion picture receipts*
Sources: See tables 13.14, 13.15.

Table 13.15. *Seasonal Variation in Receipts of First-Run Theaters in Large Cities, 1952–57*

Quarter	Total Receipts* $ (000)	Moving Average	Seasonal Relative
1952 III	33,404		
IV	31,628		
1953 I	32,535	32,985	98.64
II	32,709	34,159	95.76
III	36,730	35,106	104.63
IV	37,693	35,157	107.21
1954 I	34,051	35,250	96.60
II	31,599	35,220	89.72
III	38,588	34,970	110.35
IV	35,592	34,983	101.74
1955 I	34,147	34,770	98.21
II	31,614	34,159	92.55
III	36,870	33,784	109.13
IV	32,420	33,648	96.35
1956 I	34,319	33,402	102.75
II	30,352	33,724	90.00
III	36,166	34,004	106.36
IV	35,695	33,815	105.56
1957 I	33,284		
II	29,875		

	Quarterly Indexes			
	I	II	III	IV
1953	98.64	95.76	104.63	107.21
1954	96.60	89.72	110.35	101.74
1955	98.21	92.55	109.13	96.35
1956	102.75	90.00	106.36	105.56
Average	99	92	107	102

* 220 Theaters.
Source: "Picture grosses," *Variety*, weekly from July 1952 to June 1957.

tion pictures' largest seasonal increase has occurred during television's weakest period, the warm third quarter. And during the coldest months of the year, when television enjoys its largest audiences, the theater-receipts indexes show a decline from above to below average for the year.

Reactions of the Motion Picture Industry

Complacency

The first reaction of the motion picture industry to television was disbelief. Producers and exhibitors could not take seriously the idea that their loyal audience of 90 million people per week, which severe depression had reduced only to 60 million, could be appreciably affected by the new competition. Several types of miscalculation formed the basis of the motion picture industry's optimism.

First, the industry underestimated the potential rate of growth of television, taking encouragement from its history before 1946. Television broadcasting had actually begun in 1928, and it was tempting to project the infinitesimal development rate of the 1930s, despite the fact that underlying conditions had changed completely. Also tempting was the analogy to radio development. The early rate of television-set acquisition by the public was much higher than that of early radio-set acquisition. Why did consumers acquire television sets at a much more rapid rate than they had purchased radios?

On the demand side of the market, television emerged in a period of rising incomes and leisure, with high wartime savings available for family investment in the new medium. On the supply side, the facilities for radio broadcasting, set manufacture, and distribution were available for, and were in fact adopted for, use by the television industry. Whereas the early radio years (1922–30) had been marked by shortages of receivers, unregulated interference between broadcasting stations, and the rise and fall of scores of unsuccessful set manufacturers,[17] in 1946 radio broadcasters became television broadcasters, radio-set manufacturers began producing television receivers, radio retail outlets became television outlets, and the Federal Communications Commission (formed to regulate the radio industry) was available to supervise broadcasting. All the technical knowledge of production, distribution, and broadcasting gathered in twenty-five years of radio operations could be applied to the new industry. As a result, technological advances, in the direction of clear reception, length of life of the receiver, reduced size and cost of sets, low cost of repairs, and increased transmission distances, came much more rapidly for television than they had for radio.

The history of radio development provided other arguments for confidence on the part of motion picture executives. For one thing, direct competition from radio had never proved a serious problem to the motion picture industry. The increase in the number of radio households from 300,000 in 1922 to 35 million in 1946[18] had not interrupted the growth of motion picture audiences. Since early television fare seemed closer to vaudeville than to motion picture drama, it was easy to overlook the fact that television viewing is a more direct substitute for motion picture entertainment than radio had ever been. Further, the depressing effects of radio on *other* mass media had proved to be temporary. Newspapers, at first severely affected, had soon recovered, and their major problem had been competition for advertising rather than for the attention of the audience, a problem which the movies could not encounter. The phonograph record industry had also recovered from the severe blow of early radio competition. The Victor Company's gross income had shrunk from a high of $100 million annually to $10 million in 1932,[19] under the early impact of radio, but the record business had later found radio an ally in selling to the public. The weakness in this reasoning was later recognized by film producers, as we shall see, when they considered the possible effects of releasing their old films for television use. While the effect of hearing a record on the radio may be stimulation of its purchase by the radio audience, assuredly the viewer of an old film on television will not be inspired to pay a theater admission to see it again; and the time he spends watching it is time taken away from the theater exhibitor.

When it became evident that a good part of the motion picture audience was indeed being lured away by television (this took some time, since the motion picture industry had been notorious for its lack of accurate statistical information), producers and exhibitors took refuge in the notion that the loss would be temporary, first, because the novelty of television would wear off. During 1946 and 1947 thousands of people turned on their sets just to watch the station signals, an activity which could hardly be expected to keep them away from theaters for long. But motion picture producers underestimated the ability of the competition to develop program formats that would maintain audience interest. The television assortment of vaudeville, variety shows, panels, quiz programs, "live" drama, filmed drama, feature films, participation games, westerns, situation comedy, "spectacular" drama, and so forth, kept the television audience coming back for more each year. Average viewing time per day in television homes has increased steadily. Second, exhibitors placed their hopes in the idea that expenditures on receivers were the genuine deterrent to motion picture attendance, and that as soon as the sets had been paid for the family would return to the theaters. This belief proved to be founded on a misunderstanding of the cause of the audience's defection. Other reasons offered for believing in the eventual return of the motion picture audience from the living room included: (1) Man is basically gregarious, (2) people will tire of commercials, (3) women will demand to be taken out of the house, and (4) the quality of television shows cannot equal that of motion pictures. The last is of special interest, since this belief in the actual or potential superiority of the motion picture product formed the basis for several types of defensive development attempted by motion picture producers. One method of fighting television competition is to broaden the differences between television shows and motion pictures, in areas in which the latter are supposed to be superior. The deficiencies of television on which the motion picture producers' belief was based are:

1. *Small size of the television image.* The motion picture audience feels more directly involved in the action. The illusion is aided by the absence of distraction by commercials, family noises, and movement picked up in the peripheral vision.

2. *Limited funds.* While the television producer has only $30,000 or $40,000 to work with on most shows,[20] motion picture producers, envisioning possible gross returns of more than $10 million, can invest $5 or $6 million to procure effects beyond the capacity of the television budget.

3. *Excessive demand on writing and acting talent.* Quality is difficult to maintain in a medium which must produce so many shows. In the peak war years American motion picture producers turned out only four hundred pictures per year, whereas the three television networks must produce approximately 11,000 shows per year during prime evening hours alone.

Cost Cutting and Production Reorganization

Though there was considerable disagreement about the cause of the difficulty, the fact of decline and the need for action of some sort had become obvious by 1949. The combined net profits of the ten leading motion picture firms had declined continuously from $122 million in 1946 to $30 million in 1949.[21] The studios were still unprepared to admit the permanent nature of the decline, and therefore were not ready to consider such solutions as joining the new opposition. At a luncheon in 1949 David Sarnoff of Radio Corporation of America tried to persuade Loew's-MGM president Nicholas Schenck to put Loew's into equal partnership with RCA. Schenck demurred, and later remarked to Louis B. Mayer, "You see how hungry they are for us? Let 'em spend a little more of their own money . . . we can come in any time."[22] The cure for declining profits upon which the major studios pinned their hopes in this early stage was internal reorganization. During its years of prosperity the motion picture industry had become famous for padded payrolls and wasteful production methods.

Between 1946 and 1950 all the major studios except Metro-Goldwyn-

Mayer abandoned the "stock company" system of operation, to rid themselves of enormous fixed costs. Under the old system, each studio had its own staff of stars, producers, directors, writers, and technical people under long-term contract. Now production was reorganized on a per-picture basis, with the studios hiring a large percentage of their personnel on short-term contracts for specific productions. In 1946 the major studios had 598 actors, 160 directors, and 132 producers under term contracts. By 1957 the numbers had been reduced to 196 actors, 58 directors, and 65 producers.[23] This reorganization was also a logical result of the divorcement of studios and theaters pursuant to the 1948 Supreme Court decision. Since the studios were no longer obligated to produce large numbers of films in order to keep their theater chains supplied, they could dispense with much of the permanent staff.

This shift in studio organization encouraged the rise of the independent producer . . . stars, directors, and producers who incorporate for particular productions, and rent major studio facilities for either a fixed fee or a share of profits (usually 50 percent of net profits, or 10 percent of gross receipts). The artists themselves (actors, directors, writers) found many advantages in the new system. They could now choose their pictures and their working periods without reference to quantity commitments as under the old studio contracts. And on the financial side, they could gain two tax advantages. First, by participating in profits instead of accepting straight salaries, they could spread their incomes through time. Second, they could record large parts of the income as capital gains, which would be taxed at a lower rate.[24] (The Bureau of Internal Revenue cut off some excesses in this direction in 1956, when it ruled that holders of more than 25 percent of the stock of an enterprise using their personal services must pay taxes on income therefrom at individual rather than capital gains rates). Another advantage for the biggest stars, of course, was the elimination of the temporary monopsony power previously enjoyed by the studio holding their contract.

As the independent producers became successful enough to organize on a more or less permanent basis (e.g., Hecht-Hill-Lancaster), some became "semi-independents," in that their arrangements with the major studios were for longer periods than the single picture. The semi-independent makes contracts with a major studio for a specified number of pictures over a given number of years. He invests just enough money to qualify his company for capital gains taxation, and the studio provides the rest, with the semi-independent guaranteed a specified percentage of earnings. This gives the independent company the full facilities of a major studio on a permanent basis. These developments have now proceeded far enough so that many of the studios are in the business of renting facilities rather than in motion picture production *per se*.

Product Improvement

A. The "Big" Picture. Cost cutting is at best a temporary method of dealing with declining demand, and as the producers acknowledged that they were engaged in a permanent struggle with television for the consumer's attention, they turned to the problem of selling the product. Their line of attack was suggested by those areas of motion picture superiority listed above. Since the movies' advantage lay in the ability to procure spectacular effects by large production outlays, it was decided that the way to compete was to concentrate on the "big" picture. They reasoned that the part of the market that had shifted irrevocably to television was the audience for B- and C-grade pictures. Before 1950 each major company had included only two or three high-cost films (defined as over $1 million) per year in its production schedule. Now the major studios began to concentrate on large-scale extravaganzas, since their aim must be to offer the public what television could not provide. This policy was firmly entrenched by the 1953–54 season. Before 1953, the industry had had only one hundred "hits" that earned worldwide gross receipts of more than $5 million. (*Gone with the Wind*, the most successful, had made $35 million). In 1953 and 1954 thirty pictures were produced which each grossed more than $5 million. These costly pictures could be shown for extended runs of up to twelve weeks, at high admission prices, with full advantage taken of first-run / second-run price discrimination by confining exhibition to one theater at a time in each large population center. For example, *Ten Commandments*, made at the record cost of $13.5 million, had grossed $45 million by early 1959.[25] *Around the World in Eighty Days*, made at a slightly lower cost, earned over $50 million, and scores of others have passed the $5-million mark. *Fortune Magazine* commented (1955), "The big picture, for all its risks . . . is what everybody in the movie industry is shooting for just now . . . it is evident that the B or C picture with a low budget, undistinguished cast, poor story, and shoddy direction is on the way out, because the public refuses to pay to see it." [26]

Pursuit of this policy reduced the number of feature films produced in the United States from the 1927–47 average of 488 per year to 253 in 1954.[27] The policy was later reversed to some extent when it was found that particular subjects that attracted the adolescent audience could be safely treated on the B- or C-production level. Examples are the rock-and-roll picture and the horror picture. The increasing popularity (among producers) of horror and space pictures is also explained by their exploitation of the motion picture's advantage over television in production of special effects.

This reversal of customary evolution in other industries—i.e., the switch from a mass-produced to a custom-tailored product—proved profitable for the large studios. Twentieth Century–Fox, for example, made an $8 million profit before taxes on thirty-two pictures in 1953, and a $16 million profit before taxes on thirteen pictures produced in 1954.[28] The industry was successfully catering to a new type of audience. Since the habitual moviegoer who would turn out as a matter of course to see each double feature appearing at his neighborhood theater had been lured away by television, motion pictures now were designed to attract the family on its night out, with the expensive single feature.

Most of the ingredients of this type of feature had been in use before 1948. First, the picture should be photographed in color, since widespread color television seemed a long way off. In 1957, only 200,000 television sets (0.5 percent of all sets in use) were equipped to receive color broadcasts,[29] despite the fact that color transmission was technically available to 97 percent of television homes.[30] The major deterrent was the price of a color set, the cheapest of which was selling for $495. Second, there was a shift from original screenplays to pre-tested story properties—best selling books (e.g., *From Here to Eternity*), classics (e.g., *War and Peace*), Broadway plays (e.g., *The King and I*), and even successful television programs (e.g., *Marty*). The studios at this point bid up the screen-rights prices of Broadway plays to new highs. *The Solid Gold Cadillac* was purchased for $360,000; *Anastasia*, for $400,000; and *The Pajama Game* for a rumored $1 million.[31]

Another technique beyond the reach of television was location shooting, and this was also employed in the "big" picture. Foreign locations offered advantages other than authentic locale, such as lower labor costs, use of blocked currencies, tax advantages, and in some cases foreign subsidies.

B. Technological Innovation. The high-cost color film based on a sound story property, filmed on location and distributed for long single-feature engagements, proved effective in the competition with television. Another method of widening the gap between the television offering and the motion picture product presented itself in the larger size of the motion picture image, with its induced feeling of audience participation in the action. Why not make the screen even larger, and otherwise develop the depth illusion, to exploit this area in which television could not compete?

The first attempt to do so was a resounding success. In September 1952 Cinerama made its appearance at the Broadway Theater in New York City. The first picture (*This is Cinerama*) was a series of travel shorts and scenic displays, narrated by Lowell Thomas. Despite the traditional resistance of American audiences to travelogues, the picture played for more than three years to full houses (on a reserved-seat basis) in thirteen cities, and by 1955 had earned more than $20 million. The system projected three separate images on a wide, deeply curved screen, which produced a sense of depth by making use of the audience's peripheral vision. Normal motion pictures (and television) make use of only one-sixth of the eye's arc of vision. The system also introduced Stereophonic Sound. Speakers were placed at either side of and behind the screen, each fed by a separate sound track, so that words and music seemed to emanate from their exact point of origin.

The success of the next experiment, a three-dimensional system with complete depth illusion, was short-lived. Introduced in Los Angeles in November 1952 in a picture called *Bwana Devil*, created enough interest to be accepted for distribution by United Artists, and was followed by several "3-D" films by the major studios, the most successful of which was Warner Bros.' *House of Wax* in 1953. This system required the use of polarized spectacles by the audience, which fused two separately projected images on the principle of the stereoscope. Producers have expressed uncertainty about whether the early demise of 3-D was attributable to the annoyance of the spectacles or the low quality of the pictures for which the system was employed. At any event, audiences rapidly lost interest.

The next innovation to put in an appearance proved to be the most successful of all. In 1953 Twentieth Century–Fox introduced Cinema-Scope with *The Robe*, a picture that met all the other competitive requirements: best-selling novel, color, expensive production, location shooting, and so forth. This system employs an anamorphic lens, which compresses a wide-angle scene onto a narrow strip of film. When projected through a compensating lens, it is "spread" back to its original shape. Four-track sound is generally used, though it is optional. The curved screen is smaller than that employed in Cinerama, having a length approximately two and one-half times its height. Little if any depth illusion is produced, but the system proved to be the perfect compromise between the regular image and Cinerama. The difficulty of blending three pictures without letting the audience see the seams is eliminated by the use of only one camera and projector. Further, this system is adaptable to most theaters with relatively little expense, overcoming the serious economic defect of Cinerama, viz. that it requires a large theater and a small audience, to achieve its effects. CinemaScope's adaptability is attested by the fact that by 1957, 17,644 installations had been made in American and Canadian theaters.[32]

A successful rival to CinemaScope appeared in early 1954, introduced by Paramount Pictures in *White Christmas*. It was Vistavision, in which images are photographed horizontally on double frames and then reduced optically to 35-mm size or, in large theaters, actually projected horizontally. It was claimed that this system would improve picture quality even if projected on regular screens.

The next large studio to enter the field was Metro-Goldwyn-Mayer, which introduced Todd-A.O. via *Oklahoma* in 1956. This system is halfway between CinemaScope and Cinerama, employing one camera and projector, with the photographing done through a wide-angle lens on 65-mm film. MGM has also experimented with Panavision, another 65-mm film method. This system is designed for compatibility with all the others, since prints can be made in the proper size for projection by Cinema-Scope, Todd-A.O., Vistavision, and Cinerama installations. Up to seven sound tracks can be carried.

Other companies now rushed in to provide anamorphic systems compatible with CinemaScope. Warner Bros. introduced Warner-Superscope, RKO settled for just plain Superscope. Other CinemaScope imitations included Vistarama, Cinepanoramic, Camerascope, Vidoscope, and Delrama. Two more imitations of the original Cinerama also appeared: National Theatre Company's Cinemiracle (*Windjammer*, first shown in New York City in 1958), also using three films and projectors, but with the merging lines gone and with more mobile equipment than its ancestors; and Walt Disney's Circarama, the ultimate depth system in which eleven images are projected on a circular screen completely surrounding the audience. This is by no means the end of the list of names. Other assorted wide-screen systems proposed or introduced were Superama, Sonoptic, Platorama, Polyvision, Amp-O-Vision, Photorama, Perfect Tone, Scenic Scope, Paravision, and Metrovision.

Was this deluge a series of *inventions* fortuitously developed at the precise moment that the motion picture industry needed to be rescued from television competition? Assuredly not. Investigation shows that these developments represent *innovations* based on old inventions, called forth from inglorious obscurity by the pressing competition with television.

The principle of anamorphosis, which makes possible the presentation of wide-screen images on a single film, was patented in 1862 and demonstrated first in 1898. Dr. Sidney Newcomer conducted a demonstration for the film industry in 1930, and found them uninterested. Professor Henri Chretien had better luck in 1931, when Paramount Pictures took an option on his similar system. When they failed to develop it, Chretien exhibited it at the Paris Exhibition of 1937, but still could find no buyers. In 1952 Spyros Skouras of Twentieth Century–Fox finally acquired the rights to the system and renamed it CinemaScope. Another successful special-lens process by which film images could be "blown up" to four times their regular size was developed in 1925 by Lorenzo del Riccio. Called Magnascope, the process was generally reserved for spectacular effects at the climax of the picture. It was so used in eight films during the 1920s.[33]

The multiprojection idea underlying Cinerama and its imitators dates back equally far. In 1896 Raoul Grimoin-Sanson demonstrated a system he called Cineorama, which made use of ten cameras and projectors that cast their images on a huge circular screen. With one camera and projector added, this emerged as Disney's *Circarama* sixty years later.

In 1921 George W. Bingham exhibited a wide-angle projection system he called Widescope, which employed two films projected side by side. In 1925 a French variation called the Triptych Screen (three regular-sized screens side by side) was used by Claude Autant-Lara and Abel Gance for *Pour Construire un Feu* (1925) and later for *Napoleon* (1927). A 1939 version demonstrated by Fred Waller at the New York World's Fair, called Vitarama, used eleven projectors strapped together to project an image on a curved screen surmounted by a quarter dome. After use during World War II as a gunnery training device, this system reappeared in 1952 as *Cinerama*.

The use of film larger than 35 mm has a similar history. In 1920 Professor J. Louis Peck of France demonstrated a huge curved screen at the New York Rivoli Theater, doing scenes from Paramount's *Everywoman*. Critics were excited about the good focus and "absence of eyestrain." The Germans introduced 42-mm film at about this time, in a system called Tri-Ergon which had a premiere at the New York Cameo Theater. Another experiment with large film widths was made by Warner Bros. in 1930 (for *Kismet*) and 1931 (*The Lash*), in 65 mm. MGM performed a similar experiment with *Billy the Kid* in 1930, calling the system *Realife*. The Paramount version was Magni-Film, used in 1929 for *You're in the Army Now*. Oddly enough, another system developed in 1928 by George Hill and Professor Alberini, in which the film was shot and projected horizontally, was rejected as impractical. This system reappeared twenty-five years later as Glamorama, and shortly thereafter as Vistavision.

The largest film width experimented with was a system called Natural Vision, which employed 70-mm film projected on two screens, one behind the other, for a wide-screen stereoscopic effect. Used first in 1925 for *The American*, this system reappeared in 1929 sans stereoscopic effect as Twentieth Century–Fox's Grandeur process, used for three films. This system might have become standard, except that exhibitors became involved at this juncture with the introduction of sound, whose installation costs discouraged the introduction of 70-mm equipment.

As for the history of the stereoscopic "true three-dimension" effect requiring spectacles, perhaps *Time* magazine made the most telling comment, when they said the system was based on a "simple optical illusion whose principle was known to Euclid and whose practice put grandfather to sleep on Sunday afternoons."[34]

This brief history points to the conclusion that the successful introduction of wide-screen projection from 1952 to 1960 was in response to television competition, rather than the result of randomly occurring technological advances.[35]

Production of Film for Television Use

A. New Nonfeature Film. As television programming has developed, there has been a continuing shift from "live" production to the use of films. The percentage of program time taken up by filmed shows, increasing every year, was estimated in April 1958 as 50 percent for the Columbia Broadcasting System, 35 percent for the American Broadcasting Company, and 45 percent for the National Broadcasting Company. It was closer to 65 percent for stations not affiliated with networks, and higher still for commercials on all stations.[36] During the 1957–58 season 694 filmed television series were available to stations and advertisers in the catalogues of syndicating companies. The bulk of these (417) were half-hour drama and situation-comedy shows. More than forty specialized firms are engaged in the distribution (to individual stations, networks, or directly to advertisers) of syndicated television films. Examples are Official Films, Inc., Ziv-TV Programs, Inc., National Telefilm Associates, and the Guild Films Company. Most of the firms so engaged start out performing only the distribution function, but eventually turn to actual production. Their product is usually offered first to the television networks, and later for re-runs to national advertisers. Network exposure recovers the production costs quickly, and increases the value of the film when re-run. The re-run is usually necessary for profits, though production costs are low, compared to the costs of theater-film production at the large studios.

A half-hour film is usually completed in about three days, the amount of time a major Hollywood studio is reputed to have devoted to a single reaction shot of Irene Dunne in pre-television days.[37]

The principal reason for using film instead of "live" presentation is lower cost.[38] Since a filmed show may be presented in numerous markets (including overseas) and at scattered times, and may be reshown subsequent to first appearance, production costs are spread. In addition, quality is improved, as compared with "live" shows, in several ways: first, more action, outdoor scenes, and special effects are possible. Second, the chance of on-camera accidents is eliminated. Third, the larger potential audience permits the use of well-known stars. These advantages have a familiar ring. We have already discussed them in another connection, as the reasons for Hollywood's concentration on the "big" picture in competing with television. To some extent television found the adaptation of motion picture technique a natural step in program development.

In early years the use of film by television stations was restricted largely to newsreels, commercials, and an occasional old feature film. In 1960 most of the dramatic and comedy series that formed the bulk of evening entertainment was presented on film. Approximately two-thirds of the time between 7:30 P.M. and 11:00 P.M. was occupied by filmed programs.[39] Annual film output in the United States for 1956 was estimated by the Society of Motion Picture and Television Engineers as follows:[40]

	Percentage of *Total Footage*
Theater Films (features, shorts, newsreels)	4
Nontheatrical Film (industrial, etc.)	25
Television Film:	71
Kinescope Programs	15
Network Shows Originating on Film	15
Syndicated Film Shows	41
	100

Thus over 70 percent of film footage was produced for television, even excluding commercials.[41]

For some time the Hollywood studios were not included among those firms producing films for television use. Rather, the majority of production was carried on by newly formed enterprises, such as Desilu Productions, Inc., Ziv-TV Programs, Inc., and Official Films, Inc. The striking success[42] of such firms may be attributed in part to Hollywood's delay in entering the field. There were several reasons for this forbearance, despite the motion picture studios' position as the most experienced film-makers. First, general sentiment in Hollywood was that television was an enemy that could be overcome by the methods already discussed: internal reoganization, concentration on high-cost feature production, and technological development. Any major studio that provided the opposition with the means to further injure motion picture attendance would be looked on as a traitor. Second, the new specialized firms could produce television footage more cheaply than the major studios, since they did not start with the same large fixed costs. That is, the most efficient scale of enterprise was smaller for television-film production than it had been for motion picture production. Third, most network shows were originating in the East, far removed from Hollywood facilities.

Gradually, however, these obstacles were removed. The studios finally came to acknowledge the seriousness of their situation, and saw that their policy of noncooperation with television could not succeed. At the same time, they had now rid themselves of large parts of their fixed costs, and were able to organize production units that could turn out television film as cheaply as the independent companies. Furthermore, the networks had begun to originate a majority of their programs from the West Coast, attracted by cheaper land and the availability of star performers. The completion of the coaxial cable linking both coasts in 1951 finally made it possible for shows originating on the West Coast to reach the large eastern audiences. By 1957 the migration of television production facilities had progressed far enough for *Printers' Ink* to state, "Television is becoming an industry with New York showrooms and a West Coast plant."[43]

In 1955 the major Hollywood studios entered the field by producing filmed dramas which they cosponsored on television: "Warner Bros. Presents," "The Twentieth Century–Fox Hour," "Disneyland," and the "MGM Parade." One of the reasons for doing so was their hope that by advertising feature pictures they could stimulate waning theater attendance. During this period every hour of film made by the studios contained nine minutes of promotion material for the studio's forthcoming theater features. (The commercial sponsor usually took another six minutes.) But the old doubts about the wisdom of cooperation returned when a private survey showed a decline of from 17 to 20 percent in motion picture attendance in areas in which these programs were shown.[44]

There was no turning back now, however. Columbia Pictures organized a subsidiary, Screen Gems, to produce and distribute films for television. In 1955 the new subsidiary accounted for $6 million of Columbia's $88-million gross receipts.[45] Within the next year the other major studios likewise organized subsidiaries to produce films for television, as follows:

Parent Firm	Subsidiary
Allied Artists Pictures Corp.	Interstate Television Corp.
Columbia Pictures Corp.	Screen Gems, Inc.
Republic Pictures Corp.	Hollywood TV Service, Inc.
RKO Teleradio Pictures, Inc.	RKO Television Corp.
Twentieth Century–Fox	Twentieth Century–Fox Television Productions, Inc.
Universal Pictures Corp.	Universal International Films, Inc.
Walt Disney Pictures	Walt Disney Productions
Warner Bros.	Sunset Productions

Metro-Goldwyn-Mayer began production for television in 1957. RKO (in 1957) and Republic (in 1958) abandoned feature-film production to devote their facilities entirely to television film.

B. Old Feature Films. The application of Hollywood facilities and experience to the production of films for television had proved inevitable and profitable. Still the major studios rejected another possible source of income, the sale of rights to their libraries of old feature films. Producers and exhibitors both felt that such release could be the death blow to motion picture attendance. The latter group, now separated from production and distribution income by court order, were particularly vociferous in their objections. They would not share in the proceeds, and would bear the full brunt of the effects, of any such sale. In addition, they felt that many small television stations would not be able to survive without this cheap source of programming. The television networks seemed to share this belief, and showed little interest in purchasing rights to old movies, which could become (as they did subsequently) an effective substitute for network affiliation.

From 1947 through 1954 the only feature films available on television, with few exceptions, were those made by motion picture companies that had gone out of business since producing them, foreign films, and other films so old that they offered little threat of competition to exhibitors. The use of feature films as regular television fare was seriously hampered by the lack of sufficient numbers for regular programming.

During this period the studios were being exposed to increasingly tempting propositions, made all the more attractive by declining incomes from traditional sources. Furthermore, the libraries being bid for had long ago been written off the books, so that the sale revenue would constitute pure windfall profit. Then in late 1955 doubt was cast upon their policy by the experience of Walt Disney, who found that his television series ("Disneyland") was stimulating theater attendance at new Disney movies. The producers' united stand was finally broken in December 1955 by RKO, which (subsequent to its purchase by the General Tire Company, discussed below) was ready to convert entirely to the production of television films and therefore was no longer directly concerned with box-office effects of its actions. RKO Teleradio Pictures sold the rights to 750 feature films and one thousand short subjects to the C and C Television Corporation, a distributor, for $15.2 million. The C and C Corporation in turn sold the 750 features as a package (estimated price: $600,000) to individual television stations, selling the rights in perpetuity. Later transactions between distributors and stations (or advertisers) did not usually follow this pattern, in that rights were leased for limited time periods, and feature films marketed individually or in smaller groups.

In early 1956 Columbia Pictures released 104 feature films and a large number of short subjects to its television subsidiary, Screen Gems, for distribution to television stations, and Paramount released 1,600 short subjects to National Telefilm Associates, a distributor, for $4 million. In February of the same year Warner Bros. sold the rights to 800 feature films and 1,800 short subjects to Associated Artists Production Corp., a distributor, for $21 million. In November 1956 Twentieth Century–Fox made the best bargain for the period under discussion, selling 390 feature films to National Telefilm Associates in return for $30 million, plus a 50 percent stock interest in the NTA Film Network, a wholly owned subsidiary of the distributor, whose operations are discussed below.

Metro-Goldwyn-Mayer was next, distributing its own film rights directly to individual television stations, releasing 770 features and 900 short subjects for a total of $25 million. Republic Films also used its own subsidiary (Hollywood TV Service, Inc.) to distribute 74 of its old features. National Telefilm Associates, by this time the largest distributor of feature films for television, purchased 40 feature films from the J. Arthur Rank Organization and Sir Alexander Korda, and ten features from David O. Selznick (for $1 million), and in late 1956 leased 52 more features from Twentieth Century–Fox, for $2.3 million. In 1957 Universal Pictures leased the rights to 600 feature films to Screen Gems for $20 million. In February 1958 Paramount, the last major holdout, leased 750 features to MCA-TV, a subsidiary of the Music Corporation of America, for $50 million.

By the middle of 1958 an estimated 9,500 Hollywood feature films were available for television showing,[46] and their exhibition occupied approximately 25 percent of all sponsored television time.[47] Viewers spent 462 million hours per week watching old movies, more than four times the hours spent at motion picture theaters.[48] Early successes, such as New York's "Late Show" and "Million Dollar Movie" had shown that regular programming of Hollywood films could attract large audiences and important sponsors. Since all of the films released had been produced before 1948, a large part of the television audience was too young to have seen them.

The most common method of distribution has been sale of rights to individual television stations, which then sold time on regularly scheduled film programs. Some distributors, however, obtained payment from stations partly in the form of station time, which they could then resell to advertisers. As evidence of the size and stability of the audience for old films, advertisers' purchases have increased in size, some buying sponsorship of entire groups of feature films for a year's showing. In 1956 National Telefilm Associates signed 130 stations, each contracting for a minimum of one and one-half hours per week, to compete with the three major television networks in the area of national advertising, offering feature films only. The saving on rent for coaxial cables (the NTA stations receive their films via Railway Express) made their competition effective.

On the negative side, many theater owners blamed the free movies available on television for the bulk of the loss of theater audience. In New York City, for example, as of February 1958, 85 different films per week, in 175 separate showings, were available to the television audience. Table 13.16 shows the feature-film libraries held in 1958 by New York television stations.

From the theater exhibitors' point of view the worst was yet to come, with the release of post-1948 films. Experience had indicated a strong positive relation between date of release and size of audience, for the televised feature film. The obstacle to the release of films made after 1948 has been the demands of various Hollywood guilds (writers, actors, directors, and technical personnel) for a share in the proceeds. Early agreements between the studios and guilds stated that payment of royalties would not be sought for any films produced before 1 August 1948. Later on the studios began to come to terms on payments for post-1948 films released to television, and the trickle of newer films inevitably became a stream. In January 1957, for example, the Screen Actors Guild accepted

Table 13.16. *Feature Film Libraries of New York Television Stations, 1958*

Studio of Origin	WCBS-TV	WRCA-TV	WOR-TV	WNTA-TV	WABC-TV	WABD	WPIX	Total
				Station				
MGM	723							723
Paramount	700							700
Warner Bros.	287		26	26		120		459
Columbia-Univ.	160	13			123	100		396
Twent.-Cent.-Fox	50	38		102			52	242
RKO		22	700	30		30		782
United Artists	33	74				40		147
Republic		140						140
Miscellaneous	197		674	8	50	110	164	1,093
Total	2,150	287	1,400	166	173	400	216	4,792
Telecast at least once	400	200	600	100	153	400	216	2,069

Source: "Shortage of post-48's . . . ," *Sponsor Magazine*, 12:44, 13 Sept. 1958.

an offer of $615,000 as royalties on eighty-two RKO Radio Pictures made between 1948 and 1950, while the Screen Directors Guild (later known as Directors Guild of America) and the Screen Writers Branch of the Writers Guild of America accepted $235,000 each.[49]

In two other cases, the guilds were sidestepped. The major distributor of post-1948 films was United Artists Television, Inc., a subsidiary of United Artists Corporation. Their first issue of 39 feature films was made in August 1956, the second, consisting of 52 features, in August 1957, and the third, with 25 American and 40 foreign films, in April 1958. Since United Artists was not a studio, but merely financed and distributed the productions of independent producers, this company had little to fear from the threat of boycott with which the guilds restrained regular producers. In the second case, Republic Pictures released 218 post-1948 films to the National Broadcasting Company in February 1958, and were immediately served with separate notice of "cancellation of contract" by the actors, directors, and writers guilds.[50] Since Republic was abandoning feature film production, the guilds' action was ineffectual.

Theater exhibitors were not alone in their disapproval of the increasing use of feature films on television. The television networks regarded the trend as a threat to their domination of programming. Many feature-film shows turned up in the prime evening hours formerly reserved for network programs. Small stations, hitherto reliant on network affiliation because they could not afford live productions capable of attracting large audiences, found feature films a cheap and effective substitute for the network show. And some national advertisers abandoned sponsorship of network programs in favor of feature movies at individual stations. In 1956, for example, the Revlon Company dropped an NBC show to sponsor feature films at thirty stations, at a cost of $3 million. The networks themselves purchased film rights for showing on a local basis at their wholly owned stations, but did not use them in network broadcasting.[51] David Sarnoff, NBC president, warned NBC affiliates that if they gave up network shows for feature films, television would turn into a "national movie screen, [just as] some radio stations have become national phonographs."[52]

The Economics of the Television
Market for Theatrical Movies

Barry R. Litman

Television networks have started purchasing the rights to motion pictures before the theatrical showing, usually during the filming or editing stage of the picture.[1] While this change in bargaining strategy received little publicity, it nonetheless has the potential to enhance the collective monopoly power of the three networks vis-à-vis the movie producers. Using the economic model of oligopoly as a framework, this article will contrast the markets for regularly scheduled programming and theatrical movies, to show how this change in bargaining strategy can be viewed as a logical extension of the networks' tightly controlled market for regular series programming.

The television networks can properly be classified as an oligopoly—a market structure of a few competitors in which each firm must be aware of how its behavior affects its rivals and what type of reaction it can expect from them. Different theories of oligopolistic behavior arise from different assumptions concerning how rivals react. At the one extreme is the possibility of a vigorous competition among the firms in every area to increase or to maintain one's market share or both. Firms will court the favor of consumers by lowering prices, maintaining high quality standards, and over time introducing new products and refining old ones. Those firms which are not technologically progressive or cost efficient can expect their market shares to dwindle and financial repercussions to occur. In this scenario, the industry will perform very well from an efficiency standpoint and in fact not too dissimilarly from the economic ideal of the perfectly competitive market structure. In the perfectly competitive model, each firm is so small and powerless that it becomes a slave to the forces of the marketplace. Firms must always be innovative and cost-efficient. In the long run, all excess profits will be dissipated as new firms enter the industry, increase the supply of product, and thereby drive down the price.

At the other extreme is the possibility of a "shared" monopoly among the firms. In this scenario, the firms come to realize that every price cut, every new advertising campaign, and every new product innovation results in reaction in kind from one's competitors. While the firm initiating the action may achieve a gain in sales, that gain will be short-lived once the other firms match these price cuts or additional advertising expenditures. In fact, it is frequently true that such action leads to a price or advertising war. When all the dust has settled, relative market shares may be just about the same, but costs have risen, prices have fallen, and profits have significantly decreased.[2]

After a few of these price or advertising wars, it becomes clear to all competitors that it is a wiser policy to cooperate with each other than to fight it out in the trenches. If everyone "agrees" to maintain high product prices, low input prices, or limited advertising expenditures, then the industry as a whole can generate high profits, and each firm's share of those profits will be "greater" than in a cycle of rivalrous behavior. Of course, direct consultation with competitors over prices, output, territorial exclusivity or the like is illegal under SECTION 1 of the Sherman Antitrust Act. Nevertheless, as the oligopoly matures and the firms come to know and trust each other, a "meeting of minds" can occur, and each competitor acquires the ability to predict with near certainty the behavior of its rivals under differing economic conditions.

Certain common cooperative practices become routinized and regularized in the industry, and no open consultation need occur for the oligopolists to communicate to each other the beneficial policy for the entire industry. Price leadership and standardized markup procedures are two common devices for such "signaling" in an industry.[3] If this type of tacit cooperation operates smoothly, the end result may be a "shared" monopoly which generates higher prices for the consumer and a tendency for the industry to maintain the status quo rather than be innovative.

The television networks have maintained a position somewhere between the two extremes of competition and "shared" monopoly. There is a wide variety of areas in which the networks can choose to compete or cooperate. Cooperation would be expected in those areas which are so visible that cheating is easily detected and retaliation can be quick.[4] These would include advertising prices, commercial minutes per hour, station affiliation payments, and the percentage of original versus repeat programming.

There is evidence to corroborate a spirit of cooperation in these profit spheres. The networks follow similar policies in setting and changing advertising prices. Although not obvious from the varying prices per minute of network prime-time programs, the similarity is evident when the program ratings are taken into account and prices per thousand viewers are compared.[5] The networks also follow a pattern of administered price leadership whereby the industry leader usually initiates changes in the price level (price per thousand viewers) while the internal structure of prices remains constant. Such a system of price signaling facilitates industry coordination.

The same cooperative behavior is also followed in the affiliation area. The prices paid by the networks for clearing time will be pretty much the same for all affiliated stations in comparably sized markets. Since data on actual affiliate compensation are considered proprietary, it is necessary to look at a proxy variable to show similarity of prices. The best proxy variable is the "network station rate," the value which the network places on viewers in a market which is incorporated as "time" charges in the price charged to national advertisers. A casual examination of network station rates within any market or across markets of similar size demonstrates the similar network behavior in this area.[6]

With respect to the amount of commercialization per hour, the three networks all abide by the standards in the National Association of Broadcasters Code. The code permits different amounts of time for commercialization during the broadcasting day. For example, during prime time, six minutes of commercialization is the maximum permissible for the networks. By agreeing to this commercialization limit, the networks have the capability to restrict the supply of advertising minutes, raise prices, and narrow the range of competition.

In contrast to these profit areas, it is very difficult for networks to cooperate on the "quality" of programming, since the ingredients of a successful program are so unpredictable, and cheating could not be effectively policed. Thus, the competitive impulse will more probably surface in the sphere of programming. But rivalry over ratings need not drain away network profits. As long as networks compete only in the programming sphere, while cooperating in the other revenue-generating areas, they can place a lower limit below which profits will not fall.[7]

A most fruitful area for cooperation has been the financial side of programming. The networks took over the responsibility for programming from the national advertisers in the 1950s. The networks claimed that this shift of responsibility was made to accommodate the advertisers who could no longer afford the rising costs of sole or alternate sponsorship; the advertisers insisted that the networks made the change for themselves. Regardless of who instituted the policy, the net result was a drastic decrease in the number of buyers of prime-time pilots from between fifty and one hundred national advertisers to the three networks. Program producers were now forced to pass through the narrow network bottleneck or face the prospect of not being on the air.

In this market for regularly scheduled programs, the networks understand that their bargaining advantage is greatest in the initial developmental stages of a television show, when the quality of the scripts and pilot is of unknown value and the future success of the program is uncertain. At this stage, venture capital is scarce because the investment is so risky. Once a show becomes a hit, however, it can command a high price on the open market because its network cannot risk its being bid away by another network. To prevent such competitive bidding, the networks have developed a series of parallel steps in the buying process which, if commonly followed, will increase the uncertainty of product quality and thereby enhance their power relative to their suppliers.

After looking over the story idea, but before funding the script, the networks and program producers sign a "pilot and series" contract which stipulates not only what share of the costs the network will pay for the pilot, but also gives the network the renewal option at a set fee for each year up through the fifth year or longer. In the past there was normally a price escalation of about 5 percent per year built into the options, but in recent years the more typical procedure is to set out the exact dollar prices for the entire length of the contract.[8] Therefore, the networks have locked the producers into a set price even before the pilot is shot or the series is accepted and normally from twelve to eighteen months before the season begins. This practice effectively eliminates competitive bidding for hit shows.

In supplying the scarce venture capital and taking the risk of programming, the networks incur the losses associated with flop shows but reap the bonanzas accompanying hit programs. In the strong bull market for network advertising during the past decade, the profits from hits have greatly exceeded the losses from flops. It may be argued that this step process of program procurement is necessary for the networks to conduct business, and that this practice was thrust upon them through advertiser reluctance to provide development funds. Nevertheless the central question is how long the contract must be for a network to recover its developmental expenditures and whether the five- to seven-year contracts cause *unreasonable* restraints on trade. The same fixed length—fixed fee contracts are used even when the program is a spin-off (e.g., "Maude," "Rhoda") from a highly successful program and is accepted without a pilot. In sum, by insisting on long-term contracts, the networks as a group are able to prevent competitive bidding for hit programs, limit price increases to the rate of inflation or less, and reap the large profits accompanying the hit programs.

To further enhance this spirit of cooperation, the networks also have had a common understanding that once any network becomes seriously involved in the consideration of an idea as evidenced through the financing of a script or pilot, it achieves a virtual lifetime monopoly to the rights of the series or spin-offs even if it never purchases the show or cancels the show during the lifetime of the contract.[9] If the program does last beyond the contract expiration date, the program producers can negotiate with the other networks, but the original network retains the right of first refusal, which means it can match any offer and retain the series. In practice there have been only a handful of pilots and a small number of series which have transferred from one network to another. Again, the effect of this practice is to eliminate any competition for ideas (even rejected ones) by binding the program producer to the original network.

Producers are also bound by other network practices in the areas of deficit financing, syndication, and subsidiary rights. The networks have historically forced the program producers to deficit finance during the network run. The rule of thumb for each new episode of a half-hour comedy show is that the costs are about $180,000 but the network pays only about $160,000 for the show. According to Grant Tinker, producer for MTM Productions: "In effect, you're subsidizing the network. . . . We're all straining to achieve a sale with only three networks and we usually end up doing it for the price they offer."[10] Since the industry shakeup of 1976, the problem of deficit financing has been significantly lessened as the networks have bid up the price of new prime-time programs.

Sometimes the deficits can be reduced by concurrent sales to suitable foreign markets, but it appears that the producers must look toward the syndication market to reap any satisfactory profit. Success there is also limited because a program ordinarily needs to have at least one hundred episodes to have any value in syndication. This is because series re-runs are usually "stripped" on a daily basis, whereas the original series was produced on a weekly basis.[11] In the past, there was an average of thirty-nine new episodes produced per year, but owing to higher production costs the average today is from twenty-two to twenty-four. Therefore, according to Tinker and others,[12] a show must last for almost five years on network television before it can be assured of a successful run in syndication, and the odds are about one in ten that the show will last that long.

Before the enactment of the Prime-Time Access Rules,[13] the networks were able to extract valuable subsidiary rights in the syndication market from the suppliers. Allegedly those who refused to go along with the networks were systematically excluded from access to prime time. These subsidiary rights included domestic distribution rights, foreign distribution rights, merchandising rights, and profit shares from the syndication markets.[14] While the networks claimed that such subsidiary rights were their reward for the risks of network programming, many producers testified[15] in the hearings of having to look toward the syndication markets to recoup their losses from the network run.[16] Since the syndication markets are such an important source of revenue, it seems clear that the program producers did not willingly surrender their subsidiary rights.

Given the seemingly unprofitable position of television producers, it is not surprising that there has been a significant exit of producers from the industry in recent years. There are now only nineteen principal program suppliers as compared to twenty-seven several years ago.[17] For those who choose to stay, "there may be some type of egotistical reward ["psychic income"] that accrues from being part of the Hollywood scene and having a show carried on network television."[18] More practically speaking, these producers are driven by the hope of creating that uniquely successful program which will later turn into a syndication bonanza.[19]

By cooperating with each other and standardizing the rules of the negotiations, the networks collectively have a great deal of power over producers of regularly scheduled programming. This power has been illustrated by identical policies towards the deficit financing of programs, the extraction of subsidiary rights and profit shares, the fixed fees and favorable contract options, their "gentlemen's agreement" not to tamper with each other's properties, and the exit of significant prime-time suppliers from the market. In the area of regular series programming, the networks have had the advantage in dealing with program producers when the uncertainty of quality is at its highest level. At the same time the networks have been able to bind series to long-term contracts and thereby eliminate inter-network competition for hit programs. Thus, the networks have become profitable because they have been able to control both sources of potential profit—profit from uncertainty of program quality and profit from inter-industry coordination.

These two sources of power are intricately intertwined. The tight oligopoly structure of the networks acts as a bottleneck which narrows down the number of potential sources of access ("gatekeepers") for program producers. The profit-maximizing incentive for oligopolists to coordinate their behavior inhibits the emergence of significant inter-network competition for programming. The uncertainty over quality, large number of competing producers, and scarcity of venture capital make the producers unable to resist this network power.

Theatrical movies represent a different species of network programming because specific knowledge exists concerning their value in the theatrical market. The knowledge includes data on the box-office gross and rentals accruing to the distributor, as well as the performance of the movie in the various award categories. This information has been shown in previous studies to be an important determinant in explaining the expected rating of these films on prime-time television.[20] The known "quality" of theatrical movies, in reducing the uncertainty and risk to the networks, also enables the movie companies to demand prices reflecting the marginal worth of their movies to the networks.

The major movie companies also have more bargaining power because of a stronger position in the movie industry as producer-distributors than as television series suppliers. As table 14.1 indicates, the major movie producer-distributors clearly dominate the theatrical movie industry. Collectively, these companies accounted for 89.1 percent of the domestic rentals in 1978, with each of them contributing at least a 10 percent share. This highly concentrated market structure should enable the producers to dominate their industry[21] and bargain effectively with the networks over theatrical movie rental terms.

On the other hand, the picture is quite different in the prime-time television program market (see table 14.2). The major movie companies accounted for only one-third of TV airtime in 1978, while independent packagers supplied the majority of the programs. As Owen[22] has noted,

Table 14.1. *Market Shares of Domestic Movie Distributors, 1978 (in percentage)*

Major movie companies	
Paramount	23.8
Universal	16.8
Twentieth Century–Fox	13.4
Warner Bros.	13.2
Columbia	11.6
United Artists	10.3
	89.1
Independents	
Buena Vista	4.8
AIP	1.4
Others	4.7
	10.9

Source: *Variety*, 10 Jan. 1979, p. 3.

Table 14.2. *Supplier Market Shares of Regularly Scheduled Prime-Time Network Series, Fall 1978 (in percentage)*

Major movie companies	
Universal	18.6
Twentieth Century–Fox	4.9
Paramount	3.9
Warner Bros.	3.9
Columbia	2.0
	33.3
Networks	9.8
Independents	
Spelling-Goldberg	11.8
Lorimar	8.8
MTM	7.8
T.A.T.-Tandem	5.9
Miller-Milkis	2.9
Others	19.7
	56.9

Source: *Variety*, 14 September 1977, p. 34.

the major movie companies have no economic advantage in this area since the supply industry is competitive owing to a well-developed rental market for inputs, minimal economies of scale, and easy entry. Their only possible advantage is the minor leverage they could exert by tying movie sales to acceptance of television series.

For financial success, a theatrical movie primarily depends on rentals earned in the domestic and foreign theaters. The sale of television rights is only a secondary consideration. This is in contrast to the financial requirement of TV program producers to obtain network financing, make the network sale, and remain on the network long enough to create value for the series in the syndication market. In short, the movie companies have a greater independence in their financing and more potential profit centers. This flexibility should translate into greater bargaining strength with the networks over theatrical movie rights.

It would still be possible for the networks to tacitly agree to hold down prices for movies of known quality. For example, the networks could set up a bidding pool which would designate which one of them was to be the "highest" bidder for the next hit movie to reach the market. In this way, they could bind each hit movie to a single buyer and would probably obtain more favorable contract terms. But the success of such a price-fixing cartel would require open discussions among the networks and a complex allocation scheme. The risk of antitrust detection would be very high, which probably explains why network competition has been the rule in this sphere of programming.

Movie companies have been able to obtain high and increasing prices for their films since the early sixties. The prices for theatrical movies have always been two to three times higher than the prices of regularly scheduled programs of comparable quality, offering further evidence that movie producers have greater bargaining leverage than series producers. Movie prices started to rise because of increasing network demand and inter-network rivalry for theatrical movies. The average price of a theatrical movie rose from $100,000 for two network runs in 1961 to around $800,000 by the end of 1967.[23] During this period the number of hours of prime-time movies increased from two in 1961 to fourteen in 1968. In the mid-seventies, the prices once again skyrocketed owing to a shortage of acceptable movies for television.[24] This shortage resulted from the fact that the four-year stockpile of network features amassed during the late sixties ran out around 1972 or 1973; the trend in the seventies toward more R- and X-rated pictures resulted in a smaller percentage of acceptable features. In addition, the major movie studios cut back their production significantly and concentrated their efforts on fewer high-budget films. This shortage of acceptable theatrical features for TV is further demonstrated by the decrease in the time elapsed between theatrical release and first network telecast. In 1972, the average (mean) number of years elapsed was almost six;[25] today it is 3.74, with many features being shown in less than two years.

Around 1966 and 1967, the networks attempted to stabilize theatrical movie prices by producing their own theatrical movies and made-for-television movies. This vertical integration into the production sphere resulted in some eighty theatrical movies during 1967–71 and 40 to 50 percent of their yearly requirements of made-for-television movies. The effect of such a large foreclosure of product was devastating and sent a clear message to the movie producers that hereafter prices would be stabilized. Private and public antitrust litigation (*Columbia Pictures, Inc.* v. *ABC and CBS*, complaint filed in U.S. District Court, Southern District of New York, 1972, and *U.S.* v. *CBS, NBC, ABC*, complaint and brief filed in U.S. District Court, Central District of California, 1974), as well as an inferior product, caused the networks to leave the production industry in 1972. Since then, competition for the limited quantity of available theatrical movies has once again caused prices to increase. To counteract this problem, the networks have increased their requirements for made-for-television movies to all-time record levels. While the increased demand for these features has increased their prices, they cost less than half the rental fee for a theatrical movie.[26]

The rationale behind the recent network strategy of purchasing television rights before the theatrical release is to obtain commitments by the movie producers at an early stage in the production process when the quality is uncertain, the risk is high, and the television value is indeterminate. In this way, the networks should find it easier to bind themselves to specific producers and thereby reduce inter-network competition over theatrical movies. It is of course a risk for the networks because they will be wedded to the flops along with the hits, but it is a risk that has been shown to be acceptable and profitable with regularly scheduled programming.

Because of the market concentration in the movie industry and the numerous revenue-generating centers, it will be much more difficult for the networks to dominate the movie producers as they do the program producers. Rather, one should expect that this form of "hedging" will stabilize prices in the industry at a level somewhat in excess of the current minimum purchase price for a low quality theatrical movie. The real danger for movie producers lies in becoming too dependent on the networks as a source of initial financing for their pictures or engaging in long-term multiple picture contracts with individual networks. These two actions will reduce their bargaining power and limit the amount of inter-network competition.

A statistical model can be used to measure the effect of "quality" in the networks' negotiation of prices for theatrical programs and series. To do this, an equation can be estimated which includes several independent variables affecting price, the dependent variable. Multiple regression analysis can then be used to determine how much of the variance in price each independent variable explains.

The expected price of a theatrical film sold to the networks will depend upon the physical characteristics of the film as well as its "quality" in the theatrical market. The dependent variable in the first estimation equation is the price paid for theatrical films in 1966 and 1967.[27] All of the contracts specified two network runs.

Four independent variables are used—movie length, age, box-office value, and ratings. Generally speaking, longer pictures are thought to be more attractive to television viewers since more and higher quality resources are used in them. Also, the longer the movie, the less filler that needs to be added; and if sufficiently long, it may run past the scheduled time and thereby bring in more advertising revenue.

Second, newer movies should have more of an appeal than older ones.

The older a movie (other things being equal), the greater the probability that the subject matter will be out of date and the smaller will be the publicity carryover from the theatrical run. The data on price, length, and age come from the negotiated contracts.

Third, theatrical rentals accruing to the film distributor are the most precise measure of a film's box-office value. The data on theatrical rentals come from the annual January editions of *Variety*, which list all films earning over $1 million in rentals. The films valued below $1 million in the sample have been assigned a value of $500,000. Theatrical rentals have been either inflated or deflated by the consumer price index for indoor movie admissions (1967=100) to take account of the inflationary trend in prices over the last thirty years. Thus, a film earning theatrical rentals of $1 million in 1960 is not equivalent to one earning comparable rentals in 1967. In 1967 prices, the former would have a value of $1,538,462, while the latter's value would be $1 million.

Fourth, to measure the intrinsic artistic appeal of the films, star ratings of the New York film critics[28] were used. While such a measure of film "quality" is obviously subjective, as long as the method of evaluation is consistent, it will give a measure of *relative* quality which is desired in this case.

The results are presented in table 14.3 and generally confirm the expectations.[29] Movie length is positively correlated with the contract price. Each minute drives up the contract price by $3,847. As expected, age is negatively correlated with contract price. According to the analysis, each additional month of elapsed time between theatrical release and contract purchase drives down the price by $723.

Adjusted theatrical rentals are very highly correlated with contract price, lending much strength to the argument that the prior theatrical run ("quality") has a significant impact on the expected television rating and therefore on the contract price. Each $1 million in adjusted rentals leads to an additional $26,900 in the television price.

Finally, "star ratings" are not significantly related to contract price. This suggests that critically acclaimed films (which are not successful at the theater box offices) have a low expected rating in the television market and consequently do not command a very high television price. Forty percent of the variation in price is explained by these four variables.

The same procedure is used to estimate a price equation for regularly scheduled programs. The dependent variable is the network price paid for regularly scheduled programs during the 1977–78 season.

Four independent variables were used—program length, seasons running, production costs, and rating. Longer programs can be expected to have higher production costs, thereby necessitating higher prices. Sec-

Table 14.3. *Regression on Prices of Theatrical Movies (N = 162) Sold to TV Networks in 1966–67 (in $ thousands)*

Independent variables	Non-Standardized coefficients	Standard error	F	R^2
Movie length (minutes)	3.847	.771	24.8[†]	.240
Age when purchased (months)	−.723	.344	4.4[*]	.241
Adjusted theatrical rentals ($ millions)	26.922	4.557	34.9[†]	.374
Star ratings (no. of stars)	20.293	27.388	.5	.401
Constant term	181.583	102.814	3.1[*]	

Note: R^2 due to successive addition of independent variables.
[*] Significant at .05 for a one-tail test.
[†] Significant at .01 for a one-tail test.

ond, as mentioned above, the networks increase their prices to program producers by a constant amount or percentage for each additional year that they pick up the option to the program; hence, the longer running series should be more costly. The data on price, length, and age came from *Variety* (14 September 1977, p. 34). Third, higher production costs caused by on-location shooting or special effects should result in higher prices for these programs.

Fourth, "quality" was measured by using the average rating of the program in the previous season as shown in *Variety* (27 April 1977, p. 50). Since the new programs have no previous track record, the average rating (16.1) for all new shows during the previous season (1976–77) has been used as a proxy variable for these programs.

The results are presented in table 14.4 and very closely confirm the expectations.[30] Program length is very highly correlated with contract price. Each minute on the air increases the price by $6,350. Since the programs are shown in multiples of thirty-minute segments, each additional thirty minutes of airtime drives up price by $190,500. The number of previous seasons on the network is also positively correlated with contract price. Each additional year drives up the price by $4,715. On location shooting or special effects or both also drive prices higher by $17,753. Finally, the coefficient for rating in the previous season is not statistically significant in the estimation equation. This confirms the analysis that the networks do not renegotiate the price of a series according to program success; rather, they adhere to their long-term, fixed-fee con-

Table 14.4. *Regression on Prices of Regularly Scheduled Programs (N = 74) Sold to TV Networks in 1977–78 Season (in $ thousands)*

Independent variables	Non-standardized coefficients	Standard error	F	R^2
Program length (minutes)	6.350	.167	1447.2[†]	.947
Number of previous seasons on air	4.715	1.809	6.8[†]	.957
On location shooting or special effects (binary variable)	17.753	7.414	5.7[†]	.960
Rating in previous season (rating points)	1.259	.845	2.2	.962
Constant term	−47.202	18.111	6.8[†]	

Note: R^2 due to successive addition of independent variables.
*Significant at .05 for a one-tail test.
[†]Significant at .01 for a one-tail test.

tract policy.[31] Ninety-six percent of the variation in price is explained by these independent variables.

This analysis has shown that television networks have the upper hand in bargaining with the producers of regularly scheduled programming because the networks assume the high risks of new program development. As a *quid pro quo* for their risk capital, the networks fix program prices on a long-term basis before the true program quality is known and its value established in the market. These practices are still in effect because there are only three sources of access, venture capital is scarce for such high risk programming, and the program supply industry is relatively competitive. Furthermore, through a series of systematic parallel cooperative practices, the networks attempt to eliminate all competition among themselves for these programs and thereby force the producers to accept their terms. This hypothesis is partially confirmed by regression analysis, which shows no statistically significant relationship between price and program "quality."

On the other hand, such domination has eluded the networks in the market for theatrical movies of known quality. This market has always been very competitive, with frequent bidding wars for box-office hits. Regression analysis demonstrates that, unlike the situation for regularly scheduled programming, there is a high correlation between price and adjusted theatrical rentals. The new bargaining strategy of bidding for such movies before their theatrical release is a logical extension of the networks' activities in the regular programming market and can be expected in the long run to adversely affect the negotiating power of the movie companies.

PART SIX

America's Role in the International Film Industry

Film Conglomerate Blockbusters: International Appeal and Product Homogenization

Joseph D. Phillips

The American film industry's search for formulas with international appeal has led to an increasing reliance on standardized "spectaculars." A small number of film companies have traditionally dominated the American film industry and in turn the international film market outside the socialist countries. This situation has resulted from the size of the U.S. market for films, the historical advantage that this has given the U.S. film companies, and the nature of the film industry. These circumstances have tended toward a resurgence of concentration and centralization in the film industries of the advanced capitalist countries and toward a greater homogenization of the product.

When Roger Lewis, the former vice president in charge of advertising, publicity, and exploitation at United Artists, went into independent film production in 1961, he began to put together the picture *The Pawnbroker*. He did not have the money to take an option on the book, but he had a director who was interested in it, and the two of them got actor Rod Steiger excited about doing the film. Metro-Goldwyn-Mayer started to advance some money to develop a screenplay, but soon decided to withdraw from the project. This left Lewis with a choice between suing a major film company and trying to go on by himself. He then went to his old company United Artists and presented the project to David Picker. Lewis's account of what happened follows:

> At that time, I had it budgeted for about $400,000. David liked it very much, fought through management for it, and finally got a

reluctant okay—on the condition that I would see one more person in the company who wanted to talk to me about the project.

The person turned out to be David's uncle, and he said to me, "Look, before we go ahead there are two things I think you are going to have to change." I asked him what they were.

"Well, first you have to eliminate all references to the concentration camps."

I said, "Well, I don't know how . . ." I was trying to be very reasonable, because I was about a year and a half behind and $30,000 in hock at this time. "How would you motivate it?"

And he said, "Well, find some other injustice."

"What injustice?"

"You always argue too much. You don't want to think about it."

I said, "I'll be very glad to think about it, but I don't know what to think about."

"Maybe he was sent to prison unfairly."

"It won't work," I said, "It's got to be an epic wrong."

"Well, think about it," he said, and I said I would.

Then he said, "There's one more thing." I asked him what it was.

"Does he have to be a Jew? After all, there were other people in concentration camps. You had to sell pictures for a long time. You know people don't want to go see pictures about Jews in concentration camps."

"No, he doesn't have to be a Jew," I said, "and he doesn't have to have been in a concentration camp. He doesn't even have to run a pawnshop. He can run a saloon. We'll make it a Western!"

The deal didn't go through.[1]

The film did get produced. Ely Landau put up the money for it from independent sources and got Sidney Lumet to direct it. Lewis disagreed with some of the things Lumet did with the flashbacks, but he had to yield ultimate control to Landau, who had put up the money.

The story illustrates the problem of independent film production in the United States. Lewis says: "Ideally, the producer has sufficient stature and muscle to be able to command financing without sacrificing control of his picture. But he seldom has. When you are dealing with anywhere from a million to eight million dollars of somebody else's money and that money is being put up by businessmen, the pressures to modify, alter, and compromise are bound to be enormous, and they are very hard to withstand. Even when the pressures are unspoken. Even when the producer has the authority on paper to make all the decisions himself. It is very difficult for the independent producer to work within the economic dynamics of the film industry as it exists today." [2]

This is hardly the outcome that was heralded when the motion picture industry was shaken up by the antitrust decisions in the late 1940s and the rising competition of television that began to be felt about the same time. At that time the expectations was that independent production would blossom and creative talent would no longer be ruled by the business offices of the majors.

Before 1948 the motion picture industry in the United States was dominated by five major companies, the "Big Five"—Paramount, Twentieth Century–Fox, Warner Bros., RKO, and Loew's (MGM)—and the "Little Three"—Columbia, Universal, and United Artists—with the last engaged only in distribution of films made by independents. These eight turned out practically all the high rental films. The top eight operated film exchanges throughout the United States and in many foreign countries. Their control of distribution was the key to their dominance in the industry. Certain trade practices—block booking, blind buying, formula deals, franchises, master agreements—and ownership of the majority of the better theaters gave them control of exhibition as well. As distributors they released 95 percent of all feature films and got 95 percent of film rentals. This control affected independents in both production and exhibition.

The *Paramount* decision in 1948 and the related antitrust settlements separated ownership of theaters in the United States from production and distribution and prohibited most of the trade practices that had given the Big Five such a dominant position. These antitrust actions, coupled with the decline in attendance resulting from the competition of television, produced major changes in the structure of the industry, some of which are still taking place.

The development of the conglomerate form of business organization left its mark on the U.S. motion picture industry. In 1966 Paramount became a part of Gulf & Western Industries, Inc. United Artists was acquired in 1967 by Transamerica Corporation, a conglomerate mainly centered in insurance and other financial services. Warner Bros. was acquired in 1969 by Kinney National Service, Inc., a conglomerate engaged mainly in entertainment and communications fields; theatrical and TV film rentals accounted for 39 percent of total revenues in 1972, when the name of the parent organization was changed to Warner Communications, Inc. MGM was not acquired by a conglomerate; it became one. It is now concentrating on profitable television programs and Las Vegas hotel and gambling operations. In September 1973 it announced that it would make only six to eight "special" movies a year.[3] At the same time MGM became the first major U.S. motion picture company to withdraw from film distribution, assigning its domestic distribution rights to United Artists for ten years and its foreign distribution rights to Cinema International, a joint venture of Paramount and MCA.[4] As recently as 1981, however, MGM became involved in distribution once again by acquiring United Artists from Transamerica Corporation. Of the former Big Five, only Twentieth Century–Fox was still primarily a motion picture producer and distributor in the early 1970s. Film rentals and TV programs provided 70 percent of its income in 1972.

Independent production did expand, mostly because stars and directors formed their own production companies. The principal reason for this development was the tax saving that such high-income persons could obtain by operating their own production companies. A less important reason, probably, for going into independent production was the expectation that it would result in greater artistic freedom. However, many participants and observers of the industry have questioned the significance of this development. Robert Gessner has remarked: "Although the economic base shifted in the 1950s, the cultural superstructure remained solidly attached to box office values. Men of talent had been conditioned by formula, and upon risking their own money and reputations, they played the new game in the safe style of the old one. . . . On the whole, the product of a company dominated by an actor or director cannot be distinguished from the run-of-the-mill product of a major manufacturer. . . . The banker began to suspect that the artist (actor, director, or writer-producer) was not interested so much in creating a new art as in accumulating new money."[5]

The editor of one of the principal trade journals of the movie industry had a simpler explanation for the symbiotic relationship: "Many observers have erroneously reasoned that the rise in independent film production in Hollywood has been at the expense of the major studios. It isn't generally realized that most of the films produced independently not only rely on the distribution facilities of the big companies, but also count on them for their financing.[6]

The structure of distribution in the industry in the early 1970s is indicated in Table 15.1. It resembles that of the years preceding the Paramount decision. Some of the names have changed, but the top ten distributors got about 95 percent of gross receipts in 1972, the same percentage as the top eight in the earlier period. The top three in 1972 received more than half of the total.

One type of production which contributes particularly to the dominance of the major film companies is the so-called blockbuster, or road-

Table 15.1. *Percentage Distribution of U.S. and Canadian Distributors'*
Gross Receipts

	1972	1971	1970
Paramount	21.6	17.0	11.8
Warner Bros.	17.6	9.3	5.3
United Artists	15.0	7.4	8.7
Columbia	9.1	10.2	14.1
Twentieth Century–Fox	9.1	11.5	19.4
MGM	6.0	9.3	3.4
Universal	5.0	5.2	13.1
Buena Vista (Walt Disney)	5.0	8.0	9.1
National General/Cinema Center	3.2	8.0	7.0
ABC/Cinerama	2.7	3.6	3.0
Others	5.7	10.5	5.1
Total	100.0	100.0	100.0

Source: David Gordon, "Why the Majors Are Major," *Journal of the Producer Guild of America*, 16, no. 2 (June 1974):11.

show, movie. This is a high-budget, major production, usually on 70 mm film and requiring special wide-screen exhibition facilities, which is released for exhibition at advanced prices and on a reserved-seat basis. In most recent years, blockbusters accounted for a large proportion of domestic box-office receipts, despite the fact that by number they constituted less than 5 percent of total domestic feature film production.[7]

The $10 million to $40 million or more that blockbusters cost to produce almost guarantees that a major film company is involved. It is very difficult to get outside investors to put up that kind of money. In any case, distribution of the film must be assured, and the majors are the big distributors.

Of course, blockbusters can flop, as *Cleopatra, Tora! Tora! Tora!* and *Hello, Dolly* amply demonstrated. And even major film companies, such as United Artists, can be forced out of the business if they have too many flops. In 1970 Sidney Lumet could say: "Because money is so tight in the movie business right now . . . the day of the blockbuster seems over."[8] The number of "roadshow" attractions declined from twelve in 1968 to one in 1971.[9]

But that situation changed very quickly. Most low-budget films did not catch fire at the box office, and many movie people concluded that the public did not find them sufficiently different from what was available on television. In late 1971 *The Godfather*, which was to break all records for gross receipts, closely followed by *The Poseidon Adventure* in 1972, restored the reputation of the big-budget film. The growing conviction of the industry that attendance at movies is now an event rather than a habit has reinforced the notion that spectaculars are the wave of the future. As David Begelman, then president of Columbia Pictures, explained: "We feel we must put out special event films because no one goes to the movies anymore as a routine exercise." [10]

Twentieth Century–Fox Film Corporation and Warner Bros. jointly produced *The Towering Inferno*, which was budgeted at $12.5 million; Universal Film Corporation budgeted *Earthquake* at $7.5 million; and Universal expected *Airport 1975* to cost about $6 million. Others of this type are on the way. Producer Irwin Allen of Twentieth Century– Fox in the middle 1970s was reported to have had some $38 million in spectaculars in the planning stages, including *The Swarm*, which depicted big bees attacking New York, and *The Day the World Ended*, which was to reproduce the 1902 volcanic eruption that devastated the island of Martinique.

As the *Wall Street Journal* correspondent summarized it: "In short, the big-budget, old-time cinematic spectacle filled with high-priced stars, throngs of extras and eye-popping visual and aural excitement is back." [11] If in part the motivation is to distinguish it from television, the effect is to make film production more dependent on the sources of big money.

Fashions in movies change, of course, and there may be a swing away from blockbusters if a number of them should result in big losses. The vice-president for West Coast production of United Artists questioned whether the big-budget pictures would pay off. "My feeling is that we should stay away from trend movies—'disaster' trend movies or any other kind of trend movies." However, United Artists released *Juggernaut*, a film about passengers aboard a ship on which a bomb has been hidden. [12] Any movement away from blockbusters seems likely to be temporary, given the structure of the industry and the nature of the market. Those with the power to make the key decisions in the industry will tend to return to this form as a competitive strategy.

There are, of course, films made for special audiences. The chairman of the board of American International Pictures contends that "today the audience is fragmented; and with the exception of the big and successful picture that may by its special elements appeal to many different groups, one must take aim at a special group in order to be successful." [13] In the United States, the tendency in the years since television became generally available has been for movie theater audiences to be made up mainly of young people. According to a recent survey made for the Motion Picture Association of America, nearly three-quarters of movie admissions are purchased by persons between twelve and twenty-nine years of age, although they constitute only two-fifths of the population. Those persons over twelve years of age who go to movies regularly (defined as more than twelve times a year) constitute only 23 percent of the population, but they buy 86 percent of the tickets.[14]

A number of producers have tried to find formulas for films that would appeal to this youth audience, or at least a profitable fraction of it. A series of beach movies was the result of one formula used. Occasionally a producer will hit upon a low-budget combination of story and actors that has great appeal for a large segment of this audience. *The Graduate* was one, *American Graffiti* another. But it is too diverse a section of the population for this to happen often, so the tendency is to rely heavily upon the standard ingredients of a best seller and superstars.

Other special audiences have been the objectives of such film types as sex movies, westerns, black films (e.g., *Shaft*), and Disney films. Because these audiences, in varying degree, are limited in numbers, the films designed for them tend to be relatively low-budget ventures. Most of these films bring in correspondingly low returns for their producers.

It is clear that the risk of financial loss in producing commercial films is great. The production cost of the average feature made by the major U.S. companies increased from about $400,000 in 1941 to $2,200,000 in 1972. A few cost much more, as noted above, so of course many fall below the average. Joseph E. Levine, president of Avco-Embassy, claims that only "one out of 20 pictures makes it now" compared with pre-TV days when "nine out of ten earned money."[15] Presumably, he means that one out of twenty is very profitable. Wilton R. Holm, a vice-president of the Association of Motion Picture and Television Producers and the executive director of the Motion Picture and Television Research Center, in Hollywood, says that only 30 percent of the pictures made today actually make money.[16] According to A. H. Howe, vice-president of the Los Angeles headquarters of the Bank of America and the person in charge of motion picture credit activity for that bank, "it is only the occasional hit that makes a large profit, but that hit can bring in more than anything seen in the history of the business. Odds against that hit are great, but when it comes, jackpot!"[17]

The distributor, usually a major film company, is typically the one who takes the risk. Although the distributor often tries to spread the risk by bringing in outside investors who underwrite a share of the costs and who participate in any profits, it is the financial backing and the agreement to distribute the finished film by the major film company which is crucial. According to Howe, the backing of a major motion picture company in the form of a guarantee is probably sufficient for a producer to obtain a bank loan equal to the entire production budget at a rate within 1½ percent above the prime lending rate of commercial banks.[18]

Foreign markets have long been important to the U.S. movie industry. World War I stopped production of films in Europe, while the U.S. movie industry moved ahead rapidly. By 1918 most of the films shown throughout the world were made in Hollywood. In the 1920s they filled three-quarters of the world's screen time.

Before World War II, foreign film rentals accounted for one-fourth to one-third of total receipts of U.S. filmmakers. As U.S. movie attendance declined with the expansion of television set ownership in the postwar years, the importance of foreign markets for American films increased. In 1952 they accounted for 42 percent of total receipts. The most rapid growth occurred in Latin America, the Middle East, and Asia. The share of Europe in total foreign receipts dropped to 50 percent in 1952, or about $80 million, of which Britain accounted for $25 million and Italy $15 million.[19]

In recent years, foreign markets have generated 51 to 55 percent of total motion picture rental income of U.S. film companies. Jack Valenti, the president of the Motion Picture Association of America (and also of the Motion Picture Export Association) claims that "our industry generates a larger proportion of its revenue overseas than any other large American industry."[20] Data compiled by the U.S. Department of Commerce on "the U.S. share of film and television tape rentals, derived from the showing of U.S.-produced film and television programs abroad,"[21] indicate that these rentals rose from $120 million in 1950 to $215 million in 1955, then declined to $184 million in 1960. After that year they increased irregularly to $299 million in 1972, then fell to $285 million in 1973.[22] This revenue is received almost exclusively by the major film companies that belong to the Motion Picture Export Association. In 1968 they had over 700 foreign offices employing more than 16,000 people. The association supported their activities through its nine offices on five continents. Valenti cites estimates that 25 million to 30 million people outside the socialist countries see the average U.S. film abroad during its period of release, and that U.S. movies occupy half the screen time in the nonsocialist world.[23]

Britain has always been the largest single foreign market for Hollywood. Of the feature films registered by the Board of Trade, those from the United States regularly outnumber British features and those from any other country. They accounted for 40 percent of the total in 1964, dropped to 34 percent in 1967, and rose to 39 percent in 1971, while so-called British features ranged between 19 and 23 percent.[24]

However, many of the British films are produced or at least partially financed by U.K. subsidiaries of U.S. movie companies or by other American investors. The generally increasing dependence of the British film industry on U.S. film financing is indicated by the rise in the share of British first features and co-features exhibited on two main circuits that were wholly or partially financed by U.S. investors from 43 percent in 1962 to 88 percent in 1968.[25] In 1970 there was a sharp reduction in U.S. investment in British film production. It dropped from £31.2 million in 1969 to £17.5 million. (The British subsidiaries of major American companies accounted for 67 percent of this U.S. investment in 1969 and 73 percent in 1970.) The cutbacks in film production and employment that resulted made painfully clear how dependent on U.S. capital the local industry had become.[26]

This domination of the British film industry by the U.S. majors has been documented in a number of publications by Thomas H. Guback.[27] He has also presented evidence on the powerful economic role of the U.S. majors in the Italian and French film industries, citing data which indicate that almost 42 percent of the total rentals paid by French exhibitors to distributors went to seven U.S. companies in 1972, that at least one-fourth of the 1972 Italian-French co-productions involved a U.S. film company subsidiary as producer, and that U.S. subsidiaries contribute about half of the annual budget of ANICA, the Italian motion picture trade association.[28]

All of this only serves to demonstrate the relatively greater domination of the international film industry by the U.S. majors today compared with earlier periods, despite the many measures adopted by foreign governments to protect and encourage their respective domestic film industries. It is ironic that U.S. film company subsidiaries get most of the subsidies which the British government provides and many of those which the Italian and French governments offer in an effort to make their film producers competitive with the U.S. filmmakers, and that the latter can so easily penetrate the barriers of quotas and tariffs and film-time requirements. But in societies where private property is sacred, the most that can be asked is that it take up a local address and follow the local customs.

What role do foreign film companies play in the U.S. film market? It is difficult to determine in many cases what constitutes a foreign film vis-à-vis the United States. Clearly, films made by U.S. film companies on location abroad are not foreign films. Less clearly, films made by foreign subsidiaries of U.S. film companies or by other foreign companies with U.S. financing primarily for North America's audiences are not foreign films. However, many films are shown in the United States that are classified as foreign. Estimated payments from the United States for foreign film and television tape rentals rose from $4 million in 1950 to $15 million in 1960 and have ranged between $10 million and $13 million each year since then.[29] These are certainly insignificant amounts when compared with U.S. film rentals abroad.

The rentals obtained by distributors of foreign films in the United States increased from $40 million in 1959 to $71 million in 1965.[30] The payments they make to foreign film companies are, of course, much smaller than their rentals, which cover distribution costs and profits. In 1965 there were about 85 distributors of foreign films in the United States. About 500 theaters showed such films regularly and a larger number on occasion. In 1963, 805 foreign films were released in the United States, rentals for which were estimated at $69 million.[31]

The early 1960s seem to have been the peak period for foreign films in the United States. At that time many of them were much freer and more sophisticated than U.S. films, and some viewers still find them more satisfying. A fascination with anything foreign may also have been a factor. With the appearance of U.S. films that covered the same subject matter and uncovered the same areas of anatomy, the popularity of foreign films declined. The "art theater" circuit disappeared, making it more expensive to distribute foreign films. The college market seems to be the most important outlet now.[32]

It is evident from these data that foreign film producers have not succeeded in making a very big dent in the U.S. market. There is no evidence that foreign film companies play any significant part in production, financing, or distribution of films in the United States. Many foreign producers, directors, writers, and actors have, of course, been employed in Hollywood, but U.S. companies have been their employers.

The dominant position of the U.S. motion picture industry in the world market is compounded of several elements. First, U.S. films are the most widely distributed throughout the world. Second, the distribution organizations that the major U.S. film companies established to market their product throughout the world are the most extensive and the most effective in the world. Producers in other countries often find they must distribute their films through one of them if they want to reach the largest number of customers. Thus the U.S.-owned distributor subsidiaries handle not only the foreign rentals of U.S. films, but also the distribution of many films made by foreign producers. Third, the major U.S. film companies have subsidiaries in some countries that produce films or finance production by others. These subsidiaries are the producers and distributors (and to some extent even the exhibitors) of British, French, Italian, and other national films or they are the source of financing of such films. This domestic corporate citizenship enables them to meet the requirements for access to subsidy and other benefit programs designed to promote the domestic industry. It also permits production of films that are free from quota limitations or tariffs which the country may impose on imported films.

The reasons for this dominance in the non-socialist world by the U.S. film industry are to be found in the very large capital resources available to the U.S. film industry and their concentrated form. In part these are a function of the large market for films in the United States, which is supplemented by the industry's foreign sales, and in part they are a function of the vast capital accumulation in the U.S. economy as a whole. The large unit costs of production inherent in feature film making, especially of the blockbuster or spectacular type, and the crucial position of the distributor in the marketing of films give an enormous advantage to the major U.S. film companies. It does not seem probable that their dominant position will be undercut. On the contrary, it seems likely that the process of concentration and centralization will go on.

The structure of the industry and the nature of its market provide a strong incentive to produce films that will sell not only in the domestic, but also in the international market. Since the U.S. market is much the largest in the nonsocialist industrial countries, it serves as the lowest common denominator. U.S. film producers must aim for this market, even while mindful of the potential foreign audience scattered in many different countries. The foreign subsidiaries of U.S. film companies, of course, often produce films primarily for U.S. audiences, again keeping in mind the foreign market. When they finance production by foreign filmmakers, the product may tend to have a somewhat more local theme, but in most cases they will choose projects that seem to have audience potential in the United States and it is hoped in Third World countries. Even foreign film companies that are not dependent on U.S. financing plan on international distribution, especially in the United States, if they seek large returns.

The search for a product that has international appeal tends toward homogenization of the medium. The great weight of the U.S. market and the U.S. film industry tends to give the increasingly homogenized product a cultural bias. One formula that seems to possess a high probability of market success is the adventure story, often involving a disaster of enormous proportions. This formula appears to have great international audience potential. It calls for blockbuster treatment involving investment of great lumps of capital, which, of course, the major U.S. film companies are best able to provide. Thus the tendency toward concentration of the industry and homogenization of the product is reinforced.

Film as International Business:
The Role of American Multinationals

Thomas H. Guback

The symposium on the International Flow of Television Programs held in May 1973 at the University of Tampere (Finland) demonstrated the rapidly growing interest in the nature and consequence of the circulation of video materials among nations.

As the conference progressed, one point that became apparent was the extent to which the relatively new and highly conspicuous international trade in television programs has grown along lines already traced by the circulation of theatrical motion pictures over the last half century. It would seem as if the international film business had provided the prototype or model for television, and that would not be too surprising for in the United States, at any rate, many of the same companies are engaged in both fields.

Allied Artists, Avco–Embassy, Columbia, Disney, MCA (Universal), MGM, National General, Paramount, Twentieth Century–Fox, United Artists, and Warner Bros. are important Hollywood companies which also deal in television programs for domestic and foreign consumption. Indeed, the member companies of the Motion Picture Association of America (the above, minus Disney and National General) supplied 70 percent of the prime-time programming on the three national commercial television networks during 1972—predominantly series produced directly for television, but also feature films made for theatrical distribution or especially for video.[1] The same companies (members of the Motion Picture Export Association of America [MPEAA]) also are estimated to account for about 80 percent of television program exports from the United States. These amount to some 50,000 program hours annually, and might well run over 100,000 if data were available from more vigorous accounting methods.[2] Hollywood, then, is not just a film capital, but a telefilm capital as well.

As one might expect, the similarity between production and distribution of film and telefilm also is apparent in the forms of financing, specifically in the rise of co-production in the making of television series. This method brings together capital from at least two sources, usually in different countries, to cover production expenses. While this kind of financing is relatively new to television, it is nonetheless increasing, and for a number of reasons. The cost of making splendid, showcase series can exceed the investment possibilities of one producer or television company, but the project can be realized if the financial burden is shared between two. In some cases, international financing of series can give one of the producing partners access to a market which hitherto had been relatively closed to it. This is true, for example, in the case of Anglo-American productions which for the British producer open the United States, a market traditionally difficult to crack for any foreign producer. That appears to be one of the motives behind the series on the British Empire which united the British Broadcasting Corporation and Time-Life. The latter, it should be added, seemed to have its attention on the possibilities of extensions from the series into other forms of software—a new highly visual magazine influenced by television and material for video cassettes.

In 1972 there were 153 co-produced programs on BBC television, compared with 77 the previous year. The motive was not so much cultural exchange, but more the sharing of the production costs. Many were bilaterally produced, but others involved up to thirteen different organizations.[3] As Terry Hughes of the International Broadcast Institute in Great Britain has pointed out: "We will find co-production becoming far more important because it is the only way in which you can raise enormous sums of money to make not only TV programs but also to spin off into the other areas of new technology."[4]

Although co-production of telefilm series is still somewhat unusual, for theatrical motion pictures it is the dominant method in Europe and has been since the middle sixties. Official co-production in the European film industries takes place under terms set by treaties among nations, the first of which was signed in 1949 by France and Italy. In the years since, proliferating agreements have brought together many of the important filmmaking nations of the world. France, for instance, has treaties in force covering co-production with eighteen countries. From 1960 to 1972, she made 1,191 co-productions as against 744 films completely French.[5]

Similar figures confirming the importance of co-production could be presented for other countries in Western Europe. What they do not show, however, are films made by two or more partners not covered by bilateral treaties. Usually these involve American filmmakers as the United States is not party to any co-production agreements, although American film subsidiaries abroad which come to have legal status as "foreign" production companies would necessarily fall under terms of treaties tying the host country to others. In actuality then, the number of pictures financed by two or more international partners is somewhat greater than just the number of co-productions. In the future, it is not totally unlikely that we will see co-ventures between even the United States and the Soviet Union, if the optimism of MPAA President Jack Valenti is a guide.[6]

Another similarity between film and telefilm which cannot be overlooked is the American hegemony throughout much of the world. A cross-section of the international flow of images would show American products dominant, while their position on video and film screens, the consumer end, is equally impressive. And where American programming is not the dominant television fare in a country, then it is often at least the bulk of imported material.

In Latin America about half of the programs are imported and most of those from the United States. As a result, a third of *total* programming time is filled by shows originating in this country. In some nations, Guatemala and Nicaragua in particular, half of *all* programming is American in origin while in Chile, Mexico, Venezuela, and Peru it is about one-third. The United States also provides about three-quarters of the foreign programs on television in Argentina and Colombia and about 60 percent of those in Uruguay.[7] Although importation of series and feature films for use on television is much less in Western Europe, the same pattern is evident. Of imports, often two-thirds to three-quarters are from the United States, with commercial systems relying more on such material than do noncommercial operations. Thus, aside from the socialist nations, the content of the international trade in television material is heavily weighted with products from America.

Startling as that may seem for television, it has been a long-established rule, if not tradition, in the American motion picture industry. Its position is summed up frankly and cogently by the MPAA: "The American movie is the world's most wanted commodity."[8] With a market of more than eighty countries, the American film occupies more than 50 percent of world screen time and accounts for about half of global film trade.[9] At every moment of the day, there is an American picture being shown someplace on earth. Upwards of 30 million people around the world see the average American film during its period of release outside the socialist countries.[10] Economically, the MPAA estimates that American films annually make a favorable contribution in our balance of trade in excess of $200 million.[11]

Although film and television material demonstrate many parallels, we must be on guard against assuming that one is the carbon copy of the other. The trade in telefilm, at least for American companies, is likely to remain the small brother that it is and might never grow to truly rival the commerce in theatrical films. According to industry estimates, the world-wide television sales of MPAA member companies equal about one-third of the total gross revenue derived from theatrical exhibition.[12] Evidence suggests, furthermore, that the world market for American television series did not expand during the early seventies and if anything contracted perhaps as much as 15 percent in terms of dollar billings between 1970 and 1971 alone.[13] Some competition came from other nations in the syndication business, while former importers gradually came to produce greater shares of their own programming as their television operations matured, thus reducing their reliance upon the United States. Pressure to use indigenous talent in locally made shows also contributes to reduction of imports.

Precisely how this affected American producers in actual dollar terms is hard to pin down. There is a paucity of reliable statistics about the American communications industry, and what data there are originated with the industry itself. The Federal Communications Commission did not solicit data on the nationality of filmed material presented on television nor on the magnitude and value of American telefilm exports. The kinds of economic questions posed by the Department of Commerce were often worked out by it in consultation with the MPAA. Reporting techniques are such that one cannot even discern the box-office receipts of American pictures in their domestic market for the department lacks a definition of "American film." As far as its estimates of the total motion picture box office are concerned, these are "projections based on experience, historical trends, and judgmental factors used in conjunction with unpublished forecasts of various economic indicators," according to the department.[14]

Granting the difference in market size for film and telefilm, one still must acknowledge that practices in the production and distribution of theatrical motion pictures serve as well the telefilm segment of the entertainment industry. Seen in still larger terms, furthermore, the international flow of film not only parallels but is part of the general flow of commerce around the world. Film has a place in the culture industry whose principles are fundamentally those of other manufacturing or service industries motivated by gain.

Motion pictures have become goods to be manufactured and marketed, while their flow around the globe is guided by simple commercial imperatives. What is exported by one nation and imported by another— or more correctly, what is traded among businesses—is hardly based on any form of cultural policy. The kinds of considerations that guide trade between, say, the United States and Western Europe, are overwhelmingly economic in nature. This means that the films which are available at any moment on screens stem from commercial decisions rather than from consideration of aesthetic quality or more detached concerns about where a society ought to be going and how to get there. In the absence of a cultural policy, company accounts and management loyalty to stockholders become the arbiters, for philanthropy and service to the public (contrary to our popular, media-reinforced myths) are not intrinsic characteristics of the business system.

Much attention has been devoted to multinational corporations, their seemingly, sudden rise, and the kinds of consequences they have for societies around the world. Yet the multinational corporation has been the basis of the American film industry for perhaps the last sixty years. In this way, film has not only set the pattern for telefilm, as we saw earlier, but it has provided an example of what one could expect from industry in general.

American motion picture companies not only export their products overseas, they also have subsidiaries which make, distribute, and exhibit films abroad. These chains of businesses were forged in the decades before World War II and strengthened in the decades after, so that American film companies now have some 700 foreign offices employing 16,000 people. There is perhaps no industry in the United States which is so heavily dependent upon foreign markets as is the film industry. By the late 1960s foreign earnings represented about 53 percent of total film rentals. Indeed, the film industry derives a larger portion of its revenue from overseas than does any other large American industry.[15]

While American conglomerates often have been the corporations which have become multinational, the film companies were such before some of them were absorbed by conglomerates. It is not surprising that in the House Judiciary Committee's 1971 study of conglomerates one finds among the sample companies Gulf and Western Industries, which acquired Paramount Pictures in 1966 and Desilu Productions the following year. In examining a list of impressive subsidiaries, the study pointed out that had it not been "for participation and accommodation by the banks, it would have been impossible for G&W to maintain its merger and acquisition program."[16] Another conglomerate, National General, in a reversal of the pattern, began as the owner and operator of the Twentieth Century–Fox theater chain which was spun off from the parent corporation to comply with an antitrust judgment. From there National General spread to banking, insurance, book publishing, and so forth, and after receiving a court order amending an antitrust ruling, into film production and distribution at home and abroad.

The film companies are just a few of the 3,400 or so American corporations with interests in some 23,000 businesses overseas.[17] The value of their gross output makes American enterprises abroad the third largest economy (of sorts) in the world, behind only the United States itself and the Soviet Union.[18] Seventeen of the world's twenty largest multinationals (ranked by sales) are American. These seventeen had combined sales in 1970 greater than the GNP of France, the United Kingdom, or the People's Republic of China. In fact their sales make them the fifth largest economic power in the world.[19] As such they have been shown to affect the international money market and rates of exchange among currencies.

Western Europe, particularly the European Economic Community, constitutes the largest foreign market for American motion pictures. It is also the area in which American film companies have concentrated their overseas production capacity, especially in Great Britain, Italy, and France. Not surprisingly, this is the region in which American business in general has made substantial investments. Their magnitude demonstrates the strength of America's commercial movement abroad.

According to the U.S. Department of Commerce, the book value of American private investment abroad in 1950 was $19.0 billion; a preliminary figure for 1971 put the worth at over $130.0 billion, a more than six-fold increase in only twenty years. In the same way, the value of American direct private foreign investment (branches and subsidiaries of American firms) was $11.8 billion in 1950, but about $86.0 billion in 1971.

As to geographical areas, Europe (excluding the Eastern bloc) attracts an important and growing share of American investment, about one-third of the total. The worth of our direct private investment there was estimated by the Department of Commerce to be more than fifteen times greater in 1971 than it was in 1950. The six original members of the Common Market accounted for the greatest increase. In 1950 direct investment there was valued at $637 million, but by 1971 it was estimated to be worth $13.6 billion, a more than twenty-fold growth (and larger than our investment the same year in the nineteen republics of Latin America). By contrast, the value of American direct private investment in the rest of Europe, including the United Kingdom, increased less than thirteen times, from $1.1 billion in 1950 to about $14.0 billion in 1971.

To look at this another way, one can consider the present composition of the European Economic Community. In 1971, the book value of American direct investment in the Original Six plus the soon-to-be-members—

Denmark, Ireland, and the United Kingdom—was about $23.0 billion, or about twice as much as the 1950 value of American direct investment *in the world.*[20] The United Kingdom's entry, moreover, is the realization of American hopes and political manipulation for it gives the many U.S. firms in Britain easy access to the important Continental market constituted by the other members. As revealed by McGeorge Bundy, special assistant for National Security Affairs to Presidents Kennedy and Johnson: "If we had a single agreed tactical hope it was that Britain would secure admission to the Community. Nonetheless we had just enough wit to keep from shouting this hope aloud."[21]

The international expansion of American business has been actively encouraged and aided by the government. The Webb-Pomerene Export Trade Act of 1918 was one of the earliest efforts to stimulate exporting by small- and medium-size firms at a time when few companies, including the largest, were concerned much with foreign markets. Agitation for it began around the turn of the century when copper interests lobbied Congress. The act permitted domestic competitors to cooperate in trade by forming export associations which might otherwise have been held illegal under the Sherman and Clayton antitrust acts. In effect, this exemption allowed American companies to combine and to fix prices and allocate customers in foreign markets.

More than fifty years of experience with this legislation has shown, according to one government study, that the major beneficiaries rarely have been firms that needed associations to cope more effectively with the strength of foreign competitors. Nor did the power of foreign cartels seem to be a reason prompting formation of associations. "More often than not," the Federal Trade Commission has observed companies "exercising the right [to form export associations] were least in need of it, being capable of supporting export programs on their own accounts and, in fact, typically doing so."[22] Furthermore, the study cited a few products—sulphur, potash, carbon black, and *films*—and assumed that their export prices had been effectively influenced by such associations. (As if to confirm this, industry sources claim that despite civil war in Nigeria and political upheaval in Ghana, American film earnings in West Africa in 1967—when companies were trading through the Motion Picture Export Association—were triple those of prior years when companies individually distributed pictures.[23])

The survey pointed out that in 1962, the only year for which data were presented, export associations founded under Webb-Pomerene legislation handled twelve product lines. In three—sulphur, carbon black, and motion pictures—these associations accounted for more than half the total value of exports of such products. Moreover, the FTC revealed that for America's theatrical and television film exports, over $290 million worth (an estimated 80 percent of total film exports) was accounted for by associations founded under the Webb-Pomerene Export Trade Act. The position of film was outstanding and unique because the other eleven products *combined* had less than $208 million in assisted exports. To look at this another way, nearly 60 percent of *all* Webb-assisted exports were reported by film companies belonging to four associations. One of these, the Motion Picture Export Association of America, alone reported $270 million in assisted exports—in other words, the bulk of film exports and more than the other eleven product lines *put together*.[24] Thus the present chief beneficiary of the Webb-Pomerene Act is the film industry, specifically the members of the MPEAA.

Perhaps it was for this reason the FTC study observed that "firms currently obtaining the greatest assistance from Webb associations are, because of their size, also most capable of supporting independent export programs." It is also obvious that the cooperative activity by Webb association members—usually large firms operating in domestically concentrated markets—is more likely to have adverse effects on competition in the domestic market than would cooperative activity by fringe producers in concentrated markets or by producers in unconcentrated markets."[25]

But encouragement of export trade was not just a feature of the early years of this century, nor have communication products themselves been overlooked. It is hardly a secret that during World War II the Department of State already was making plans for the postwar international spread of our print and film media, and of Tin Pan Alley music as well. The Informational Media Guaranty Program, established in 1948 as part of the Economic Cooperation Administration, permitted the converting of certain foreign currencies into dollars at attractive rates providing the exported information materials earning the money reflected the best elements of American life.

This was a decided advantage to American media, particularly film companies, for it allowed them to distribute products in difficult currency areas with complete assurance that a portion of the resulting revenue would become available to them in dollars. American media products therefore went forth into the world with the rank of ambassador. Film companies alone received almost $16 million between the end of 1948 and mid-1966. Print media also received considerable payments (over $2 million each to Reader's Digest and Time, Inc., for instance), prompting Senator Allen Ellender to complain that the IMG "is a Fund primarily to benefit a chosen few of our large publishing houses located in New York City."[26]

Aid to overseas expansion of American business has taken other forms.

The Revenue Act of 1971 included provisions permitting the establishment by an American business of a Domestic International Sales Corporation as a subsidiary to handle foreign sales. The DISC purchases from the parent and sells abroad. If the DISC derives at least 95 percent of its revenue from overseas sale, lease, or rental transactions, and other qualifications concerning incorporation are met, it can defer tax on up to half of its export income. These tax-deferred retained earnings can be used in export development activities or can be lent to domestic producers of export products. However, they become taxable if they are distributed to stockholders. In essence, the program's effect is to defer taxation in 50 percent of export earnings, a feature which led the European Commission late in 1972 to declare that this is equivalent to a tax exemption on exports and a violation of GATT (General Agreement on Tariffs and Trade).

There is no list available of companies conforming to criteria of the DISC program because the Department of the Treasury, with which appropriate documents must be filed, considers such information to be confidential. However the DISC scheme was designed, according to then Treasury Secretary John Connally, "especially to encourage smaller businesses, which may have had little or no export experience, to export"—a rational resembling that of the Webb-Pomerene Export Trade Act.[27]

Further aid to the international expansion of American business has been provided by the Overseas Private Investment Corporation, authorized in 1969 but formally organized in January 1971. OPIC is a wholly owned government corporation with majority private sector representation on its board of directors, although it is an agency of the United States, under policy guidance from the Secretary of State. Its objective is the more effective investment of American private capital and know-how in friendly developing countries and areas. It seeks to accomplish this by insuring American companies against loss owing to certain political risks of currency inconvertibility, expropriation, war, revolution, and insurrection. It also provides direct-dollar and foreign-currency loans for financially sound, new investments or expansions of existing projects.

The corporation has already placed part of its expropriation insurance liability with private underwriters. During Fiscal 1972, OPIC reinsured $289 million of its then-current coverage with Lloyd's of London and others, including the USSR's Black Sea and Baltic Insurance Company.[28] Political risk insurance has covered some two-thirds of American private investment (excluding petroleum) in eligible developing countries, or about $500 million annually. At the end of Fiscal 1972, OPIC's maximum potential liability was $2.3 billion for expropriation, based upon its more than 700 insured clients in eighty countries. During that year it paid Anaconda almost $12 million in full compensation for the expropriation of its investment in a Chilean mine. It also received, but rejected, a claim from IT&T for $92 million for its holdings in the Chile Telephone Company. As a lender, OPIC had more than $200 million outstanding by mid-1972. Considering all its programs, OPIC has helped encourage more than $4 billion of direct American investment abroad.[29]

These are just a few of the ways in which government directly aids international business. Of course, there are less dramatic and more routine methods on the embassy level when foreign service officials assist American companies abroad in overcoming a variety of local political and trade obstacles. In the case of film, it is clearly understood they are "ambassadors of good will" and of great asset to our foreign propaganda program. For the industry, however, the imperatives are commercial and it maintains a tenacious hold on its markets.

Advantageous trade terms for American films often have been the product of pressure exerted by companies, and not only on their foreign counterparts. As Jack Valenti, MPAA/MPEAA president (and former White House aide to Lyndon Johnson) has observed: "To my knowledge, the motion picture is the only U.S. enterprise that negotiates on its own with foreign governments."[30] It is not surprising that the MPEAA is often called "the little State Department" for its duties nd methods often parallel that government agency. The film association has offices or representatives in sixteen foreign cities while boards composed of representatives from member companies exist in thirty-eight. When American pictures keep half a country's theaters open and generate an important share of entertainment tax revenue, the threat of a market boycott through withholding of films can bring foreign adversaries to terms. It is hard to comprehend quite all the consequences of this, but according to Valenti, foreign governments earn more income from the showing of American films (through import, admission, and income taxes) than do the producers of those films.[31]

One factor contributing to the worldwide strength of American films is the virtual monopoly of international distribution achieved by American companies. There is no European company, for example, with the stature of, say Paramount or Twentieth Century–Fox. In effect, this locus of power means that a handful of distributors decide, by and large, which pictures circulate internationally among major filmmaking nations. As these companies also are important in financing production through distribution guarantees, they exert considerable influence on the kinds of pictures made for global audiences.

Even within markets the role of American distributors is substantial. During 1972 in France, a major Continental market, of the 364.5 million francs (close to $75 million) paid by exhibitors to distributors, almost 42 percent went to 7 American companies. The remainder was divided among the 115 French distributors.[32] This is not exceptional for data from other European countries demonstrate substantially the same situation. In 1970 7 American distributors in Great Britain were estimated to have received 84 percent (about $44 million) of all film rentals.[33]

Another important feature of the European cinema is the extensive American financing of European films. These are not simply American films shot on location to deplete accumulations of blocked and unexportable earnings, as was the case in the years after World War II. Rather, these pictures meet all criteria for being granted British, French, Italian, or another nationality and thereby qualify to receive subsidy payments from various national aid schemes. The extent of American participation is such that in the decade up to 1972, two of every three 'British' features exhibited on the country's two main circuits were partially or entirely financed by American subsidiaries. In fact, American companies were financially involved in almost five times more British films than was the British government's chosen instrument, the National Film Finance Corporation.[34] In this respect, the British film industry is little more than an appendage of Hollywood and American companies. It is an example of what has been happening more recently in other industries: American companies export their production plants to take advantage of lower paid foreign labor and often tax incentives from foreign governments. "Runaway production"—a term coined a quarter of a century ago in the film industry—now is applicable to automotive, electronics, and a host of other manufacturing fields. It has led some to wonder whether America of the future will not be simply a service economy, or as described in a report prepared for the AFL-CIO Maritime Trades Department—"a nation of hamburger stands" with "citizens busily buying and selling cheeseburgers and root beer floats."

In European film industries, the extent of American investment is usually obscure because data from these countries do not distinguish adequately between locally financed and American financed pictures. Moreover, foreign subsidiaries of Hollywood companies usually acquire the nationalities of their host countries, making it difficult to identify the precise nationality of the source of money. Further, American subsidiaries not only make pictures abroad under their own names but they can supply finance to foreign producers as well, or guarantee loans made by foreign banks. It is evident that companies themselves are not especially helpful to a researcher, for they are reluctant to release details of business practices for public scrutiny. As a result, American investment is masked in dozens of nominally "national" and co-produced films. One can scan the list published annually by the Centre National de la Cinématographie (or Italy's Unitalia or Spain's Uniespana) of completely national and co-produced pictures and not find a single reference to *American invest-ment.* Nor do these nations have official co-production treaties with the United States. Yet behind the names of producers and their addresses in Paris, Rome, or Madrid often stand American subsidiaries or American production loans.

One recent case is *Ultimo Tango a Parigi*, an Italian-French picture, in the ratio 60 : 40 as far as financing is concerned, co-produced under terms of the treaty between those two nations. While the film fulfills the *legal* definition of an Italian-French co-production, it is in reality an Italian-American co-venture, and not simply because the male lead is Marlon Brando or a third or so of the dialogue is in English. Closer inspection of the French producer reveals it to be Productions Artistes Associés, a sub-sidiary of United Artists. According to the production contract of 10 Janu-ary 1972, the "French" producer contributed 40 percent of the estimated budget of 714,000,000 lire (about $1.2 million) with United Artists re-ceiving world distribution rights. The box office was to be divided 60 : 40, except for Italian and French speaking areas where all receipts were to be paid to the Italian or French producer, respectively. Other terms spec-ified that the film was to be made under the Italian-French film agreement and that the principal role was to be given to Brando, who was to be re-munerated for his services by the Italian producer, P.E.A., to which Ber-nardo Bertolucci had transferred his scenario rights. The contract also stipulated that the production subsidies in Italy and France were to be paid respectively to the Italian and French producer.

The Last Tango in Paris is not an isolated case. At least one-quarter, maybe more, of the 1972 Italian-French co-productions involved an American subsidiary as producer.[35] In virtually all cases its contribution to the estimated budget was only 20 percent, the legal minimum, but enough to secure "French" nationality for the film and thereby access to the production subsidy in France, about 13 percent of the picture's do-mestic box-office receipts.

There can be no denying that the subsidies to production in Great Brit-ain, Italy, and France have been important factors in attracting Ameri-can investment to those film industries, although the quantity of pay-ments cannot be determined with any precision. It has been estimated, however, that for every dollar-equivalent of subsidy paid in France to American subsidiaries, they receive two in Italy and probably four in the United Kingdom. In some instances, through complex international co-production arrangements, American producers have been able to accrue subsidies from three countries for one film, covering as much as 80 percent of its production cost. It is not surprising then that through the 1960s, American financed films abroad rose from about 35 percent to 60 percent of the total output of American producers, although the early 1970s have seen a slight decrease in such activity overseas. Towards the end of the 1960s, American motion picture interests were investing an estimated $100 million per year in films made outside the United States.[36] That figure is quite reasonable because the Italian industry released data revealing that in the decade to 1967, American companies spent a yearly average of $35 million to acquire and to finance Italian features and to make their own films in Italy.[37]

The position of American subsidiaries in that country is such that they contribute about half the annual budget of ANICA, the Italian motion picture trade association.[38] One of the recent achievements of ANICA was a campaign for tax reform, which became effective in 1973. According to the association's managing director, Carmine Cianfarani, this legislative victory represented the equivalent of $15 million in additional remittances to home offices by American companies in Italy.[39] However, through voting power in ANICA, American members can block certain moves that could make Italian companies more competitive in their own home market. In 1972, for example, American distributors there released twenty-four Italian films that were among the biggest box-office attractions in the country. For reasons such as these, some Italians consider their film industry has been "colonized" by American interests.

The American involvement in the financing and distributing of European films—quite apart from the large quantity of authentic made-in-USA films on European screens—had wide political, social, and economic consequences which I have examined at length elsewhere.[40] Suffice it to say that preference is given to those kinds of pictures whose international marketing possibilities seem most satisfactory. Consequently, films are made for world markets rather than local ones, and this results in the closing of channels to the expression of indigenous cultural characteristics and the submerging of regionalisms in the mix demanded by international commerce. Further, the dependence of European film economies on American corporations means that Europeans have lost effective control of their industries, and thus of their own artistic destinies.

Those who are concerned only with the shadows on the screen and not their source are judging ends and disregarding means, for *how* something is done inevitably affects *what* is done. Europeans cannot lose control of the economic end of film-making and expect to retain autonomy in the cultural or social spheres. As a publication of the European Community Information Service has observed, the creation of Europe's Continental market "has quickened the growth of American style corporate society on the old Continent," though the transition is hardly completed.[41] There is no question that the British film industry, and to a slightly lesser extent the Italian and French, have lost their autonomy by becoming tied to, and relying upon, American finance and distribution.

Some have hoped the framework of the Common Market would provide the mechanism and model for increasing relations and trade among film industries of member states, eventually leading to commercial and economic integration. However, it is unrealistic to believe that a *European* film industry can be constructed on *American* investment. What will be built is a large European market without internal trade restrictions, but the principal beneficiary will be American subsidiaries who will produce in the market and employ local talent, but only as long as they consider it profitable. Lacking any intrinsic loyalty to their host nations, these subsidiaries will manage investment and production according to their own demands and not the economic, cultural, or artistic needs of foreign countries. Some observers believe that as multinationals they will not even exhibit any loyalty to the United States. As the chairman of the American-owned Ronson's British subsidiary has been quoted as affirming: the executive "must set aside any nationalistic attitudes and appreciate that in the last resort his loyalty must be to the shareholders of the parent company and he must protect their interests even if it might appear that it is not perhaps in the national interest" of the host country.[42]

Whereas a decade or two ago, American film companies might have weighed their policies in terms of motion picture economy, it is evident today that as parts of "leisure time" divisions of conglomerate corporations which themselves are multinational, fields far removed from the cinema can effect film policy. Universal marketing strategy, worldwide monetary patterns, speculation in Euro-dollars, corporate investment in district lands, or global industrial warfare—and how they are assessed by American multinationals—can be reasons influencing the ways in which corporations allocate resources by shifting men, material, and capital to meet their own needs. The major film industries in Europe cannot escape the shock waves from this because they have lost their sovereignty to huge international companies, over which no country or any citizens can exercise power.

Acceptance of American investment has not solved, as some seem to think, the economic difficulties of European film industries. It has only postponed the day of reckoning, for these problems are endemic to a private market economy, regardless of the extent of state aids and subventions, whose presence only serve to confirm the inadequacies. There is continuous talk of establishing an American production subsidy or instituting tax incentives to lure more filmmaking to Hollywood. The

American industry implies that it is not subsidized—at least in the United States. Yet its record over the last quarter century clearly indicates that it has availed itself of subsidies in foreign countries.

It is indeed a curious progression of events. The deluge of American films in Europe, most especially in the postwar period, restricted the market for those made locally by industries struggling to recover from the war. In an effort to help, governments created subsidy schemes to rejuvenate production, whereas mandatory screen quotas assured that a portion of theater time would be available for these films. But the chief beneficiaries, it seems, have been American subsidiaries abroad which garner important shares of production subsidies while screen quotas assure their films a reserved place in foreign theaters.

It is not to be seen as curious, however, that few voices in European film industries have attacked this intervention, for the short run American investment has meant a new source of production capital, utilization of studios, and access to the American market for selected films (even if little of the resulting revenue finds its way back to Europe). Even some left-wing entertainment trade unions in Europe have uttered only muffled, symbolic cries of protest while quietly appreciating more stable conditions, although the reduction of American finance in Britain in 1970 produced an unemployment crisis of sorts and served to spotlight anew the array of dangers. But the long run will demonstrate how this false prosperity, if it can be called prosperity, has no foundation beyond the immediate policies of a dozen or so American film companies, some of which are themselves subject to conglomerate strategies.

What one British producer has said about the United Kingdom could apply equally to other nations: "We have a thriving film production industry in this country which is virtually owned, lock, stock and barrel, by Hollywood."[43] And it must be remembered, of course, that when American producers went abroad, they did not consider it "runaway production," but just good business. When they leave England, or some other country, it will be for the same reason.

Cultural Dependency in Canada's Feature Film Industry

Manjunath Pendakur

In 1925 D. W. Griffith advised Canadians, "You should not be dependent on either the United States or Great Britain. You should have your own films and exchange them with those of other countries. You can make them just as well in Toronto as in New York." More than half a century later, Canada's screens are still dominated by imported feature films, most of which come from the United States.[1]

This is not to say Canada does not produce its own feature films. After a decade of public assistance to production through the Canadian Film Development Corporation, the number of films produced in the country is steadily rising. A generation of actors, producers, and directors has been created, some of whom have won international acclaim. But faced with tough competition from U.S. films in the domestic and international markets, profitability for films made in Canada is severely limited. While the branch plants of U.S. film distribution companies and their affiliated theater circuits are thriving in Canada, the same cannot be said of independent, Canadian-owned enterprises in production, distribution, and exhibition.[2]

An argument commonly heard in the Canadian film industry is that moviegoers in Canada freely chose U.S. films over Canadian and other films because the former have superior box-office ingredients, such as stars, sets, and so forth. This myth of consumer sovereignty masks the film-distributing companies' ability to create demand through massive advertising. Moreover, audiences can only be formed for films that are effectively available to them. The free-choice argument is hollow because it assumes free and open competition between American and Canadian film production and distribution companies for theatrical markets.

To understand why Canada is the biggest foreign consumer of American films, one must go beyond the images and sounds of that medium. It is necessary to investigate the ownership and policies of the dominant firms in the Canadian film market to understand why Canada is dependent on imported films and why profitability for films made in Canada is limited in the domestic and foreign markets.

Equally important, the reasons for Canada's dependency on imported U.S. films cannot all be found within the Canadian film industry. The problem is more complex than that. It has to be seen in the larger context of Canada's economic, political, and military dependence on the United States. The post-World War II take-over of Canada's resource industries and the reduction of Canadian economy to the status of a U.S. satellite have been well documented.[3] In addition, one cannot ignore the fact that the U.S. government has recognized and used film and other media exports as tools of mass persuasion since at least 1946 in order to help achieve its foreign policy goals.[4] However, the discussion here is limited to the economic relations that exist between the Canadian and U.S. film industries, and their impact on indigenously produced films in Canada. I shall argue that concentration of ownership in the distribution and exhibition sectors of the industry, and certain monopolistic market relationships between the dominant theater circuits and dominant distributors, are detrimental to the growth of an indigenous film industry.

An old adage in the film industry is that if you control distribution, which is the marketing end of the business, you can control your revenues, and thereby your profits. The Canadian distribution sector is firmly in the hands of the large, integrated U.S. production-distribution companies, which are members of a cartellike trade association—the Motion Picture Export Association of America (MPEAA).[5] Table 17.1 presents 1977 data for Canadian film and videotape distribution revenues which reveal a high degree of concentration in the Canadian distribution market. Among the eighty-three distribution companies operating in Canada that year, the eight largest corporations—all of them subsidiaries of U.S. production-distribution firms—took in 77.8 percent of the total rental revenues from the sale of film and videotape productions. These eight corporations are, in alphabetical order: Disney/BuenaVista; Columbia Pictures of Canada; Metro-Goldwyn-Mayer, Ltd.; Paramount Films Distributing (Canada), Ltd.; Twentieth Century–Fox Film Corp.; United Artists Corp., Ltd.; Universal Films (Canada); and Warner Bros. Distributing (Canada), Ltd.

The imbalance in the market share of these companies can be seen more clearly if their average annual rental revenues are compared with those of the small Canadian-owned companies. The eight U.S. majors had an average revenue of $12.9 million in Canada, whereas the seventy-five

Table 17.1 *Canadian Distributors of Film and Videotape Productions by Revenue Size Group, 1977*

Size of receipts	Establish-ments (N)	Sale and rental of film and videotape productions (in $)
Less than $50,000	13	$298,000
$50,000–99,999	9	$662,000
$100,000–249,999	14	$2,511,000
$250,000–499,999	11	$3,483,000
$500,000–999,999	9	$6,716,000
$1,000,000–4,999,999	19	$40,700,000
$5,000,000 and over	8	$103,209,000
Total	83	$157,579,000

Source: Statistics Canada, Annual, No. 63–207 Ottawa, 1977

Canadian distributors had only $725,000 average annual rental revenue. Those eight U.S. companies paid 67.1 percent of their gross rental income as royalties to the producers of films they distributed that year. No Canadian producer received *any* royalties from those eight companies.

Canada has always been a lucrative market for the U.S. majors, and the available data show that Canada's importance as a market for U.S. films is growing every year. Table 17.2 presents comparative data on the ten top foreign markets for the major U.S. distributors in the years 1970–77. Since 1974, Canada has been the number one market for U.S. films. According to *Variety* (2 August 1978), gross rental billings (money received by distributors from exhibitors for the showing of films) by the MPEAA companies in the Canadian market have nearly quadrupled from $16.8 million (U.S.) to $64.3 million (U.S.) between 1963 and 1977.

The exhibition sector in Canada is characterized by a high degree of concentration of economic power in the two largest circuits—the Famous Players Ltd., and Canadian Odeon Theatres Ltd.[6] Famous Players is 100 percent owned by a leading U.S. producer-distributor, Paramount Pictures, which in turn is a fully owned subsidiary of Gulf & Western Industries, Inc., a U.S.-based transnational industrial conglomerate. Odeon was a 100-percent owned subsidiary of Rank Organisation, a British multinational conglomerate, until 1978. It is now a fully owned Canadian corporation.

Although ownership is important, it does not tell the whole story about Canadian theatrical exhibition. Of the 1,633 screens in 1977, which

Table 17.2. *Top Foreign Theatrical Film Markets for Major U.S. Distributors,*
1970–77 (in U.S. $ millions)

Country	1970	1971	1972	1973	1974	1975	1976	1977
Canada	27.4	29.4	38.7	39.9	54.4	63.2	60.8	64.3
Italy	32.4	34.5	39.1	46.1	47.7	56.4	45.0	39.6
Australia	18.0	17.8	21.6	26.3	38.1	—	—	—
Japan	20.2	20.2	23.9	31.4	37.1	56.7	52.2	48.9
United Kingdom	38.1	33.2	39.6	32.2	36.5	—	—	—
West Germany	20.8	20.7	23.7	33.4	35.0	45.7	41.3	51.7
France	29.8	24.3	29.0	37.0	35.0	54.6	51.9	46.5
Spain	14.7	14.8	16.2	17.0	20.8	—	—	—
South Africa	13.9	12.4	12.2	16.2	16.8	—	—	—
Brazil	17.4	15.6	15.3	16.7	16.7	—	—	—

Source: Motion Picture Export Association of America as reported in various issues of *Variety*.
Note: The missing data for Australia, the United Kingdom, Spain, South Africa, and Brazil were unavailable.

included regular theaters and drive-ins, Famous Players controlled 418 screens and Odeon operated 236 screens.[7] In other words, 40 percent of Canada's screens were in the control of these two circuits. Independent theater operators, including chains and single theaters, had 979 screens, or 60 percent of the country's total. However, as Table 17.3 shows, their share of the national theatrical revenue was significantly lower than that of the two largest circuits. As a matter of fact, although the independents had more than twice as many screens as Famous Players, and more than four times as many screens as Odeon, in 1975 they collected an average per screen gross revenue of $92,505—45 percent less than that of Famous Players and 57 percent less than that of Odeon.

It is not simply the number of screens the two circuits operate that establishes them in a position of dominance in the business, but rather the location of their theaters and their command of first-run U.S. films. Most of the holdings of the two chains are in prime urban markets such as Montreal, Toronto, Vancouver, Edmonton, Calgary, and Winnipeg, whereas the independents are located in rural areas of Canada and certain suburbs of the cities.

Furthermore, the two chains have concentrated their operations in the province of Ontario, which is the largest market for motion pictures in Canada. For instance, in 1976 the seating capacity in that province was greater than in any other province. Gross receipts from admissions in Ontario were $70,822,000, or 37 percent of total Canadian admission receipts, and exceeded box-office receipts of any other province in the

Table 17.3. *Average per Screen Gross Revenue Shared by Two Major Circuits and Independents, 1975*

Circuit	Number of screens*	Gross admission revenue	Average per screen revenue
Famous Players	418	$70,303,000	$168,188
Odeon	236	$50,543,000	$214,127
Independents	979	$90,563,000	$92,505
Total	1633	$211,400,000	$129,454

Source: For Famous Players, The Bryce Commission Papers for Odeon, Auditor's Report, Consolidated Financial Statements, 31 Oct. 1975; other data are from Statistics Canada, *Annual*, 1977.
* These are 1977 data, as 1975 data on number of screens were unavailable.

country.[8] Ontario had a total of 480 screens in 1976, of which 380 were regular theaters and 100 were drive-ins, making up 30 percent of all screens in Canada. Famous Players controlled 38.7 percent of Ontario's theaters, and Odeon controlled 19 percent.[9] Thus, the two largest circuits in Canada controlled an overwhelming portion of the biggest market in the country. Their holdings in the Ontario market increased by 14.7 percent between 1963 and 1976, indicating that the two dominant circuits are trying to concentrate their operations further in that market.

As a consequence of their dominant position, the two major circuits collect the greatest portion of the box-office revenue in Canada. As indicated in table 16.3, although the two circuits together controlled only 40 percent of the total number of screens in the country, their share of total Canadian box-office revenue was 57 percent. To understand how they remain in a dominant position, I will turn to the relationships between the major circuits and the U.S. major distributors.

The existing market relationships between the dominant exhibitors and dominant distributors in Canada date back to the early 1940s. George P. Destounis, the current present of Famous Players, explained[10] how the two circuits monopolized first-run films of all the leading American distributors: "Well, it's been an historical fact that . . . the major distributors aligned themselves with either one circuit or the other. People like Paramount and Warners and United Artists will play 100 percent Famous and people like Columbia and two thirds Universal and one third Fox would play Odeon."

The exclusive right to play a certain distributor's films, a monopolistic practice, is still in vogue in Canada. The net effect of the practice is that it reduces competition between the two major circuits for films. It does not mean, however, that the two major circuits do not compete for audiences in the various markets where they both have theaters. But there seems to be no real competition for films between them.

This pattern of allocation of first-run films of the U.S. majors is of great mutual advantage to the dominant distributors and the dominant circuits in Canada. Except for some minor internal shifts, these market relations have not changed since the early forties. The major circuits claim that these shifts are indicative of a certain level of competition between the distributors and the exhibitors in Canada. For example, in 1975 Universal moved its films to Odeon, and in the same year, United Artists switched over to Famous Players.[11] But these are only internal shifts within the existing market structure. Furthermore, as Wayne Case, Columbia Canada's president, explained,[12] these minor shifts are not easy to make: "Changes cannot be made, even if, for any reason, Columbia wished to switch. Famous is totally booked up with commitments from other major companies and probably couldn't handle the additional business. Every one is locked into the system without much margin for maneuvering."

As shown earlier, the system to which Case refers on the one hand produces bounties to the vertically integrated American majors and their affiliated circuits in Canada, and on the other hand keeps the Canadian-owned unintegrated distribution and exhibition enterprises in an uncompetitive position in the market. If Columbia, one of the U.S. majors, has complaints about the system, it is not hard to imagine the plight of smaller Canadian distributors, and hence Canadian filmmakers, in gaining access to the domestic theatrical markets.

In this mutually advantageous system, the major circuits in Canada have allowed the leading U.S. distributors to practice block and blind booking. In block booking, the exhibitor agrees to buy a package of films which may consist of one or two potential box-office hits, and the rest second-rate pictures. Blind booking is a policy of obtaining playdates whereby the theater operator has had no chance to see the film because it may still be in production. These two policies have serious consequences for the ability of Canadian distributors to compete on an equal basis with the American majors for playdates in the domestic market. When I asked the president of Odeon Theatres whether the American majors offer him one or two potentially successful pictures and ten inferior ones as a package, he replied: "No, it's . . . not done quite as rudely as that. But if you tell him, I don't want [that package], we have had *Jaws*. . . . Come see me when next time you have a good one. He will just say, look chum, I am not going to see you next time when I got a good one. You want my next good one, you look after these, which you know is fair enough."[13] This method of distribution is block booking in essence. It was declared illegal in the U.S. under the Sherman Antitrust Act by the U.S. Supreme Court in 1948 (*United States* v. *Paramount Pictures*, 66 F. Supp. 323, 330 S.D.N.Y. [1946]). No such precedent exists in Canada under Canadian combine laws.[14]

Block booking creates a minimum market for all films distributed by a U.S. major in Canada. Furthermore, it helps distributors to spread their losses over several films. A film sold in a block by an American major distributor also gains entry into the theaters operated by the independents, because the publicity resulting from a picture's box-office performance on the major circuits helps to draw the audience for the independents' theaters. In effect, a second-rate film sold by a U.S. major has better chances of reaching a larger audience, and thereby maximizing its revenues, if it is sold in a block. However, this policy affects the Canadian-made films adversely because of resulting market preemption for films released by major American distributors.

While the U.S. majors have significant access to and control of the Canadian theatrical markets, Canadian filmmakers have been unable to market their films through the majors in any significant numbers. Between 1968 and 1978 Canada produced 448 films.[15] However, according to the Canadian Motion Picture Distributors Association,[16] only 14 of them were distributed by the U.S. majors.[17] In comparison, a total of 100 Canadian films were distributed by 8 independent Canadian-owned distributors in the domestic market between 1967 and 1977.[18]

The independents have thus by and large taken the financial risks involved in distributing Canadian films, and as a result they have been important to the development of the indigenous production sector in Canada. But in the absence of open competition for playdates between the majors and the independents, access to the domestic market for Canadian films, let alone foreign markets, has been severely restricted. This does not mean, however, that Canadian films do not get shown in the theaters across the country—they do. But under the existing market relationships, when Canadian films are shown in Canadian theaters they do not seem to get the best exposure.

In the motion picture business, one of the most important considerations in distributing a film is finding what are called the key playdates, such as Christmas, Thanksgiving, Easter, and the summer months, in first-run houses located in the major markets. These dates assure a certain degree of box-office success for films released during those periods. The commercially attractive playdates in both major circuits in Canada are penciled in at least eight to eighteen months in advance of the release of a U.S. major's picture.[19]

Moreover, when the major U.S. distributors release a big-budget picture (which includes most films), their contracts with the circuits call for a certain amount of what is called "committed playing time." This in effect locks in not just the best dates, but almost the entire fifty-two weeks in a year. The victims in this system of monopoly are the independent distributors, and thereby Canadian producers. Occasionally, a major's film does not do as well as was expected at the box office. Then the circuits might request that the distributor remove the picture from the theaters. But the circuits' theaters are still committed to the agreed playing time in the contract. The U.S. distributor may wish to release another film for those remaining weeks, or agree to use the weeks at another time. Only under these circumstances do independent distributors get playing time for their pictures. Since most of the Canadian pictures are being distributed by the independents, they have to wait for a "hole" in the schedule of the two chains.[20]

When I asked the president of Odeon Theatres why the major theater chains discriminate against the independent distributors, and thereby against Canadian pictures, he replied: "I have to say from a purely commercial point of view, the people who are entitled to my spare playing time, are the people who provide us the 5 or 6 blockbusters, if they got other things that have not been played, as against somebody who has provided me with nothing . . . to me that's not only fair but it's logical. You know, if you are a Canadian producer and you don't have to be releasing through an American major distributing company, and you think, your picture is the greatest, and you tell him no, you can't get a Christmas date with Famous because they are all tied up with United Artists, Metro, Warners, Columbia, Universal, and so forth, you turn around and say, Jesus Christ, this is a conspiracy. I am being discriminated against because I'm a Canadian. You are not being discriminated against because you are a Canadian, you are being discriminated against because your picture is no . . . good."[21]

This statement indicates a collective judgment in the Canadian distribution/exhibition system which applies to almost all forthcoming Canadian films. The system is structured to exclude almost all Canadian films *except by chance*. The traditional argument is that if it is a "good" Canadian film, it will get played. In other words, it is not the structure of the industry and the market relationships that preclude Canadian films in the national market, but it is their poor "quality." This argument is largely a myth perpetuated by the dominant distributors and exhibitors in Canada.

Many Canadian films, such as Claude Jutra's *Mon Oncle Antonie* and Don Shebib's *Goin' Down the Road*, did not receive commercial distribution in Canada until they won impressive international awards.[22]

As table 17.4 indicates, none of the seven top-grossing Canadian pictures produced between 1968 and 1978 was released in Canada during the best playing times. Furthermore, when a Canadian film is doing well at the box office, despite all the odds against it, the circuits may terminate the showing because of the locked-in booking with an American film distributor. A recent example of this practice was the case of *In Praise of Older Women*, which had grossed $24,000 the previous week from a key theater, when Famous Players abruptly ended the film's showing in order to accommodate *The Boys From Brazil*, a U.S. distributor's film.[23]

Independent distributors are thus at the mercy of the major theater chains in Canada. They are seldom prepared for release when the circuits call. They seldom have the choice of theater(s) that might maximize a film's grossing potential. Publicity materials may not be ready, owing to lack of time. As a result, the Canadian picture is released "cold," without the necessary prerelease publicity, planning, or timing.[24] As can be expected, the result is often disastrous to that film.

Some independent distributors have found it so difficult to operate within the system that they have gone into the theater business them-

Table 17.4. *Release Dates for Seven Top-Grossing English Canadian Feature Films in Three Key Canadian Markets*

Title	Toronto	Montreal	Vancouver	Gross box office (as of 15 Nov. (1978)
Apprenticeship of Duddy Kravitz	April 1975	April 1975	May 1975	$2,200,000
Black Christmas	Oct. 1974	Oct. 1974	Nov. 1974	$2,000,000
Why Shoot the Teacher	—	—	—	$1,800,000
Who has Seen the Wind	Nov. 1977	Nov. 1977	Nov. 1977	$1,200,000
Shadow of the Hawk	Aug. 1976	Aug. 1976	Aug. 1976	$1,000,000
Rabid	April 1977	April 1977	—	$910,000
Lies My Father Told Me	Oct. 1975	Sept. 1975	Nov. 1975	$875,000

Source: Canadian Film Development Corporation.

selves. New Cinema Enterprises, a newcomer in the industry dealing mainly in art films and Canadian films, has leased three theaters since 1975 after finding it impossible to get dates for its pictures in the major theater circuits.[25] The rest of the independents, who do not have the necessary capital to acquire theaters, have to wait in line to get playdates for their pictures.

The monopolistic system of distribution and exhibition in Canada, and its adverse impact on unintegrated Canadian-owned companies in distribution and production, has developed over the last sixty years only to the mutual advantage of the major U.S. distribution corporations and their affiliated circuits in Canada. Assured profits for both these parties is the main goal of these relationships. Underdevelopment in the indigenously controlled production/distribution sector is perpetuated by lack of participation for Canadian capital in production, lack of access for Canadian films to Canadian screens, nonavailability of the best playing dates, and extraction of profits by the American majors without any significant investment in Canadian feature films.

Canada is perhaps the only country in the capitalist world that has allowed free access to its feature film market and ownership of its screens by foreign multinational firms without *any* control over the market. Traditional barriers, such as screen quotas and box-office levies, are shunned by the Canadian federal government. It has pursued a policy of voluntary participation by the U.S. multinationals to yield screen time for Canadian films. The role of the state in the underdevelopment of Canadian cinema and the perpetuation of the dependency status of Canada on imported films from the U.S. needs careful study. But any serious national film policy must first deal with structural and market constraints for Canadian films within the domestic market, if Canada is to have a viable feature film industry of its own.

The Common Market Film Industry:
Beyond Law and Economics

Don R. Le Duc

The European film industry was described by Konrad Bieberstein, West German minister of economics, as a "horse and buggy" business in competition with the automobile.[1] Although this analogy is neither original nor completely accurate, it does suggest one explanation for the failure of Western European film companies to share in the general prosperity of the Common Market.[2]

Film remains a nationally oriented, nationally marketed commodity during an era when fundamental laws and economic policies of the Common Market are designed to encourage, if not compel, mass production and distribution across the entire European Economic Community. Despite the fact that nine nations of Western Europe have now combined economically to form a single market of 260 million people, filmmakers and distributors within these nations continue to operate as if the national trade barriers of the past remained firmly in place.

Why have European film companies been inclined to spurn this wider European Community market, content instead to remain sheltered within national law and nurtured through governmental grants? And more directly, how have Common Market film producers and distributors been able to avoid prosecution for violations of European Community laws which prohibit national subsidies or restrictions upon the flow of goods, services, labor, or capital among member states of the community?

The Common Market Cinema Industry Committee (CICCE) has responded to the economic question by contending that film, unlike other industries, cannot transcend cultural barriers and thus is incapable of benefitting from a combined market consisting of nine distinct nations with seven different major languages. Yet, as they make this argument,

361

the CICCE is pressing the Common Market for protection against feature films made for an American audience, transcending these same nine national borders to attract more than 40 percent of the total theater box-office revenues earned within the European Community.[3]

The CICCE also has denied that the European film industry enjoys any special legal status within the Common Market, asserting that film is simply acting in reliance upon certain "exemptions" from European Community regulations granted the industry during the 1960s. As this assertion is being made, however, exemptions previously granted to a wide variety of industries have been revoked, while film continues to receive extensions of time for developing a program for voluntary compliance with Common Market law.

If answers to these fundamental questions are somewhat inconclusive, the problem may lie in assumptions implicit in the questions themselves. Is it accurate to assume, for example, that an economically backward film industry will of necessity be less valuable to a nation than a modern, mass appeal-oriented film system? Similarly, must law be compelled to overlook any distinctions in the nature of those industries intimately related to national identity, as opposed to those which simply produce or distribute goods for general use?

If these assumptions can be challenged in the case of the film industry, then it may be more useful to examine the actual economic and legal status of European film from a broader perspective than that offered by either economics or law alone. Viewing national film within the context of Common Market policy during the past two decades may suggest applications of economic and legal theory particularly relevant to this mass medium. On a larger scale, it may also suggest how national and international regulatory bodies might apply such special principles to a more extensive range of mass media issues in the future.

The European Economic Community, which was formed by the Treaty of Rome in 1957, marked a radical departure from economic nationalism of the past. The treaty pledged its six member states to:

—the elimination, as among member states, of custom duties and of quantitative restrictions on the import and export of goods and all other measures having equivalent effect. . . .

—the abolition, as among member states, of obstacles to freedom of movement of persons, services and capital.

—the institution of a system ensuring that competition in the Common Market is not distorted.[4]

These and other pledges described as "principles" of the European Community in ARTICLE 3 of the treaty became fully effective on 31 December 1969. Yet, even during the transitional period, as national manufacturing, agricultural, and service industries adjusted to each new stage of the merger, the commission (the executive body of the Common Market) began legal actions to compel compliance with these basic principles.

As early as 1963, for example, the commission was successful in having the Court of Justice of the European Community strike down as illegal a national tariff of a member state found to be in violation of Treaty of Rome provisions (*Van Gend en Loos* vs *Netherland* [26–62], *Common Market Law Reports* [cited hereafter as *CMLR*], 1963–64, pp. 85–86; see also *Costa* vs *ENEL* [6/64], *CMLR*, 1964–65, pp. 197–98). Similarly, in 1964 the commission was able to establish the principle that freedom of movement of workers required that member states repeal any laws reducing social benefits paid to nationals working in other member states (*Mrs. Hoekstra-Unger* vs *Bestuum van de Bedrijfsvereniging von Detailhandel em Ambachten* [75–63], *Common Market Reports* [CCH], 1964, p. 7377).

During the mid-1960s the commission appeared somewhat less vigorous in its campaign for compliance with basic Treaty of Rome principles. The merging of both the European Coal and Steel Community and the European Atomic Energy Community with the Economic Community tended to complicate the enforcement role of the commission. But an even more divisive force emerged from clashes between Gaulist France and other member states. These political conflicts led to a shift in power from the bureaucratic commission to the far more nationally oriented Common Market Council of Ministers, but as the decade ended, the commission appeared to regain the initiative.[5]

When the Treaty of Rome became fully effective in 1970, the commission was not only vested with enforcement responsibility for nearly every phase of economic activity occurring in existing member states, but also faced the prospect of expanding national membership which would raise the cumulative GNP of its domain to a level closely rivaling that of the United States.[6] Under these circumstances, prompt action was necessary to establish broad and generally applicable principles of Common Market law, lest the sheer weight of specific legal questions raised by each section of the treaty overwhelm the commission.[7]

Although direct tariffs against the flow of member state goods have all but disappeared, ingenious indirect restrictions having an "equivalent effect" have now been challenged successfully in a wide range of cases before the Court of Justice. Measures as innocuous as labeling requirements of unusual complexity which are applicable only to imported goods, or special standards for all nondomestic products, have been found by the court to operate as tariff restrictions rather than consumer protection laws, and thus to be void in effect.[8]

Since 1970 the commission has challenged various national laws which have the equivalent effect of a tariff in actions involving more than fifty different European industries. In 1976 alone, the agency commenced more than 100 actions before the Court of Justice to overturn restrictions upon the movement of goods among Common Market nations, but during this entire period not one film-related law or practice has been challenged.[9]

There seems little question that a number of film laws and several common practices in the field are more restrictive in nature than those "equivalent effect" laws and practices already challenged in other industries.[10] Foreign film licensing requirements, for example, tend to be far more burdensome and much less closely related to national interest than prescription-drug licensing laws. Yet the latter have been struck down while national bureaucracies continue to impose cumbersome filing requirements upon foreign film distributors. Similarly, taxes imposed on certain categories of film, such as "pornographic" films in France,[11] seem clearly in conflict with the uniform taxation provisions of the• Treaty of Rome, and yet such measures have never been challenged by the commission.

If anything, the commission and the Court of Justice have been even more stringent in voiding national laws which impose even the slightest citizenship qualification upon any type of employment. The court struck down a French law which set a quota of French employees for each French merchant ship, despite evidence that this quota was not followed in actual practice (*French Merchant Seamen* [167/73], *CMLR*, 1974, p. 216). Even in the professions, the court has held that no law may relate competency to nationality, so that a qualified "advocate" or attorney must be admitted to practice without regard for citizenship (*Reyners* vs *Belgian State* [2/74], *CMLR*, 1974, p. 305).

Soon after the *French Seamen* case, the French and Danish film industries entered into a co-production agreement which established a specific quota of French and Danish film workers to be employed in each co-production effort. In response to "unofficial" expressions of concern from commission officials, the French film representatives simply declared that the agreement paralleled a number of other co-production agreements already in effect among other Common Market film groups, and would not be modified until those other agreements were also modified. To date the commission has made no effort to bring this clear violation before the Court of Justice.[12]

Government grants-in-aid or subsidies to domestic industries have been approved by the commission only in special circumstances, because of their general tendency to "distort competition" within the European Community. Thus a recent effort of the Italian government to aid its textile industry in the expansion of worker benefits to conform to European Community standards was challenged by the commission and struck down by the court because this special treatment tended to favor the Italian industry unfairly in competition with other Common Market textile producers (*Aids to Italian Textile Industry* [173/73], *CMLR*, 1973, p. 593). In at least six of the nine Common Market nations, some type of national subsidy exists, offering special production loans, tax remissions, or theater box-office tax rebates to domestic films qualifying for such favored treatment.[13] Rather than face head-on this apparent violation of Economic Community law, the commission has simply asked that these subsidies operate uniformly throughout the Common Market nations. Even this mild request has been ignored with impunity by the European film industry.[14]

A recent memorandum prepared by the Internal Marketing section of the EC Commission lists numerous other national film practices and programs which appear to be in direct violation of Common Market law. These include restrictions upon investment and marketing rights, as well as the tariff, labor, and subsidy violations already detailed. Yet despite these allegations, the commission still awaits some proposal from the European film industry indicating how it intends to achieve eventual compliance with European Community law. In 1968 the commission granted the film industry certain exemptions from Common Market law in order to allow the industry time to make these adjustments, but by 1973 it seemed clear that nothing would be done without further commission pressure.

In that year the commission became more specific, recommending that film producers and distributors work through their national bureaucracies to seek abolishment of export aids designed to encourage film sales to other member states, import restrictions imposed upon film from other member states, and to work towards uniformity in, if not the termination of, existing domestic film aid systems.[15]

When the next two years brought no improvement in the situation, the commission convened an informal meeting with CICCE in 1975. This meeting was to inform the group that the commission's success in its anticompetitive enforcement campaigns, coupled with Court of Justice decisions supporting the campaign, made it imperative that the film industry move quickly to end its violations of law, or face concerted commission action.[16]

By 1977, finally aware that European film producers and distributors were either unwilling or unable to work for voluntary compliance with Common Market rules, the commission again convened a meeting with CICCE. It demanded that the industry come up with some means of guaranteeing free circulation of film within the Economic Community, and with some system for abolishing aid schemes and labor quota systems based upon nationality.

In June 1977 Dimitri Balachoff, president of the CICCE, publicly presented a plan to encourage international cooperation in the film industry. The plan called for (a) all films originating in the Common Market to be subject to the same taxation in every member nation, (b) all films originating in the community to enjoy a single level of state aid in their country of origin and a uniform rate of aid in all other member nations, and (c) films originating in a Common Market nation to obtain supplemental aid in each country supported by taxes to be levied against box-office receipts, television rights paid for feature films, and taxes paid on television receivers. This plan, which also included a proposal for limiting the number of feature films which could be shown on domestic television systems each year, was destined to "unite" the European film industry as never before. Within days the British, Italian, and German trade organizations were attacking the plan as unrealistic, utopian, and beyond Balachoff's authority as head of the CICCE. The clamor for his resignation as leader of the organization grew louder and louder.[17]

With the failure of the Balachoff plan to create the consensus necessary for voluntary reform, national CICCE delegations have already begun efforts to reduce the pressures of the commission upon film industry operations. The Italians are attempting to shift issues of film competitive practices to the European Communities Parliament, a body with extremely limited powers. At the same time the French delegation, by striving to convince the Council of Ministers to assert jurisdiction, hopes to argue their case to a much more nationalistic forum.[18]

Whatever the eventual outcome of these political maneuvers, the fact remains that for the past two decades of Common Market existence, the film industry has been virtually unique in being able to operate without liability for violation of any of the primary legal principles of the Treaty of Rome. Even if the commission should move to challenge certain film industry activities in the future, this period of forebearance already suggests a special status for film enjoyed by no other European industry.

In the economic realm, apparent financial prosperity disguises underlying money problems of the Common Market film industry. Feature films earn approximately $600 million annually in Common Market nations, and at least 200,000 people are employed by the industries of the nine nations of the European Community.[19] These figures, however, tend to obscure patterns of attrition and stagnation which are eroding the financial foundation of film in several European nations.

The first level of obfuscation arises from divergent definitions of "nationalism" for purposes of providing loans, grants, or tax benefits to "domestic" film activities. There is no uniform, Common Market-wide standard setting the degree of national financing, production participation, and distribution rights necessary for qualification. As a result, it is not possible to determine from these gross revenues what portion of earnings is actually available to support further filmmaking in Western Europe, and what portion is diverted directly through multinational corporations or indirectly through covert agreements to interests outside the community.[20]

A second barrier to analysis involves the complex, cartellike arrangements among European film companies themselves, which tend to prevent revenues from being distributed evenly across the entire range of film companies operating within the Common Market. Small companies have difficulty surviving in this environment, which is becoming even more hostile as interest rates for film loans in some European nations are rising to 20 or 25 percent per year.[21]

In reality, then, gross revenues suggest little about either the funds generated for new European films, or the number of European film companies sharing in these revenues.

Finally, gross revenues reflect inflationary trends that diminish their value, but do not suggest the massive decrease in theater attendance that has occurred over the past two decades. Between 1956 and 1973, film attendance in Common Market nations decreased by almost two-thirds. A 600-percent increase in Common Market television households during the same period is obviously responsible for a substantial portion of this loss, with CICCE officials contending that 95 percent of their audience for each European Community film now views it on television, rather than in a film theater.[22]

Sentiment appears almost unanimous that in all Common Market nations, with the possible exceptions of Italy and France, film faces the most severe financial crisis since World War II, with no real solution in sight.

In an effort to discover remedies for the financial ills, the CICCE conducted a precise analysis of those films from the United States which had been most successful in European theaters. The study revealed what most filmmakers had suspected—that films made in the United States were in general far more carefully designed for mass appeal than their European counterparts. American films, for example, were produced with budgets five to ten times as large as the typical European film, and tended to stress general, basic themes rather than the more particularized statements of national filmmakers in Europe. In addition, dialogue represented only 30 to 40 percent of the total film content of an American film, while most European films contained 60 to 70 percent dialogue. Thus, American films not only are less likely to be culturally bound in theme, but they are also less expensive and less difficult to convert for domestic consumption through dubbing or subtitling.[23]

The study gave European filmmakers an opportunity to reaffirm their cultural superiority by pointing out quite correctly that to reduce American competition by copying its qualities would be to sacrifice the very qualities they were attempting to preserve. Yet this exercise in self-righteousness did nothing to lessen the underlying economic difficulties the research had been commissioned to solve.

In reality, however, any improvement in the economic conditions being experienced by most European film companies would appear to demand something far more drastic than even a fundamental modification of film production or treatment. Nationalism in European film is maintained and enforced by a broad range of powerful political interests. Any effort to lower barriers in order to unify European film production efforts would confront not only the national film producers, distributors, and exhibitors, but strong trade unions, equipment manufacturers, banking institutions, and even a rather militant and well-organized national bureaucracy closely allied with the industry being regulated.[24]

There is little question that these national coalitions have been responsible for the hesitancy of the European Community Commission to challenge practices which seem clearly in violation of Common Market law. It could be argued, however, that these same coalitions are depriving film of the financial independence essential for artistic integrity.

The Balachoff Plan, precisely because it was designed to free film from a number of national controls, acted as a catalyst to unite the national interests in opposition. Government film administrators opposed the $320 million annual production revenue pool which would provide domestic film companies with an alternative source of funding, while film companies with close government relations were hostile to possible competition for funds previously earmarked for their organizations. Labor unions feared a reduction of their influence over local film hiring practices if foreign workers could compete for national jobs, and foreign film distributors saw in this unification the creation of a more powerful bargaining entity to face in future negotiations.

The commission itself has proposed several plans for unification, including, as in Balachoff's proposal, inducements for cooperation such as a market-wide effort to limit television usage of feature films and increase the price paid for each film, to reduce VAT taxes imposed upon film in some Common Market nations, and to provide low-interest-rate loans for film production. Even such potential benefits have not been able to overcome nationalistic resistance to a broader, Common Market orientation for film.[25]

National interests in film may remain powerful enough in the immediate future to thwart any efforts to consolidate political and economic power at the Common Market level, but they appear to lack the capacity as national entities to control either those domestic television or foreign film distribution forces which continue to erode their financial position. Thus, while they may be successful in rejecting either an "American" approach to film production or a European Communities' approach to film financing and marketing, the price that must be paid for such rejection is growing dependence upon national governments for political protection and economic support. Under these circumstances, it might be difficult to judge which alternative truly offers the greatest guarantee of artistic integrity.

The growing dependence on government results in part from the effect of Common Market laws upon the national film archives. Even the most superficial of legal studies would criticize the lack of uniformity evident in the treatment of the Common Market film industry. National tariffs, restrictive trade and labor agreements, and government subsidies prevalent in film have been challenged and voided in numerous other industries. Inability to conform to these general legal standards has compelled each national film industry to seek the protection of its government, and thus to become even more dependent upon that government for survival. A sudden shift in government position, or even less vigorous government support, could leave the industry exposed to massive legal attack. In essence, then, rather than encouraging broad cooperative effort across the Common Market, these laws have forced the film industry to become a ward of the state, more vulnerable and thus more committed to national control than ever before.

During the 1960s, while the commission was still in the process of drafting regulations pursuant to the Treaty of Rome and deciding on enforcement policies to test before the Court of Justice, special rules could have been drafted for the film industry, which traditionally had operated with a far greater range of internal controls and protections than other industries. A timetable could have been adopted to serve as a schedule for controlling the implementation of Common Market laws. This would have allowed time for conformance to the law and for offering inducements to lessen the opposition of national interest groups. But instead of enforcing specific and special rules for film, the commission gradually exempted certain film practices from prosecution, and requested cooperation in achieving eventual compliance from those same interest groups which saw the entire Common Market structure as a threat to their own positions.

Once the grace period had ended without result, and Court of Justice decisions compelled total compliance of all industries without exemption, film was suddenly left without any legal defense against commission action. Yet, because of the close political relationship between film and national governments, the commission continues to threaten film without taking action, thereby constantly reinforcing the dependence of film upon national governments for protection. Thus, the end result of failing to be flexible in application of general legal principles in this field has been to transform film more completely than ever before into a nationally dominated mass medium.

The irony of the situation is that there would appear to be far more advantages for European film in strong organization at the Common Market level than in continuing operation at the national level. At present, sheltered by bureaucratic rules, coerced by trade union restrictions, and nurtured by domestic subsidies, no national film industry has the independence or autonomy necessary, for example, to demand of its government protection from government-owned or -controlled domestic television competition, or to obtain restrictions upon film imported from the United States.

The divisiveness of nationalism limits economic or political options, while unity at the Common Market level would provide leverage against national policies designed to produce (or at least resulting in) further dependence upon national administrations. In the final analysis, then, the major criticism of Common Market law as it pertains to film would seem to be not that it has been applied improperly, but that it was not shaped specifically to encourage an economic union of benefit both to the film industry and to the European Community.

It might well be suggested that financial salvation of national film in the Common Market lies in increasing earnings through emphasis upon the production of mass appeal features. While this solution might reduce film company dependence upon national financing, it would also tend to reduce the attraction of European film as a unique product of national culture. The fact that one type of economic solution may not be feasible, however, does not indicate that no means for improving the financial independence of film exists. Financial studies tend to view film as an "industry" defined by its traditional production, distribution, and exhibition mechanisms. It might be more useful, instead, to isolate from this total industry mechanism those elements of film as a mass medium which make it unique, in order to determine whether any or all portions of the existing industry structure are necessary to preserve that uniqueness. It is true, of course, that it is "existing structures" rather than "unique elements" which generate political pressure, but until such an assessment is made, there will not even be a justification for policies that might attempt to reduce the dependence of film upon any nonessential structures in the production or distribution process. If it should be found, for example, that the element which makes film unique is its mode of production alone, then some other mode of delivery might be encouraged to strengthen film's economic efficiency, and thus reduce its degree of dependence upon government grants or protection.

Thus, in the last analysis, the cruel analogy of the German Economic Ministry official[26] may in fact be accurate. Perhaps in this era of television dominance, with direct broadcast satellite distribution looming just ahead, the narrow and somewhat archaic foundation of domestic theater box-office receipts supporting national feature film efforts in Western Europe must be expanded to include other channels, in order to provide sufficient revenues for continued production of such films in the future.[27] Here again it would seem that regional organization at the level of the Common Market, or possibly the European Broadcasting Union, would be far more likely to be able to develop and provide such services than individual European governments.

The purpose of this study has not been to assess the validity of any specific legal or economic solution to the problems facing European film today. Rather it is to suggest that in this case, as in all future studies attempting to discover the factors shaping functions of mass media, it is essential to seek relationships more complex than those posited by either law or economics alone. Legal analysis assumes that statutes or regulations should require all those within the same legal classification to assume the same legal responsibilties. In cases where this may not be equitable, it is important to establish that the unique characteristics of film or some other mass medium require a separate legal classification. Similarly, traditional economic analysis assumes that the proper concern for each industry is to increase efficiency and thereby increase profitability. To the extent that this approach overlooks other considerations of vital importance, it is obligatory to develop techniques for isolating those characteristics and to indicate their unique value.

Lacking such a perspective, future debates are likely to replicate much of the somewhat sterile argumentation now taking place in Western Europe about the "privileged" status of film, or mass production methods to increase its popular appeal. If such dialogue often appears simplistic or elemental, it may simply reflect a failure to perform the essential process of synthesis necessary to make legal and economic principles directly applicable to mass media policy formulation.

Notes
Bibliography
Contributors
Index

Notes

1. Vitascope/Cinématographe: Initial Patterns of American Film Industrial Practice

1. Gordon Hendricks, *The Kinetoscope* (New York: Beginnings of American Film, 1966), p. 3; Memo, "Kinetograph Case: 1900," Edison National Historic Site, West Orange, N.J. (hereafter cited as Edison Archive).
2. Terry Ramsaye, *A Million and One Nights: A History of the Motion Picture* (New York: Simon, 1926), p. 119.
3. Thomas Edison to Eadweard Muybridge, 8 Feb. 1894, Edison Archive.
4. Hendricks, *Kinetoscope*, p. 79.
5. Raff to Thomas R. Lombard, 31 May 1895, Raff and Gammon Collection, Baker Library, Harvard Univ. (hereafter cited as Raff and Gammon Collection).
6. Ibid.
7. George Sadoul, *Louis Lumière* (Paris: Editions Seghers, 1964), p. 148.
8. Raff to Messrs. Daniel and Armat, 17 Jan. 1896, Raff and Gammon Collection.
9. Oliver Read and Walter L. Welch, *From Tin Foil to Stereo* (New York: Bobbs-Merrill, 1959), p. 110.
10. Raff and Gammon to M. Hendersholt, 4 Apr. 1896, Raff and Gammon Collection.
11. Vitascope Company Catalogue, 1896, Crawford Collection, Museum of Modern Art.
12. A. F. Reiser to Edison Kinetoscope Co., 29 Feb. 1896, Raff and Gammon Collection.
13. Raff and Gammon to Armat, 21 Mar. 1896, Raff and Gammon Collection.
14. Raff and Gammon to A. Bial, 7 Apr. 1896, Raff and Gammon Collection.
15. Maxwell F. Marcuse, *This Was New York* (New York: Carlton Pr., 1965), p. 199.
16. *New York Journal*, 4 Apr. 1896, clipping in Raff and Gammon Collection.
17. *New York Dramatic Mirror*, 4 July 1896, p. 17; 11 July, p. 17; 18 July, p. 17.
18. Robert Grau, *The Theatre of Science: A Volume of Progress and Achievement in the Motion Picture Industry* (New York: Broadway Pub. Co., 1914), p. 9.
19. A. F. Reiser to Raff and Gammon, 8 May 1896, Raff and Gammon Collection.
20. P. T. Kiefaber to Raff, 11 June 1896, Raff and Gammon Collection.
21. A. Holland to Raff, 9 Sept. 1896, Raff and Gammon Collection.
22. Sadoul, *Lumière*, p. 67.
23. Hixom and Wollam to Raff and Gammon, 23 June, 1896, Raff and Gammon Collection.
24. A. F. Reiser to Raff and Gammon, undated but filed with 1896 letters, Raff and Gammon Collection.
25. Hixom and Wollam to the Vitascope Co., 28 Aug. 1896, Raff and Gammon Collection.
26. Sadoul, *Lumière*, p. 41.
27. Hendricks, *Kinetoscope*, p. 140.

28. Raff and Gammon to Maguire and Baucus, 25 Aug. 1896, Raff and Gammon Collection.
29. Sadoul, *Lumière*, p. 134.
30. Reiser to Vitascope Co., 24 Nov. 1896; Hixom and Wollam to Raff and Gammon, 9 Dec. 1896, both in Raff and Gammon Collection.
31. Sadoul, *Lumière*, pp. 135–36.

2. Motion Picture Exhibition in Manhattan, 1906–1912: Beyond the Nickelodeon

1. Eugene L. Connelly, "The Life Story of Harry Davis," *Pittsburgh Sun-Telegraph*, 3 Jan. 1940; Alexander Parker, "Fifty Years Ago," *Box Office*, 4 June 1955, pp. 20–21.
2. See Benjamin B. Hampton, *A History of the Movies* (New York: Covici, Friede, 1931), pp. 44–48; Lewis Jacobs, *The Rise of the American Film* (New York: Harcourt, 1939), pp. 55–57; Robert Sklar, *Movie-made America* (New York: Random, 1975), pp. 14–20, 30–32; Garth Jowett, *Film: The Democratic Art* (Boston: Little, 1975), pp. 31–42.
3. Jacobs, p. 56.
4. Sklar, pp. 14–17.
5. Hampton, pp. 45, 47.
6. Joseph H. North, *The Early Development of the Motion Picture: 1887–1909* (New York: Arno Pr., 1973), p. 239.
7. Sklar, p. 30.
8. Russell Merritt, "Nickelodeon Theatres: 1905–1914; Building an Audience for the Movies," in Tino Balio, ed., *The American Film Industry* (Madison: Univ. of Wisconsin Pr., 1976), p. 60.
9. Russell Merritt, "Nickelodeon Theatres," *AFI Reports*, May 1975, p. 4.
10. Douglas Gomery, "A History of Milwaukee's Movie Theatres," unpublished paper, pp. 3–5.
11. Thomas Kessner, *The Golden Door: Italian and Jewish Immigrant Mobility in New York City, 1880–1915* (New York: Oxford Univ. Pr., 1977), p. 5.
12. The principal sources of data for this study were the listings of "Moving Picture Exhibitions" of *Trow's Business Directory of Greater New York* for the years 1906–12, inclusive, and theatrical and motion picture trade journals from the period. It is, of course, possible that these listings are not exhaustive. However, the 1908 *Trow's* list was compared with a similar one prepared by Edison employee Joseph McCoy in July 1908 and found to correlate highly. The McCoy list is contained at the Edison Archive.
13. *Variety*, 26 Jan. 1907, p. 12.
14. Kessner, p. 131; Thomas M. Henderson, *Tammany Hall and the New Immigrants* (New York: Arno Pr., 1976), pp. 17–19.
15. Kessner, p. 136.
16. *Insurance Maps of the City of New York Borough of Manhattan* (New York: Sanhorn Map Co., 1905).
17. Alvin F. Harlow, *Old Bowery Days* (New York: Appleton, 1931), pp. 367–401.
18. Helen Campbell, Thomas W. Know, and Thomas Byrnes, *Daylight and Darkness; or, Lights and Shadows of New York* (Hartford: The Hartford Pub. Co., 1895), p. 211.
19. *Variety*, 19 Dec. 1908, p. 13.
20. Henderson, p. 78.
21. Ibid., p. 49.
22. Quoted in Grace Mayer, *Once upon a City* (New York: Macmillan, 1958), p. 58.

23. Henderson, p. 20.
24. Charles Lockwood, *Manhattan Moves Uptown: An Illustrated History* (Boston: Houghton, 1976), p. 306; Gilbert Osofsky, *Harlem: The Making of a Ghetto* (New York: Harper, 1963), p. 89.
25. Osofsky, p. 79.
26. *New York Clipper*, 29 Apr. 1889.
27. Quoted in Grace Mayer, p. 29.
28. Grace Mayer, p. 50.
29. Lockwood, p. 319.
30. Kessner, pp. 28–31.
31. Ibid., pp. 30–31.
32. *Variety*, 9 Nov. 1907, p. 5; 15 Dec. 1907, p. 33.
33. Ibid., 14 Dec. 1907, p. 13; 15 Feb. 1908, p. 4; 29 Feb., p. 6; 14 Dec. 1907, p. 33.
34. Hampton, p. 116; Jacobs, p. 167; Jowett, *Film*, p. 31.
35. *Moving Picture World* (hereafter cited as *MPW*) 15, no. 9, 28 Aug. 1909, p. 288.
36. Ibid., 16 Nov. 1907, p. 593.
37. Ibid., 4 May 1907, p. 124.
38. Ibid., 29 Aug. 1908, p. 152.
39. *Variety*, 19 Dec. 1908, p. 13; 12 Dec. 1908, p. 12; 1 Oct. 1910, p. 10.
40. Bosley Crowther, *The Lion's Share* (New York: Dutton, 1957), pp. 23–39.
41. *MPW*, 11 Sept. 1927, p. 2.
42. *Variety*, 28 Aug. 1909, p. 8. Fuller discussion of the rise of small-time vaudeville and its interaction with "high class" vaudeville and legitimate theater is contained in Robert C. Allen, *Vaudeville and Film 1895–1915: A Study in Media Interaction* (New York: Arno Pr., 1980).
43. *Variety*, 11 Dec. 1909, p. 7.

3. Monopoly in Motion Picture Production and Distribution: 1908–1915

1. See particularly Edison v. American Mutoscope & Biograph Co., 151 Fed. 767 (2d Cir. 1907); Edison v. American Mutoscope & Biograph Co., 144 Fed. 121 (C.C.S.D.N.Y. 1906); American Mutoscope & Biograph Co. v. Edison Mfg. Col., 137 Fed. 262 (C.C.D.N.J. 1905); Edison v. American Mutoscope & Biograph Co. 127 Fed. 361 (C.C.S.D.N.Y. 1904); Armat v. Edison, 125 Fed. 939 (2d Cir. 1903); Edison v. Lubin, 122 Fed. 240 (3d Cir. 1903); Edison v. American Mutoscope Co., 114 Fed. 926 (2d. Cir. 1902); Edison v. American Mutoscope Co., 110 Fed. 660 (C.C.S.D.N.Y. 1901); Edison v. Schneider, 100 Fed. 1007 (C.C.S.D.N.Y. 1900).
2. Record, vol. 3, p. 1514 United States v. Motion Picture Patents Co., in the District Court of the United States for the Eastern District of Pennsylvania (hereafter cited as Record). Vols. 1 through 7 available at the Law Library, Univ. of California, Los Angeles, Calif. Microfilm of the transcript is also available at the Princeton Univ. Library.
3. Ramsaye, pp. 471–72.
4. Record, vol. 1 at 21.
5. Ibid., vol. 7 at 3479.
6. Ibid., vol. 1 at 12.
7. Ibid., vol. 7 at 3895–3900.
8. See ibid., vol. 6 at 3326.
9. Ibid., vol. 7 at 3487.
10. Ibid.

11. It is noteworthy that no attempt was made to control the activities of the film laborato-
    ries whose function it was to develop the negatives and print motion picture positives
    for distribution to theaters.
12. Record, vol. 1 at 558–82.
13. See W. K. Laurie Dickson, "A Brief History of the Kinetograph Kinetoscope and the
    Kineto-Phonograph," *Journal of the Society of Motion Picture Engineers*, 1933,
    pp. 442–44. But see Goodwin Film & Camera Co. v. Eastman Kodak Co., 207 Fed. 351
    (W.D.N.Y. 1913), in which Rev. Hannibal Goodwin was found to have prior rights to
    the basic process of manufacturing flexible film per se, which resulted in an out-of-
    court settlement of $5 million by Eastman to the Goodwin estate.
14. Record, vol. 7 at 3488–3514.
15. By terms of an amended agreement, dated 6 June 1912, with the licensed manufac-
    turers and importers, the licensees were required to pay royalties directly to the
    licensor.
16. In addition to the manufacturers and importers mentioned previously, the Gaumont
    Company was licensed, by terms of an agreement dated 2 March 1909, to manufacture
    and lease "talking motion pictures." Record, vol. 1 at 398–420. The Kinemacolor
    Company of America, by terms of an agreement dated 4 Aug. 1913, was licensed to
    manufacture and lease colored motion pictures, Record, Vol. 3 at 1335–51. However,
    neither of these ventures amounted to much in those early days.
17. Record, vol. 7 at 3513.
18. See ibid., vol. 7 at 3517–19.
19. Ibid., vol. 1 at 87–94.
20. Ibid., vol. 7 at 3520.
21. Ibid., vol. 7 at 3518.
22. Ibid., vol. 7 at 3519.
23. Ibid., vol. 1 at 66.
24. Ibid., vol. 7 at 3521.
25. According to the testimony of Harry M. Marvin, vice-president of the Motion Picture
    Patents Company, there were approximately 6,000 exhibitors in the United States in
    1909, and he estimated that three or four thousand of these became licensees. How-
    ever, those remaining outside the fold were for the most part, no doubt, small and
    relatively unimportant. Ibid., vol. 1 at 27.
26. See ibid., vol. 1 at 41.
27. Ibid., vol. 1 at 109.
28. Ibid., vol. 1 at 105.
29. Ibid., vol. 1 at 51.
30. Ibid., vol. 1 at 93, 762.
31. Ibid., vol. 1 at 104.
32. One of the early announcements to exhibitors stated that the objectives of the Motion
    Picture Patents Company were: (1) "To insure to the manufacturer a fair and reason-
    able price for his film so as to enable him to maintain and improve the quality of his
    pictures." (2) "By reason of the high quality of . . . (licensed) pictures . . . to eliminate
    the cheap and inferior foreign films which have been forced upon the market." (3) "To
    prevent the renter from supplying scratched and worn out film." (4) "To furnish . . . an
    adequate variety and supply of first-class subjects." (5) "To afford the legitimate ex-
    hibitor protection from ruinous and' unfair competition by refusing to license or sup-
    ply licensed film to a new exhibitor attempting to start a show where not required by
    public demand and where the competition would injuriously affect an existing li-
    censed theatre." Ibid., at 98.

33. Ibid., at 258.

34. Ibid., vol. 3 at 1737.

35. Ibid., vol. 2 at 931; vol. 3 at 1571.

36. Ibid., vol. 1 at 393–94.

37. For supporting evidence, see for example, 1 Record 29, 36, 45, 47, 50, 52; 2 Record 930 (circulars to film rental exchanges); 1 Record 60–61, 64, 66, 69, 71–82; 3 Record 1299–1300, 1302 (exchange bulletins); 1 Record 448–49, 451–54, 456–65, 2 Record 672, 688, 692, 694, 696, 805–8, 819, 823, 1040, 1044, 1047, 1064–66, 1070–71, 1074–76, 1130, 1142, 1164, 1219–20, 1225, 1227–28; 3 Record 1280 (letters to individual exchanges). See also 1 Record 87, 95, 97, 99; 2 Record 1061 (circular letters to exhibitors); 1 Record 104–5, 108, 111–12, 114–17; 3 Record 1571 (exhibitors' bulletins); 1 Record 455; 2 Record 864–65, 868, 876, 901, 903, 975, 1020–22, 1073, 1086, 1159, 1166, 1242; 3 Record 1373, 1406, 1421 (letters to individual exhibitors).

38. Record, vol. 1 at 301–2.

39. Ibid., vol. 3 at 1305.

40. Ibid.

41. See ibid., vol. 7 at 3535–39.

42. See ibid., vol. 8 at 3463; vol. 3 at 1351–55, 1357–1423.

43. Ibid., vol. 7 at 3540–51.

44. See p. (7).

45. Record, vol. 3 at 1362–89.

46. See ibid., vol. 7 at 3552–58.

47. See "Roosevelt African Pictures Turn out Splendidly," *The Film Index*, 19 Mar. 1910, p. 1, and "Roosevelt Pictures Release—April 18," *The Film Index*, 26 Mar. 1910, p. 1.

48. Record, vol. 1 at 53–58, 188–90.

49. For example, Carl Laemmle, who later organized Universal Film Company, withdrew from the combine in April 1909 and took his seven exchanges with him. 3 Record 1439. *The Film Index*, 1 May 1909, p. 3.

50. See Record, vol. 1 at 77–78, 282.

51. Ibid., vol. 6 at 3161–62.

52. Ibid., vol. 1 at 202–7.

53. Ibid., vol. 6 at 3220.

54. Ibid., vol. 1 at 188–99.

55. Ibid., vol. 2 at 672–73; vol. 3 at 1698.

56. Ibid., vol. 2 at 691–93.

57. Ibid., vol. 1 at 199–200.

58. Ibid., vol. 6 at 3159, 3156.

59. Ibid., vol. 1 at 188–90.

60. Ibid., vol. 2 at 208.

61. See *MPW*, vol. 11; p. 106.

62. See W. W. Hodkinson, "Picture Theatre Management," *The Film Index*, 19 Mar. 1960, p. 8; 26 Mar. 1910, p. 8.

63. Record, vol. 1 at 548–49.

64. The division of net profit among the companies for 1911, after payment of dividends on preferred and common stock, was as follows: Pathé-Frères, $164,965.92; Vitagraph Company of America, $149,919.35; Thomas A. Edison, Inc., $122,771.31; Selig-Polyscope Co., $109,703.03; Biograph Co., $104,907.61; Essanay Film Manufacturing Co., $102,316.70; Lubin Manufacturing Co., $101,370.65; Kalem Co., $90,833.31; George Kleine, $77,308.54; George Méliès, $31,483.56.

65. Record, vol. 6 at 3197–99.

66. Ibid., vol. 5 at 2890; vol. 1 at 533–35.
67. Ibid., vol. 2 at 1120.
68. *MPW*, vol. 4, p. 187.
69. Grau, p. 44.
70. See *MPW*, vol. 4, pp. 231, 359, 588.
71. Between 1909 and 1911, the Patents Company brought twenty-one suits under the camera patent, no. 12037, ten suits under the Latham (loop) patent, no. 707,934. In 1912 and 1913 three suits were reportedly brought under camera patent reissue no. 13329. Because of delays, technical reversals, and genuine weaknesses in patent position, the Motion Picture Patents Company gained little permanent relief from the legal actions directed against alleged infringers of its letters patent, although it undoubtedly had a temporary adverse effect on independent efforts. Record, vol. 6 at 3170–71, 3391–92.
72. According to a list of exchanges whose licenses were cancelled or terminated by the Motion Picture Patents Company, fifteen of these licenses were cancelled in the first six months of 1909. Therefore, in a real sense the Patents Co. was an important contributor to the independent problem. Ibid., vol. 1, at 188–90.
73. See *MPW*, vol. 4, pp. 387, 480–81.
74. Ibid., vol. 5, p. 681.
75. See Record, vol. 3 at 1433–56; vol. 7 at 3517–21; vol. 6 at 3341–46; vol. 1 at 389; vol. 2 at 824–26, 886, concerning replevin suits; and Ramsaye, pp. 525, 494, 533, concerning the trust's extralegal means of repossessing films.
76. See *MPW*, vol. 4, p. 511; Record, vol. 3 at 1426–58.
77. See *MPW*, vol. 4, pp. 134, 151, 658, 538.
78. Ibid., pp. 110, 319, 607.
79. Ibid., p. 690; vol. 5, p. 586; see also Record, vol. 3 at 1735; vol. 5 at 2991 concerning "raiding of personnel."
80. *MPW*, vol. 5, p. 866.
81. John Drinkwater, *The Life and Adventures of Carl Laemmle*, New York: Putnam's, 1931; *MPW*, vol. 8, p. 4.
82. Although during the shortage conditions of early 1909 it appears that independent prices were higher both at the manufacturer and at the exchange levels, there was a strong tendency as the independent product became more plentiful for prices to seek lower levels. See *MPW*, vol. 4, p. 436; Record, vol. 4 at 2274, 2279, 2283.
83. *MPW*, vol. 4, pp. 424, 436, 618; vol. 5, p. 36.
84. See ibid., vol. 5, p. 410; vol. 6, p. 213, concerning rule violations. The "going price" for unlicensed films at that time was about ten cents per foot net, for regular releases, which was approximately the same as the standing order price charged by licensed manufacturers on regular (not noninflammable) stock after taking into account the 10 percent discount. *MPW*, vol. 6, pp. 15, 164, and 839.
85. Ibid., vol. 6, p. 549; vol. 5, 2872; vol. 6, p. 1027.
86. Ibid., pp. 724, 893, 1037.
87. Ibid., vol. 7, pp. 74–75; vol. 6, p. 839.
88. Record, vol. 5 at 2874–76; 3026–27.
89. *MPW*, vol. 12, pp. 34, 707.
90. Ibid., pp. 807, 911; Record, vol. 5 at 2870.
91. Less than two weeks later, Adam Kessel, Jr., and C. O. Baumann, owners of the New York Motion Picture Company and the Bison brand, deserted Universal and went over to the other camp. *MPW*, vol. 13, p. 525; see also Record, vol. 5 at 2866–67, concerning profitability of independent motion picture activity.

92. Although motion picture production costs varied then as now, the typical cost of producing films, or manufacturing, as it was then known, at that time was approximately $1 per negative foot, i.e., $1,000 per reel. According to Motion Picture Patents Company figures the number of places in the United States in which motion pictures were exhibited, as of 18 Dec. 1911, totaled 11,441, which included 6,236 licensees and 5,205 nonlicensees. This, of course, was in addition to the hundreds of legitimate theaters scattered throughout the country which were used to present live attractions. Record, vol. 5, at 3032–33.

93. Albert E. Smith and Phil Koury, *Two Reels and a Crank*, (Garden City, N.Y.: Doubleday, 1952) pp. 217–18 and George Pratt, "A Myth Is As Good As a Milestone," *Image*, no. 47 (Nov. 1957): 210.

94. Pratt, "Myth," p. 210; *MPW*, vol. 16, pp. 496–97; Ramsaye, p. 607.

95. Record, vol. 3 at 1631–32.

96. *MPW*, vol. 21, p. 272.

97. See Record, vol. 4 at 1914; *MPW*, vol. 11, 1212.

98. *MPW*, vol. 14, p. 675.

99. United States v. Paramount Pictures, Inc. 66, Fed. Supp. 323, 334 (S.D. N.Y. 1976).

100. Smith, Koury, p. 259.

101. Adolph Zukor, *The Public is Never Wrong*, (New York; n.p., 1953), p. 61.

102. Ibid., pp. 73–74, 87.

103. *MPW*, vol. 19, pp. 323, 965; vol. 21, p. 844.

104. Ibid., p. 186.

105. United States v. Paramount Pictures, Inc. 334 U.S. 131, 156–57 (1948).

106. *MPW*, vol. 20, p. 1268.

107. Ibid., vol. 21, p. 264.

108. Smith, p. 260.

109. *MPW*, vol. 21, pp. 181–85.

110. Record, vol. 3 at 1632; vol. 4 at 2237, 2282, 2366.

111. Zukor, p. 126, and Smith, p. 259.

112. *MPW*, vol. 19, p. 787, and *MPW*, vol. 20, p. 371.

113. *MPW*, 30 Dec. 1916, p. 4256.

114. Ibid., p. 4260.

115. Zukor, p. 180.

116. Famous Players–Lasky Corp. 11 F.T.C. 108, 187, 203, 205 (1927).

117. Zukor, pp. 195.

118. See Ralph Cassady, "Impact of the Paramount Decision on Motion Picture Distribution and Price Making." *Southern California Law Review* 31 (1958) 150.

119. See *The Federal Antitrust Laws*, Commerce Clearing House, 1952.

120. Statutes, vol. 26 (1890), at 209.

121. See Record, vol. 7 at 3565.

122. Record, vol. 1 at 7.

123. United States v. Motion Picture Patents Company, 225 Federal (E.D. Pa. 1915) 800–11.

124. It is interesting that the collusive activities of the independently-controlled Motion Picture Distributing and Sales Company apparently did not disturb the government.

125. The court found that: "A further inducement and motive was (and these were also ends in view) the wish to relieve each other from the odium of infringement, to end contests which hampered the development of the art, to protect the morals of the public by the prevention of the exhibition of suggestive or otherwise improper pictures, to promote the progress of this branch of dramatic art by improving the character of shows both in the artistic merits and mechanical perfection of the display, and

generally to supply what, up to that time, the state had neglected to furnish, a regulating and governing authority over the entire motion picture business." United States v. Motion Picture Patents Co. 225 Federal (E.D. Pa. 1915) 800–11.

126. The Méliès Manufacturing Company was found by the court not to be a party to the combination, ibid.

127. Ibid.

128. Record, vol. 7 at 3923–27.

129. See Motion Picture Patents Co. v. Universal Film Manufacturing Co. 235 Federal (1916) 398.

130. 38 Statutes (1914) 730–31.

131. Motion Picture Patents Co. v. Universal Film Manufacturing Co. 243 U.S. (1917) 502, 518.

132. See Famous Players-Lasky Corp., 11 F.T.C. (1927) 187.

4. Hollywood's Movie Star System: A Historical Overview

1. See *New York Times*, 27 Feb. 1910, p. 8, and 7 Mar. 1910, p. 9; and Gerald D. McDonald, "Origin of the Star System," *Films in Review* 4 (Nov. 1953):449–58.

2. See F. M. Scherer, "Product Differentiation, Market Structure, and Competition," *Industrial Market Structure and Economic Performance* (Chicago: Rand McNally, 1970), chap. 14, pp. 346–78. It has been argued that each movie star is a monopoly, a unique personality, which is quite different from laborers in industries with less product differentiation. See Sidney R. Finkel and Vincent J. Tarascio, *Wage and Employment Theory* (New York: Ronald Pr., 1971), pp. 111–12.

3. See Thomas Simonet, *Regression Analysis of Prior Experience of Key Production Personnel as Predictors of Revenues from High Grossing Motion Pictures in American Release* (New York: Arno Pr., 1980).

4. Jeanne Thomas Allen, "The Decay of the Motion Picture Patents Company," *The American Film Industry*, ed. Tino Balio (Madison: The Univ. of Wisconsin Pr., 1976), p. 132; Lewis Jacobs, *Rise of the American Film* (New York: Harcourt, 1939), pp. 86–89; Ramsaye, p. 523; Hampton, p. 89.

5. Ralph Cassady, Jr., "Monopoly in Motion Picture Production and Distribution: 1908–1915," *Southern California Law Review* 32, no. 4 (Summer 1959):369. [reprinted herein, p. 51]

6. In Nov. 1910 an article in *MPW* indicated that it had only been in the last year that movie stars had been revealed to the public. *MPW* 7, no. 20 (12 Nov. 1910):1099.

7. Ibid., 6, no. 2 (15 Jan. 1910):50.

8. *Saint Louis Post-Dispatch*, Sunday, 27 Feb. 1910, p. 9.

9. Ibid., "Sunday Magazine," 6 Mar. 1910, p. 4.

10. "We Nail a Lie," *MPW* 6, no. 10 (12 Mar. 1910):635.

11. See Drinkwater.

12. Reported in *MPW* 6, no. 20 (21 May 1910):825. In a letter to me, 14 Jan. 1981, Thomas Gunning suggests that a feature article on Florence Turner actually appeared in the *New York Sun* in 1909. If true (I am unable to verify it), Vitagraph may have instituted the star system one year earlier than has generally been supposed.

13. *MPW* 7, no. 4 (23 July 1910):188.

14. Ibid., no. 13 (23 Sept. 1910):680.

15. Alexander Walker, *Stardom: The Hollywood Phenomenon* (New York: Stein, 1970), p. 37; McDonald, p. 452.

16. Salary information obtained from Tino Balio, *United Artists: The Company Built by the Stars* (Madison: Univ. of Wisconsin Pr., 1975), pp. 14–21; see Walker.

17. *Historical Statistics of the United States, Colonial Times to 1970,* U.S. Bureau of the Census, Washington, D.C., Series H 878–93, "Personal Consumption Expenditures for Recreation: 1909 to 1970," not adjusted for inflation (estimated for 1909 from combined category), still an increase of 150 percent if adjusted for inflation.

18. Balio, *United*, p. 15. *See also* Cassady [reprinted herein, p. 44]

19. Ibid.

20. Ibid., pp. 25–26.

21. Ibid., pp. 30–51, 73.

22. Ibid., p. 103.

23. See Aljean Harmetz, *The Making of "The Wizard of Oz"* (New York: Knopf, 1977), pp. 101–34; Walker, p. 244.

24. U.S. v. Paramount Pictures, Inc., U.S. #334, U.S. Supreme Court Records, Briefs, 1947, no. 79–86, pp. 3169 and 1797.

25. Balio, *United*, 98–99. For other views upon the emergence of Hollywood Unions, see chap. 11, Douglas Gomery, "Hollywood, the National Recovery Administration, and the Question of Monopoly Power"; Murray Ross, *Stars and Strikes* (New York: Columbia Univ., Pr., 1941), pp. 89–174.

26. Walker, p. 251.

27. Paul K. Perry, "Marketing and Attitude Research Applied to Motion Pictures." Paper given at International Gallup Conference, New Delhi, India (26 Mar. 1968).

28. Letter from Paul K. Perry, vice-president, Marketing and Attitude Research, The Gallup Organization, Inc., to Thomas Simonet, 22 Mar. 1978.

29. *Continuing Audit of Marquee Values,* Jan. 1942, contained in *Gallup Looks at the Movies,* (microfilm by American Institute of Public Opinion and Scholarly Resources, Wilmington, Del. 1979).

30. *Variety,* "Thirty-seventh Anniversary Issue," Jan. 1943, p. 58. See Gorham Kindem, "Hollywood's Movie Star System and the Film Industry in the 1940's," *Readings in Mass Communication: Selected Proceedings of the Fourth International Conference on Culture and Communication* (New York: Ablex, forthcoming).

31. Thomas Simonet, "Performers' Marquee Values in Relation to Top-Grossing Films" (paper delivered to the Society for Cinema Studies, Temple Univ., 5 Mar. 1978).

32. Ibid., p. 6.

33. Ibid., p. 7.

34. David Shipman, *The Great Movie Stars, The International Years* (New York: St. Martin's, 1972), pp. 502–3.

35. *Film Daily Year Book of Motion Pictures* (hereafter cited as *FDY*) *1918–1970.* See also Douglas Ayer et al., "Self-Censorship In the Movie Industry: An Historical Perspective on Law and Social Change," *Wisconsin Law Review* 3 (1970) 797.

36. Paul Newman reportedly bought himself out of his five-year contract with Warner Bros. (which guaranteed him $17,500 per film but loaned him out to other studios for $75,000 per film) for $500,000 in the late 1950s, and then supposedly received $200,000 for *Exodus.* Shipman, p. 388.

37. See Andrew Sarris, *The American Cinema, Directors, and Directions: 1929–1968* (New York: Dutton, 1969).

38. See Bruce Austin, "Motion Picture Attendance and Factors Influencing Movie Selection among High School Students," unpublished paper presented to the University Film Association 33d Annual Conference, 13–17 August 1979, Ithaca, N.Y. See also "Hollywood's Newspaper Advertising: Stereotype of a Nation's Taste," in *Mass Culture,*

edited by Bernard Rosenberg and David M. White (New York: Free Pr., 1957), pp. 443–50.

39. See Michael Pye and Lynda Myles, *The Movie Brats: How the Film Generation Took over Hollywood* (New York: Holt, 1979); Douglas Gomery, "Review: *The Movie Brats*," *Screen*, 21, no. 1 (Spring 1980):15–17.

40. *Variety*, 1 Oct. 1980, p. 7; 26 Nov. 1980, p. 3.

41. Lee Cedric Garrison, Jr., *Decision Processes in Motion Picture: A Study of Uncertainty*. Ph.D. diss., Stanford Univ., 1971.

42. See Simonet, *Regression*.

43. See Simonet, "Marquee Values," p. 8.

44. See David Kehr, "A Star Is Made," *Film Comment* 15, no. 1 (Jan.–Feb. 1979):7–12. See also Garth Jowett and James M. Linton *Movies as Mass Communication*, (Beverly Hills: Sage, 1980) pp. 79.

5. Dividing Labor for Production Control: Thomas Ince and the Rise of the Studio System

1. This paper is a result of a seminar in social and economic problems in American film history conducted by Douglas Gomery, Fall 1977, at the Univ. of Wisconsin–Madison. I would like to thank the members of the seminar for their suggestions and help in formalizing these ideas. I also appreciate further research leads given me by members of the Society for Cinema Studies at the 1978 conference, where a draft of this paper was read.

2. George Mitchell, "Thomas H. Ince," *Films in Review* 11 (Oct. 1960):464–68; "The 'IMP' Company Invades Cuba," *MPW* 8, no. 3 (21 Jan. 1911): 146.

3. Kalton C. Lahue, *Dreams for Sale: The Rise and Fall of the Triangle Film Corporation* (South Brunswick and New York: A. S. Barnes, 1971), pp. 61, 65–66, 71; "Los Angeles Letter," *MPW* 25, no. 8 (21 Aug. 1915):1301; "Forty-Three Acres for Incity," *MPW* 27, no. 6 (12 Feb. 1916):958.

4. Jacobs, pp. 162, 205–6; Lahue, *Dreams*, p. 46; Eric Rhode, *A History of the Cinema: From Its Origins to 1970* (New York: Hill and Wang, 1976), p. 58.

5. Harry Braverman, *Labor and Monopoly Capital: The Degradation of Work in the Twentieth Century* (New York: Monthly Review Pr., 1974), p. 54.

6. Ibid., p. 59.

7. Ibid., p. 63.

8. Ibid., p. 75.

9. Adam Smith, quoted in ibid., pp. 76–77.

10. Ibid., p. 107.

11. For a Marxist analysis of these effects, see also Ernst Fischer, *The Essential Marxist*, trans. Anna Bostock (New York: Seabury Pr., 1970), pp. 15–51.

12. Braverman, p. 125.

13. Ibid., p. 260.

14. Peter Milne, *Motion Picture Directing* (New York: Falk, 1922), p. 136.

15. Braverman, p. 125.

16. Everett McNeil, "Outline of How to Write a Photoplay," *MPW* 9, no. 1 (15 July 1911):27.

17. "Doings in Los Angeles," *MPW* 12, no. 10 (8 June 1912):913; "Doings in Los Angeles," *MPW* 14, no. 1 (5 Oct. 1912):32.

18. Mitchell, pp. 469–70.
19. W. E. Wing, "Tom Ince, of Inceville," *New York Dramatic Mirror* 70, no. 1827 (24 Dec. 1913):34; also in George C. Pratt, *Spellbound in Darkness: A History of the Silent Film*, rev. ed. (Greenwich, Conn.: New York Graphic Society, 1973), pp. 144–45.
20. Aitken Brothers Papers, Scenarios, Manuscript Collection (Wisconsin Center for Film and Theater Research, Madison, Wis.), Boxes 1–9.
21. Milne, p. 140; Jacobs, p. 204; Arthur Knight, *The Liveliest Art: A Panoramic History of the Movies* (New York: Macmillan, 1957), p. 38; Edward Wagenknecht, *The Movies in the Age of Innocence* (Norman: Univ. of Oklahoma Pr., 1962), p. 175; Lahue, *Dreams*, p. 45; Rhode, p. 58.
22. Wing, p. 34; Milne, p. 140; William S. Hart, *My Life East and West* (Boston and New York: Houghton, 1929), pp. 206–7.
23. For example, *The Iron Strain* (1915) costs were $2737.56 per reel (six reels) and $2.73 per foot.
24. Mitchell, p. 468.
25. "Doings in Los Angeles," *MPW* 15, no. 7 (15 Feb. 1913):668.
26. Wing, p. 34; Jean Mitry, *Histoire du cinéma: Art et Industrie, Vol. I: 1895–1914* (Paris: Editions Universitaires, 1967), p. 440; Mitry, *Vol. II: 1915–1925*, pp. 88–89; Hart, p. 213; Lahue, *Dreams*, p. 40.
27. "William S. Hart," *MPW* 22, no. 7 (14 Nov. 1914):920; Mitry, *II*, pp. 88–89; Lahue, *Dreams*, p. 40; Ad, *MPW* 25, no. 2 (10 July 1915):333.
28. Lahue, *Dreams*, p. 45.
29. Kalton C. Lahue, *Mack Sennett's Keystone: The Man, the Myth, and the Comedies* (Cranbury, N.J.: A. S. Barnes, 1971), p. 244.
30. Mitchell, pp. 472–73; Mitry, *I*, p. 440; "Los Angeles Letter," *MPW* 25, no. 9 (28 Aug. 1915):1466; "Ince's Big Picture Completed," *MPW* 27, no. 10 (11 Mar. 1916):1638; "Los Angeles Letter," *MPW* 25, no. 8 (21 Aug. 1915):1301; "Triangle Appoints a General Manager," *MPW* 25, no. 8 (21 Aug. 1915):1303; "Triangle Opening Announced," *MPW* 25, no. 10 (4 Sept. 1915):1622; "Manufacturers' Exposition," *MPW* 25, no. 5 (31 July 1915):820.
31. "Manufacturers' Exposition," *MPW* 25, no. 5 (31 July 1915):820; Aitken Brothers Papers, Scenarios, Boxes 1–9.
32. "Los Angeles Letter," *MPW* 25, no. 7 (14 Aug. 1915):1144.
33. George Blaisdell, "Mecca of the Motion Picture," *MPW* 25, no. 2 (10 July 1915):216.
34. Aitken Brothers Papers, Correspondence, Boxes 10–14.
35. Braverman, p. 260.
36. Milne, p. 136.

6. The Movies Become Big Business:
Public Theatres and the Chain-Store Strategy

1. Alfred D. Chandler, *The Visible Hand* (Cambridge, Mass.: Harvard Univ. Pr., 1977), pp. 233–37; Thomas C. Cochran, *Two Hundred Years of American Business* (New York: Delta, 1977), pp. 116–17; William E. Leuchtenburg, *The Perils of Prosperity* (Chicago: Univ. of Chicago Pr., 1958), p. 192; Godfrey M. Lebhar, *Chain Stores in America, 1859–1962* (New York: Chain Store Pub. Co., 1963), pp. 24–64.
2. Monopsony power results when a firm is one of a limited number of buyers of a certain input, and thus can bargain for a lower purchase price.

3. Walter S. Hayward and Percival White, *Chain Stores*, 3d ed. (New York: McGraw, 1928), pp. 1–14, 571; William S. Darby, *Story of the Chain Store* (New York: Dry Good Economist, 1928), pp. 41–59; Chandler, pp. 208, 236–39; Godfrey M. Lebhar, *The Chain Store: Boon or Bain* (New York: Harper, 1932), pp. 25–32.

4. Many inputs made up any exhibitor's product; B&K did not hold a comparative advantage in them all. For example, although B&K used large-scale advertising, and by all accounts was successful at it, it did not innovate any new advertising techniques.

5. Paul F. Cressey, "Population Succession in Chicago: 1898–1930," *American Journal of Sociology* 44 (1938), p. 59; Homer Hoyt, *One Hundred Years of Land Values in Chicago* (Chicago: Univ. of Chicago Pr., 1933), pp. 225–29; Chicago Plan Commission, *Forty-Four Cities in the City of Chicago* (Chicago: Chicago Plan Commission, 1942), pp. 27–28; *Exhibitor's Herald*, 15 June 1918, p. 22.

6. Chicago Historical Society, Arthur G. Levy Collection, "Largest Motion-Picture Theatres in Chicago and Vicinity," 12 July 1935 (mimeo.), n.p.; Michael Conant, *Antitrust in the Motion Picture Industry* (Berkeley and Los Angeles: Univ. of California Pr., 1960), pp. 154–55; Chicago Recreation Commission, *The Chicago Recreation Survey, 1937;* Vol. 2: *Commercial Recreation* (Chicago, 1938), pp. 36–37; Hoyt, *One Hundred Years of Land Values in Chicago*, pp. 227–31, 262.

7. *MPW* 38, no. 1 (5 Oct. 1918):67; R. W. Sexton and B. F. Betts, eds., *American Theatres of Today* (New York: Architectural Book Pub. Co., 1927), p. 1; "Uptown Theatre," *Marquee* 9 (Second Quarter 1977), pp. 1–27; Theatre Historical Society, *The Chicago Theatre* (Notre Dame, Ind.: N.p., 1975); *Motion Picture News*, 9 Apr. 1921, pp. 2485–86; John W. Landon, *Jesse Crawford* (Vestal, N.Y.: The Vestal Pr., 1974), p. 37.

8. Fred Wittenmeyer, "Cooling of Theatres and Public Buildings," *Ice and Refrigeration*, July 1922, pp. 13–14; Oscar E. Anderson, *Refrigeration in America* (Princeton: Princeton Univ. Pr., 1953), p. 223; Margaret Ingeles, *Willis Haviland Carrier* (New York: Country Life Pr., 1952), p. 64.

9. "Air Conditioning System in Motion Picture House," *Ice and Refrigeration* 69 (Nov. 1925), pp. 251–52; "Heating, Ventilating, and Cooling Plant of the Tivoli Theatre," *Power Plant Engineering* 26 (1 Mar. 1922), pp. 249–55; *Variety*, 9 Sept. 1925, p. 30; 10 June 1925, p. 31.

10. Arthur Mayer, *Merely Colossal* (New York: Simon, 1953), p. 71; Ira Berkow, *Maxwell Street* (Garden City, N.Y.: Doubleday, 1977), p. 201; David Wallerstein, interview held in Slinger, Wis., 28 Aug. 1977; "Uptown Theatre Personnel List," *Marquee* 9 (Second Quarter 1977), p. 28; Carrie Balaban, *Continuous Performance* (New York: A. J. Balaban Foundation, 1964), pp. 54–55, 95.

11. *Exhibitor's Herald and Motography*, 21 Dec. 1918, p. 25; Barney Balaban and Sam Katz, *The Fundamental Principles of Balaban and Katz Theatre Management* (Chicago: Balaban and Katz, 1926), pp. 69–73.

12. *New York Times*, 18 Sept. 1966, p. 18; *Variety*: 12 Apr. 1923, p. 30; 12 July 1923, p. 27; 1 Nov. 1923, p. 26; 8 Nov. 1923, p. 21; 8 Dec. 1922, p. 37; 29 Mar. 1923, p. 30; 23 Sept. 1925, p. 32.

13. This merger was part of a general trend toward vertical integration in the U.S. film industry between 1925 and 1930. Paramount/Publix was the largest and, I think, the most important of the new combinations.

14. *Variety*, 28 Oct. 1925, p. 27; Mason Miller, "Famous Players in Transition Period," *The Magazine of Wall Street* 23 Apr. 1927, p. 1178; *Variety*, 26 June 1929, p. 5; "Review of Operations—Paramount Famous Lasky," *Commercial and Financial Chronicle*, 21 Apr. 1928, p. 2490.

15. It is impossible to more than estimate the number of theaters in the Publix chain at any one time because of extremely complicated real estate arrangements and sometimes secret deals.

16. U.S., Congress, Senate, Temporary National Economic Committee, *The Motion Picture Industry—A Pattern of Control*, Monograph 43, 76th Cong., 3d sess., 1941, pp. 10, 12, 15; *FDY, 1931*, pp. 823–44; *FDY, 1927*, pp. 649–71; *Variety*, 7 Aug. 1929, pp. 3–4, 50; *Wall Street Journal*, 11 June 1927, pp. 1, 4.

17. Howard T. Lewis, ed., *Cases on the Motion Picture Industry* (New York: McGraw, 1930), p. 516; Arthur Mayer, p. 102; *Variety*, 7 Aug. 1929, p. 10; *Film Daily*, 26 Aug. 1927, pp. 1, 4.

18. Joseph P. Kennedy, ed., *The Story of the Films as Told by Leaders of the Industry* (New York: A. W. Shaw, 1927), p. 275; Lewis, ed., *Cases*, pp. 516–19; Arthur Mayer, pp. 106–11; Jesse L. Lasky, *I Blow My Own Horn* (Garden City, NY: Doubleday, 1957), p. 241; U.S., Congress, *A Pattern of Control*, pp. 10–15.

19. *Variety*, 7 Aug. 1929, p. 10; *New York Times*, 10 July 1927, p. 24; *Film Daily*, 21 Nov. 1926, pp. 1, 18; *Film Daily*, 8 Apr. 1926, pp. 1, 6; *Barrons*, 11 Nov. 1926, p. 10; Lewis, ed., *Cases*, p. 519; Kennedy, pp. 276–77; Ben M. Hall, *The Best Remaining Seats* (New York: A. N. Potter, 1962), pp. 207–9.

20. *Variety*, 10 Apr. 1929, p. 41; A. Raymond Gallo, "Presentation Acts," *The Motion Picture Almanac, 1929* (New York: Quigley Publications, 1929), pp. 129–30; Carrie Balaban, pp. 94–95.

21. Katz eventually dropped the school; other circuits were hiring away recent graduates, while contributing nothing to the cost of the education.

22. *Variety*, 18 Jan. 1961, p. 4; *Film Daily*, 14 Jan. 1926, p. 1; *Film Daily*, 26 Feb. 1926, p. 1; *Film Daily*, 30 July 1926, pp. 1–2; Lewis, ed., *Cases*, pp. 519–20; Kennedy, pp. 266–70.

23. *Variety*, 7 Aug. 1929, p. 4.

24. Ibid., pp. 10, 189; *New York Times*, 25 June 1927, p. 15; Arthur Mayer, pp. 107–8; Lewis, ed., *Cases*, pp. 520–21.

25. Arthur Mayer, p. 105; Lewis, ed., *Cases*, p. 521.

26. Kennedy, pp. 265, 270–72; *Variety*, 7 Aug. 1929, p. 10; *Variety*, 18 Jan. 1961, p. 4; Lewis, ed., *Cases*, pp. 521–22.

27. Legally the Paramount Famous Lasky Corporation and Publix were two distinct entities until 24 Apr. 1930. Then the name was formally changed to the Paramount Publix Corporation.

28. *Film Daily*: 8 Apr. 1929, p. 1; 16 Apr. 1929, pp. 1, 4; *Variety*: 14 May 1930, p. 4; 29 May 1929, p. 30; 26 Sept. 1928, p. 19; 7 Aug. 1929, p. 10; Hall, pp. 251–53.

29. *Variety*: 12 Sept. 1928, p. 57; 11 July 1928, p. 4; *Barrons*: 21 Oct. 1929, p. 15; 26 May 1930, p. 9; *Variety*: 19 June 1929, p. 65; 28 Aug. 1928, p. 27; 11 Sept. 1929, p. 5; *New York Times*, 22 Sept. 1929, 2:14; *Barrons*, 26 Aug. 1929, p. 29; *Variety*: 2 Oct. 1929, pp. 1, 4; 16 Oct. 1929, p. 35.

30. *Barrons*: 7 Nov. 1932, p. 16; 28 Oct. 1929, p. 15; *Variety*, 9 Oct. 1929, p. 6; *Moody's Manual of Industrials, 1932* (New York: Moody's Investor Service, 1932), p. 2427; *Moody's Manual of Industrials, 1933* (New York: Moody's Investor Service, 1933), p. 3048.

31. *New York Times*, 3 Nov. 1932, p. 31; *Film Daily*: 18 Nov. 1930, pp. 1, 4; 10 Apr. 1931, pp. 1–2; 20 Aug. 1931, p. 1; *Variety*: 18 Mar. 1931, p. 20; 29 Apr. 1931, p. 7.

7. The "Warner-Vitaphone Peril":
The American Film Industry Reacts to the Innovation of Sound

1. Lewis Jacobs, *The Rise of the American Film* (New York: Harcourt, 1939), p. 298.
2. Ibid., p. 299.
3. Benjamin B. Hampton, *History of the American Film Industry* (New York: Covici, Friede, 1931; reprint, Dover, 1970), pp. 378–83.
4. For example, Harry M. Geduld, *The Birth of the Talkies: From Edison to Jolson* (Bloomington: Indiana Univ. Pr., 1975), pp. 152–53, accepts Green without reservation and quotes Green's account verbatim.
5. Fitzhugh Green, *The Film Finds Its Tongue* (New York: Putnam, 1929), pp. 79–81.
6. William I. Greenwald, "The Impact of Sound upon the Film Industry: A Case Study of Innovation," in *Explorations in Entrepreneurial History* 4 (May, 1952):182; N. R. Danielian, *A. T. & T.: The Story of Industrial Conquest* (New York: Vanguard, 1939), pp. 140–41.
7. For a review of these failures see Douglas Gomery, "The Coming of Sound to the American Cinema: A History of the Transformation of an Industry" (Ph.D. diss., Univ. of Wisconsin-Madison, 1975), pp. 26–47.
8. General Talking Pictures Corporation et al. v. American Telephone and Telegraph Co. et al., 18 F. Supp. 650 (1937), Record at 2627–30, 2828–30.
9. U.S., Congress, House. Committee on Patents, *Pooling of Patents. Hearings Before the Committee on Patents H.R. 6250 and H.R. 9137*, 68th Cong., 1st sess., 1924, p. 1343; U.S., Federal Communications Commission. *Staff Report on Electrical Research Products, Inc., Volume II, Report B* (Pursuant to Public Resolution No. 8, 74th Cong.), 1937, p. 161; General Talking Pictures, 18 F. Supp. 650, Record at 2630–31. Post later sued Western Electric for compensation for his investments. He collected $18,000.
10. General Talking Pictures, 18 F. Supp. 650, Record, pp. 2633–36; Electrical Research Products, Inc. v. Vitaphone Corporation 171A. 738 (1934), Affidavit of Waddill Catchings, p. 3; Koplar (Scharaf et al., Interveners) v. Warner Bros. Pictures, Inc. et al., 19 F. Supp. 173 (1937), Record, p. 367. See Gomery, "Coming of Sound," pp. 118–34 for more on the Rich-Warner Bros. meeting.
11. General Talking Pictures, 18 F. Supp. 650, Record at 2672, 2831–32.
12. *New York Times*, 1 Oct. 1926, p. 8; Koplar, 19 F. Supp. 173, Record at 480–84; *New York Times*, 1 Oct. 1926, p. 8; General Talking Pictures, 18 F. Supp. 650, Exhibit C, letter, John E. Otterson to Harry Warner, 28 Sept. 1926, Exhibit D, letter, Harry Warner to John E. Otterson, 2 Oct. 1926.
13. *Variety*, 20 Oct. 1926, p. 51; *Electrical Research Products*, 171 A. 738, Answer, pp. 23–24; Koplar, 19 F. Supp. 173, Record at 484–85.
14. General Talking Pictures, 18 F. Supp. 650, Record at 2671–77.
15. Ibid., at 2678.
16. U.S., Congress, *Pooling of Patents*, p. 1349; Koplar, 19 F. Supp. 173, Record at 491–92; U.S., Federal Communications Commission. *Telephone Investigation Exhibits* (Pursuant to Public Resolution No. 8, 74th Cong.), 1936–37, Exhibit 1606, pp. 20–22 and Exhibit 1605, p. 55.
17. General Talking Pictures, 18 F. Supp. 650, Record at 2680–83, 2834; F.C.C., *Telephone Exhibits*, Exhibit 1605, p. 55.
18. For more on Fox, see Gomery, "Coming of Sound," pp. 175–83.
19. Koplar, 19 F. Supp. 173, Record at 489.
20. Maurice D. Kahn, ed., *FDY, 1929*, p. 489.

21. General Talking Pictures, 18 F. Supp. 650, Exhibit 105.

22. Charles H. Hession and Hyman Sardy, *Ascent to Affluence* (Boston: Allyn and Bacon, 1969), pp. 611–18.

23. *Variety*, 18 May 1927, pp. 5, 26; *Wall Street Journal*: 11 June 1927, pp. 1, 4; 23 June 1927, pp. 1, 4.

24. Ross, p. 27.

25. Ibid., pp. 27–28; *Commercial and Financial Chronicle*, 25 June 1927, p. 3700; *Barrons*, 27 June 1927, p. 4.

26. *Equity*: July 1927, pp. 7–9; Dec. 1927, pp. 7–16; *Barrons*, 29 Aug. 1927, p. 1.

27. Maurice D. Kahn, ed., *FDY, 1940* (New York: Film Daily, 1941), p. 48; *Barrons*: 19 Sept. 1927, p. 19; 28 May 1928, p. 2; Lewis, ed., *Cases*, p. 320.

28. General Talking Pictures, 18 F. Supp. 650, Record at 2838–39.

29. F.C.C., *Telephone Exhibits*, Exhibit 1622, pp. 1–4; *New York Times*, 30 Aug. 1927, p. 10; *Variety*: 21 Dec. 1927, p. 115; 30 Nov. 1927, p. 11; Earl I. Sponable, "Historical Development of Sound Films," *Journal of the Society of Motion Picture Engineers* 48 (May 1947):420.

30. General Talking Pictures, 18 F. Supp. 650, Record at 2838–42.

31. Ibid., at 2841; F.C.C., Telephone Exhibits, Exhibit 1622, pp. 5–7.

32. General Talking Pictures, 18 F. Supp. 650, Record at 2846–48; F.C.C., *Telephone Exhibits*, Exhibit 1622, pp. 4–5.

33. General Talking Pictures, 18 F. Supp. 650, Record at 2716, 2847.

34. Ibid., Deposition of Edwin C. Mills, pp. 1–12; *Variety*, 28 Dec. 1927, pp. 1, 26; *New York Times*, 21 Dec. 1927, p. 29; *MPW*, 89, no. 8 (24 Dec. 1927):1; F.C.C., *Telephone Exhibits*, Exhibit 1609, pp. 19–23; United Artists Collection. O'Brien File. Manuscript Collection (Wisconsin Center for Film and Theatre Research, Madison), Box 86–5.

35. Electrical Research Products, 171 A. 738, Plea, pp. 224–27; General Talking Pictures, 18 F. Supp. 650, Exhibit 15.

36. F.C.C., *Telephone Exhibits*, Exhibit 1622, pp. 8–9, and Exhibit 1623.

37. Electrical Research Products, 171 A. 738, Affidavit of John E. Otterson, p. 182; F.C.C., *Telephone Exhibits*, Exhibit 1622, pp. 8–12.

38. U.S., Congress, *Pooling of Patents*, p. 518; General Talking Pictures, 18 F. Supp. 650, pp. 2715–16; Electrical Research Products 171 A. 738, Affidavit of John E. Otterson, p. 84; F.C.C., *Telephone Exhibits*, Exhibit 1621.

39. General Talking Pictures, 18 F. Supp. 650, Record at 2713–31, 2844–46.

40. Electrical Research Products, 171 A. 738, Affidavit of John E. Otterson, pp. 152–63; General Talking Pictures, 18 F. Supp. 650, Record at 2846–48.

41. Koplar, 19 F. Supp. 173, Record at 556–58; Electrical Research Products, 171 A. 738, Affidavit of Waddill Catchings, pp. 23–24, and Affidavit of John E. Otterson, pp. 185–86.

42. Electrical Research Products, 171 A. 738, Affidavit of Waddill Catchings, pp. 25–26, and Affidavit of John E. Otterson, pp. 186–91.

43. F.C.C., *Telephone Exhibits*, Exhibit 1622, p. 9.

44. *New York Times*, 19 Apr. 1928, p. 23; *Variety*, 2 May 1928, p. 12; General Talking Pictures, 18 F. Supp. 650, Record at 2946–47; United Artists Collection, Box 84–4.

45. General Talking Pictures, 18 F. Supp. 650, *Opinion*, p. 15.

46. *New York Times*, 16 May 1928, p. 18; *Variety*, 16 May 1928, passim; Electrical Research Products, 171 A. 738, Affidavit of John E. Otterson, pp. 192–97.

47. For more on this period, see Gomery, "Coming of Sound," pp. 254–367.

8. The Demise of Kinemacolor

1. Ramsaye, pp. 562–72.
2. Rachael Low, *The History of the British Film 1906–1914* (London: George Allen 1949), pp. 100–4.
3. Adrian Cornwell-Clyne, *Colour Cinematography* (London: Chapman, 1950), pp. 6–9. See also Roderick T. Ryan, *A History of Motion Picture Color Technology* (London: Focal Pr., 1977), pp. 26–30.
4. D. B. Thomas, *The First Colour Motion Pictures* (London: Stationery Office, 1969).
5. Ibid., p. 14.
6. *The Bioscope*, Dec. 17, 1908, p. 15.
7. Cornwell-Clyne, p. 8.
8. Thomas, p. 31.
9. *Journal of the Royal Society of Arts*, 1908, 57, No. 2, 929.
10. Edwin H. Land, "Color Vision and the Natural Image," *Proceedings of the National Academy of Science* 45 (1959):115–29, "Experiments in Color Vision," *Scientific American* (May 1959):84–99, and "The Retinex Theory of Color Vision," *Scientific American* (Dec. 1977):108–28.
11. Author's discussion with Professor Mark Hollins, perceptual psychologist Department of Psychology, The University of North Carolina at Chapel Hill.
12. The *Bioscope*, 5 Oct. 1911, p. ii.
13. Special Correspondent "News from America," The *Bioscope*, 19 Oct. 1909, p. 19.
14. See Low.
15. Thomas, pp. 14–16.
16. "Bioschemes, Limited, v. Natural Color Kinematograph Company, Limited," The *Bioscope*, 9 Apr. 1914, pp. 141–42.
17. Thomas, p. 33.
18. The *Bioscope*, 30 Apr. 1914, pp. 540–41.
19. Ibid.
20. Thomas, p. 30.
21. Ibid., p. 27. According to Thomas, Urban wrote in 1910, " 'With the life and scenery of the world, in every land upon which the sun shines, waiting to be recorded in color, time spent in finding ways and means of photographing artificial comedies and artificial tragedies by artificial light is wasted,' " and critics said of Kinemacolor dramatic films that "although the colour was almost invariably praised . . . the acting was poor and the direction worse."
22. Ibid., p. 30.
23. *MPW*, 14, no. 2 (12 Oct. 1912):161.
24. Ibid., 14, no. 3 (19 Oct. 1912):231.
25. Russell Merritt, "Dixon, Griffith, and The Southern Legend," *Cinema Journal* 12 no. 1 (Fall 1972):31.
26. *MPW*, 14, no. 3 (19 Oct. 1912):231.
27. Cassady, "Monopoly," p. 327. [reprinted herein, p. 378n.16.]
28. Thomas, p. 30.
29. *MPW*, 18, no. 5 (1 Nov. 1913):500.
30. Low, p. 101.
31. *MPW*, 18, no. 5 (1 Nov. 1913):500.
32. Ibid., 19, no. 5 (31 Jan. 1914):561.
33. *Variety*, 35, no. 2 (12 June 1914):23.
34. See Cassady, "Monopoly."

35. Thomas, p. 31.
36. According to D. B. Thomas, Kinemacolor never had a sufficient library of films to provide a theater with a twice weekly change of program. Ibid., pp. 32–33.
37. See ibid., p. 27.
38. Raymond Fielding, *The American Newsreel 1911–1967* (Norman: Univ. of Oklahoma Pr., 1972), p. 83.
39. Marvyn Scudder Manual of Extinct and Obsolete Companies, Inc. (New York: 1928), vol. 2, p. 768.
40. See William V. D. Kelly, "Natural Color Cinematography," *Transactions of the Society of Motion Picture Engineers* (Nov. 1918), pp. 38–43.
41. Ibid.
42. For a more thorough examination of Technicolor and Eastmancolor, see chap. 9.

9. Hollywood's Conversion to Color: The Technological, Economic, and Aesthetic Factors

1. Ryan, p. 16.
2. Colors were not originally recorded but were added later in one or at most two hues, when tinting and toning were combined.
3. For a more in-depth explanation of this theory, see Scherer, chap. 15, and for an application of this theory to the coming of sound, see Gomery, "Coming of Sound."
4. George E. Frost and S. Chesterfield Oppenheim, "A Study of the Professional Color Motion Picture, Antitrust Decrees, and Their Effects," *The Patent, Trademark, and Copyright Journal of Research and Education* 4 (Summer 1960):121.
5. *Moody's Industrials 1932*, p. 2595.
6. Frost and Oppenheim.
7. Substances in the film emulsion or developing solution which form color dyes during photochemical processing of the exposed film.
8. *Moody's Industrials 1949*, pp. 1252, 2625.
9. Herbert Kalmus, "Technicolor Adventures in Cinemaland," *Journal of the Society of Motion Picture Engineers* (Dec. 1938), pp. 572–74.
10. Lyne S. Trimble, *Color in Motion Pictures and Television* (Los Angeles: Lyne S. Trimble, 1954), p. 165.
11. See n. 37, below.
12. See Miles Kreuger, *The Movie Musical from Vitaphone to 42nd Street* (New York: Dover Publications, 1975), p. 257; Tom Shales, "Warner's Musicals; Busby and Beyond," in *The American Film Heritage*, ed. Tom Shales (Washington, D.C.: Acropolis, 1972), p. 82.
13. Kalmus, p. 574.
14. Tino Balio, *United Artists* (Madison: Univ. of Wisconsin Pr., 1976), p. 116.
15. Trimble, pp. 166–67.
16. *Time*, 27 May 1935, p. 28.
17. George H. Morris, "Color in 1943," *FDY, 1944*, p. 71.
18. Frost and Oppenheim.
19. *Time.*
20. Author's estimate.
21. Frank S. Taylor, "Mr. Technicolor," *Saturday Evening Post*, 22 Oct. 1949, p. 133.
22. *FDY, 1950*, p. 73.
23. Estimated from *FDY, 1940, 1950* and other sources.

24. *Variety*'s gross distributor receipts from 1941–50 (published each Jan.).

25. *Variety*, 7 Jan. 1948, p. 58.

26. Ibid., 5 Jan. 1949, p. 46.

27. *FDY, 1949*, p. 67.

28. For Selznick's description of his arguments with MGM executives about the relative merits of color for feature films, see *Memo from David O. Selznick*, ed. Ruby Behlmer (New York: Viking, 1972), pp. 168–69.

29. Based upon decline in average negative costs (the production costs of an average feature, exclusive of distribution costs, like prints and advertising) from 1948 through the mid 1950s as published in *FDY*, 1949, 1955.

30. One such promotion took the form of a short film in which a popular television star (Red Skelton) talked about the advantages of motion pictures over television as he emerged from a corner of the screen inside a small box in black-and-white to fill the entire screen in color.

31. The headline of *Variety*'s 6 Jan. 1954 issue read, "WB's 16 in '54 will cost as much as 42 Previous Pix."

32. Michael Conant, "The Impact of the Paramount Decrees," *The American Film Industry*, ed. Tino Balio (Madison: Univ. of Wisconsin Pr., 1976), p. 361.

33. See fig. 9.1.

34. *Broadcasting*, 16 Nov. 1964, p. 76.

35. *Variety*, 4 Jan. 1967, p. 98.

36. *Broadcasting*, 2 Jan. 1967, declared that 38 of 47 prime-time features would be in color on ABC (p. 84).

37. See fig. 9.1.

38. *The American Film Institute Catalogue Feature Films 1921–1930* (New York: Bowker, 1976).

39. Jacobs, pp. 506–18.

40. Erik Barnouw, *Tube of Plenty, The Evolution of American Television* (New York: Oxford Univ. Pr., 1975), p. 401. These dates are contradicted by *Broadcasting*, 2 Jan. 1967, p. 86, which stated that NBC broadcast its news in color beginning 15 Nov. 1965, but did not initiate the use of color news film until 1967. In short, in 1965, black-and-white news film was used almost exclusively on its color broadcasts.

41. Taken from *Variety*'s "All Time Rental Champs," 11 May 1977, p. 8.

10. Antitrust Policies and the Motion Picture Industry

1. Floyd L. Vaughan, *Economics of Our Patent System* (New York: Macmillan, 1925), pp. 52–58, 106–9, 121–25.

2. Ibid., p. 55.

3. U.S. v. Motion Picture Patents Co., 225 Fed. 800 (E.D. Pa. 1915), *dismissed per stipulation*, 247 U.S. 524 (1918).

4. Motion Picture Patents Co. v. Universal Film Manufacturing Co., 235 Fed. 398 (2d Cir. 1916), 243 U.S. 502 (1917).

5. Mae D. Huettig, *Economic Control of the Motion Picture Industry* (Philadelphia: Univ. of Pennsylvania Pr., 1944), p. 20.

6. William F. Hellmuth, Jr., "The Motion Picture Industry," *The Structure of American Industry*, ed. Walter Adams, rev. ed. (New York: Macmillan, 1961), p. 364; Jacobs, p. 84; Eric Johnston and Michael Linden, "The Motion Picture Industry," *The Develop-*

ment of American Industries, ed. John George Glover and William Bouck Cornell, 3d ed. (New York: Prentice-Hall, 1951), p. 937.

7. *Stanley Booking Corp.*, Docket 104, 1 F.T.C. 212 (1918).

8. Two hundred twenty features, according to "Paramount," *Fortune*, Mar. 1937, p. 90.

9. Adolph Zukor, *Variety*, 4 Jan. 1956, p. 43.

10. Figures in F.T.C. v. Paramount Famous Lasky Corp., 57 F. 2d 152, 155 (2d Cir. 1932).

11. *Famous Players–Lasky Corp.*, Docket 835, 11 F.T.C. 187 (1927).

12. 57 F. 2d 152.

13. "Restraints on Motion Picture Exhibition and the Antitrust Laws," *Illinois Law Review* (Dec. 1938), p. 429.

14. Howard T. Lewis, *The Motion Picture Industry* (New York: Van Nostrand, 1933), pp. 264–66.

15. See U.S. v. Paramount Famous Lasky Corp., 34 F. 2d 984 (S.D. N.Y. 1929); Paramount Famous Lasky Corp. v. U.S., 282 U.S. 30 (1930); U.S. v. First National Pictures, Inc., 34 F. 2d 815 (S.D. N.Y. 1929), 282 U.S. 44 (1930), 51 F. 2d 552 (S.D. N.Y. 1931).

16. Lewis, *The Motion Picture Industry* (New York: Van Nostrand, 1933), pp. 291–98.

17. Joel Swenson, "The Entrepreneur's Role in Introducing the Sound Motion Picture," *Political Science Quarterly* (Sept. 1948), p. 409.

18. U.S. v. Fox Theatres Corp., Eq. 51–122 (S.D. N.Y. 1929).

19. U.S. v. Warner Bros. Pictures, Inc., Eq. 51–121 (S.D. N.Y. 1929).

20. Lewis, *Picture Industry*, p. 307; see also Huettig, pp. 46–47.

21. Hellmuth, p. 367.

22. Daniel Bertrand, W. Duane Evans, and E. L. Blanchard, *The Motion Picture Industry—A Pattern of Control*, TNEC Monograph 43 (1941), p. 7.

23. Ibid., pp. 23–49; Hellmuth, pp. 373–77.

24. U.S. v. Paramount Pictures, Inc., 334 U.S. 131, 150 n.9, 167–68 (1948).

25. Ibid., Complaint, Eq. 87–273 (S.D. N.Y. 1938).

26. Compare U.S. v. Paramount Pictures, Inc., 66 F. Supp. 323, 341 (S.D. N.Y. 1946), "not challenged" on this point in 334 U.S., at 145. The most careful analysis is that of District Judge Leon R. Yankwich, in Fanchon & Marco v. Paramount Pictures, Inc., 100 F. Supp. 84 (S.D. Calif. 1951).

27. "The Sherman Act and the Motion Picture Industry," *University of Chicago Law Review* (Apr. 1946), p. 354.

28. *Illinois Law Review* (Dec. 1938), p. 430; Southern California Theatre Owners Ass'n., Trade Relations Committee Report, mimeo., Los Angeles, 1952, pp. 17–18.

29. West Coast Theatres, Inc., Dockets 1319 and 1320, 12 FTC 383 and 436 (1929); U.S. v. West Coast Theatres, Inc., Eq. S–10–C (S.D. Calif. 1930); U.S. v. Fox West Coast Theatres, Eq. Y–38–H (S.D. Calif. 1932).

30. U.S. v. Motion Picture Theatre Owners of Oklahoma, Eq. 1005 (W.D. Okla. 1928).

31. U.S. v. Balaban & Katz Corp., Eq. 8854 (N.D. Ill. 1928); U.S. v. Barney Balaban, Cr. 31230 (N.D. Ill. 1928).

32. U.S. v. United Theatres, Inc., Eq. 39 (E.D. La. 1932).

33. Lewis, *Picture Industry*, p. 217.

34. Marco Wolff, in *Motion Picture Distribution Trade Practices, Hearings Before a Subcommittee of the Senate Small Business Committee*, 83d Cong., 1st sess., 1953, p. 213.

35. U.S. v. Warner Bros. Pictures, Inc., 13 F. Supp. 614 (E.D. Mo. 1936), 298 U.S. 643 (1936).

36. "Warner Brothers," *Fortune*, Dec. 1937, p. 212.

37. Interstate Circuit Co. v. U.S., 306 U.S. 208 (1939).

38. Ibid., at 222.

39. North Dakota law sustained in Paramount Pictures, Inc. v. Langer, 23 F. Supp. 890 (D. N.D. 1938).

40. U.S. v. Paramount Pictures, Inc., Commerce Clearing House, *1940–1943 Trade Cases*, no. 56072.

41. See Robert W. Chambers, "Block Booking—Blind Selling," *Harvard Business Review* (Summer 1941), pp. 496–507; "Operation of the Consent Decree in the Motion Picture Industry," *Yale Law Journal* (May 1942), pp. 1175–97.

42. Compare John F. Zeller III, "Judicial Regulation of the Motion-Picture Industry: The Paramount Case," *Univ. of Pennsylvania Law Review* (May 1947), p. 665.

43. Commerce Clearing House, *The Federal Antitrust Laws with Summary of Cases Instituted by the United States*, No. 434, U.S. v. Paramount Pictures, Inc., Chicago, 1951.

44. U.S. v. Crescent Amusement Co., 323 U.S. 173 (1944).

45. U.S. v. Schine Chain Theatres, Inc., 63 F. Supp. 229 (W.D. N.Y. 1945); Schine Chain Theatres, Inc. v. U.S. 334 U.S. 110 (1948).

46. U.S. v. Griffith Amusement Co., 68 F. Supp. 180 (D. Okla. 1946), 334 U.S. 100 (1948).

47. Numbers of theaters in *FDY, 1944–55*.

48. *Variety*, 1 Dec. 1954, p. 11.

49. U.S. v. Schine Chain Theatres, Inc., Civil 223 (W.D. N.Y. 1951); U.S. v. J. Myer Schine, Cr. 6279–C (W.D. N.Y. 1954).

50. 334 U.S. at 105.

51. Ibid., at 107.

52. Ibid., at 108.

53. Joel B. Dirlam and Alfred E. Kahn, *Fair Competition: The Law and Economics of Antitrust Policy* (Ithaca: Cornell Univ. Pr., 1954), p. 68.

54. Huettig, p. 144.

55. U.S. v. Paramount Pictures, Inc., 66 F. Supp. 323, 70 F. Supp. 53 (S.D. N.Y. 1946).

56. Ibid., 334 U.S. 131, 148 (1948).

57. Ibid., at 164.

58. Ibid., at 175.

59. Ibid., 85 F. Supp. 881 (S.D. N.Y. 1949).

60. Loew's, Inc. v. U.S., 339 U.S. 974 (1950).

61. *Variety*, 6 Oct. 1954, p. 15.

62. Walter Adams, "The Aluminum Case: Legal Victory—Economic Defeat," *American Economic Review* (Dec. 1951), pp. 915–16 n. 3.

63. Walter Adams, "Discussion," *American Economic Review*, Papers and Proceedings, May 1955, p. 523.

64. Compare John Balaban, president of Balaban and Katz, *Variety*, 21 Mar. 1956, p. 16.

65. Abram F. Myers, chairman of Allied States Association, in *Motion-Picture Distribution Trade Practices—1956, Hearings Before a Subcommittee of the Senate Small Business Committee*, S. Rept. 2818, 84th Cong., 2d sess., 1956, p. 4. (Cited hereafter as Senate Hearings, 1956).

66. Ibid., p. 14.

67. Youngclaus v. Omaha Film Board of Trade, 60 F. 2d 538 (D. Neb. 1932).

68. 282 U.S. 30 and 44.

69. Bigelow v. RKO Radio Pictures, Inc., 327 U.S. 251 (1946); Richard G. Kruger, "The Jackson Park Antitrust Case: A Business Use of the Antitrust Laws," *Current Economic Comment*, College of Commerce, Univ. of Illinois, Urbana, Apr. 1954, pp. 37–44.

70. Louis Phillips, general counsel of Paramount Pictures Corp., Senate Hearings, 1956, p. 455.

71. Robert Coughlan, "Now It Is Trouble That Is Supercolossal in Hollywood," *Life*, 13 Aug. 1951, p. 103.

72. *Variety*, 7 Dec. 1955, p. 9.

73. Of the 41 who replied, 15 had been chosen at random from phone directories, 13 suggested by Theatre Owners of America, 8 by a large producer, 5 by Allied States Association.

74. Statement of the late Alfred Starr.

75. *Variety*, 16 May 1956, p. 61.

76. American Broadcasting-Paramount Theatres, Inc., Annual Report, 1954, p. 11.

77. Charles M. Reagan, general sales manager of Loew's, Inc., Senate Hearings, 1956, pp. 365–67.

78. See Freeman Lincoln, "The Comeback of the Movies," *Fortune* 51 (Feb. 1955): 127–31+.

79. "RKO: It's Only Money," ibid., May 1953, p. 212.

80. Eugene V. Rostow, "The New Sherman Act: A Positive Instrument for Progress," *University of Chicago Law Review* (June 1947), p. 599; John R. McDonough, Jr., and Robert L. Winslow, "The Motion Picture Industry: United States v. Oligopoly," *Stanford Law Review* (Apr. 1949), pp. 397–98.

81. *Variety*, 4 Nov. 1953, p. 22.

82. See *Motion Picture Herald*, 15 Jan. 1955, p. 17.

83. *Variety*, 3 Nov. 1954, p. 3.

84. Annual Report of Chairman and General Counsel, Allied States Association, 1946, p. 7; Harry Brandt, president of Independent Theatre Owners Association, Senate Hearings, 1956, p. 255.

85. *Variety*, 7 Oct. 1953, p. 5.

86. Ibid., 7 Apr. 1954, p. 20; 26 May 1954, p. 5; 18 Aug. 1954, p. 5.

87. *Motion Picture Herald*, 28 Aug. 1954, p. 14.

88. Don Carle Gillette, "Hollywood Plunge: Theatre Owners Brave the Perils of Movie-Making," *Barron's*, 20 Dec. 1954, p. 5.

89. *Variety*, 8 Feb. 1956, p. 3.

90. Abram F. Myers, Senate Hearings, 1956, p. 29.

91. Calculated from *Motion Picture Theatres: 1954*, report of Sindlinger & Co., Inc., Independent Analyst, Ridley Park, PA, to Council of Motion Picture Organizations, p. 90.

92. *Variety*, 4 Jan. 1956, p. 84.

93. Leo F. Wolcott, Senate Hearings, 1956, p. 36.

94. Louis Phillips, ibid., p. 434.

95. Interview, *U.S. News and World Report*, 5 Mar. 1954, pp. 38–39.

96. Huettig, pp. 69–70.

97. Compare report to stockholders of Leonard H. Goldenson, president of American Broadcasting–Paramount Theatres, Inc., 20 Oct. 1954, p. 3.

98. Of the forty-one theaters answering the questionnaire in the present study, twenty-eight could effect occasional adjustments before 1948 and twenty-one still can.

99. Senate Hearings, 1956, p. 41.

100. Sidney E. Samuelson, president of Allied Independent Theatre Owners Association of Eastern Pennsylvania, *Problems of Independent Motion-Picture Exhibitors*, Report of Senate Small Business Committee, S. Rept. 835, 83d Cong., 1st sess. 1953, p. 393. (Cited hereafter as "Senate Hearings, 1953".)

101. Assistant Attorney General Stanley N. Barnes, ibid., p. 652.

102. *Variety*, 13 Aug. 1952, pp. 5, 16.

103. Ibid., 12 Jan. 1955, p. 18.

104. Ibid., 27 June 1951, p. 5; Charles J. Feldman, general sales manager of Universal Pictures Corp., Senate Hearings, 1953, p. 548; idem, Senate Hearings, 1956, p. 474.
105. *Variety*, 10 Mar. 1954, p. 15.
106. Ruben Shor, Senate Hearings, 1956, p. 181.
107. See *Variety*, 22 June 1955, p. 10; *Motion Picture Herald*, 11 Sept. 1954, p. 12.
108. Senate Hearings, 1953, p. 12.
109. *Motion Picture Herald*, 30 July 1955, p. 13.
110. Senator Guy M. Gillette of Iowa, Senate Hearings, 1953, p. 14. The number is given as 5,000, but this is evidently a misprint since Iowa had only 500 theaters in 1948, according to a study by the National Association of Real Estate Boards, ibid., p. 948.
111. Louis Phillips, Senate Hearings, 1956, p. 450.
112. Compare "Loew's Inc.," *Fortune*, Aug. 1939, p. 106.
113. Albert Hanson, in Senate Hearings, 1953, p. 10.
114. Cecil Vinnicof, ibid., p. 111.
115. Sidney A. Samuelson, ibid., p. 784.
116. Jay Emanuel, in *Motion Picture Exhibitor*, 9 June 1954, p. 7.
117. Charles M. Reagan, Senate Hearings, 1953, p. 527; Charles J. Feldman, ibid., p. 547.
118. Answers of twenty-two out of forty-one on this study's questionnaire.
119. Senate Small Business Rept., 1956, p. 26.
120. Trial testimony of William Zimmerman, sales executive of RKO, quoted in Brief for the Respondents, Theatre Enterprises, Inc. v. Paramount Film Distributing Corp., Supreme Court, Oct. term 1953, p. 13.
121. United Paramount Theatres, Inc., Annual Rept., 1952, pp. 13–14.
122. *Variety*, 9 Jan. 1952, p. 17.
123. Ibid., 1 Sept. 1954, p. 7.
124. Ibid., 17 Oct. 1951, p. 18; Spyros P. Skouras, ibid., 2 Jan. 1952, p. 7; Alfred Starr, ibid., 12 Nov. 1952, pp. 4, 85; Charles J. Feldman, ibid., 5 Jan. 1955, p. 43.
125. Allied States Association bulletin quoted in ibid., 1 Sept. 1954, p. 7.
126. Senator Hubert H. Humphrey of Minnesota, Senate Hearings, 1956, p. 79.
127. Philip Marcus, Senate Hearings, 1953, p. 654; compare Antitrust Division memorandum, ibid., p. 676.
128. Stanley N. Barnes, ibid., p. 649.
129. Senate Hearings, 1953, p. 19.
130. Ibid., 1956, p. 47.
131. Ibid., pp. 54–57.
132. *Variety*, 8 Aug. 1956, p. 16; 15 Aug. 1956, p. 24.
133. Eleven answers to the questionnaire sent out in this study.
134. *Motion Picture Herald*, 26 May 1956, p. 18.
135. Trueman T. Rembusch, Senate Hearings, 1956, p. 71.
136. Walter Reade, quoted in *Variety*, 1 Feb. 1956, p. 15.
137. Trueman T. Rembusch, Senate Hearings, 1956, p. 71.
138. 66 F. Supp., at 330.
139. *Variety*, 26 May 1954, p. 7.
140. Ibid., 16 Feb. 1955, p. 3.
141. Y. Frank Freeman, vice-president of Paramount Pictures Corp., Senate Hearings, 1956, p. 349.
142. *Motion Picture Herald*, 22 Sept. 1956, p. 18.
143. *Variety*, 9 Nov. 1955, p. 61.
144. Huettig, p. 95.
145. *Variety*, 17 June 1953, p. 3.

146. Ibid., 6 Feb. 1952, p. 21.

147. Milgram v. Loew's, Inc., 192 F. 2d 579 (3d Cir. 1951).

148. William Goldman Theatres, Inc. v. Loew's, Inc., 150 F. 2d 738, 743 (3d Cir. 1945).

149. Milwaukee Towne Corp. v. Loew's, Inc., Commerce Clearing House, *1950–1951 Trade Cases*, no. 63660 (N.D. Ill. 1950).

150. Milgram v. Loew's, Inc., 94 F. Supp. 416, 418, 419 (E.D. Pa. 1950).

151. Moses Lasky, "The Long Bow, or Lucretius, Book IV, Line 817," *California Law Review* (Oct. 1955), p. 599.

152. Michael Conant, "Consciously Parallel Action in Restraint of Trade," *Minnesota Law Review* (June 1954), pp. 805–6.

153. Theatre Enterprises, Inc. v. Paramount Film Distributing Corp., 346 U.S. 537 (1954). Justice Clark delivered the opinion of the Court.

154. Compare Fanchon & Marco, Inc. v. Paramount Pictures, Inc. 133 F. Supp. 839 (S.D. N.Y. 1955); Robbinsdale Amusement Corp. v. Warner Brothers Pictures Distributing Corp., 141 F. Supp. 134 (D. Minn. 1955).

155. *Variety*, 26 Jan. 1955, p. 5.

156. *FDY, 1956*, p. 91.

157. Senate Hearings, 1956, p. 29.

158. Donald Dewey, "Romance and Realism in Antitrust Policy," *Journal of Political Economy* (Apr. 1955), p. 95, n. 5.

159. See especially dissent of Commissioner Frieda Hennock in FCC Docket 10031, *Decision in Matter of the Applications of Paramount Television Productions, Inc.* (cited in Hellmuth, p. 400); also letter of Attorney General James P. McGranery to F.C.C. (Department of Justice press release, 12 Jan. 1953); Adams, *American Economic Review* (May 1955), p. 524.

160. Hellmuth, p. 399.

161. Ruth A. Inglis, "Need for Voluntary Self-Regulation, in The Motion Picture Industry," *Annals of the American Academy of Political and Social Science* (Nov. 1947), pp. 53–54.

162. Otto Preminger, producer, quoted in Art Buchwald's column, *New York Herald Tribune*, 10 Nov. 1953, p. 27; Father Paul J. Hayes, cited in *Newsweek*, 8 Aug. 1955, p. 51.

163. Huettig, p. 122.

164. Compare Spyros P. Skouras, *Variety*, 2 Jan. 1952, p. 7.

165. Albert E. Sindlinger, cited in ibid., 8 Dec. 1954, p. 3.

166. U.S. v. Technicolor, Inc., Civil 7507–WM, Consent Judgment about Eastman Kodak Co. (S.D. Calif. 1948), *1948–1949 Trade Cases*, No. 62338.

167. U.S. v. Technicolor, Inc., Consent Judgment about Technicolor, Inc. (S.C. Calif. 1950), *1950–1951 Trade Cases*, No. 62586; *Business Week*, 11 Mar. 1950, p. 25; *FDY, 1951*, p. 63.

168. See *Variety*, 19 Dec. 1951, pp. 7, 14; and *Wall Street Journal*, 11 Aug. 1952, p. 11.

169. U.S. v. Starlite Drive-In, Inc., 204 F. 2d 419 (7th Cir. 1953).

170. U.S. v. Alliance Theatre Corp., Civil 493 (S.D. Ind. 1952): Department of Justice press release, 9 Sept. 1955.

171. F.T.C. v. Motion Picture Advertising Service Co., 344 U.S. 392 (1953).

172. Acting Assistant Attorney General Newell A. Clapp, letter to *New York Times*, 20 Aug. 1952, p. 24.

173. *Motion Picture Herald*, 17 Sept. 1955, p. 13.

174. U.S. v. Twentieth Century–Fox Film Corp., 137 F. Supp. 78 (S.D. Calif. 1955).

175. *Variety*, 14 Mar. 1956, pp. 3, 75.

176. Department of Justice press release, 6 Mar. 1956.

Notes to Pages 198–208

177. *International Motion Picture Almanac*, 1956, p. xii.

178. F.T.C. v. Paramount Famous Lasky Corp., 57 F. 2d 152, 155 (2d Cir. 1932).

179. *FDY, 1956*, pp. 103, 105.

180. Huettig, p. 29.

181. Hellmuth, p. 395.

182. Charles R. Metzger, "Pressure Groups and the Motion Picture Industry," *Annals* (Nov. 1947), pp. 110–15; Leo C. Rosten, "Movies and Propaganda," ibid., p. 117.

183. Keynote speech at convention of Allied States Association of Motion Picture Exhibitors, *Variety*, 7 Oct. 1953, p. 16.

184. *Motion Picture Herald*, 21 Apr. 1956, p. 13.

185. "What's Playing at the Grove?" *Fortune*, Aug. 1948, p. 134.

11. Hollywood, the National Recovery Administration, and the Question of Monopoly Power

1. Sklar, p. 167.

2. Ibid., pp. 168–69.

3. Ibid., pp. 167–71; Jowett, *Film*, pp. 244–46. Tino Balio has examined United Artists' involvement in the NRA in his *United* pp. 97–100. His analysis is based, in part, on an earlier version of this paper; see p. 296. Balio summarizes his work on the NRA and United Artists in his edited volume *The American Film Industry* (Madison: Univ. of Wisconsin Pr., 1976), pp. 216–17.

4. The source is attorney Louis Nizer's book, *New Courts of Industry: Self-Regulation under the Motion Picture Code* (New York: Longacre Pr., 1935). Nizer worked for the film industry's monopolists and found their activities praiseworthy. His book is quite biased in favor of the status quo, as one might expect.

5. See Patricia F. Bowers, *Private Choice and Public Welfare* (Hinsdale, Ill.: Dryden Pr., 1974), pp. 1–201, for a summary of the neoclassical position. Roughly, for economic questions Jowett is the conservative and Sklar the liberal; both work primarily from a neoclassical framework.

6. For a critique of the neoclassical model, see James O'Connor, *The Fiscal Crisis of the State* (New York: St. Martin's, 1973), pp. 1–39; for a summary of theory of the state in Marxist economics, see Paul M. Sweezy, *The Theory of Capitalist Development* (New York: Monthly Review Pr., 1970), pp. 239–53; and for a rereading of the theory of the state in Marxist economics, see Antony Cutler et al., *Marx's Capital and Capitalism Today* (London: Routledge & Kegan Paul, 1978), 2:243–54.

7. Clair Wilcox and William G. Shepherd, *Public Policy Toward Business* (Homewood, Ill.: Richard D. Irwin, 1975), pp. 159–62; Harold S. Sloan and Arnold J. Zurcher, *A Dictionary of Economics*, rev. (4th ed.) New York: Barnes & Noble, 1964), p. 334; Will H. Hays, *The Memoirs of Will H. Hays* (Garden City, NY: Doubleday, 1955), pp. 323–63; Raymond Moley, *The Hays Office* (Indianapolis: Bobbs-Merrill, 1945), pp. 25–51.

8. Robert F. Himmelberg, *The Origins of the National Recovery Administration* (New York: Fordham Univ. Pr., 1976), pp. 1–222; Bernard Bellush, *The Failure of the NRA* (New York: Norton, 1975), pp. 45–46; Ellis W. Hawley, *The New Deal and the Problem of Monopoly* (Princeton: Princeton Univ. Pr., 1966), pp. 10–11, 36–43.

9. The legend of "fourth-largest" began in the late 1920s; *Variety*, 27 June 1933 (p. 5), quoted one source: "Some fool [the source said] back in 1927 put it in the bonnet of the U.S. Chamber of Commerce that pictures were fourth largest. Of course that is ridiculous" Using total sales, I estimate for 1933 the industry ranked somewhere be-

tween thirty-seventh and forty-fifth largest. In terms of total assets, the U.S. film industry ranked even lower. See Huettig, p. 56; Ferdinand Lundberg, *The Rich and Super Rich* (New York: Lyle Stuart, 1968), pp. 938–46.

10. L. S. Lyon et al., *The National Recovery Administration* (Washington, D.C.: Brookings, 1935), p. 11; Arthur M. Schlesinger, Jr., *The Coming of the New Deal* (Boston: Houghton, 1958), pp. 98–99; Bellush, pp. 1–52; Irving Bernstein, *Turbulent Years* (Boston: Houghton, 1969), pp. 34–36; Hawley, pp. 53–72; Wilcox and Shepherd, pp. 616–17.

11. It must be noted that, despite public solidarity, the Hays group continually fought amongst themselves. Each firm wanted the most relative monopoly power and fought to select strategies for the group which would guarantee both the monopoly position and maximum profits. See, for example, Warner Bros. objections in *Variety*, 4 July 1933, p. 5.

12. *Variety*: 6 June 1933, p. 7; 13 June 1933, p. 5; 20 June 1933, p. 5; 27 June 1933, p. 4; A. B. Momand, *The Hays Office and the NRA* (Shawnee, Okla.: Shawnee Printing Co., 1935), pp. 1–35; Conant, *Antitrust*, p. 85. Will Hays' own version is most illuminating; see Hays, p. 448. Hays suggests that Owen D. Young, president of General Electric, was the candidate for industry overseer.

13. U.S., National Recovery Administration, Division of Review, *Work Materials No. 34— The Motion Picture Industry*, by Daniel Bertrand (Washington, D.C.: Government Printing Office, 1936), pp. 37–39; *Variety*: 19 Sept. 1933, pp. 5, 29; 28 Nov. 1933, p. 1; and 12 Dec. 1933, p. 5; Jack Alicoate, ed., *FDY, 1934*, p. 597.

14. Under the 5 percent (5–5–5) system, exhibitors were permitted to cancel 5 percent of a block of films without payment, another 5 percent with half payment, and a final 5 percent with full payment, but with extended playing time on the other features, provided the block included all the features released by the distributor during a single season.

15. Using the motion picture code's definition, a *bank night* was "a plan under which the people in the community sign their names without charge in a book, each line of which is numbered. On a certain night the winning number is drawn in the theater and the lucky holder, whether he be in the theater or outside may go to a bank in the town the next morning, and receive the $25.00 or $50.00 which have been deposited there for this purpose."

    Race night was "a plan by which each patron entering the theater gets a number from one to ten. During the performance a short subject showing a race involving ten contestants is exhibited, and those holding the number which represents the winner receive a package containing various household and toilet articles."

    Screeno was "a plan whereby each patron is given a card containing five vertical and horizontal lists of numbers on the screen. An indicator whirls around a dial and stops at a number. The patrons having the number, cross it off. The first person securing a consecutive series of numbers, either horizontally or vertically calls out 'Screeno' and is entitled to a cash prize." Nizer, pp. 64–65.

16. U.S., Congress, Senate, Temporary National Economic Committee, *The Motion Picture Industry—A Pattern of Control*, Monograph 43, 76th Cong., 3d sess., 1941, pp. 7–8; U.S., N.R.A., *Work Materials No. 34*, pp. 40–57; Nizer, pp. 148–302; William I. Greenwald, "The Motion Picture Industry: An Economic Study of the History and Practices of a Business," Ph.D. diss., New York Univ., 1950, p. 145–52; Michael Mayer, "The Exhibition Contract," in A. William Bluem and Jason E. Squire, eds., *The Movie Business: American Film Industry Practice* (New York: Hastings, 1972), pp. 210–13.

17. Sklar, pp. 170–71; Balio, *United*, pp. 216–17; Nizer, pp. 243–48; *Variety*, 27 June 1933, p. 5; U.S., National Recovery Administration, "Report Regarding Investigation to

Be Made by the President in His Executive Order of November 27, 1933, Approving the Code of Fair Competition for the Motion Picture Industry," by Sol A. Rosenblatt (Washington, D.C.: G.P.O., 1934), pp. 1–13.

18. Ross, 1941, pp. 89–119; Hugh Lovell and Tasile Carter, *Collective Bargaining in the Motion Picture Industry* (Berkeley: Univ. of Calif. Inst. of Ind. Relations, 1955), pp. 40–50; Louis B. Perry and Richard S. Perry, *A History of the Los Angeles Labor Movement, 1911–1941* (Berkeley: Univ. of California Pr., 1963), pp. 318–61; Gomery, "Coming of Sound," pp. 305–16.

19. Bellush, pp. 142–46; *Motion Picture Herald*, 26 May 1934, p. 18; *Variety*, 2 Jan. 1934, p. 4; Wilcox and Shepherd, pp. 618–19; U.S., N.R.A., "Hearings Held Before the National Recovery Review Board in the Matter of the Motion Picture Code," vols. 1–4 (Washington, D.C.: G.P.O., 1934); U.S., Congress, Senate, Finance Committee, *Investigation of the N.R.A.: Hearings Before the Senate Finance Committee* (Pursuant to Senate Resolution No. 79, vol. 2, 74th Cong., 1st sess.), 1935; Hawley, pp. 91–110.

20. *Variety*: 29 May 1935, p. 1; 5 June 1935, p. 7; Bellush, pp. 168–75; Conant, *Antitrust*, pp. 95–97; "Arbitration in the Motion Picture Industry," *American Arbitration Journal* 5 2 (Spring, 1941):178–94; Hawley, pp. 283–360.

21. Of the eight Hollywood monopolists, six still dominate the industry. Only Howard Hughes' odd behavior with RKO caused that firm to drop from power. Loew's left voluntarily. See David Gordon, "Why the Movie Majors are Major," *Sight and Sound* 42 (Autumn 1973):194–96.

12. Self-censorship in the Movie Industry:
A Historical Perspective on Law and Social Change

1. The first movie censorship case was Block v. Chicago, Illinois #239, pp. 251, 87 N.E. 1011 (1909). See Richard S. Randall, *Censorship of the Movies: The Social and Political Control of a Mass Medium* (Madison: Univ. of Wisconsin Pr., 1968), pp. 11–12.

2. Ibid., pp. 77–143.

3. Ibid., pp. 18–25; 236 U.S. 230 (1915).

4. John Sargent, "Self-Regulation: The Motion Picture Production Code 1930–1961," Ph.D. diss., Univ. of Michigan, 1963, pp. 5–15.

5. Ibid., pp. 16–38.

6. Randall, pp. 204–5.

7. See Moley, pp. 25–127; Murray Schumach *The Face on the Cutting Room Floor* (New York: Morrow, 1964); Jack Vizzard, *See No Evil* (New York: Simon, 1970); Randall, pp. 198–214; Sargent, pp. 35–84, 107–8; *Variety*, 9 Oct. 1968, p. 9, col. 3.

8. See Sargent, pp. 107–8; Moley, pp. 226–54; Schumach, pp. 279–92; and Vizzard, pp. 366–81.

9. See Conant, *Antitrust*, chap. 2 and 3; Temporary National Economic Commission, "The Motion Picture Industry—A Pattern of Control," Monograph No. 43, 1941.

10. See Ralph Cassady, Jr., and Ralph Cassady III, *The Private Antitrust Suit in American Business Competition: A Motion-Picture Industry Case Analysis* (Los Angeles: Bureau of Business and Economic Research, U.C.L.A., 1964).

11. United States v. Paramount Pictures, 334 U.S. 131 (1948).

12. See Robert Coughland, "Now It Is Trouble That Is Supercolossal In Hollywood," *Life*, 13 Aug. 1951, p. 103.

13. *Moody's Industrials, 1950*, p. 2774.

14. Ibid., p. 665.
15. Freeman Lincoln, "The Comeback of the Movies," *Fortune*, Feb. 1955, p. 128.
16. Conant, Antitrust, p. 4.
17. Ibid., p. 13.
18. Ibid., pp. 4, 12–15.
19. *FDY, 1969*, pp. 97–98.
20. Samuel Goldwyn, "Movies Best Years Ahead: Television Is no Threat," *U.S. News and World Report*, 5 Mar. 1954, p. 38.
21. *FDY, 1949*, and *FDY, 1957*.
22. Coughlan, p. 107.
23. Lincoln, p. 128.
24. Gordon Stulberg, "Hollywood Transition," *Saturday Review*, 28 Dec. 1968, p. 20.
25. Milton Mackaye, "The Big Brawl: Hollywood vs. Television," *Saturday Evening Post*, 19 Jan. 1952, pp. 17–19.
26. See Hollis Alpert, "Retrospective," *Saturday Review*, 27 Nov. 1965, p. 45; Goldwyn, pp. 38–43.
27. Goldwyn, p. 38.
28. *Variety*, 22 Jan. 1958, p. 11, col. 5.
29. John Kenneth Galbraith, *The New Industrial State*, (Boston: Houghton, 1967) p. 356.
30. Ibid., pp. 97–108.
31. See Stulberg.
32. Galbraith, p. 384.
33. *Variety*, 22 Jan. 1958, p. 10.
34. Anthony Schillaci, "Film As Environment," *Saturday Review*, 28 Dec. 1968 p. 8; *MPAA Annual Report, A Year in Review*, June 1968, p. 13.
35. *FDY, 1969*, p. 98.
36. Ibid., p. 99.
37. *International Motion Picture Almanac*, 1969, p. 60.
38. *FDY, 1950–60*; See also John E. Twomey, "Some Considerations on the Rise of the Art-Film Theatre," *The Quarterly of Film, Radio, and Television*, Spring 1956, p. 240; Edouard de Laurot and Jonas Mekas "Foreign Film Distribution in the U.S.A.: An Interview with Thomas J. Brandon," *Film Culture*, no. 7, 1956, pp. 16–17; and Dallas W. Smythe, Parker B. Lusk, and Charles A. Lewis, "Portrait of an Art-Theatre Audience," *The Quarterly of Film, Radio, and Television 8*, Fall 1953, pp. 28–50.
39. *Variety*: 7 Jan. 1970, p. 25; 1 Apr. 1970, p. 11.
40. See Randall, pp. 116–18.
41. Conant, *Antitrust*, pp. 113–14.
42. Randall, pp. 201–2.
43. Interview with Jack Valenti by Gene Bates, Washington, D.C., 15 Aug. 1969.
44. *Daily Variety*, 20 Mar. 1970, pp. 34, 35.
45. United States v. Paramount Pictures, 334 U.S. 131, 166 (1948).
46. See Note, "Private Censorship of Movies," *Stanford Law Review*, 22 (1970) 618. The author indicates that if government boards utilized MPAA standards and procedures, they would be unconstitutional.
47. 343 U.S. 495 (1952).
48. Ibid., pp. 501–2.
49. Roth vs. United States, 354 U.S. 476 (1957).
50. Freedman v. Maryland, 380 U.S. 51, 58, 59 (1965).
51. "(U)nless such film or a part thereof is obscene, indecent, immoral, inhuman, sacri-

legious, or is of such a character that its exhibition would tend to corrupt morals or incite to crime, (the Motion Picture Division) shall issue a license therefore." Quoted in Joseph Burstyn, Inc. v. Wilson, 343 U.S. 495, 497 (1952).

52. Ibid., pp. 504, 505.
53. Burstyn has been memorialized in Alan F. Westin, "The Miracle Case: The Supreme Court and the Movies," Inter-University Case Program No. 64, 1961.
54. See Conant, *Antitrust*, pp. 113–14; Randall, pp. 208–10; Schumach, pp. 36, 40, 68–70; and Vizzard, pp. 151–58.
55. *Censorship*, Autumn, 1964, p. 33; *American Civil Liberties Union, 39th Annual Report* (1958–59), p. 21.
56. Randall, p. 162.
57. Ibid., pp. 206, 212–13.
58. See Richard Corliss, "The Legion of Decency," *Film Comment*, Summer 1968, pp. 24–61; Schumach, pp. 84–93; and Randall, pp. 160–62, 186–198.
59. *American Civil Liberties Union, Report on Civil Liberties*, (Jan. 1951–June 1953), p. 22.
60. Randall, p. 162.
61. Schumach, p. 89–90.
62. Interview with Henry Herx, Director of Educational Services, National Catholic Office for Motion Pictures, New York, 11 July 1969.
63. *National Decency Reporter*, Jan.–Feb. 1969, masthead.
64. Ibid., July–Aug. 1969, p. 14. The defendant in the landmark case of Jocabellis vs. Ohio, 378 U.S. 184 (1964), believed that the CDL was the major cause of his arrest and the seizure of *The Lovers*, Randall, p. 164.
65. William B. Lockhard and Robert C. McClure, "Literature, the Law of Obscenity, and the Constitution," *Minnesota Law Review* 38 (1954) 295, 311.
66. *Censorship Today*, Feb.–Mar. 1969, p. 48.
67. *Variety*, 23 Oct. 1968, p. 20, col. 1.
68. *American Civil Liberties Union, 43rd Annual Report* (1962–63), p. 19.
69. Schumach, pp. 95 and 99.
70. *American Civil Liberties Union, Report on Civil Liberties* (Jan. 1951–June 1953), p. 23.
71. *Censorship Today*, June–July 1969, p. 46; *Daily Variety*, 13 Jan. 1969, p. 1. col. 1.
72. *Variety*, 24 Dec. 1969, p. 18, col. 1. Note, "Entertainment: Public Pressures and the Law," *Harvard Law Review*, 71 (1957) 326, 362–63.
73. Schumach, pp. 99–107, 357; Note, *Harvard Law Review*, p. 357.
74. Note, "Extralegal Censorship of Literature," *New York University Law Review*, 33 (1958) 989, 993.
75. Schumach, p. 83.
76. Ira H. Carmen, *Movies, Censorship, and the Law*. Ann Arbor: Univ. of Michigan Pr., 1966. pp. 125, 184; Randall, pp. 77–81.
77. Note, *Harvard Law Review*, pp. 332–33.
78. Randall, p. 92.
79. Ibid., p. 90.
80. Carmen, pp. 186–99.
81. Ibid., p. 241.
82. Ibid., p. 302.
83. 390 U.S. 676 (1968).
84. Ibid., p. 690.
85. Randall, pp. 173–78.

86. *Variety*: 10 Sept. 1969, p. 6, col. 2; 3 Dec. 1969, p. 21, col. 5.
87. *American Civil Liberties News*, Sept. 1969, p. 1.
88. *Variety*: 22 Oct. 1969, p. 26, col. 2; 29 Oct. 1969, p. 26, col. 1; 11 Mar. 1970, p. 15, cols. 2–3.
89. *Variety*: 5 Mar. p. 3, col. 3; 22 Oct. 1969, p. 26, col. 2; *Censorship Today*, Oct–Nov. 1969, p. 26.
90. *Variety* 29 Oct. 1969, p. 26. col. 2.
91. *Censorship Today* 1, no. 3, p. 17.
92. Ibid., pp. 54–55.
93. *Variety*, 26 Mar. 1969, p. 26. col. 2.
94. Ibid., 12 Nov. 1969, p. 4. col. 5.
95. Schumach, pp. 107–16.
96. Interstate Circuit, Inc. v. Dallas, 390 U.S. 676 (1968), 691–703. For an excellent analysis of the case, see Samuel Krislov "From Ginzburg to Ginzgerg: The Unhurried Children's Hour in Obscenity Litigation, *1968 Supreme Court Review* 153, pp. 170–75, 185–87.
97. Interstate Circuit, Inc. v. Dallas, 247 Texas (1965–66).
98. Interstate Circuit, Inc. v. Dallas, 390 U.S. 676 (1968).
99. 390 U.S. 629 (1968).
100. Ibid., p. 636.
101. Krislov, p. 176.
102. *FDY, 1969*, p. 384.
103. *Variety*, 22 May 1968, p. 4, col 4; *FDY, 1969*, p. 99.
104. For a list of NATO affiliates, see *FDY, 1969*, pp. 390–95.
105. Letter from IFIDA to authors, 16 Jan. 1970.
106. *FDY, 1969*, p. 1014; *Variety*, 9 Oct. 1968, pp. 3, 9.
107. See *Variety*, 24 Apr. 1968, pp. 3, 14.
108. See *Variety*: 1 May 1968, p. 7, col. 3; 22 May 1968, p. 4, col. 4 and 5; see Nizer; *Variety*, 1 May 1968, p. 20, col. 2 and p. 7, col. 4 and 5.
109. *Variety*, 15 May 1968, p. 3, col. 3 and p. 13, col. 1.
110. Ibid., 22 May 1968, p. 4, col. 5; see pt. 4.
111. Ibid., p. 4. col. 5.
112. Ibid., 29 May 1968, p. 7, col. 1; *Daily Variety*, 18 Mar. 1970, p. 1, and col. 2.
113. *Variety*: 5 June 1968, p. 4, col. 3; 12 June 1968, p. 3, col. 2.
114. Ibid., 12 June 1968, p. 29, col. 1.
115. Dallas, Tex., Review Code #46A-4(d) (1960).
116. *Variety*, 26 June 1968, p. 1, col. 3.
117. Ibid.: 18 Feb. 1970, p. 6, col. 4; 11 Feb. 1970, p. 4, col. 2; 26 June 1968, p. 16. col. 1.
118. Ibid.: 9 Oct. 1968, p. 9, cols. 4–5; 16 Oct. 1968, p. 3, col. 3.
119. Ibid., 26 June 1968, p. 16. col. 1.
120. Ibid., 11 Feb. 1970, p. 4. col. 1.
121. Ibid., 21 Jan. 1970, p. 16. col. 2.
122. Ibid., Jan. 28, 1970, p. 4, col. 1.
123. Paragraph IX of the complaint in Tonylyn Prod., Inc. v. Motion Picture Association, Inc., C.D. Calif. complaint filed 9 Feb. 1970.
124. *Ibid.*
125. *Variety*, 3 July 1968, p. 5, col. 4.
126. Ibid.: p. 15, col. 4; 24 June 1970, p. 2, col. 4.
127. Ibid., 14 Aug. 1968, p. 5, col. 3.
128. Ibid., 18 Sept. 1968, p. 3, col. 3.

129. Ibid., 9 Oct. 1968, p. 3, col. 3.
130. *Hollywood Reporter*, 30 Mar. 1970, p. 1, col. 3; *FDY, 1969*, pp. 625–30; *Variety*, 29 July 1970, p. 2, col. 4.
131. See Note (Roy E. Bates and Peter Herman), *Stanford Law Review* 22 (1970) 618. The author concludes that the code's standards and procedures, if adopted by governmental agencies or courts, would be unconstitutional.
132. *Variety*, 12 Nov. 1969, p. 1, col. 1 (excerpts courtesy of MPAA, Washington, D.C.).
133. See *Variety*, 17 Dec. 1969, p. 3, col. 4; and 24 Dec. 1969, p. 7, col. 4.
134. Ibid., 17 Dec. 1969, p. 14, col. 1.
135. Ibid., 11 Mar. 1970, p. 26, col. 5.
136. Eugene Picker estimates that 2 percent of the nation's circulations restricts X and sometimes R films. *Variety*, 22 July 1970, p. 4. col. 4.
137. The survey by Young Nato covered 3,164 out of 13,000 exhibitors. *Variety*, 19 Nov. 1969, p. 20, col. 1.
138. *Variety*, 18 Feb. 1970, p. 6, col. 4–5; see also Tropic Film Corporation v. Paramount, MPAA, -F. Supplement- (S.D. N.Y. 1970); *Daily Variety*, 3 Aug. 1970, p. 3, col. 4.
139. Ibid.
140. *Variety*, 9 Apr. 1969, p. 26, col. 2.
141. Ibid., 5 Nov. 1969, p. 22, col. 1.
142. See *Hollywood Reporter*, 6 Feb. 1970, p. 1, col. 3.
143. Interview of Leonard Kastle by William F. Buckley on "Firing Line," KQED-TV, Channel 9, San Francisco, Calif., 12 Apr. 1970, 9:00–10:00 P.M.
144. *San Francisco Examiner*, 7 Dec. 1969, sec. B, p. 4, col. 3; *Variety*: 5 Nov. 1969, p. 4, col. 1; 12 Nov. p. 4, col. 1; Note, *Stanford Law Review* 22 (1970) 618.
145. *Variety*: 21 Jan. 1970, p. 3, col. 1; 18 Mar. 1970, p. 5, col. 1.
146. See *Daily Variety*, 17 Feb. 1970, p. 1. col. 2–3; *Variety*: 25 Feb. 1970, p. 5, col. 3; 20 May 1970, p. 22, col. 2; 22 July 1970, p. 6, col. 4; 10 June 1970, p. 3, cols. 4–5; 15 July 1970, p. 18, col. 5.

13. The Effects of Television on the
Motion Picture Industry: 1948–1960

1. These companies in 1946 produced over 70 percent of all American feature films, and received over 95 percent of all film-rental income. Gordon S. Watkins (ed.), *The Motion Picture Industry* (Philadelphia: American Academy of Political and Social Sciences, 1947).
2. American Academy of Political and Social Sciences.
3. U.S., Department of Commerce, *Survey of Current Business*, July 1957, and *National Income Supplement to the Survey of Current Business*, July 1947 and July 1954.
4. *FDY, 1957*.
5. "Is Television Killing the Movies?" *Advertising Agency Magazine* 49 (9 Nov. 1956): 49. There were five hundred respondents.
6. Advertising Research Foundation, Inc., *U.S. Television Households by Region, State, and County, March 1956* (New York: Advertising Research Foundation, Inc., 1956).
7. The method of combination in 1956 was to fit a least-squares linear regression equation using the Census county estimates as dependent variable and A. C. Nielsen Co. estimates of the same counties as independent variable (Nielsen's estimates covered all U.S. counties). Estimates for counties other than the original 435 were then made on the basis of the equation, subject to adjustment to bring regional totals into agreement with those estimated by the Census bureau.

8. Advertising Research Foundation, Inc., *U.S. Television Households by Region, State, and County, June 1955* (New York: Advertising Research Foundation, Inc., 1955). See table 13.3.

9. Ibid. The estimating procedure differed from that followed in the 1956 survey, in that the dependent variable used in the regression was an average of two sets of county estimates arrived at independently by the National Broadcasting Co. and *Television Magazine*.

10. The statement of significance is based on R. A. Fisher's z-transformation (see Mordecai Ezekiel and Karl A. Fox, *Methods of Correlation and Regression Analysis* (New York: John Wiley and Sons, 1959). The term *significant* as here used indicates a probable minimum value greater than zero for the correlation coefficient in the universe from which the sample has been taken. Correlation coefficients presented hereafter are significant at the 0.01 confidence level, unless otherwise stated.

11. Total U.S. population was 146,093,000 in 1948, and 161,191,000 in 1954. U.S., Bureau of Census, *Statistical Abstract of the United States: 1957* (Washington, D.C.: U.S. G.P.O. 1957).

12. "Things May Be Looking Up for the Movie Theaters," *Barron's* 38 (23 June 1958):3.

13. A. C. Nielsen Co., *Nielsen Television Index* (New York: A.C. Nielsen Co., monthly to subscribers).

14. There is a common belief, which the above data contradict, that the fall (Oct., Nov., Dec.) is television's best season. This results from the frequent use of data on advertising expenditures or program costs or both as an indirect measure of the television audience. As an example, the series "Television Advertising—Cost of Facilities," appearing monthly in the *Survey of Current Business* (compiled by Publishers Information Bureau), yields seasonal indexes of:

	Quarter		
I	II	III	IV
Seasonal Index 104	98	90	108

But this series represents total gross time charges for network television advertising, and the assumption that advertising outlays are always proportional to the size of the television audience is not justified, since factors other than audience size may be important to sponsors. For example, the automobile companies, accounting for almost 10 percent of network television advertising, advertise heavily in the fourth quarter, when new models appear.

15. The Census Bureau surveys show:

Percent of Households with Television Sets

Date	In Metropolitan Areas	Outside Metropolitan Areas
June 1955	78	50
Feb. 1956	82	59
Aug. 1956	84	63
Apr. 1957	87	70
Jan. 1958	89	75

Source: U.S., Bureau of the Census, *Housing and Construction Reports*.
(Washington, D.C.: U.S. Government Printing Office, 1958).

16. In addition, increased use of home air-conditioners has probably offset any effects of

increased air-conditioning in motion picture theaters. Nine and one-half million room air-conditioners were sold between 1948 and 1958. ("Manufacturers' Sales and Retail Value of Appliances," *Electrical Merchandising*, Statistical and Marketing Issue, Jan. 1959).

17. See Lloyd R. Morris, *Not So Long Ago* (New York: Random, 1949) for an interesting account of these early trials.

18. "Statistics of the Radio-TV-Electronics Industries," *Tele-Tech* 15 (Jan 1956):68.

19. Helen B. Shaffer, "Movie-TV Competition," *Editorial Research Reports* (18 Jan. 1957), p. 45.

20. The 244 network television programs produced during 1956 had a mean cost of $34,000 and a median cost of $33,000. Most expensive was the NBC "Hallmark Hall of Fame," at $210,000. "Television Magazine Data Book, 1957," *Television Magazine*, Mar. 1957.

21. *FDY, 1950.*

22. Reported in "Film Is Replacing Live Shows, Commercials," *Sales Management* 75 (20 Nov. 1955):42.

23. *FDY, 1947* and *FDY, 1958.*

24. For example, William Holden contracted to appear in *Bridge on the River Kwai* in return for 10 percent of gross revenues, with the proviso that returns be paid to him at the maximum rate of $50,000 per year. Since the picture has grossed almost $30 million, the producers are paying Holden out of interest earned by the $3 million obligated to him.

25. *Time*, 20 Apr. 1959.

26. "Comeback of the Movies," *Fortune* 51 (Feb. 1955):127.

27. *FDY, 1957.*

28. "Comeback of the Movies," p. 127.

29. U.S., House of Representatives, Committee on Interstate and Foreign Commerce, *Report on Network Broadcasting* 85th Cong., 2d sess., H. Rept. 1297, Union Calendar 509, 27 Jan. 1958).

30. "NBC Radio Sales Up 41 Percent," *Broadcasting Magazine* 54 (13 Jan. 1958):60.

31. "Getting Them Back to the Movies," *Business Week*, 22 Oct. 1955, p. 58.

32. *International Motion Picture Almanac, 1958* (New York: Quigley Publications, 1958).

33. "The Big Parade," "Old Ironsides," "North of '76," "The Thundering Herd," "Twinkletoes," "The Iron Horse," and "Wings."

34. *Time*, 8 June 1953, p. 66.

35. Another old idea whose development has been attempted recently is the motion picture with odors (of the literal variety) to supplement action and setting. "AROMARAMA" opened in New York in Dec. 1959. The film is distributed with a machine that can project forty smells to each seat in the theater.

36. "The Tape Threat," *Printers' Ink* 263 (25 Apr. 1958):25.

37. "Television: The Light That Failed," *Fortune* 58 (Dec. 1958):78.

38. Dependability is another advantage. An anonymous television producer has pointed out that "film doesn't arrive drunk."

39. "TV Goes Hollywood," *Printers' Ink* 260 (23 Aug. 1957):19.

40. "Economic Impact of the Audio-Visual Field," *Journal of the Society of Motion Picture and Television Engineers* 66 (Aug. 1957):458.

41. "Videotape," introduced commercially during the 1958–59 season, provides an alternative method of permanently recording television programs. Both sound and picture

are recorded on magnetic tape, and are reproduced with better fidelity than offered by regular film. Furthermore, the process is only two-thirds as expensive as filming a "live" show. For these reasons this development may lead to increased "live" programming as opposed to the use of syndicated film, since it reduces the cost of reshowing such programs. In particular, the television networks have adopted this method to "delay" live programs intended for broadcasting in different time zones at the same local time.

42. The leader, Ziv-TV, grossed $42 million in 1958. The company employs 3,500 people and uses ten Hollywood sound stages to produce thirty-two syndicated shows.

43. "Television Goes Hollywood," *Printers' Ink* 260 (23 Aug. 1957):19.

44. "Study Blames Television for Theater Drop," *Broadcasting Magazine* 54 (3 Feb. 1958):58.

45. "Box-Office Upturn," *Barron's* 36 (5 Mar. 1956):11.

46. "Paramount's Effect on Television," *Sponsor* 12 (22 Feb. 1958):37.

47. "Uncertainties That Blur Motion Picture Outlook," *Magazine of Wall Street* 101 (15 Feb. 1958):634.

48. Study by Sindlinger and Co., reported in *Broadcasting* 54 (3 Feb. 1958):58.

49. "Movie-Television Competition," *Editorial Research Reports*, 18 Jan. 1957, p. 45.

50. "Hard Times for Movie Makers," *Financial World* 109 (5 Mar. 1958):18.

51. An unsuccessful exception was the American Broadcasting Co.'s "Famous Film Festival," consisting mainly of British pictures.

52. Speech before executives of affiliated stations of the National Broadcasting Co., Miami Beach, Dec. 1956.

14. The Economics of the Television Market for Theatrical Movies

1. *Variety*, 8 Nov. 1978, p. 1.

2. See Scherer.

3. Ibid.

4. Bruce M. Owen, Jack H. Beebe, and Willard G. Manning, *Television Economics* (Lexington, Mass: Heath, 1974), p. 104.

5. The price per minute equals the price per thousand viewers times the number of expected viewers. One complication in this analysis is that, generally speaking, the top-rated network demands that a premium be added to its prices for its entire lineup of programs. However, as long as this premium is known and predictable, it should not affect oligopolistic consensus.

6. For example, the network base hourly rates for the three affiliates in Chicago are: WMAQ (NBC) = $4,800; WLS (ABC) = $4,900; WBBM (CBS) = $4,750. See *Television Factbook* (Washington, D.C.: Television Digest, 1978).

7. A good example of this practice is found in the auto industry, where prices have been stabilized and style changes are the only area of competition. For more detail, see Lawrence J. White, "The Automobile Industry," in *The Structure of American Industry*, ed. Walter Adams, (New York: Macmillan, 1977).

8. For example, the "Kojak" program began in 1972 at $200,000 per original episode and $20,000 for each repeat. For the sixth year of the program, the contract calls for $233,000 and $22,500, respectively. This amounts to less than a 3 percent increase per year over the six-year period. See U.S. v. CBS, NBC, ABC, complaint and brief filed in U.S. District Court, Central District of Calif. 1974, exhibit 7. Since the 1976 season,

when the degree of network competition began to intensify, the networks have been somewhat more flexible in granting higher episode prices for subsequent seasons. However, the fundamental inequality in bargaining power, which favors the networks has not been significantly eroded.

9. Federal Communications Commission, *Television Network Program Procurement, Part II: Second Interim Report by Office of Network Study* (Washington, D.C.: U.S. Government Printing Office, 1965), chap. 13.

10. *Wall Street Journal,* 27 Dec. 1977, p. 24 and *Advertising Age,* 11 Nov. 1974, p. 2.

11. Eugene Foster, *Understanding Broadcasting* (Reading, Mass.: Addison-Wesley, 1978): 267.

12. Ibid.

13. The rules forbid networks from obtaining distribution rights or profit shares in programs other than those which they have produced themselves. See Federal Communications Commission, "Prime Time Access Report and Order." 23 FCC Reports 2d 389, 1970.

14. The networks were able to obtain (a) domestic distribution rights in about 25–30 percent of their prime-time series; (b) foreign distribution rights in a similar percentage of series; (c) average domestic and foreign profit shares of 25–30 percent in 55–65 percent of their series. See Arthur D. Little, Inc., *Television Program Production Procurement, Distribution and Scheduling: Data Relating to Proposals for Rule Making in FCC Docket No. 12782* (Cambridge, Mass.: A. D. Little, 1969), pp. 46–51.

15. Federal Communications Commission, Television chap. 12.

16. Robert Crandall has argued that the networks compensated the program producers for syndication rights and profit shares with higher license prices. However, his model has several deficiencies and yields mixed results. Robert W. Crandall, "FCC Regulation, Monopsony, and Network Program Costs," *The Bell Journal of Economics* 3 (Autumn 1972):483–508.

17. *Broadcasting,* 23 Sept. 1974, pp. 15–16.

18. Dennis B. McAlpine, "The Television Programming Industry," Report from Tucker Anthony and R. L. Day (stockbrokers), New York, 1975, p. 7.

19. The data needed to calculate subsidiary income from the syndication industry are considered confidential and hence not available for research purposes. Theoretically speaking, the profit-maximizing producer will consider all sources of profit and losses before engaging in production. This stream-of-profits function will depend upon such factors as the program type, the number of years the program stays on the network, the average rating per year, and the age at first syndication. After assigning probabilities to these variables, the producer can determine his expected profit from the series. This type of analysis is a very fruitful area for future research if the data can be obtained.

20. The most important work in this area has been done by Taylor, who has shown that the expected television rating for theatrical movies significantly depends upon success in the theatrical premarket. He measured success by binary variables for film awards, top-grossing films, and the "quality" of the director. See Ryland A. Taylor, "Television Movie Audiences and Movie Awards: A Statistical Study," *Journal of Broadcasting* 18 (Spring 1974):181–86; and "Televised Movies: Directors Win Audience," *Journal of Broadcasting* 20 (Fall 1976):495–500. See also Barry Litman, "Predicting Ratings for Theatrical Movies," *Journalism Quarterly* 56, no. 3 (Autumn 1979):590–94.

21. Robert W. Crandall, "Postwar Performance of the Motion Picture Industry," *The Antitrust Bulletin* 20 (Spring 1975):49–88.

22. See Owen, Beebe, and Manning.

23. *Variety*, new season annual editions.

24. Ibid., 5 Apr. 1978, p. 3; 16 Feb. 1978, p. 1.

25. McAlpine, p. 14.

26. *Variety*: 19 Apr. 1978, p. 45; 26 Apr. 1978, p. 1.

27. These are the only contract data available and were obtained from confidential sources. One of the problems associated with the data is that the individual films are negotiated in packages of ten or more. Hence, it is possible that the price associated with each film is not truly representative of the film's quality but merely an accounting price. In particular, the prices might be "averaged out" over all the films in the package, and there would thus be little or no correlation between price and film quality. However, the fact that the coefficients of the theatrical rental variables are strongly correlated indicates either that this averaging process was not used, or if it was used, then the coefficients understate a much stronger correlation.

28. Leonard Maltin, *TV Movies* (New York: New American Library, 1974).

29. The average picture in the sample has a length of 109.83 minutes, an age of 53.76 months, an adjusted rental of $2.70 million, and a star rating of 2.56 stars. According to the estimation equation this film would be worth $689,870 in the 1966–67 television market:

$$Y = (3.87 \cdot 109.83) - (.723 \cdot 53.76) + (26.922 \cdot 2.70) + (20.392 \cdot 2.56) + 181.583$$
$$= 689.87$$

Since 1966, the price for theatrical films of average quality has nearly tripled. See *Variety*, 5 Apr. 1978, p. 3. Thus a first approximation for the current estimation equation can be found by multiplying all of the coefficients of the independent variables by a factor of three.

30. The average program in the sample has been on the air for 1.19 seasons, with a previous season's rating of 18.66. If this program was 60 minutes in length and had special effects, the expected contract price would be $380,654.

$$Y = (6.35 \cdot 60) + (4.715 \cdot 1.19) + (17.753 \cdot 1) + (1.259 \cdot 18.66) - 47.202 + 380.654$$
$$= 380.654$$

31. This expectation is not as simple or trivial as it may appear, for it is quite possible that the producers of hit shows may ask for and receive special compensation from the network which would then result in a positive correlation between price and ratings.

    Since the test here is whether there is a correlation between price and ratings for programs in the initial contract period, four shows which have been on the air over five years were eliminated from the sample. They are "All in the Family," "Hawaii Five-O," "The Carol Burnett Show," and "The Wonderful World of Disney."

15. Film Conglomerate Blockbusters:
International Appeal and Product Homogenization

1. Roger Lewis, "On the Producer," *Movie People: At Work in the Business of Film* ed. Fred Baker and Ross Firestone (New York: Lancer Books, 1973), pp. 22–23.

2. Ibid., p. 19.

3. Earl C. Gottschalk, "MGM to Sell Studio, Give Up Film Distribution," *Wall Street Journal*, 18 Sept. 1973, p. 36.

4. Leonard Sloane, "Aubrey Resigns Top Post at Metro-Goldwyn-Mayer," *New York Times*, 1 Nov. 1973, p. 63.

5. Robert Gessner, "Film," *International Encyclopedia of the Social Sciences* 5:428.

6. Lou Greenspan, "The Journal Looks at Hollywood and the State of the Industry," *Journal of the Producers Guild of America* 12, no. 1 (Mar. 1970):3–4.

7. U.S., Department of Commerce, *U.S. Industrial Outlook, 1972* (Washington, D.C.: G.P.O., 1971):439.

8. Sidney Lumet, "On the Director," *Movie People: At Work in the Business of Film* ed. Fred Baker and Ross Firestone (New York: Lancer Books, 1973):51.

9. U.S., Department of Commerce, *U.S. Industrial Outlook*, 1972, p. 380.

10. Earl C. Gottschalk, Jr., "The Spectaculars," *Wall Street Journal*, 10 Aug. 1974, p. 1.

11. Ibid.

12. Ibid.

13. Samuel Z. Arkoff, "Famous Myths of the Film Industry," *Journal of the Producers Guild of America* 11, no. 3 (Sept. 1969):6.

14. Charles Champlin, "Who's Watching?" *Journal of the Producers Guild of America* 15, no. 1 (Mar. 1973):17.

15. Stephen Grover, "Spreading the Risk," *Wall Street Journal*, 30 May 1974, p. 1.

16. Wilton R. Holm, "Management Looks at the Future," *Journal of the Producers Guild of America* 12, no. 3 (Sept. 1970):15.

17. A. H. Howe, "A Banker Looks at the Picture Business," *Journal of the Producers Guild of America* 11, no. 1 (Mar. 1969):17.

18. Ibid., p. 18.

19. William F. Hellmuth, Jr., "The Motion Picture Industry," *The Structure of American Industry* ed. Walter Adams (New York: Macmillan, 1954):380–82.

20. Jack Valenti, "The 'Foreign Service' of the Motion Picture Association of America," *Journal of the Producers Guild of America* 10, no. 1 (Mar. 1968):21.

21. U.S., Department of Commerce, *U.S. Direct Investments Abroad 1966, Part 1: Balance of Payments Data* (Washington, D.C.: G.P.O., 1971):24.

22. U.S., Department of Commerce, *Balance of Payments* (Washington, D.C.: G.P.O., n.d.):144.

23. Valenti, p. 25.

24. William Pay, "British Year in Review," *International Motion Picture Almanac, 1966–1973* (New York, Hollywood, and London: Quigley Publishing Co., 1966–73).

25. Ibid. (1972) p. 551.

26. Ibid., p. 572.

27. See Thomas H. Guback, "American Interests in the British Film Industry," *The Quarterly Review of Economics and Business* 7, no. 2 (1967):7–21; "Film as International Business," chap. 16; and *The International Film Industry* (Bloomington: Indiana Univ. Pr., 1969).

28. Guback, "Film as Business," chap. 16.

29. U.S., Department of Commerce, *Balance of Payments*, p. 144.

30. U.S., Department of Commerce, *U.S. Industrial Outlook, 1972*, p. 438.

31. Ibid., p. 171.

32. Paul Gardner, "Foreign Films, Popular in U.S. in '60s, Being Treated Like Foreigners in '70s," *New York Times*, 4 Oct., 1973, p. 1.

16. Film As International Business:
The Role of American Multinationals

1. Motion Picture Association of America and Motion Picture Export Association of America, *1972: A Review of the World of Movies* (New York: MPAA, 1973), pp. 28–29 (hereafter cited as MPAA/MPEAA).
2. Tapio Varis, *International Inventory of Television Programme Structure and the Flow of TV Programmes Between Nations* (Tampere, Finland: Institute of Journalism and Mass Communication, Univ. of Tampere, 1973), pp. 194–95.
3. International Secretariat of Entertainment Trade Unions, *Newsletter* 9, no. 1 (Jan.–Feb. 1973):5.
4. Institute of Journalism and Mass Communication, Univ. of Tampere (Finland), *Proceedings of the Symposium on the International Flow of Television Programmes* (Tampere: 21–23 May 1973), p. 62.
5. Centre National de la Cinématographie, *L'Activité Cinématographique Française en 1972*, supplement to *Bulletin d'Information*, nos. 140–41 (Apr.–June 1973), p. 2.
6. *Variety*, 25 July 1973.
7. Varis, pp. 45–61.
8. MPAA/MPEAA, p. 2.
9. U.S., Department of Commerce, *1973 U.S. Industrial Outlook* (Washington, D.C.: G.P.O., 1973), p. 433.
10. Valenti, 25.
11. MPAA/MPEAA, p. 8.
12. Ibid., p. 28.
13. Varis, p. 194.
14. Consumer Goods and Services Division, Office of Business Research and Analysis, U.S., Department of Commerce, letter to the author, 18 Sept. 1973.
15. Valenti, p. 21.
16. U.S., House of Representatives, Committee on the Judiciary, Report by the Staff of the Antitrust Subcommittee (Subcommittee No. 5), *Investigation of Conglomerate Corporations*, 1 June 1971 (Washington, D.C.: G.P.O., 1971) p. 187.
17. "U.S. Multinationals—the Dimming of America," a report prepared for the AFL-CIO Maritime Trades Department Executive Board Meeting, 15–16 Feb. 1973, as reprinted in U.S., Senate, Committee on Finance, Subcommittee on International Trade, Hearings, *Multinational Corporations*, Feb. and Mar. 1973 (Washington, D.C.: G.P.O. 1973), p. 448.
18. Leo Model, "The Politics of Private Foreign Investment," *Foreign Affairs* 45, no. 4 (July 1967):641.
19. "U.S. Multinationals," p. 475.
20. U.S., Department of Commerce, *Survey of Current Business*: 49, no. 10 (Oct. 1969): 24; 52, no. 10 (Oct. 1972):21; 52, no. 11 (Nov. 1972):28.
21. McGeorge Bundy, "Europe Still Matters," *European Community*, no. 163 (Feb.–Mar. 1973):17–18.
22. Federal Trade Commission, *Economic Report for Webb-Pomerene Associations: A 50-Year Review* (Washington, D.C.: G.P.O., 1967), p. 59.
23. "Higher Income from Abroad," *Journal of the Producers Guild of America* 10, no. 1 (Mar. 1968):30.
24. Federal Trade Commission, pp. 41, 53.
25. Ibid., p. 47.

26. U.S., Senate, Committee on Foreign Relations, Hearings, *U.S. Information Media Guaranty Program,* Mar. and Apr. 1967 (Washington, D.C.: G.P.O., 1967), p. 76.
27. Department of the Treasury, *DISC, A Handbook for Exporters* (Washington, D.C.: G.P.O., 1972), p. i.
28. Overseas Private Investment Corp., *Annual Report Fiscal 1972,* n.p., n.d., p. 4.
29. Overseas Private Investment Corp., *An Introduction to OPIC,* July 1971, p. 2.
30. Valenti, p. 22.
31. Ibid., p. 24.
32. Centre National de la Cinématographie, p. 12.
33. Association of Cinematograph, Television, and Allied Technicians, *Report of the A.C.T.T. Nationalisation Forum* (6 May 1973), p. 15.
34. National Film Finance Corp., *Annual Report and Statement of Accounts, for the Year Ended 31st March 1972* (London: Stationery Office, 1972), p. 4.
35. Centre National de la Cinématographie, *Bulletin d'Information,* no. 139 (Feb. 1973): 29–30.
36. Robert W. Gilbert, "Foreign Film Subsidies As an Aspect of Financing," *Journal of the Producers Guild of America* 10, no. 3 (Sept. 1968):6, 8.
37. Eitel Monaco, president of Associazione Nazionale Industrie Cinematografiche ed Affini, quoted in Centre National de la Cinématographie, *Bulletin d'Information,* no. 108 (Dec. 1967), p. 233.
38. *Variety,* 7 Mar. 1973. Additional details concerning American membership in European motion picture trade organizations is available in Thomas H. Guback, *The International Film Industry: Western Europe and America since 1945* (Bloomington: Indiana Univ. Pr., 1969).
39. *Variety,* 28 Mar. 1973.
40. "American Interests in the British Film Industry," *The Quarterly Review of Economics and Business* 7, no. 2 (Summer 1967):7–21; "Les Investissements Américains dans le Cinéma Européen," *Cinéthique,* Jan.–Feb. 1970, pp. 33–40; "Film and Cultural Pluralism" *Journal of Aesthetic Education* 5, no. 2 (Apr. 1971):35–51.
41. Paul Kemezis, "The Consumer and the Common Market," *European Community,* no. 159 (Oct. 1972):19.
42. "U.S. Multinationals," p. 452.
43. *Variety,* 4 May 1966, p. 1.

17. Cultural Dependency in Canada's Feature Film Industry

1. Statistics Canada, *Annual,* Nos. 63–207. Ottawa, 1977.
2. For a discussion of how major U.S. film producer/distributors invaded and occupied the Canadian theatrical film markets as early as 1920, see Manjunath Pendakur, "Canadian Feature Film Industry: Monopoly and Competition," Ph.D. diss., Simon Fraser Univ., 1980.
3. Kari Levitt, *Silent Surrender: The American Economic Empire in Canada* (New York: Liveright, 1970).
4. Herbert I. Schiller, *Communication and Cultural Domination* (White Plains, N.Y.: International Arts and Sciences Pr., 1976).
5. Created in 1945 as a legalized cartel under the Webb-Pomerene Export Trade Act of 1918, the Motion Picture Export Association of America protects the hegemony of

American major producer/distributors in foreign markets. For a detailed analysis of its activities in Canada, see Pendakur, pp. 146–54 and also chap. 8.

6. For a discussion of how Odeon theaters came to be organized as a competing circuit and how the U.S. majors reorganized the market structure to best suit their interests, see Pendakur, pp. 182–88.

7. Council of Canadian Film Makers, Documents, Hearings Before the Royal Commission of Corporate Concentration, *The Bryce Commission Papers*, 27 Apr. 1976.

8. Ibid.

9. Ibid.

10. George Destounis, Interview by Kirwan Cox for "The Great Canadian Culture Hunt" (CBC television program), 17 Mar. 1976.

11. See *Bryce Papers*.

12. *Cinemag*, Feb. 1979.

13. C. R. B. Salmon, Canadian Odeon Theatres, personal interview, Toronto, 15 Nov. 1978.

14. Canada, Bureau of Competition Policy, Department of Consumer and Corporate Affairs, *Applications of the Combines Act to Services*, Ottawa, Apr. 1976.

15. Canadian Film Development Corporation, *Annual Reports*, 1968–78.

16. This association is a branch plant of the Motion Picture Export Association of America, representing the interests of the U.S. majors in Canada.

17. Canadian Motion Picture Distributors Association, *A Submission to the Federal Department of Finance*, July 1978.

18. Association of Independent and Canadian Owned Motion Picture Distributors, *Brief Submitted to the Secretary of State*, Ottawa, 1977.

19. Jeremy Katz, former booker for Famous Players, personal interview, Kingston, Ontario, 20 Nov. 1978.

20. Daniel Weinzweig, president, Association of Independent and Canadian Owned Motion Picture Distributors, personal interview, 18 Nov. 1978.

21. Salmon interview.

22. Susan M. Crean, *Who's Afraid of Canadian Culture?* (Toronto: General Publishing, 1976), p. 89.

23. *Variety*, 14 Feb. 1979.

24. Weinzweig, interview.

25. Linda Beath, partner, New Cinema Enterprises, personal interview, 16 Nov. 1978.

18. The Common Market Film Industry:
Beyond Law and Economics

1. Quoted in Roger Watkins, "Reaction to Command-M Proposals Not Cheery at Berlin Festival," *Variety*, 6 July 1977, p. 6.

2. The terms "Common Market" and "European Communities" will be used interchangeably in this study to describe the economic organization of the nine member states of this trade union: Belgium, Denmark, West Germany, the United Kingdom, Ireland, Italy, Luxemburg, and the Netherlands. The Common Market was often called the European Economic Community (EEC) until the late 1960s, when with the merger of the EEC with two other European regional organizations for coal and steel, and atomic energy, EC, or "European Communities," was adopted as a title for all three organizations. The United Kingdom, Ireland, and Denmark joined the European Communities in 1973.

3. American films are particularly dominant in nations such as West Germany and the United Kingdom, attracting between 65–70 percent of the German theater audience, and between 80–90 percent of the United Kingdom audience. See "Common Market Maps All-Europe Policy for Films," *Variety*, 9 Feb. 1977, p. 3.

4. These general principles are restated more specifically in later chapter provisions of the treaty, with ARTICLES 12–29 dealing specifically with customs regulations, ART. 30–37 with equivalent measures, ART. 48–51 with the free movement of goods and services, and ART. 92–94 with state aids. *Treaty Establishing the European Economic Community* (Rome, 25 Mar. 1957), ART. 3.

5. Despite these political problems, however, the Common Market was able to complete its timetable for ending all international tariffs and restraints almost two years ahead of schedule. See John Newhouse, *Collision in Brussels* (New York: Norton, 1967).

6. These rough calculations of relative GNP are derived from 1974 figures supplied by the European Community Statistical Office, indicating that Common Market nations cumulatively had reached 80–85 percent of the GNP of the United States in that year.

7. This motive for immediate action was suggested during several interviews with members of the Legal Office of the EC Commission in Brussels, 10–20 June 1977.

8. Procurer de Roi vs Dassonville, the first and still most important case defining when licensing or labeling requirements may have the equivalent effect of tariff restraints, is described extremely well in the pamphlet "The Court of Justice of the European Communities" (Brussels: European Documentation-Information, 1976). The case limiting labeling restrictions on prescription drugs is *De Peijper* ([104–75], CJEC 12.5 (1976); as yet unreported in CMLR or CCH).

9. See European Economic Communities, *Tenth General Report on the Activities of the Communities in 1976* (Brussels: European Community, 1976), section on "Community Law."

10. This contention is made by Pierre Loriot, an official until recently in charge of film negotiations for Division 4, Internal Market of the EC Commission, in an internal memorandum prepared before the summer meeting of Commission and CICCE representatives in July 1977.

11. See *Variety*, 9 Feb. 1977, p. 1.

12. Ibid.

13. See, e.g., "British Eady Fund May Be Illegal in Common Market," *Variety*, 21 Jan. 1976, p. 36.

14. See Ted Clark, "Common Market's Common Trait: Stall," *Variety*, October 5, 1977, p. 51.

15. European Economic Communities, *1st Report on Competition* (Brussels: European Community, 1972), p. 137.

16. EEC, *2nd Report on Competition* (Brussels: European Community, 1973), p. 95.

17. See *Variety*: 6 July 1977, p. 37; 20 July 1977, p. 31; 13 July 1977, p. 26; and 6 July 1977, p. 6.

18. See ibid., 31 Aug. 1977, p. 1.

19. See EEC, *1st Report*, p. 137.

20. See Guback, *International Film Industry*, chap. 16.

21. See Massima Ferrara Santamaria, "Subsidy, Coproduction, Shelter in Europe Now and in the Future," *Variety*, 19 Oct. 1977, p. 104.

22. Harold Myers, "Common Market Aim: Offset U.S. Advantages," ibid., January 7, 1976, p. 18.

23. Ted Clark, "New Eurocrat Fund for Film Biz," ibid., May 18, 1977, p. 1.

24. See "Bureaucrats Stall on Film Regs: Common Market Bosses Must Act," ibid., 6 Apr. 1977, p. 2.

25. Ibid., 5 Oct. 1977, p. 51.

26. Ibid., 6 July 1977, p. 6.

27. Support would be based upon payment for viewing of specific films, possibly employing one of the scrambling-unscrambling techniques now used by pay-TV systems in the United States. For a description of the direct-broadcast satellite proposed to provide sufficient channel space for such delivery techniques by 1990, see ibid., 19 Oct. 1977.

Selected Bibliography

Trade Papers, Journals, and Yearbooks

Box Office (1932–)
Broadcasting (1931–)
Daily Variety (1933–)
Exhibitors' Herald (1914–29)
    Exhibitors' Herald-World (1929–30)
    Motion Picture Herald (1930–70)
Film Daily (1922–68)
    Wid's Daily (1915–21)
    Film and Television Daily (1968–69)
    Film TV Daily (1970)
Film Daily Year Book of Motion Pictures (FDY) (1928–69)
    Wid's Year Book (1918–22)
    Film Year Book (1922–27)
    Film TV Year Book of Motion Pictures and Television (1970)
Hollywood Reporter (1930–)
International Motion Picture Almanac (1936–51, 1956–)
    Motion Picture Almanac (1929–36)
    Motion Picture and Television Almanac (1952–55)
Journal of the Producers Guild of America (1958–)
Journal of the Society of Motion Picture and Television Engineers (1950–)
    Transactions of the Society of Motion Picture Engineers (1916–20)
    Journal of the Society of Motion Picture Engineers (1920–49)
Motion Picture Herald (1930–72)
Moving Picture World (1907–27)
    Exhibitors' Herald (1914–29)
    Exhibitors' Herald-World (1929–30)
Moving Picture World (MPW) (1907–27)
    Exhibitors' Herald (1928)
    Exhibitors' Herald-World (1929–30)
    Motion Picture Herald (1930–72)
New York Dramatic Mirror (1889–17)
    New York Mirror (1879–89)
    Dramatic Mirror (1917–22)
Variety (1905–)

Books and Articles

A. C. Nielsen Co. *Nielsen Television Index*. New York: A. C. Nielsen Co., 1951+.

Allen, Jeanne Thomas. "The Decay of the Motion Picture Patents Company." *Cinema Journal* 10 (Spring 1971):34–40; In *The American Film Industry*, edited by Tino Balio, pp. 119–34. Madison: Univ. of Wisconsin Pr., 1976.

———. "Copyright and Early Theater, Vaudeville and Film Competition." *Journal of the University Film Association* 31 (Spring 1979):5–11.

Allen, Robert C. "Contra the Chaser Theory," *Wide Angle* (Spring 1979):4–11.

———. *Vaudeville and Film 1895–1915: A Study in Media Interaction*. New York: Arno Pr., 1980.

Alpert, Hollis. "Retrospective." *Saturday Review*, 27 Nov. 1965, p. 45.

American Film Institute Feature Film Catalogues, The (1921–30, 1961–70). New York: Bowker, 1976.

Anderson, Oscar E. *Refrigeration in America*. Princeton: Princeton Univ. Pr., 1953.

Andrew, Dudley. "The Postwar Struggle for Color." *Cinema Journal* 18 (Spring 1979): 41–52.

Arkoff, Samuel Z. "Famous Myths of the Film Industry." *Journal of the Producers Guild of America* 11, no. 3 (Sept. 1969):3–7.

Balaban, Barney, and Katz, Sam. *The Fundamental Principles of Balaban and Katz Theatre Management*. Chicago: Balaban and Katz, 1926.

Balaban, Carrie. *Continuous Performance*. New York: A. J. Balaban Foundation, 1964.

Balio, Tino. *United Artists: The Company Built by the Stars*. Madison: Univ. of Wisconsin Pr., 1975.

———, ed. *The American Film Industry*. Madison: Univ. of Wisconsin Pr., 1976.

Barnouw, Erik. *Tube of Plenty, The Evolution of American Television*. New York: Oxford Univ. Pr., 1975.

Baumgarter, Paul A., and Farber, Donald C. *Producing, Financing, and Distributing Film*. New York: Drama, 1973.

Behlmer, Ruby, ed. *Memo from David O. Selznick*. New York: Viking, 1972.

Bellush, Bernard. *The Failure of the NRA*. New York: Norton, 1975.

Berkow, Ira. *Maxwell Street*. Garden City, N.Y.: Doubleday, 1977.

Bernstein, Irving. *Hollywood at the Crossroads: An Economic Study of the Motion Picture Industry*. Hollywood: By the author, 1957.

———. *The Economics of Television Film Production and Distribution*. (A report to the Screen Actors Guild.) Sherman Oaks, Calif., 1960.

———. *Turbulent Years*. Boston: Houghton, 1969.

Bertrand, Daniel; Evans, W. Duane; and Blanchard, E. L. *The Motion Picture Industry—A Pattern of Control*, TNEC Monograph 43, 1941.

Blaisdell, George: "Mecca of the Motion Picture," *MPW* 25, no. 2 (10 July 1915):216.

Bluem, A. William, and Squire, Jason E., eds. *The Movie Business: American Film Industry Practice*. New York: Hastings, 1972.

Borneman, Ernest. "Rebellion in Hollywood: A Case Study in Motion Picture Finance." *Harper's* 193 (Oct. 1946):337–43.

———. "United States Versus Hollywood: The Case Study of an Antitrust Suit." *Sight and Sound* 19 (Feb. 1951):418–20+; (Mar. 1951):448–50.

Bowers, Patricia F. *Private Choice and Public Welfare*. Hinsdale, Ill.: Dryden Pr., 1974.

Brannigan, Edward. "Color and Cinema: Problems in the Writing of History." *Film Reader* 4 (1979):16–34.

Braverman, Harry. *Labor and Monopoly Capital: The Degradation of Work in the Twentieth Century*. New York: Monthly Review Pr., 1974.

Brownlow, Kevin. *The Parades Gone By*. New York: Knopf, 1968.

Bundy, McGeorge. "Europe Still Matters." *European Community*, no. 163 (Feb.–Mar. 1973):17–18.

Campbell, Helen; Know, Thomas W.; and Byrnes, Thomas. *Daylight and Darkness; Or, Lights and Shadows of New York*. Hartford: The Hartford Pub. Co., 1895.

Campbell, Russell. "Warner Brothers in the Thirties." *Velvet Light Trap* 1 (June 1971):2–4.

Carmen, Ira H. *Movies, Censorship, and the Law*. Ann Arbor: Univ. of Michigan Pr., 1966.

Cassady, Ralph, Jr. "The Motion Picture Patents Company and Anti-Trust Law in the United States." Ph.D. diss., U.C.L.A., 1930.

———. "Some Economic Aspects of Motion Picture Production and Marketing." *Journal of Business of the University of Chicago* 6 (Apr. 1933): 113–31.

———. "Impact of the Paramount Decision on Motion Picture Distribution and Price Making." *Southern California Law Review* 31 (Feb. 1958) 150–80.

———. "Monopoly in Motion Picture Production and Distribution: 1908–1915," *Southern California Law Review* 32, no. 4 (Summer 1959) 325–90.[Reprinted herein.]

———, and Cassady, Ralph, III. *The Private Antitrust Suit in American Business Competition: A Motion-Picture Industry Case Analysis*. Bureau of Business and Economic Research, U.C.L.A., 1964.

Casty, Alan. *Development of the Film: An Interpretive History*. New York: Harcourt, 1973.

Ceplair, Larry. *The Inquisition in Hollywood: Politics in the Film Community 1930–1960*. New York: Doubleday, 1980.

Ceram, C. W. *Archaeology of the Cinema*. New York: Harcourt, 1955.

Chambers, Robert W. "Block Booking–Blind Selling." *Harvard Business Review* 19, no. 4 (July 1941) 496–507.

Champlin, Charles. "Who's Watching?" *Journal of the Producers Guild of America* 15, no. 1 (Mar. 1973): 17–18.

Chandler, Alfred D. *The Visible Hand*. Cambridge, Mass.: Harvard Univ. Pr., 1977.

Clark, Ted. "New Eurocrat Fund for Film Biz." *Variety*, 18 May 1977, p. 1.

———. "Common Market's Common Trait: Stall." *Variety*, 5 Oct. 1977, p. 51.

Cochran, Thomas C. "Media and Business: A Brief History." *Journal of Communication* 25 (Autumn 1975):155–65.

———. *Two Hundred Years of American Business*. New York: Delta, 1977.

Cogley, John. *Report on Blacklisting, I: The Movies*. Santa Barbara, Calif.: Fund for the Republic, 1956.

Conant, Michael. "Consciously Parallel Action in Restraint of Trade." *Minnesota Law Review* 38 (June 1954) 797–825.

———. *Antitrust in the Motion Picture Industry*. Berkeley and Los Angeles: Univ. of California Pr., 1960.

———. "The Impact of Paramount Decrees." In *The American Film Industry*, edited by Tino Balio, pp. 346–70. Madison: Univ. of Wisconsin Pr., 1976.

Connelly, Eugene L. "The Life Story of Harry Davis." *Pittsburgh Sun-Telegraph*, 3 Jan. 1940.

Corliss, Richard. "The Legion of Decency." *Film Comment* 4, no. 4 (Summer 1968):25–61.

Cornwell-Clyne, Adrian. *Colour Cinematography*. London: Chapman, 1950.

Coughlan, Robert. "Now It Is Trouble That Is Supercolossal in Hollywood." *Life*, 13 Aug. 1951, pp. 102–14.

Council of Canadian Film Makers, Documents, Hearings Before the Royal Commission of Corporate Concentration. *The Bryce Commission Papers* (Apr. 1976).

Crandall, Robert W. "FCC Regulation, Monopsony, and Network Television Program Cost." *The Bell Journal of Economics* 3, no. 2 (Autumn 1972):483–508.

———. "Postwar Performance of the Motion Picture Industry." *Antitrust Bulletin* 20 (Spring 1975):49–88.

Crean, Susan M. *Who's Afraid of Canadian Culture?* Toronto: General Pub., 1976.

Cressey, Paul F. "Population Succession in Chicago: 1898–1930." *American Journal of Sociology* 44 (1938):341–50.

Crowther, Bosley. *The Lion's Share.* New York: Dutton, 1957.

Cutler, Antony, et al. *Marx's Capital and Capitalism Today.* London: Routledge, 1978.

Daly, David A. *A Comparison of Exhibition and Distribution Patterns in Three Recent Feature Motion Pictures.* New York: Arno Pr., 1980.

Danielian, N. R. *A. T. and T.: The Story of Industrial Conquest.* New York: Vanguard, 1939.

Darby, William S. *Story of the Chain Store.* New York: Dry Good Economist, 1928.

De Laurot, Edouard, and Mekas, Jonas. "Foreign Film Distribution in the U.S.A.: An Interview with Thomas J. Brandon." *Film Culture,* no. 7 (1956):15–17.

Dickson, W. K. Laurie. "A Brief History of the Kinetograph Kinetoscope and the Kineto-Phonograph." *Journal of the Society of Motion Picture Engineers* (1933), pp. 442–44.

Dirlin, Joel B., and Kahn, Alfred E. *Fair Competition: The Law and Economics of Antitrust Policy.* Ithaca: Cornell Univ. Pr., 1954.

Drinkwater, John. *The Life and Adventures of Carl Laemmle.* New York: Putnam, 1931.

Ellis, Jack C. *A History of Film.* Englewood Cliffs, N.J.: Prentice, 1979.

European Economic Communities. *Treaty Establishing the European Economic Community.* Rome: E.E.C., 1957.

———. *Reports.* Brussels: E.E.C., 1972–76.

Everson, William K. *American Silent Film.* New York: Oxford Univ. Pr., 1978.

Ezekiel, Mordecai, and Fox, Karl A. *Methods of Correlation and Regression Analysis.* New York: Wiley, 1959.

Fell, John L. *Film and the Narrative Tradition.* Norman: Univ. of Oklahoma Pr., 1974.

Fielding, Raymond. *A Technological History of Motion Pictures and Television.* Berkeley and Los Angeles: Univ. of California Pr., 1967.

———. *The American Newsreel 1911–1967.* Norman: Univ. of Oklahoma Pr., 1972.

Finkel, Sidney R., and Tarascio, Vincent J. *Wage and Employment Theory.* New York: Ronald Pr., 1971.

Fischer, Ernst. *The Essential Marxist.* Translated by Anna Bostock. New York: Seabury Pr., 1970.

French, Philip. *The Movie Moguls.* London: Weidenfield, 1969.

Frost, George E., and Oppenheim, S. Chesterfield. "A Study of the Professional Color Motion Picture, Antitrust Decrees, and Their Effects." *The Patent, Trademark, and Copyright Journal of Research and Education* 4, no. 2 (Summer 1960):108–49.

Galbraith, John Kenneth. *The New Industrial State.* Boston: Houghton, 1967.

Gardner, Paul. "Foreign Films, Popular in U.S. in '60s, Being Treated Like Foreigners in '70s." *New York Times,* 4 Oct. 1973, p. 1.

Garrison, Lee Cedric, Jr. "Decision Processes in Motion Pictures: A Study of Uncertainty." Ph.D. diss., Stanford Univ., 1971.

Geduld, Harry M. *The Birth of the Talkies: From Edison to Jolson.* Bloomington: Indiana Univ. Pr., 1975.

Gessner, Robert. "Film." *International Encyclopedia of the Social Sciences* 5:426–32.

Gilbert, Robert W. "Foreign Film Subsidies As an Aspect of Financing." *Journal of the Producers Guild of America* 10, no. 3 (Sept. 1968):6–8.

Goldwyn, Samuel. "Movies Best Years Ahead: Television Is no Threat." *U.S. News and World Report* 36 (5 Mar. 1954):38–43.

Gomery, Douglas. "The Coming of Sound to the American Cinema: A History of the Transformation of an Industry." Ph.D. diss., Univ. of Wisconsin—Madison, 1975.

————. "Writing the History of the American Film Industry." *Screen* 17, no. 1 (Spring 1976):40–53.

————. "The Coming of the Talkies: Invention, Innovation, and Diffusion." *The American Film Industry*. Edited by Tino Balio, pp. 193–211. Madison: Univ. of Wisconsin Pr., 1976.

————. "Problems in Film History: How Fox Innovated Sound." *Quarterly Review of Film Studies* 1, no. 3 (Aug. 1976):315–30.

————. "Rethinking American Film History: The Depression Decade and Monopoly Control." *Film and History* 10, no. 2 (May 1980):32–38.

————. "Economic Struggle and Hollywood Imperialism: Europe Converts to Sound." *Yale French Studies* 60 (Winter 1980):80–93.

Goodman, Ezra. *The Fifty Year Decline and Fall of Hollywood*. New York: Simon, 1961.

Gordon, David. "Why the Movie Majors Are Major." *Sight and Sound* 42 (Autumn 1973): 194–96; *Journal of the Producers Guild of America* 16, no. 2 (June 1974):9–15, 24.

Gottschalk, Earl C., Jr. "MGM to Sell Studio, Give Up Film Distribution." *Wall Street Journal*, 18 Sept. 1973, p. 36.

————. "The Spectaculars." *Wall Street Journal*, 10 Aug. 1974, p. 1.

Grau, Robert. *The Theatre of Science: A Volume of Progress and Achievement in the Motion Picture Industry*. New York: Broadway Pub. Co., 1914.

Green, Fitzhugh. *The Film Finds Its Tongue*. New York: Putnam, 1929.

Greenspan, Lou. "The Journal Looks at Hollywood and the State of the Industry." *Journal of the Producers Guild of America* 12, no. 1 (Mar. 1970):3–4.

Greenwald, William I. "The Motion Picture Industry: An Economic Study of the History and Practices of a Business." Ph.D. diss., New York Univ., 1950.

————. "The Impact of Sound upon the Film Industry: A Case Study of Innovation," *Explorations in Entrepreneurial History* 4 (May 1952):178–92.

Griffith, Richard. *Samuel Goldwyn, The Producer and His Films*. New York: Simon, 1956.

————. *The Movie Stars*. Garden City, N.Y.: Doubleday, 1970.

Grover, Stephen. "Spreading the Risk." *Wall Street Journal*, 30 May 1974, p. 1.

Guback, Thomas H. *The International Film Industry: Western Europe and America since 1945*. Bloomington: Indiana Univ. Pr., 1969.

————. "American Interests in the British Film Industry." *The Quarterly Review of Economics and Business* 7, no. 2 (1967):7–21.

————. "Theatrical Film." In *Who Owns the Media?* edited by Benjamin M. Compaine, pp. 179–249. White Plains, N.Y.: Knowledge, 1979.

————, and Dombrowski, Dennis J. "Television and Hollywood: Economic Relations in the 1970s." *Journal of Broadcasting* 20, no. 4 (Fall 1976):511–27.

Hall, Ben M. *The Best Remaining Seats*. New York: A. N. Porter, 1962.

Hampton, Benjamin B. *A History of the Movies*. New York: Covici, Friede, 1931.

Handel, Leo A. *Hollywood Looks at Its Audience*. Urbana: Univ. of Illinois Pr., 1950.

Harlow, Alvin F. *Old Bowery Days*. New York: Appleton, 1931.

Harmetz, Aljean. *The Making of "The Wizard of Oz."* New York: Knopf, 1977.

Haralovich, Mary Beth. "Sherlock Holmes: Genre and Industrial Practice." *Journal of the University Film Association* 31 (Spring 1979):53–57.

Hart, Williams S. *My Life East and West*. Boston and New York: Houghton, 1929.

Hawley, Ellis W. *The New Deal and the Problem of Monopoly*. Princeton: Princeton Univ.
 Pr., 1966.

Hays, Will H. *The Memoirs of Will H. Hays*. Garden City, N.Y.: Doubleday, 1955.

Hayward, Walter S., and White, Percival. *Chain Stores*. 3d ed. New York: McGraw, 1928.

Hellmuth, William F., Jr. "The Motion Picture Industry." In *The Structure of the American
 Industry: Some Case Studies*, Edited by Walter Adams, pp. 393–429. Rev. ed. New
 York: Macmillan, 1961.

Henderson, Thomas M. *Tammany Hall and the New Immigrants*. New York: Arno Pr.,
 1976.

Hendricks, Gordon. *The Edison Motion Picture Myth*. Berkeley: Univ. of California Pr., 1961.

———. *Beginnings of the Biograph*. New York: Beginnings of American Film, 1964.

———. *The Kinetoscope*. New York: Beginnings of American Film, 1966.

Hession, Charles H., and Sardy, Hyman. *Ascent to Affluence*. Boston: Allyn and Bacon, 1969.

Himmelberg, Robert F. *The Origins of the National Recovery Administration*. New York:
 Fordham Univ. Pr., 1976.

Hodkinson, W. W. "Picture Theatre Management," *The Film Index*, 19 Mar. 1960, p. 8;
 26 Mar. 1910, p. 8.

Holm, Wilton R. "Management Looks at the Future." *Journal of the Producers Guild of
 America* 12, no. 3 (Sept. 1970):15–17.

Howe, A. H. "A Banker Looks at the Picture Business." *Journal of the Producers Guild of
 America* 11, no. 2 (Mar. 1969):15–22.

Hoyt, Homer. *One Hundred Years of Land Values in Chicago*. Chicago: Univ. of Chicago Pr.,
 1933.

Huettig, Mae. *Economic Control of the Motion Picture Industry*. Philadelphia: Univ. of
 Pennsylvania Pr., 1944.

Ingeles, Margaret. *Willis Haviland Carrier*. New York: Country Life Pr., 1952.

Inglis, Ruth A. "Need for Voluntary Self-Regulation in the Motion Picture Industry." *Annals
 of the American Academy of Political and Social Science* (Nov. 1947):153–59.

International Motion Picture Almanac. New York: Quigley Pub. Co., 1956.

Jacobs, Lewis. *The Rise of the American Film*. New York: Harcourt, 1939.

Jenkins, Reese V. *Images and Enterprise: Technology and the American Photographic Industry 1839–1925*. Baltimore: Johns Hopkins Univ. Pr., 1975.

Jeter, Ida. "The Collapse of the Federated Motion Picture Crafts: A Case Study of Class Col-
 laboration." *Journal of the University Film Association* 31 (Spring 1979):37–45.

Jobes, Gertrude. *Motion Picture Empire*. Hamden, Conn.: Archon, 1966.

Johnston, Eric, and Linden, Michael. "The Motion Picture Industry." In *The Development of
 American Industries*, edited by John George Glover and William Bouck Cornell, pp.
 935–51. 3d ed. New York: Prentice, 1951.

Jowett, Garth S. "American Domination of the Motion Picture Industry: Canada As a Test
 Case." *Journal of the University Film Association* 27 (1975):58–61, 72.

———. *Film, The Democratic Art*. Boston: Little, 1975.

———, and Linton, James M. *Movies As Mass Communication*. Beverly Hills: Sage, 1980.

Kahn, Gordon, and England, Steven. *Hollywood on Trial*. New York: Arno Pr., 1972.

Kalmus, Herbert. "Technicolor Adventures in Cinemaland." *Journal of the Society of Motion Picture Engineers* (Dec. 1938):564–85.

Kehr, David. "A Star Is Made." *Film Comment* 15, no. 1 (Jan.–Feb. 1979):7–12.

Kelly, William V. D. "Natural Color Cinematography." *Transactions of the Society of Motion
 Picture Engineers* (Nov. 1918):38–43.

Kemezis, Paul. "The Consumer and the Common Market." *European Community*, no. 159
 (Oct. 1972):19–23.

Kennedy, Joseph P., ed. *The Story of the Films As Told by Leaders of the Industry.* New York: A. W. Shaw, 1927.

Kessner, Thomas. *The Golden Door: Italian and Jewish Immigrant Mobility in New York City, 1880–1915.* New York: Oxford Univ. Pr., 1977.

Kindem, Gorham A. "Hollywood's Movie Star System and the Film Industry in the 1940s." *Readings in Mass Communication: Selected Proceedings of the Fourth International Conference on Culture and Communication.* New York: Ablex Pub. Corp., forthcoming.

Knight, Arthur. *The Liveliest Art: A Panoramic History of the Movies.* New York: Macmillan, 1957.

Knox, Donald. *The Magic Factory: How MGM Made "An American in Paris."* New York: Praeger, 1973.

Kreuger, Miles. *The Movie Musical from Vitaphone to 42nd Street.* New York: Dover, 1975.

Krislov, Samuel. "From Ginzburg to Ginzgerg: The Unhurried Children's Hour in Obscenity Litigation." 153 *Supreme Court Review* (1968).

Lahue, Kalton C. *Dreams for Sale: The Rise and Fall of the Triangle Film Corporation.* South Brunsvick and New York: A. S. Barnes, 1971.

———. *Mack Sennett's Keystone: The Man, the Myth, and the Comedies.* Cranbury, N.J.: A. S. Barnes, 1971

Land, Edwin H. "Color Vision and the Natural Image," *Proceedings of the National Academy of Science* 45 (1959):115–29.

Landon, John W. *Jesse Crawford.* Vestal, N.Y.: The Vestal Pr., 1974.

Lasky, Jesse L. *I Blow My Own Horn.* Garden City, N.Y.: Doubleday, 1957.

Lebhar, Godfrey M. *The Chain Store: Boon or Bain.* New York: Harper, 1932.

———. *Chain Stores in America, 1859–1962.* New York: Chain Store Pub. Co., 1963.

Leff, Leonard J. "A Test of American Film Censorship: *Who's Afraid of Virginia Woolf?*" *Cinema Journal* 19 (Spring 1980):40–55.

Leuchtenberg, William E. *The Perils of Prosperity.* Chicago: Univ. of Chicago Pr., 1958.

Levitt, Kari. *Silent Surrender: The American Economic Empire in Canada.* New York: Liveright, 1970.

Lewis, Howard T. *The Motion Picture Industry.* New York: Van Nostrand, 1933.

———, ed. *Cases on the Motion Picture Industry.* New York: McGraw, 1930.

Lewis, Roger. "On the Producer." In *Movie People: At Work in the Business of Film*, edited by Fred Baker and Ross Firestone. New York: Lancer Books, 1973.

Lincoln, Freeman. "The Comeback of the Movies." *Fortune*, Feb. 1955, pp. 127–31+.

Litman, Barry. "Predicting Ratings for Theatrical Movies." *Journalism Quarterly* 56 (Autumn 1979):590–94.

———. *The Vertical Structure of Television Broadcasting Industry: The Coalescence of Power.* East Lansing: Michigan State Univ., 1979.

Little, Arthur D., Inc. *Television Program Production Procurement, Distribution, and Scheduling: Data Relating to Proposals for Rule Making in FCC Docket No. 12782.* Cambridge, Mass.: A. D. Little, 1969.

Lockhard, William B., and McClure, Robert C. "Literature, the Law of Obscenity, and the Constitution." *Minnesota Law Review* 38 (1954) 295–311.

Lockwood, Charles. *Manhattan Moves Uptown: An Illustrated History.* Boston: Houghton, 1976.

Lovell, Hugh, and Carter, Tasile. *Collective Bargaining in the Motion Picture Industry.* Berkeley: Univ. of California Institute of Industrial Relations, 1955.

Low, Rachael. *The History of the British Film 1906–1914.* London: George Allen, 1949.

Lumet, Sidney. "On the Director." In *Movie People: At Work in the Business of Film*, edited by Fred Baker and Ross Firestone. New York: Lancer Books, 1973.

Lundberg, Ferdinand. *The Rich and Super Rich*. New York: Lyle Stuart, 1968.

Lyon, L. S. et al. *The National Recovery Administration*. Washington, D.C.: Brookings, 1935.

Lyons, Timothy J. *The Silent Partner: The History of the American Film Manufacturing Company, 1910–1921*. New York: Arno Pr., 1974.

McAlpine, Dennis B. "The Television Programming Industry." Report from Tucker Anthony and R. L. Day. New York, 1975.

MacCann, Richard Dyer. *Hollywood in Transition*. Boston: Houghton, 1962.

McDonald, Gerald D. "Origin of the Star System." *Films in Review* 4 (Nov. 1953):449–58.

McDonough, John R., Jr., and Winslow, Robert L. "The Motion Picture Industry: United States v. Oligopoly." *Stanford Law Review* 1 (Apr. 1949) 385–427.

Macgowan, Kenneth. *Behind the Screen: The History and Techniques of the Motion Picture*. New York: Dell, 1965.

Mackaye, Milton. "The Big Brawl: Hollywood vs. Television." *Saturday Evening Post*, 224 (19 Jan. 1952):17–19.

McLaughlin, Robert. *Broadway and Hollywood: A History of Economic Interaction*. New York: Arno Pr., 1974.

McNeil, Everett. "Outline of How to Write a Photoplay." *MPW* 9, no. 1 (15 July 1911):27.

Maltin, Leonard. *TV Movies*. New York: New American, 1974.

Marcuse, Maxwell F. *This Was New York*. New York: Carlton Pr., 1965.

Mast, Gerald. *A Short History of the Movies*. 3d ed. Indianapolis: Bobbs-Merrill, 1981.

Mayer, Arthur. *Merely Colossal*. New York: Simon, 1953.

Mayer, Grace. *Once upon a City*. New York: Macmillan, 1958.

Mayer, Michael. "The Exhibition Contract." In *The Movie Business*, edited by A. William Bluem and Jason E. Squire, pp. 210–13. New York: Hastings, 1972.

———. *The Film Industries*. New York: Hastings, 1973.

Merritt, Russell. "Dixon, Griffith, and the Southern Legend." *Cinema Journal* 12, no. 1 (Fall 1972):26–45.

———. "Nickelodeon Theatres." *AFI Reports* (May 1975):4–6.

———. "Nickelodeon Theatres: 1905–1914: Building an Audience for the Movies." In *The American Film Industry*, edited by Tino Balio, pp. 59–79. Madison: Univ. of Wisconsin Pr., 1976.

Metzger, Charles R. "Pressure Groups and the Motion Picture Industry." *Annals of the American Academy of Political and Social Science* (Nov. 1947):110–15.

Milne, Peter. *Motion Picture Directing*. New York: Falk, 1922.

Mitchell, George. "Thomas H. Ince." *Films in Review* 11 (Oct. 1960):464.

Mitry, Jean. *Histoire du cinéma: Art et Industrie*. Paris: Editions Universitaires, 1967– Vol. I:1895–1914. Vol. II:1915–1925.

Moley, Raymond. *The Hays Office*. Indianapolis: Bobbs-Merrill, 1945.

Momand, A. B. *The Hays Office and the NRA*. Shawnee, Okla.: Shawnee Printing Co., 1935.

Morin, Edgar. *The Stars*. New York: Evergree, 1960.

Morris, George H. "Color in 1943." *The Film Daily Yearbook—1944*:71.

Morris, Lloyd. *Not So Long Ago*. New York, Random, 1949.

Motion Picture Association of America and Motion Picture Export Association of America. *1972: A Review of the World of Movies*. New York: MPAA/MPEAA, 1973.

Myers, Harold. "Common Market Aim: Offset U.S. Advantages." *Variety*, 7 Jan. 1976, p. 18.

National Film Finance Corp. *Annual Report and Statement of Accounts, for the Year Ended 31st March 1972*. London: Her Majesty's Stationery Office, 1972.

Newhouse, Joh. *Collision in Brussels*. New York: Norton, 1967.

Nizer, Louis. *New Courts of Industry: Self-Regulation under the Motion Picture Code.* New York: Longacre Pr., 1936.

North, Joseph H. *The Early Development of the Motion Picture, 1887–1909.* New York: Arno Pr., 1973.

Note [Sturges, Wasley A.]. "Operation of the Consent Decree in the Motion Picture Industry." *Yale Law Journal* 51 (May 1942):1175–95.

Note [Bates, Roy Eugene, and Herman, Peter]. "Private Censorship of Movies." *Stanford Law Review* 22 (1970):618–56.

Note. "The Sherman Act and the Motion Picture Industry." *University of Chicago Law Review* 13, no. 3 (Apr. 1946):346–61.

O'Connor, James. *The Fiscal Crisis of the State.* New York: St. Martin's, 1973.

O'Connor, John E., and Jackson, Martin A. *American History/American Film.* New York: Ungar, 1979.

Ogle, Patrick. "Technological and Aesthetic Influences upon the Development of Deep Focus Cinematography in the United States." *Screen* 13 (Spring 1972):45–72.

Osofsky, Gilbert. *Harlem: The Making of a Ghetto.* New York: Harper, 1963.

Owen, Bruce M.; Beebe, Jack H.; and Manning, Willard G. *Television Economics.* Lexington, Mass: Heath, 1974.

Paletz, David, and Noonan, Michael. "The Exhibitors." *Film Quarterly* 19 (Winter 1965/66):14–40.

Parker, Alexander. "Fifty Years Ago," *Box Office,* 4 June 1955, pp. 20–21.

Pay, William. "British Year in Review." *International Motion Picture Almanac, 1966–73.* New York, Hollywood, and London: Quigley Pub. Co., 1966–73.

Pendakur, Manjunath. "Canadian Feature Film Industry: Monopoly and Competition." Ph.D. diss., Simon Fraser Univ., 1979.

Perry, Louis B., and Perry, Richard S. *A History of the Los Angeles Labor Movement, 1911–1941.* Berkeley: Univ. of California Pr., 1963.

Phillips, Joseph D. "Film Conglomerate 'Blockbusters.'" *Journal of Communication* 25 (Spring 1975):171–81.

Powdermaker, Hortense. *Hollywood, the Dream Factory.* Boston: Little, 1950.

Pratt, George. "A Myth Is As Good As a Milestone." *Image* (Nov. 1957):210.

———. "No Magic, No Mystery, No Sleight of Hand." *Image* 8 (Dec. 1959).

———, ed. *Spellbound in Darkness: A History of the Silent Film.* Rev. ed. Greenwich, Conn.: New York Graphic Society, 1973.

Price, Waterhouse and Company. *The Motion Picture Industry.* New York: Price Waterhouse, 1917.

Procurer de Roi vs Dassonville. "The Court of Justice of the European Communities." Brussels: European Documentation-Information, 1976.

Pye, Michael, and Myles, Lynda. *The Movie Brats: How the Film Generation Took over Hollywood.* New York: Holt, 1979.

Ramsaye, Terry. *A Million and One Nights: A History of the Motion Picture.* New York: Simon, 1926.

Randall, Richard S. *Censorship of the Movies: The Social and Political Control of a Mass Medium.* Madison: Univ. of Wisconsin Pr., 1968.

Read, Oliver, and Welch, Walter L. *From Tin Foil to Stereo.* Indianapolis: Bobbs-Merrill, 1959.

Rhode, Eric. *A History of the Cinema: From Its Origins to 1970.* New York: Hill and Wang, 1976.

Ross, Murray. *Stars and Strikes: Unionization of Hollywood.* New York: Columbia Univ. Pr., 1941.

Rosten, Leo C. *Hollywood: The Movie Colony, the Movie Makers.* New York: Harcourt, 1941.

―――. "Movies and Propaganda." *Annals of the American Academy of Political and Social Science* (Nov. 1947):116–24.

Ryan, Roderick T. *A History of Motion Picture Color Technology.* London: Focal Pr., 1977.

Sadoul, Georges. *Louis Lumière.* Paris: Editions Seghers, 1964.

―――. *Histoire du Cinéma Mondial.* Paris: Flammarion, 1949.

Sands, Pierre Norman. *A Historical Study of the Academy of Motion Picture Arts and Sciences, 1927–1947.* New York: Arno Pr., 1973.

Santamaria, Massima Ferrara. "Subsidy, Coproduction, Shelter in Europe Now and in the Future." *Variety,* 19 Oct. 1977, p. 104.

Sargent, John. "Self-Regulation: The Motion Picture Production Code, 1930–1961." Ph.D. diss., Univ. of Michigan, 1963.

Sarris, Andrew. *The American Cinema, Directors, and Directions, 1929–1968.* New York: Dutton, 1969.

Schary, Dore. *Case History of a Movie.* New York: Random, 1950.

Scherer, F. M. *Industrial Market Structure and Economic Performance.* Chicago: Rand, 1970.

Schillaci, Anthony. "Film As Environment." *Saturday Review,* 28 Dec. 1968, p. 8.

Schiller, Herbert I. *Communication and Cultural Domination.* White Plains, N.Y.: International Arts and Sciences Pr., 1976.

Schlesinger, Arthur M., Jr. *The Coming of the New Deal.* Boston: Houghton, 1958.

Schumach, Murray. *The Face on the Cutting Room Floor.* New York: Morrow, 1964.

Seabury, William Marston. *The Public and the Motion Picture Industry.* New York: Macmillan, 1925.

―――. *Motion Picture Problems: The Cinema and the League of Nations.* New York: Avondale, 1929.

Sexton, R. W., and Betts, F. F., eds. *American Theatres of Today.* New York: Architectural Book Pub. Co., 1927.

Shales, Tom, ed. *The American Film Heritage.* Washington, D.C.: Acropolis, 1972.

Shaffer, Helen B. "Movie-TV Competition." *Editorial Research Reports,* 18 Jan. 1957, pp. 43–61.

Shickel, Richard. *Movies: The History of an Art and an Institution.* New York: Basic, 1964.

Shipman, David. *The Great Movie Stars, The International Years.* New York: St. Martin's, 1972.

―――. "Performers' Marquee Values in Relation to Top-Grossing Films." Paper delivered at the Society for Cinema Studies Conference, Temple Univ., 5 Mar. 1978.

Simonet, Thomas S. *Regression Analysis of Prior Experience of Key Production Personnel as Predictors of Revenues from High Grossing Motion Pictures in American Release.* New York: Arno Pr., 1980.

Sinclair, Upton. *Upton Sinclair Presents William Fox.* Los Angeles: Sinclair, 1933.

Sklar, Robert. *Movie-made America: A Social History of American Movies.* New York: Random, 1975.

Slide, Anthony. *American Film History Prior to 1920.* Metuchen, N.J.: Scarecrow, 1978.

―――. "The Evolution of the Film Star." *Films in Review* 25 (Dec. 1974):591–94.

Sloan, Harold S., and Zurcher, Arnold J. *A Dictionary of Economics.* Rev. 4th ed. New York: Barnes, 1964.

Sloane, Leonard. "Aubrey Resigns Top Post at Metro-Goldwyn-Mayer." *New York Times,* 1 Nov. 1973, p. 63.

Bibliography 427

Smith, Albert E., and Koury, Phil. *Two Reels and a Crank.* Garden City, N.Y.: Doubleday, 1952.

Smythe, Dallas W.; Lusk, Parker B.; and Lewis, Charles A. "Portrait of an Art-Theatre Audience." *The Quarterly of Film, Radio, and Television* 8 (Fall 1953):28–50.

Sponable, Earl I. "Historical Development of Sound Films," *Journal of the Society of Motion Picture Engineers* 48 (May 1947):420.

Stanley, Robert. *The Celluloid Empire: A History of the American Motion Picture Industry.* New York: Hastings, 1978.

Sterling, Christopher H., and Haight, Timothy R. *The Mass Media: Aspen Institute Guide to Communication Industry Trends.* New York: Praeger, 1978.

Strauss, William V. "Foreign Distribution of American Motion Pictures." *Harvard Business Review* 8 (Apr. 1930):307–15.

Strick, John. "The Economics of the Motion Picture Industry: A Survey." *Philosophy of the Social Sciences* 8 (Dec. 1978):406–17.

Stulberg, Gordon. "Hollywood Transition," *Saturday Review* 51 (28 Dec. 1968):20.

Suber, Howard. "The Anti-Communist Blacklist in the Hollywood Motion Picture Industry." Ph.D. diss., U.C.L.A., 1968.

Survey of Current Business, July 1956.

Sweezy, Paul M. *The Theory of Capitalist Development.* New York: Monthly Review Pr., 1970.

Swenson, Joel. "The Entrepreneur's Role in Introducing the Sound Motion Picture." *Political Science Quarterly* 63 (Sept. 1948):404–23.

Tailleur, Roger. "Kazan and the House Un-American Activities Committee." *Film Comment* 4, no. 1 (Fall 1966):43–59.

Talbot, Frederick A. *Moving Pictures: How They Are Made and Worked.* Philadelphia: Lippincott, 1923.

Taylor, Frank S. "Mr. Technicolor." *Saturday Evening Post,* 22 Oct. 1949, pp. 26–27, 131–34.

Taylor, Ryland A. "Television Movie Audiences and Movie Awards: A Statistical Study." *Journal of Broadcasting* 18 (Spring 1974):181–86.

———. "Televised Movies: Directors Win Audience." *Journal of Broadcasting* 20 (Fall 1976):495–500.

Theatre Historical Society. *The Chicago Theatre.* Notre Dame, Ind.: N.p., n.d.

Thomas, D. B. *The First Colour Motion Pictures.* London: Her Majesty's Stationery Office, 1969.

Trimble, Lyne S. *Color in Motion Pictures and Television.* Los Angeles: By the author, 1954.

Twomey, John E. "Some Considerations on the Rise of the Art-Film Theatre." *The Quarterly of Film, Radio, and Television.* (Spring 1956):239–47.

U.S., Department of Commerce. *Balance of Payments.* Washington, D.C.: G.P.O., n.d.

———. *U.S. Direct Investment Abroad, 1966, Part 1: Balance of Payments Data.* Washington, D.C.: G.P.O., 1971.

U.S. Industrial Outlook, 1965, '70, '72. Washington, D.C.: G.P.O., 1964, 1969, 1971.

U.S., Federal Communications Commission. *Television Network Program Procurement, Part II: Second Interim Report by Office of Network Study.* Washington, D.C.: G.P.O., 1965.

U.S., Federal Trade Commission. *Economic Report for Webb-Pomerene Associations: A 50-Year Review.* Washington, D.C.: G.P.O., 1967.

Valenti, Jack. "The 'Foreign Service' of the Motion Picture Association of America." *Journal of the Producers Guild of America* 10, no. 1 (Mar. 1968):21–25.

Vardac, A. Nicholas. *Stage to Screen.* Cambridge, Mass.: Harvard Univ. Pr., 1949.

Varis, Tapio. *International Inventory of Television Programme Structure and the Flow of TV Programmes Between Nations.* Tampere, Finland: Institute of Journalism and Mass Communication, Univ. of Tampere, 1973.

Vaughan, Floyd L. *Economics of Our Patent System.* New York: Macmillan, 1925.

Vizzard, Jack. *See No Evil.* New York: Simon, 1970.

Wagenknecht, Edward. *The Movies in the Age of Innocence.* Norman Univ. of Oklahoma Pr., 1962.

Walker, Alexander. *Stardom: The Hollywood Phenomenon.* New York: Stein, 1970.

Wallis, Hal B., and Higham, Charles. *Starmaker.* New York: Macmillan, 1980.

Warner, Jack L. *Jack of All Trades.* London: W. H. Allen, 1975.

Wasko, Janet. "D. W. Griffith and the Banks: A Case Study in Film Financing." *Journal of the University Film Association* 30, no. 1 (Winter 1978):15–20.

Watkins, Gordon S., ed. "The Motion Picture Industry." *Annals of the American Academy of Political and Social Science* 256 (Nov. 1947):1–236.

————, ed. *The Motion Picture Industry.* Philadelphia: American Academy of Political and Social Science, 1947.

Watkins, Roger. "Reaction to Common-M Proposals not Cheery at Berlin Festival." *Variety,* 6 July 1977, p. 6.

Wenden, D. J. *The Birth of the Movies.* New York: Dutton, 1974.

Westin, Alan F. *The Miracle Case: The Supreme Court and the Movies.* Inter-University Case Program, no. 64 (1961).

White, Lawrence J. "The Automobile Industry." In *The Structure of American Industry,* edited by Walter Adams, pp. 311–56. New York: Macmillan, 1957.

Wilcox, Clair, and Shepherd, William G. *Public Policy Toward Business.* Homewood, Ill.: Richard D. Irwin, 1975.

Williams, Henry. "Economic Changes in the Motion Picture Industry As Affected by Television and Other Factors." Ph.D. diss., Indiana Univ. 1968.

Wing, W. E. "Tom Ince, of Inceville." *The New York Dramatic Mirror* 70, no. 1827 (24 Dec. 1908):34.

Wittenmeyer, Fred. "Cooling of Theatres and Public Buildings." *Ice and Refrigeration,* July 1922, pp. 13–14.

Wright, Basil. *The Long View.* New York: Knopf, 1974.

Zeller, John F., III. "Judicial Regulation of the Motion-Picture Industry: The Paramount Case." *University of Pennsylvania Law Review* 95 (May 1947) 662–75.

Zukor, Adolph. *The Public Is Never Wrong.* New York: N.p., 1953.

Contributors

Jeanne Thomas Allen is Associate Professor of Communications, Temple University, and author of articles on film history.

Robert C. Allen is Assistant Professor of Radio, Television, and Motion Pictures, University of North Carolina. He is author of *Vaudeville and Film 1895–1915: A Study in Media Interaction*; *Film History: Theory and Practice*, with Douglas Gomery (forthcoming); and articles on film history.

Douglas Ayer was Associate Professor of Law, Stanford University, and is now a doctoral candidate in history at Stanford University and an Institutional Research Analyst at Menlo College.

Roy E. Bates is an attorney with Farella, Braun, and Martel in San Francisco.

Ralph Cassady, Jr., was Director, Bureau of Business and Economic Research, and Professor of Marketing, University of California, Los Angeles.

Douglas Gomery is Associate Professor of Communications Arts and Theatre, University of Maryland. He is author of *High Sierra* and *Film History: Theory and Practice*, with Robert C. Allen (forthcoming), and articles on film history and economics.

Thomas Guback is Research Professor of Communications, University of Illinois. He is author of *The International Film Industry: Western Europe and America Since 1946* and articles on the American industry's economic structure, trade practices, and history.

Peter J. Herman is President of Citizens for Effective Public Policy and an attorney in California and Hawaii.

Gorham Kindem is Associate Professor of Radio, Television, and Motion Pictures, University of North Carolina. He is author of *Toward a Semiotic Theory of Visual Communication in the Cinema*; *Introduction to Television and Film Production* (forthcoming); and articles on film history and theory.

Don R. Le Duc is a communications attorney, Professor of Communications, University of Wisconsin, and research coordinator of a project analyzing West European mass media policies for the Council for European Studies at Columbia University. He is author of *Cable Television and the FCC*, and several studies on the impact of Common Market law upon European telecommunication and film industries.

Barry R. Litman is Associate Professor of Telecommunications, Michigan State University. He is author of *The Vertical Structure of Television Broadcasting Industry: The Coalescence of Power* and articles on film and television economics.

429

Manjunath Pendakur is Assistant Professor of Radio, Television, and Film, Northwestern University, and author of articles on the film industry and international communication issues.

Joseph D. Phillips is Professor of Economics, University of Illinois. He is author of *Little Business in the American Economy*; co-editor with Herbert I. Schiller of *Super-State: Readings in the Military-Industrial Complex*; and articles on business and economics.

Janet Staiger is Assistant Professor of English, University of Delaware, and author of articles on film history.

Fredric Stuart was Professor of Business, Hofstra University. He authored *Effects of Television on the Motion Picture and Radio Industries* and books and articles on market structure and computer programming.

Simon N. Whitney was Professor of Economics, New York University, and author of books and articles on antitrust policy.

Index

Index

447

United Artists: censorship of films distributed by, 238; conglomerate's acquisition of, 327; distribution of independently produced films by, 190; exhibitor bidding and, 183; formation of, 83, 163; French subsidiaries of, 347; financing of independent productions by, 325–26; Little Three and, 165; "Loew's split" and, 182; membership in MPAA and MPEAA of, 239, 336; number of films released between 1932 and 1955 by, 198; numerous flops by, 329; PCA and, 218, 228–29; percentage distribution by, 329; sale of feature films to television by, 307; sound adoption by, 119, 122–23, 131; spectaculars by, 330; use of 3-D by, 297. See also Little Three
United Artists Corporation, Ltd. (Canada), 352, 355–56
United Kingdom, 341, 354, 414 n.3
United Paramount Theatres Corporation, 173
United States Census of Business, 263–90
United States v. Crescent Amusement Company (1944), 171
United States v. First National, 174
United States v. Griffith Amusement Company, 170–72
United States v. Motion Picture Patents Company (1916), 64–68, 69, 161–62
United States v. Paramount-Famous Lasky, 174
United States v. Paramount Pictures, Inc. (1938), 170, 174, 212
United States v. Paramount Pictures, Inc. (1946), 58, 172–90, 193–95
United States v. Paramount Pictures, Inc. (1948): Canadian absence of similar antitrust cases, 357; effects on independent production, xix, 327; effects on movie content, 221, 224–26, 228–29; effects on movie industry profits, 257–60; negotiations concerning consent decrees, 172–73; preconditions for, 212; proscription of block booking by, 61; relations to self-censorship, 218–19; reopening of, 212; star system and, 80, 88; treble damage suits following decrees of, 191. See also Antitrust; Department of Justice; Divorcement; Sherman Act; Supreme Court

United States v. Schine Chain Theatres, Inc., 170–72
United States v. Technicolor. Inc. (1948 and 1950), 153, 195–96, 397 n.166., 397 n.167
Universal Film Manufacturing Company, 54, 63, 163
Universal Films (Canada), 352, 355–56
Universal International Films, Inc., 63, 303
Universal Pictures: decrees against theater chain associated with, 170–71; formation of, 163; Little Three and, 165; membership in MPAA and MPEAA, 239, 336; number of films released between 1932 and 1955, 198–99; PCA and, 218; percentage of total U.S. distribution by, 329; receivership of, after Great Depression, 166; refusal of, to rent out studio space to independents, 190; "RKO's split" and, 182; sale of feature films to television by, 197, 304–5; sound adoption by, 119–20; 122, 124, 126, 131; television series supplying by, 315. See also Little Three
Unsatisfied, The, 252

Valenti, Jack, 217, 225, 240, 332, 338, 345
Valentino, Rudolph, 83
Van Gend en Loos v. Netherland (1962), 363
VAT taxes, 369
Vaudeville: comparison to television and film of, 220; complete "acts" for, by Lumière Company, 9–11; Edison, Vitagraph Company of America, and 11; interaction between legitimate theater and "small-time" and "high class," 377 n.42; "live" entertainment at picture palaces and, 19–21, 106–9, 111, 113–14; nickelodeon theaters and, 12, 15, 21–22; popularity of, 3, 6–7; short films for, 3–11, 113, 121–22; small-time vaudeville and middle class audiences for, 19–24; television use of techniques from, 292. See also Exhibition, vaudeville and film
Venezuela, 338
Vertical integration, 61–64
Veterans of Foreign Wars, 230
Victor Company, 292